Black Families

This book is dedicated to my husband,
John Lewis McAdoo, Ph.D.
1935–1994

Black Families

Third Edition

Edited by
Harriette Pipes McAdoo

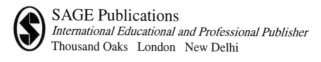

SAGE Publications
International Educational and Professional Publisher
Thousand Oaks   London   New Delhi

For information address:

SAGE Publications, Inc.
2455 Teller Road
Thousand Oaks, California 91320
E-mail: order@sagepub.com

SAGE Publications Ltd.
6 Bonhill Street
London EC2A 4PU
United Kingdom

SAGE Publications India Pvt. Ltd.
M-32 Market
Greater Kailash I
New Delhi 110 048 India

Printed in the United States of America

Library of Congress Cataloging-in-Publication Data

McAdoo, Harriette Pipes.
    Black families / editor, Harriette Pipes McAdoo.—3rd ed.
        p.   cm.
    Includes bibliographical references and index.
    ISBN 0-8039-5572-3 (acid-free paper).—ISBN 0-8039-5573-1 (pbk. : acid-free paper)
        1. Afro-American families.   I. Title.
    E185.86.B525 1996
    305.896'073—dc20   96-9989

This book is printed on acid-free paper.

97 98 99 00 01 02 10 9 8 7 6 5 4 3 2

Contents

Foreword

Few people know as much, care as much, or spend as much time thinking about African American families as Harriette Pipes McAdoo. With her husband, John, and their children to inspire her, she has pioneered in bringing into scholarly focus this wide-ranging area of knowledge and concern. Low-, middle-, high-, and no-income families; single-parent, two-parent, grandparent, and blended families; functional families and less functional families—all are here in the third edition of this most enduring book, *Black Families.*

Dr. McAdoo and her collaborators have done it again. They have opened up to the discerning reader the ways in which African American families exist, survive, overcome adversity, and reach remarkable levels of achievement.

The reader will not find here *the* African American family; anyone in search of such will surely be disappointed. The reader will find an appreciation for complexity and diversity as well as searches into what holds these families together and enables them to soar above the odds. Whether the reader is a student, teacher, activist, policy maker, parent, or child, whether male or female, old or young, Black or otherwise, he or she will find this book to be a movable and memorable feast.

Personally, I am grateful to Harriette and her colleagues for bringing us this new edition. It is an enormously valuable instrument for my teaching, writing, and parenting.

Andrew Billingsley

Preface to the Third Edition

This edition of *Black Families* goes to press at a period in which Black families are faced with growing problems: isolation from the economic mainstream, public schools that are becoming even less successful than in the past, increasing violence in our communities, more children being reared in families by women alone, and a growing conservatism on the part of policy makers. When one looks at African American families, it is tempting to focus on these problems, for they are life threatening and seem overwhelming. But families in all groups in U.S. society today are facing changes. Babies in all groups are being conceived outside of marriage, divorce is rampant, unemployment of parents is becoming a factor in all segments of our society, and senseless violence is increasing everywhere.

At the same time, many African Americans are experiencing greater successes in achieving real power and sustained upward mobility. Some families are entering into their seventh and eighth generation of upper-middle-class status. Yet even the parents of those families are now faced with the problem of raising children who seem not to be embracing the values of hard work and achievement that motivated them. Many middle-class families are facing the reality that their children may not be as successful and may even fall into lower classes, unless the parent generation supports them. Thwarted mobility and the changing marketplace have taken their toll, and middle-class status has become even more unstable.

The majority of African American families are neither in dire poverty nor among the affluent. They are not on the nightly news as having been shot, and they are not featured in *Jet* magazine among the elite. Most African American parents are hardworking people who go to their jobs every day and are attempting to rear their children into adults. It is often overlooked that the members of many families in poverty, including those headed by single mothers, are working every day. The solid working-class stratum is too often overlooked. People in this stratum may be poor because of wage and job inequities, but they are not on welfare. This is the group from which the upwardly mobile will come. This is the group that has maintained stability and is under great pressure to remain employed and self-sufficient, free of government assistance.

Never before has it been so obvious that the Black experience involves more than one reality. The title of this book is *Black Families,* and not *The Black Family,* precisely because the diversity of experiences among African Americans, both economic and social, is increasing every day. Despite media attempts to present us as all of one social class, usually lower, it is important to understand that the common element of African descent does not determine exactly what the life patterns of individuals will be. It does mean, however, that it has become more difficult to excel in the present environment.

It is clear that, as a group, African Americans are no longer essential to the economic survival and productivity of the United States, as they were during the period of enslavement. At that time their free labor helped establish major pools of wealth that still exist today. Nor are they as essential as they were during the period of industrial growth or during the two world wars. As the United States has moved into a global economy with greater emphasis on technology, and as jobs have become more precious due to industrial reorganization and downsizing, there is even less need for large numbers of low-skilled and less-educated people in the workforce. As a group, African Americans and other people of color have become unnecessary to the world economy. They have become disposable since the end of enslavement, the automation of production, and the discovery of the profitability of using cheap labor abroad.

These changes come at the same time that drugs are flowing freely into the Black community, AIDS and other destructive illnesses are increasing, and the ganglike behavior of our youth is growing. This may or may not be coincidental. Regardless, the sum experience of the current generation of Black youth has been more negative than positive. The crises in which that portion of our community finds itself are probably as great as those faced during enslavement.

In this third edition of *Black Families,* we continue to explore the experiences of Black families, ranging from the African continent, through historical accounts, and on to the essential issues of today. The contributors present up-to-date reviews of the literature and explore the dimensions of Black family life from many angles. As in previous editions, the chapters are divided into five major areas: historical and theoretical conceptualizations, family patterns, socialization within families, gender relations, and advocacy and family policy.

Many of the authors who contributed to the second edition were asked to join in this venture. All are scholars whose work is among the best in this field, and I want to express my appreciation for their efforts as they faced competing responsibilities. We have all grown older, but wiser, and our writings reflect this maturing knowledge. As time has passed, we all have experienced growth and decline in our families, which is as it should be. Three new contributors have also joined us in this edition: Rose Merry Rivers, John Scanzoni, and Beverly Tatum. Their chapters and their special insights add depth to this volume, and I welcome them to this collective effort.

A few of the chapters here remain basically as they were in earlier editions, for they have become true classics and it would not do to tamper with them too much. Some of the other contributors have updated their earlier chapters, but most have written entirely new essays for this edition.

As I note in my introduction, readers will notice that the terms used to discuss ethnic groups vary from chapter to chapter; for instance, contributors use both *African American* and *Black*. This diversity of preferences reflects the diversity that is so important to the field, and this is as it should be. Previously, the word *Negro* was used throughout the chapter by my father, William Pipes, but on his deathbed he changed by hand almost every *Negro* to *Black,* and that is how his chapter appears in this volume.

There may be even greater need today than there was in the past to look at the unique experiences in African American history, to find the reasons behind many current problems. In this edition, the contributors and I have attempted to do just that. Only by knowing our history, both African and American, will we be able to understand just what is happening in the present society. This edition of *Black Families* should be very significant both for the knowledge it imparts and for the understanding of and appreciation for African American families to be gained from it.

Preface to the Second Edition

Significant changes have occurred in the lives of Black families across the nation during the past 6 years. Major policy changes at the federal and local levels have truncated governmental programs that had contributed to the vulnerability of many of our families and the occupational and educational avenues that are open for members of Black families. While some Blacks have benefited from earlier governmental programs of support and have been upwardly mobile, many others have fallen deeper into despair.

Governments have become more conservative and apparently less interested in supporting the striving toward stability and equality of family members of color. Verbal assertions of the need for economic self-sufficiency have run parallel to policy decisions that have limited the opportunities of families to remove themselves from dependency, the prevailing preference for white over Black has continued, has intensified, and has led to more overt demonstrations of structural and personal ethnocentrism and racism.

A decade that began with hope has not lived up to expectations. The need is even greater now to understand the economic situations, cultural patterns, and socialization practices of Black families. The African American patterns of mutual support and coping strategies that were so effective in the past are more important now than ever. The authors of chapters in the second edition of *Black Families* have continued to make important contributions in their various fields. All the contributors have been actively living their own family lives, as can be seen by comparing their descriptions in the 1981 edition and this 1988 edition. We are all 7 years older and, we hope, wiser. During this period babies have been born, marriages have ended, spouses have passed, children have married, a Ph.D. degree was completed, tenure and professorships were earned, important awards were received, jobs have ended, and important professional positions have been assumed. These significant life changes are often reflected in the work of the authors.

Since the first edition was published, two of the contributors have died: my father, William Harrison Pipes, and one of my dearest friends, Marie Ferguson Peters. Both of them are dearly missed by me and by many of us.

This revised volume grew out of the need to bring the content current with ongoing research and literature, to reflect the demographic changes that have occurred in the past 6 years, and to expand the topic into newly relevant areas. Many of the classic chapters remain as they were. The new authors reflect the issues that have come to the forefront during the 1980s. Four new contributors have joined us: John Hope Franklin, Joyce Ladner, Julianne Malveaux, and Audrey Chapman. Their chapters have added special insights and depth to the volume. We welcome them to our collective effort. We hope that this Sage Focus Edition will contribute to greater understanding of the lives of Black families and the issues that must be addressed to successfully prepare us for the next generation of Black Families.

Acknowledgments

This volume has been a long time coming. The chapters were almost all compiled just before the unexpected illness and subsequent death of my husband, John Lewis McAdoo. The events following his death and the emotional roller coaster on which my family and I found ourselves precluded my finishing the volume for some time. After a lengthy process, however, it is now finally completed.

Many persons have helped in the completion of this new edition. The contributors are foremost, for the many hours they have devoted. I feel very good about their efforts and think they will be proud, as I am, of the third edition. Each author has made significant contributions to the field of African American family studies. A diversity of viewpoints on Black families is presented, which adds spice to this book. The authors represent many different areas of study and approach African American families from many different perspectives. I want to thank my contributors for their patience and thoughtfulness. I also especially want to thank my next-door neighbor and editor, Elizabeth Johnston, for her constant willingness to work with me in bringing these chapters together.

The real impetus for my writing about Black families grew from my own experiences of living within my family of orientation, which was made up of the Pipes family of Mississippi and the Russell family of Kentucky. My grandparents—Hezekiah Winter Pipes, Ada L. Causey Pipes, Harvey Clarence Russell, Harriett Tucker Russell, and Julia Jones Russell McClain (the maternal grandmother I knew)—left important legacies for me, especially my parents. William Harrison Pipes and Anna Howard Russell Pipes, my parents, left me with memories of love, encouragement, and respect and love for education and African American history.

My family of procreation has been composed, most importantly, of my husband of 32 years, John Lewis McAdoo, a very special loving companion, and our children. John and I worked together on our family, in our writing and research, and in our interactions with people from all over the world. He was a wonderful father to our four McAdoo children: Michael Garnett, John Lewis III, Julia BethAnn, and David Harrison Pipes. Our family has grown with their marriages to Marsu Cartmill, Thomas Poole, and Wanda Smith. We have been further delighted with our three grandchildren: Joseph Brandon, William, and John IV, the last born only a month before John's death. These individuals have provided me with all the love, support, complexities, child-rearing traumas, frustrations, and pride that could be found in any family.

I would like also to acknowledge the support of my siblings, Willetta Ada Pipes Ewing and William Howard Pipes. Willetta brought Paul Ewing and Kahmara and Paul Russell Ewing into our lives. All the members of my extended family, those who have passed on and those who are living, have had special places in my life: Aunt Bessie Russell Stone; Uncles Harvey and George Vance; Aunt Randa Russell; Aunt Hattie Pipes Peagues; my cousins Mildred Peagues Beadle, Alfred Stone, and Randa Stone Hailstock; and my younger cousins Denny, John, George, and Lisa Russell. The new family members I have discovered while doing my continuous family oral history will join our family together in one continuous line.

My special thanks go to Elsie Zdanis, who typed the entire first edition of *Black Families,* and whose organizational skills were instrumental in that effort and even into this third edition. Other peers and friends, who remain anonymous, did blind reviews of the chapters and provided important feedback to all of us. Finally, I want to thank my Sage editor through two editions and the beginning of the third, Mitch Allen, and my present editor, Peter Labella. Both have had the patience of Job as deadlines were missed during a traumatic year.

Introduction

A decade that began with hope has not lived up to expectations. The need to understand the economic situations, cultural patterns, and socialization practices of Black families is even greater now than it has been in the past. Significant changes have occurred in the lives of Black families across the United States during the past decade. Major policy changes at the federal and local levels have truncated government programs that had contributed to the vulnerability of many of our families and have limited the occupational and educational avenues open to African Americans. Although some Blacks benefited from earlier government programs of support and have been upwardly mobile, many others have fallen deeper into despair. Governments have become more conservative and apparently less interested in supporting the striving toward stability and equality of families of color. Verbal assertions of the need for economic self-sufficiency have run parallel to policy decisions that have limited the opportunities of families to remove themselves from dependency. The prevailing preference for White over Black has continued, even intensified, and has led to more overt demonstrations of structural and personal ethnocentrism and racism. The African American patterns of mutual support and coping strategies that were so effective in the past are more important now than ever.

The study of African American family life has undergone periods of intense activity and periods of quiescence. At one point it was possible to indicate the one expert in the field and later the three or four, but an infusion of new researchers has increased the production of studies, books, and views on the Black family. This increased activity has been helpful for the field.

When one is asked to make a definitive statement about "the Black family," it is now more difficult to respond. The diversity of Black families, their value systems, and their lifestyles, makes it impossible for any one person to be "the expert" on Black families. This is as it should be.

This book addresses some unresolved issues concerning African American families. The original impetus for the first edition of *Black Families* came out of my frustration at not being able to find a book on Black families to use in my graduate classes at Howard University. I grew tired of teaching my family and child development courses from piles of reprints and library assignments. There were excellent individual works on Blacks, but they were all scattered around and difficult to assemble for a single course. I felt a strong need to assemble one volume of writings from the work of the excellent scholars in the field that could be used for a survey course on Black families or as a supplement to family studies courses. Several volumes have been written on African American families in the 15 years since the first edition of *Black Families* was published, but none is as useful for instruction in upper- or graduate-level courses. *Black Families* ties the family unit together as family members attempt to survive economically, develop relationships in order to procreate and rear children, and move as advocates for their children and other family members. Some of the best thinkers on American Black families were asked to prepare chapters that tie together the major issues, theories, and empirical findings in their areas. These contributors were carefully selected from a variety of disciplines, regardless of philosophical orientation, race, or agreement with my own biases.

Many of the contributors to this third edition of *Black Families* also wrote chapters that appeared in previous editions, and they have continued to make important contributions in their various fields. They have been actively living their own family lives, as one can see by comparing their biographical sketches in the 1981 and 1988 editions with those in this one. We are all several years older and, we hope, wiser. During this period, some of the authors had babies, marriages ended, spouses passed away, children graduated from college, children married, grandchildren were born, a Ph.D. was completed, tenure and professorships were earned, important awards were received, jobs ended and began, and important professional positions were assumed. These significant life changes are reflected in the work of the authors.

Since the first edition was published, three of the contributors have died: my father, William Harrison Pipes; my husband, John Lewis McAdoo; and one of my dearest friends, Marie Ferguson Peters. All of them are deeply missed by me and by many others.

This revised edition grew out of the need to bring the content current with ongoing research and literature, to reflect the demographic changes that have occurred in the past several years, and to expand the topics into newly relevant areas. Many of the classic chapters remain very nearly as they appeared in previous editions, whereas the new authors reflect issues that have come to the forefront during the 1990s.

Lack of consensus keeps the field of Black family studies lively, volatile, and continuously open to new interpretations as new and old data are incorporated by those writing in the field and those of us living it. The diversity of schools of thought reflects the diversity of Black life experiences and is reflected in the title of this book: *Black Families* rather than *The Black Family*. No attempt is made in this volume to represent all sides of each issue, nor have all the chapters been selected to promote any one prevailing view, interest group, or sociopolitical orientation. A careful reading of the chapters reveals fundamental unresolved—and some probably unresolvable—differences in frames of reference represented by the authors.

This diversity is also reflected in the manner in which racial and ethnic labels are handled in the various chapters. Conformity in usage is customary in an edited book, but readers will note some variation here. During periods of flux, racial labels, as well as decisions about whether or not to capitalize those terms, become more than just matters of editorial style; they are often intended as political statements or as expressions of personal racial pride or individuality. The history of our own life experiences, professional training, and ideological stances have affected all our perceptions of families. Conformity to an imposed style would have violated these expressions. Therefore, reflecting the diversity within the field of the study of Black families, the authors have made their own decisions regarding the use of *Black, black, White, white, African American, Afro-American,* and *Negro* in their own chapters.

Demythologizing Black Families

As interdisciplinary researchers, scholars studying African American families have been able to go beyond the negative stereotypical views held about these families. Unfortunately, the wider society has not made this journey, and many of us are continually called upon to speak against the negative images of Black families—images often held by persons who are in positions to make policy and programmatic decisions that can have direct effects on the lives of Black families. Therefore, some of our creative energies are continually channeled into reactionary activities when we would prefer to concentrate on more creative theoretical and empirical examination of Black family life.

Demythologizing negative images of the Black family is an ongoing process that probably will continue for generations, for the ethnocentric concepts held by the mainstream social science literature about Black families will persist. The one main change that has occurred is that fewer writers are able to make blatant conjectures about Black families and remain unchallenged. Publishers and editors of professional journals, the "gatekeepers" of much of the literature on African Americans, have become more sensitized to these issues. Although the process of putting myths to rest is essential, we must not sacrifice our other efforts to achieve this one objective. This volume represents a move to continue the examination of Black families on a conceptual level and to test some of the theories that have been brought forth. It also is an effort to give a complete review of relevant works on a given area within each chapter and to gather the most current facts and figures known about Black families.

Diverse Conceptualizations

There have been major divisions within the field of African American family studies. The major disagreement has focused on whether Black families differ from other families in any way other than their greater level of poverty. One view is that Black families are what they are simply because they are poor; if poverty were removed, then there would be a convergence of values and structure among all families. Another view is that poverty, plus the experiences of slavery and Reconstruction, has left an indelible mark on Black families that persists today. Still another view is that Black families are unique because of the remnants of African culture that have been maintained and adapted to discrimination. These divisions among Black scholars are now evolving into the "Africanist" and "empiricist" schools, with growing polarity between the two. The chapters in this volume reflect both points of view and should move us closer to the answer to some of the age-old debates about the African American family. The real "truth" will probably be an amalgamation of many scholars' views.

There is no denying the soul-satisfying comfort that comes from identification with a known ethnic lode of culture, whether it is retained directly from the old country or re-created in part within the new country. Too often the emotional desire for ethnic identification has caused many writers to go far beyond their data or knowledge to create cultural links that may be tenuous. Although this provides a needed grounding in an emotional place of origin, it often is not based on a clear understanding of history.

The work of Herskovits (1941), Nobles et al. (1976), Pipes (1951), Semaj (1980), Sudarkasa (1980), and Walker (1980) has contributed to study in this direction. The links between African and African American families have become more obvious as scholars have refined their analyses and as more writers have joined the effort with skills and expertise in cross-cultural analysis. The danger to be avoided is the romantic belief that a return to Africanist practices will somehow eradicate the problems that beset contemporary Black families, such as plural marriages within a society that makes adequate support of even one average Black family difficult. There may be few, if any, one-to-one direct carryovers, but the common patterns found in non-Western families on the African continent, in the Caribbean, and in isolated areas of rural America make it impossible to deny some cultural continuities.

At the same time, there is some clear validity in the view of those who feel that poverty and discrimination are the major factors impinging on Black families. These scholars attempt to focus on the variables of Black family life in the here and now. As we can only reconstruct what may have been retained from Africa or acquired during enslavement, these researchers argue, we should emphasize at this point only on what we can measure now. This pragmatic approach assumes that historians and other researchers will eventually be able to piece together more of the patterns that are now only speculation. Meanwhile, we can focus on doing good descriptive studies and move into more theoretical work.

There is so much value that can and will result from the investigations of these two schools of emphasis that there is no need for antagonism between the two. Yet this tension may be the impetus that will generate even greater endeavors. Serious scholars will have to keep abreast of the dynamic debates and explorations that will come from the concentration on cultural continuities and from the separate approaches.

Key Scholarship in the Field

This volume on African American families continues in the same vein as
W. E. B. Du Bois's *The Negro American Family* (1908) and Robert Staples's
edited book *The Black Family: Essays and Studies* (1971). In these books
Du Bois and Staples brought together what they felt reflected the best work
done at that time on Black families. This volume does not give a historical
portrayal of Black families, but concentrates on the contemporary family.
The history of Black families has been succinctly presented elsewhere by
noted writers and should be familiar to readers; these include the works of
Du Bois (1967), Quarles (1964), Blassingame (1972), Lammermeier (1973),
Bennett (1975), Gutman (1976), Pleck (1979), Haley (1976), and Drake
(1980). In addition, there are large-scale studies with which the reader should
also be familiar, such as the work of Scanzoni (1971), Heiss (1971), and
James Jackson and others at the University of Michigan Institute of Social
Research.

Following the beginning made by Du Bois, Frazier remains the undisputed
leader in the social science study of Black families (see, e.g., Frazier 1939).
Although there is not total agreement with some of his analyses about family
life, the clearness of his methodology, observations, and analyses and the
vacuum that existed before his works place him in a position that even his
opponents have had to respect. The next wave of work was spearheaded by
the key writers in the field: Billingsley, with *Black Families in White America*
(1968) and Hill, with *The Strengths of Black Families* (1971). These works
articulate the essence of where we were and where we hoped to go in the
field. Although they were not the only voices of that period, Billingsley and
Hill became the main spokesmen on Black families. Their theoretical and
descriptive works provided a springboard for many of the writings on Black
families during the 1960s and 1970s.

Sources of Black Family Research Data

Highlighting the traditional leaders in the field of Black family research
is difficult, for at the same time other scholars in different fields were making
similar observations, but their works were never picked up in the popular or
professional press. A review of many of the early Negro journals, newspapers, and writings in literature, anthropology, religion, education, and

social organizations makes one aware of the mass of beautifully documented works scattered over the country and lost to scholars.

Even today, dissertations are being written that break new ground, but for a variety of reasons the findings they contain are not being made known to others in the field. The doctoral dissertations and master's theses found in the Howard University library, and materials in its Moreland Room, are probably the richest untapped source of information on Black life. Many of the master's theses done in the first half of this century are far superior to dissertations currently being done in the major universities. They are the result of students' striving for excellence and the Ivy League-trained professors who came to Howard, attracted by the caliber of minds on the campus and who, because of racism, could not obtain positions on non-Black campuses. They demanded and received a level of scholarship that would be difficult to replicate today with few exceptions.

Across the country there are resources for Black family research that are being tapped only slightly: Atlanta and Fisk Universities are two of these. Much of the archival work being done is occurring at larger universities that are able to provide the resources needed by archivists, historians, and oral historians. The Smithsonian Institution has become another focal point during the present period.

Other continuing resources for data on African American family life are the Black publications put out by professional organizations and a dedicated group of scholars (e.g., *Journal of Black Psychology, Black Scholar, Journal of Behavior and Social Scientist, Western Journal of Black Studies*). The problems these publications confront, however, are the costs and energy required to maintain their efforts without needed university or institutional support. Graduate students' work may not be exposed, and their professors are not familiar with them. These sources of data, in essence, have not been "validated" by the mainstream and thus are denied to graduate students, Black and white, who want to use them as their main theoretical bases. This lack of validation limits students' use of these sources, but frees writers and editors to take directions that are supportive of scholarly examination unhindered by the acceptability of organized mainstream scholarship.

It would be wrong to assert that only Black institutions and researchers are advancing Black family studies. Several professional organizations have supported the efforts of scholars studying Black families. The National Council on Family Relations, for which I served as president in 1994, has sponsored the *Journal of Marriage and the Family* and *Family Relations*.

The first of these took leadership with its "Decade Reviews" written by Robert Staples and others as well as a groundbreaking special issue on Black families edited by Marie Peters. Black families had been so ignored in the major professional social science journals that this special issue significantly increased the number of articles published on the subject. The National Association of Social Workers has done likewise by sponsoring a special journal issue, edited by June Hopps, on people of color. Several other special issues have further disseminated the work on Black families.

Although these target issues have made special contributions, it is unfortunate that articles on Black family studies are not regularly included in many major journals. There have been more articles in the past two years, however—*Child Development, Developmental Psychology,* and *Journal of Adolescence* have all included such articles, for example. For a variety of ethnocentric reasons as well as lack of knowledge about the great amount of work being done in this field, editors have not routinely included work on or by Blacks. Important reviews of the literature written by people who are not of color usually ignore significant research by African Americans. This situation may be improved in the future with the more active participation of Blacks and other people of color in professional organizations and the professional publication process.

Meanwhile, the reality is that many social scientists do not value the diversity found in African American families. The attitudes often encountered by African American researchers require that active participation and support of the Black-oriented and other professional publication efforts must be continued. It will be necessary for researchers to continue expending their energies actively on both fronts for the foreseeable future.

Roles Played by Professional Meetings in Black Family Research

The major professional organizations often are the validators of the field and control the academic and professional futures of young researchers and, indirectly, funds for their research efforts. Therefore, a continuation of the integration of knowledge of African American family life is required to include it in the mainstream literature that will be available to all researchers. At the same time, the freedom to take unpopular positions and make exploratory thrusts generally does not exist within mainstream journals. These efforts are possible only within journals or institutions that have gone beyond such debates as "Are Black families really a valid subject area?" "Are these really just polemic exercises?" "Are we giving too much emphasis to people of color?" "Can't we just focus on 'good research' and forget about all this race business?"

There are other places where the needed dialogue has become traditional. The annual meetings of the National Association of Black Psychologists have become a rallying point for many researchers to expound upon and refresh their own concepts on African American families. The annual conferences held at the University of Louisville on Black families have become another exciting venue for those of us immersed in the field. The conference's selected themes each year bring attendees up-to-date on many activities going on across the country. These meetings allow "older" researchers in the field to come together and speak with one another, to meet younger re-searchers, and to return home stimulated to continue their concentration on families.

In past years, symposia have been presented at the National Council on Family Relations by some of the contributors to this volume (Staples, Peters, Nobles, both McAdoos, Hill, Johnson) on Black families. At each biennial meeting of the Society for Research on Child Development, contributors to this volume (Harrison, Peters, and McAdoo) have organized and presented information on the African American family and child. There has been a definite effort in these two organizations to bring together those who are doing work on Black families and those who are working with Black children, for the problems and concerns of one affect the other, both directly and indirectly.

Similar efforts have continued over the years at other major professional meetings. Seminars have been organized by myself and by Marie Peters at the Groves Conference on Marriage and the Family, where I have served on the board of directors for several years. These have brought together some of the key Black and other minority researchers to focus on one theme each year. Widespread cross-fertilization has grown out of these efforts, which have allowed researchers and writers from all races to come together and share information. They have had some influence on those who are writing the textbooks to be used in college classrooms throughout the country and have brought together for the first time researchers from different disciplines who may never attend the same professional conferences. In addition, cau-cuses, sections, special interest groups, and other subdivisions of these organizations specifically for Blacks and other people of color are contributing to the professional socialization of Blacks and the dissemination of information on Black family life.

There was a period when a poor piece of scholarship was heard and then quietly ignored, for a researcher who focused on Black families often came under so much attack from those in the profession that it was considered contrary to "the code" to speak out against poor work (Welsing 1970). We are no longer within the reactionary frame of reference in which it was felt unwise to differ with the "leaders." We have to be able to give and receive criticism within the field on any piece of research that is presented. Efforts at internal critiques have been found in recent years among a small group of researchers who come together annually to make presentations and be critiqued in closed sessions at the Conference on Empirical Black Psychology. Papers have become stronger as a result. This process assists younger researchers who feel they are unable to get this type of support at their diverse academic institutions and agencies. Papers are presented, honestly critiqued, edited, and then are ready for publication.

In addition to the sometimes esoteric dialogues held at professional meetings, the real-world problems of families are continuing to be addressed by those in the community who are providing leadership in family advocacy organizations. At their seminars, annual meetings, and media briefings, and in publications, they are acting as watchdogs, monitoring the erosion of Black family resources. They have made evaluations and designed programs and public education efforts in order to allow communities and parents to take an active part in bettering the conditions of their families. Some of the major organizations that are involved in such efforts are the Children's Defense Fund, NAACP, Urban League, National Black Child Development Institute, and National Council of Negro Women. Representatives from these key organizations have pointed out areas where efforts should be targeted and have developed agendas that can be followed in each community.

Personal Reflections

One of my special delights in editing this volume has been the in-depth study I was able to make of my father's book that led to the excerpt presented herein. I had quickly read the book for interest in high school and as an undergraduate, mostly looking for good references, so I felt I knew its contents. But it was only after going over the book repeatedly to select one of the sermons for this volume that I really had a chance to see all the richness included in *Say Amen, Brother!* The Georgia sermons are a vivid reminder of the central role the rural "Black Belt" churches played throughout the South. With the growing interest developing in oral history of the Black experience, several persons and major libraries have made copies of these now rare sermons. Over the years, mobility, education, and "sophistication" have gradually changed this preaching style. These sermons provide a direct link to the religious patterns found immediately after and probably during enslavement.

When I was a child, my parents, Bill Pipes and Anna Russell Pipes, would take me, their Victor recording machine, and a Brownie box camera down old dusty roads to little churches to participate in all-day church meetings, in order to make the recordings that are included in this chapter. I have vague memories of these experiences, and I grew up with the pictures and the recordings of the sermons, which are now in the archives at the University of California at Berkeley.

It is typical for children of authors to take their parents' works for granted and not pay them the attention they deserve, as these books have always been around on their bookshelves. My children had that experience when they were in college. They paid no attention to the stacks of papers and books all over the house as they grew up, until they were in a class and saw one of their parents' articles listed in a bibliography. They were amazed that anyone would bother to read them, let alone think that the papers they had to eat around on the dining room table were worth their effort to read. Just as I was, they were pleasantly surprised and delighted when they finally sat down and really began to understand what their parents had been doing all those years. This process was particularly poignant for me because my father died during the last stages of the production of the first edition of this book in 1981.

References

Bennett, L. 1975. *The Shaping of Black America.* Chicago: Johnson.

Billingsley, A. 1968. *Black Families in White America.* Englewood Cliffs, NJ: Prentice Hall.

Blassingame, J. 1972. *The Slave Community Plantation Life in the Ante-Bellum South.* New York: Oxford University Press.

Drake, S. C. 1980. "Anthropology and the Black Experience." *Black Scholar* 11(7):2-31.

Du Bois, W. E. B. 1908. *The Negro American Family.* Cambridge: MIT Press.

————. 1967. *The Philadelphia Negro: A Social Study.* New York: Schocken.

Frazier, E. F. 1939. *The Negro Family in the United States.* Chicago: University of Chicago Press.

Gutman, H. G. 1976. *The Black Family in Slavery and Freedom, 1750-1925.* New York: Pantheon.

Haley, A. 1976. *Roots: The Saga of an American Family.* New York: Doubleday.

Heiss, J. 1971. *The Case of the Black Family: A Sociological Inquiry.* New York: Columbia University Press.

Herskovits, M. J. 1941. *The Myth of the Negro Past.* New York: Harper.

Hill, R. H. 1971. *The Strengths of Black Families.* New York: Emerson-Hall.

Lammermeier, P. J. 1973. "The Urban Black Family of the Nineteenth Century: A Study of Black Family Structure in the Ohio Valley, 1850–1880." *Journal of Marriage and the Family* 35:440-56.

Nobles, W. W., et al. 1976. *A Formulative and Empirical Study of Black Families.* DHEW Publication OCD-90-C-255. Washington, DC: Government Printing Office.

Pipes, W. H. 1951. *Say Amen, Brother!* New York: William-Frederick.

Pleck, E. H. 1979. *Black migration and Poverty: Boston 1865–1900.* New York: Academic Press.

Quarles, B. 1964. *The Negro in the Making of America.* New York: Collier.

Scanzoni, J. 1971. *The Black Family in Modern Society.* Boston: Allyn & Bacon.

Semaj, L. 1980. "Meaningful Male/Female Relationships in a State of Declining Sex Ratio." *Black Books Bulletin* 6.

Staples, R. E., ed. 1971. *The Black Family: Essays and Studies.* Belmont, CA: Wadsworth.

Sudarkasa, N. 1980. "African and Afro-American Family Structure." *Black Scholar* 11(8):37-60.

Walker, S. 1980. "African Gods in America: The Black Religious Continuum." *Black Scholar* 11(8):25-36.

Welsing, F. 1970. *The Cress Theory of Color Confrontation and Racism.* Washington, DC: Welsing.

PART I

Historical and Theoretical Conceptualizations of African American Families

We begin the discussion with an overview of the history of Black families in America. As only he is able to do, John Hope Franklin presents a beautiful statement of the experiences of African American families. He highlights the attempts of enslaved men to be reunited with their wives and children when they had been sold away. He emphasizes the importance of the strong family tradition to the community of enslaved Africans, as the families continued with two parents despite impoverishment.

Niara Sudarkasa's work on African and African American family organization brings knowledge from an anthropological viewpoint and relates it to policy issues. Sudarkasa gives an overview of West African family structure and relates it to the American experience during and after enslavement. She points to the disintegration of poor families due to economic factors, and she ends with a discussion of traditional African American family values that are similar to West African values.

The Africanist versus "culture of poverty" debate is continued in the chapter by William Harrison Pipes. It is amazing that the chapters by Sudarkasa and Pipes were written 40 years apart, given that they address many of the same issues and arguments: the sources of Black American family and religious or cultural values. Although their fields of emphasis differ—one in anthropology and the other in speech and literature—their conclusions are the same. This shows that we are still arguing the same arguments. Many recent writers are not familiar with the writings of the Negro intellectuals before the turn of the century and during the first half of the twentieth century. The fact that certain issues are still introduced in 30-year cycles reflects the importance of these issues to Black life and identity. The review of authors whose works are often unavailable today adds much to the present literature.

Discussion of the diverse conceptualizations of the Black family continues with the reflective analysis of Jualynne Elizabeth Dodson, who reviews the work of writers whose viewpoints are based in the three major schools of thought on Black families: pathological or dysfunctional, cultural relativity, and social class as main determinant. For each school, Dodson provides an in-depth review of the major writers and the chief beliefs held by those in the school, presented within a historical context. Her analysis is invaluable because it sets the stage for the chapters that follow, some of which have been written by authors who represent one of the three identified schools of thought. Dodson stresses the need for further empirical research before we can make any definitive statement about the cultural origins of Black family life. She presents within her reflective analysis a schema of the minimum requirements needed to evaluate the Black family effectively.

In his chapter, psychologist Wade W. Nobles focuses on the importance of the parent-child relationship in the African American family and the need for the family to be geared to prepare children for a unique type of existence in a hostile, racist societal environment. Writing from a strong Afrocentric perspective, Nobles gives a sound background for the scientific racism that formed the groundwork that has allowed one group to receive preferential treatment over another. He explores the changes that have occurred in social scientists' coverage of the Black family and the seminal work of Billingsley, Hill, and Staples. He uses the centuries-long enslavement of Africans as an analogy for the existence of African Americans today. The supportive network of the extended family has been used to protect African American children, and Nobles outlines three domains that must receive attention if children are to realize their potential: a sense of history, a strong sense of family, and a sense of the need and power of spiritual beliefs. His work ties neatly into the chapter by Sudarkasa on the extended family and that by Pipes on the importance of religious participation. Nobles ends his chapter with the assertion that for the family to be able to perform its responsibilities, it is imperative that the state be supportive of the family. Nobles also adds an element of spirituality that one does not often find in the family literature. He presents the cultural base but also supports the later chapters in this volume by Hill and Edelman, on the importance of parents' operating within knowledge of the political system in providing for children, but not at the expense of leaving the spiritual or cultural components of their lives to chance.

Leanor Boulin Johnson effectively rounds out the discussion on diverse conceptualizations of the Black family with her empirical study of the theoretical frameworks that have been presented in the sociology and social work journals with the widest circulation during the period 1965–1978. She first presents two conceptual frameworks on the value orientations of the Black family, as presented by Walter Allen and Robert Staples, that are similar to those found in Dodson's reflective analysis. Allen's three stages show the changes in orientation that the literature has taken as it has gone from a deviant view to an equivalent view, and finally to a cultural relative view of the Black family and its function. Staples's four stages relate to the changes in emphasis from looking at families only as victims of poverty, to seeing them as pathological, to the reactionary stances of the 1960s, and finally to the emphasis on functionality of families, regardless of structure. Both Allen and Staples note the clear value of the later stages in comparison with the earlier stages. Johnson has analyzed all the articles related to the Black family found in 10 journals, applying both typologies to each. This extremely useful analysis indicates that less than 1% of all empirical studies published in these journals in the time period of her research related to the Black family, and most of those were in special issues edited by Blacks or in Black journals. Social work journals during her period of study were surprisingly negligent in their coverage of Black families. Earlier articles tended to stress deviance, and later ones, especially those by Black re-searchers, tended to focus on Black uniqueness, without comparison with white family norms. Johnson lists all of the articles surveyed and provides ratings of the articles' value orientations and the topics covered. These ratings should be useful for researchers who want to avoid relying on earlier studies that used the cultural deviant or pathological framework to describe Black families.

African American Families

A Historical Note

JOHN HOPE FRANKLIN

The family is one of the strongest and most important traditions in the black community. How much of this tradition is based in African custom and how much was developed in the New World is impossible to determine. It is doubtless some of both.

There is no question that early in their sojourn on this continent, enslaved Africans evinced their concern about the family unit. Their loyalty to the family defied the efforts of slave owners to promote a casual attitude among blacks toward this all-important institution. A great deal has been written about gentlemen slave owners who would not separate families, but the evidence clearly refutes this. "I think it is quite probable that this [run-away] . . . has succeeded in getting to his wife who we carried away last spring out of my neighborhood," one advertisement read. A Florida owner advertised for a 14-year-old who had escaped and was trying to reach Atlanta, where his mother was supposed to be. Another runaway was said to be no doubt lurking in a certain vicinity near her children. Still another escapee was believed to be near Savannah, where he had a wife and children. Literally thousands of examples are known of slaves running away in search of members of their families. The attachment was real, and the warmth of their relationships persisted, despite their separation by the so-called gentlemen who claimed they never did such things.

The family was important to the slave community, if for no other reason than the lack of other institutions to which slaves could openly be committed. In the quiet and intimacy of the family, slaves could provide the mutual support so necessary to withstand the abuses and cruelties of slavery. They married early and, if necessary, frequently—usually with the encouragement of the owner, especially if the prospects were bright for numerous offspring, which, of course, were additional capital for him.

Many slave men preferred to marry women from other plantations. As John Anderson put it, "I did not want to marry a girl belonging to my own place, because I knew I could not bear to see her ill-treated." Henry Bibb put it even more eloquently: "If my wife must be exposed to the insults and licentious passions of wicked slave drivers and overseers; if she must bear the stripes of the lash laid on by an unmerciful tyrant; if this is to be done with impunity, which is frequently done by slaveholders and their abettors, Heaven forbid that I should be compelled to witness the sight."

At the end of the Civil War, freedmen searched frantically for family members separated by slavery. Some wrote the Freedmen's Bureau seeking assistance in locating loved ones. One man who had moved to Pittsburgh in the antebellum period asked the Bureau in Greenville, South Carolina, to help him find his parents. Some freedmen, not knowing where to turn or what to do, simply got on the road and began to search for their wives, husbands, or children. Some were successful; some were not. Some discovered that their mates had remarried, having given up hope of reunion. In those early years following emancipation, nothing was more poignant than the sight of separated families attempting to reestablish their relationships. The institution of slavery had not destroyed the black family.

Given that many slaves had been married by the mere consent or even suggestions of their owners, they sought at the end of the war to make their marriages legal and their children legitimate. In 1866, for example, 9,452 former slaves from 17 North Carolina counties registered their marriages by entering their names on the marriage records and paying a fee of 25 cents. Herbert Gutman (1976), who discovered the North Carolina records, tells us that many couples took the next step and participated in secular or religious marriage ceremonies. That this rural and illiterate population, fresh from slavery and living in the aftermath of a devastating war, could turn from their urgent activities and numerous anxieties to legitimate their marriages tells us something of the extent to which the sense of family was a part of the very fabric of the Afro-American community.

Family stability in the black community survived Reconstruction and was alive and well at the end of the nineteenth century. In the 1880s, most rural and urban southern blacks lived in husband- or father-present households and subfamilies. During those years, however, the number of women over 40 years of age heading father-absent households and subfamilies increased. In some instances the husband had died. In others, he went away to work. The practice persisted, moreover, for young, single mothers to live with their parents or other adults, thus relieving them of the responsibility of heading a household. Gutman (1976) points out that in 1900 the kin-related household was the norm, and the size of the household had hardly changed since the end of Reconstruction. Long marriages continued to be common among rural and urban southern blacks, "and so was the attachment of parent to child."

It is remarkable that the great migration of blacks to the urban North during World War I and subsequent years did not adversely affect the stability of the black family to any significant degree. In Manhattan, for example, where the black population increased rapidly between 1905 and 1925, the black family remained intact, although it differed in characteristics from the southern rural and urban black families of a generation earlier. There were many foreign blacks—mostly West Indian—and understandably more boarders and lodgers than one saw in the South. Also, the simple nuclear household tended to decline in importance, whereas extended and augmented households increased in importance.

Surprisingly, with all these changes during these crucial years, no significant increase in male-absent households or subfamilies occurred. In 1925, for example, six of seven black households had either a husband or father. As Herbert Gutman (1976) concludes in *The Black Family in Slavery and Freedom:*

> At all moments in time between 1880 and 1925—that is, from an adult generation born in slavery to an adult generation about to be devastated by the Great Depression of the 1930s and the modernization of southern agriculture afterward—the typical Afro-American family was lower-class in status and headed by two parents. This was so in the urban and rural South in 1880 and in 1900 and in New York City in 1905 and 1925. It was just as common among farm laborers, sharecroppers, tenants, and northern and southern urban unskilled laborers and service workers. It accompanied the southern blacks in the

great migration to the North that has so reshaped the United States in the twentieth century.

The strong family tradition among blacks thus survived the slave system, then legal segregation, discrimination, and enforced poverty. Finally, black families had to contend with racially hostile governmental and societal practices, policies, and attitudes. These forces ultimately weakened a family fabric that had for generations proved unusually resilient, even in the face of awesome adversity. Indeed, until the 1960s, a remarkable 75% of black families included both husband and wife. However, in a study published in 1983, the Joint Center for Political Studies (1983) concludes:

> Since the 1960s, rapid urbanization, and especially ghettoization, has had a devastating impact on many black families. As large numbers of blacks migrated to large cities from rural areas, black males have often been unable to find work, and government policies and other social forces further sapped family strength. These trends proceed apace today, aided by the widespread failure even to recognize the pressures on the black family as central to other problems and by the failure to devise both preventive and healing strategies.

References

Franklin, J. H. 1987. *From Slavery to Freedom: The History of Negro Americans.* New York: Knopf.

Gutman, H. G. 1976. *The Black Family in Slavery and Freedom, 1750-1925.* New York: Pantheon.

Joint Center for Political Studies. 1983. *A Policy Framework for Racial Justice.* Washington, DC: Author.

African American Families and Family Values

NIARA SUDARKASA

All over the United States, families are changing. The American ideal of the nuclear family, composed of two parents and their children, is only one of many different types of family groupings occupying single households today. Various permutations of the stepfamily, resulting from the marriages of couples with children from previous marriages, are commonplace. The numbers of households composed of single mothers and their children have increased dramatically over the past 25 years. Single parenting by men is also on the rise, as is the incidence of parenting by couples of the same gender.

Public policy discussions and debate over these changes have not focused on the economic, demographic, and sociological forces underlying them. Rather, these discussions have tended to portray changes in family structure as moral failures that signal the breakdown in the fabric of our society. Thus, instead of seeking to understand and assess these emerging forms of the family in order to influence their development, the public is warned against

AUTHOR'S NOTE: The original version of this chapter was included in Niara Sudarkasa et al., eds., *Exploring the African-American Experience* (Lincoln, PA: Lincoln University Press).

(a) the "alarming disintegration" of the nuclear family and (b) the "loss of traditional family values."

No fewer than three U.S. presidents have identified the disintegration of the family and the loss of family values as issues of national concern. Former presidents Ronald Reagan and George Bush (along with former vice president Dan Quayle) exhorted the country to "return to traditional family values." President Bill Clinton is focusing efforts on restoring and strengthening the nuclear family. An attentive observer will recognize right away that these different emphases are actually two stanzas of the same lament for the "demise" of the American family.

And no matter what particular "spin" is given to this theme, the stated or unstated premise is the same: Something is "wrong" with families throughout America, but there is "more wrong" with Black families than with any others. Although families in various ethnic groups and at various income levels are recognized as undergoing change, only the African American family is consistently described as being "in crisis." Other families are "in transition." African American families are portrayed as being "on the brink of collapse."

Starting from this premise, a number of journalists, scholars, and public officials have gone on to lay the blame for the relatively high incidence of crime that occurs in certain Black neighborhoods on the "disintegration of the Black family" and the "absence of family values." Despite the persuasive evidence and arguments presented by William Julius Wilson in his book *The Truly Disadvantaged* (1987), that poverty and unemployment are the fundamental causes and predictors of high crime rates among African Americans, we still hear that the Black family is the "root cause" of these social problems. This notion of the "pathological" Black family, traceable to the work of Daniel Patrick Moynihan (1965) and others, still dominates thinking about the form and function of African American families, and still misinforms public policies supposedly designed to assist those families.

My primary goal in the present essay is to place the recent changes in African American family structures in their historical context, to promote a better understanding and more accurate interpretation of these changes. I ask: What do we know about the earliest African American families, and what do we know about the changes these families have undergone from the period of slavery to the present day? The discussion begins with an overview of West African family structure, because most of the enslaved population brought to America came from West Africa. Understanding the family structure brought with them by the Africans who came to America in chains is essential to an understanding of what happened to these families as they adapted and evolved during slavery and afterward.

Obviously, we cannot explain African American families only by reference to their West African cultural antecedents. By the same token, we cannot understand African American families without taking into account the West African family structures out of which they evolved. Scholars from E. Franklin Frazier ([1939] 1966) to Andrew Billingsley (1992) have emphasized the adaptive nature of African American families. Indeed, African American families, like all families, are adaptive institutions. Thus, in analyzing the changing structure of African American families, one must examine the contexts and conditions that influenced those changes. Slavery, segregation, urbanization, changing economic conditions, changing educational opportunities, changing demographics, housing options, welfare restrictions, and other public policies must all be taken into account. Yet one cannot begin to speak of the adaptation of any structure to any condition unless one knows what the structure was to begin with. In the case of African American families, we first must understand the African family structures that were brought to America in order to analyze, appreciate, and assess how those structures adapted and changed over time. In that way, we can better interpret what we see today.

In the first part of this essay, I provide an overview of the African extended family out of which African American families evolved and discuss some aspects of the transformation of African families into African American families during the period of slavery and beyond. Given space constraints, in reviewing African family structures and in seeking to interpret some of the changes that occurred in America, I must greatly simplify many complex aspects of family organization, and I can only allude to or abbreviate certain lengthy scholarly debates. Readers are encouraged, therefore, to trace the various arguments back to the publications in which they were first set forth.

In the second and third sections of this essay, I call attention to special aspects of African American household and family organization and outline the changes that have occurred in these structures in the past 30 years. Drawing on data found in Billingsley's recent book *Climbing Jacob's Ladder* (1992), I highlight the extraordinary decline in two-parent households, the phenomenal increase in female-headed households, and the increase in households with individuals living by themselves. In this connection, I cite K. Sue Jewell's *Survival of the Black Family: The Institutional Impact of*

U.S. Social Policy (1988) to support the view that many of the changes in African American family structure that have occurred in the past 30 years are linked directly to welfare policies and programs, especially the program known as Aid to Families with Dependent Children. The central argument in Jewell's copiously documented and cogently argued book is that female-headed households have proliferated as a result of welfare policies that discourage or disallow the presence of males in the home (see also Sudarkasa 1981, p. 46; 1993).

Of the various changes in family structure documented by Billingsley and Jewell, the most far-reaching is the proliferation of female-headed households, especially two-generational households in which women are living alone with their children. Most writers, including Billingsley and Jewell, attribute the phenomenal increase in this type of household to the breakdown of the nuclear family. I suggest that this is also the result of the breakup of the multigenerational female-headed household that was common before the welfare system encouraged and enabled young mothers to live alone with their children (Sudarkasa 1993). The implications of this point are very important. Instead of focusing solely on strengthening and rebuilding nuclear families, we should also acknowledge the benefit of reconnecting and strengthening multigenerational female-headed households, which have proven in the past that they, too, can be a source of stability and upward mobility within the African American community.

In the fourth part of this essay, I take up the issue of "family values" from an African American perspective. Virtually every historian or sociologist writing on the African American experience, whether Black or White, has remarked on the importance of families in the lives of African Americans. Many scholars, including myself, consider the family, especially the extended family, to be the institution most responsible for the survival of African people in the United States and elsewhere in the Americas. Some might argue for the primacy of the church, because of its centrality in the lives of African American families, but even they would have to acknowledge the more pervasive role of immediate and extended families themselves in providing for the well-being of their members.

How could these families so revered by African Americans become so reviled by our White American compatriots? How could anyone who knows the historical (and the present-day) dynamics in African American families maintain that they have no "family values"? One part of the answer is clear. Most White Americans know little or nothing about African American families beyond the negative stereotypes portrayed in the entertainment and news media and sensationalized in the press. Another part of the answer is that many White Americans, like many other people of European descent, still cling to nineteenth-century notions about the racial superiority of their group and the cultural superiority of their institutions. To the extent that African families and those of their descendants differ from the European ideal of the nuclear family, they have been denigrated by many without so much as a thought that they might gain something by studying these institutions.

In discussing African American family values, I first refer to some of the values that other scholars of Black family life have identified as important through their research. I then discuss seven values that emerged from my research as guiding principles for interpersonal relations within African families. I indicate that some of these clearly survived as guiding principles in African American families of the past and, to some extent, of the present. I go on to suggest that these "Seven Rs," as I call them—respect, responsibility, reciprocity, restraint, reverence, reason, and reconciliation—hold out promise as principles that can be universally embraced by all those seeking to strengthen African American families and communities today.

In the concluding section of the essay, I reiterate the need to get away from pejoratives in describing and analyzing African American families. Instead, I suggest that we need to focus on understanding their dynamics in order to develop and implement policies that can have truly positive effects on their future. The final point I make is that all social ills in the Black community cannot and should not be laid at the doorstep of the African American family. As many persons have said, and as Andrew Billingsley puts it in *Climbing Jacob's Ladder* (1992), "Societies make families" just as "families make societies." Billingsley goes on: "The so-called black family crisis is not of their own making; nor is it the worst crisis they ever faced and survived" (p. 79). In my judgment, this is both a justifiable conclusion from the evidence on the history of Black families in America and an appropriate starting point for analyses and action designed to address the problems they face.

African Roots of the African American Family

To understand African American families today, one must understand their evolution over time. Fundamentally, they grew out of African institutions brought to the Americas by enslaved populations over a period of centuries.

Over time, the transplanted African families evolved into African American families, Afro-Caribbean families, Afro-Brazilian families, and so forth. In the various countries or regions where the enslaved Africans were settled, they were forced to accommodate and adapt to whatever European laws and traditions prevailed. Nevertheless, the similarities evident in family life among people of African descent throughout the Americas are a testament to the strength and viability of the extended family, which is one of the two most important bases for kinship groupings throughout sub-Saharan Africa (the other being the lineage).

Not surprisingly, throughout the Americas, surviving features of African family structure tend to be strongest among the lower-income segments of the Black population. The greater the income and the higher the formal education of Africa's descendants, the more their family organization and other sociocultural attributes are intentionally or unintentionally patterned after those of the European-derived dominant group. There is no question that, everywhere, formal education and exposure to the dominant group have tended to validate and reinforce the culture and lifestyles of that group.

African extended families were (and are) large multigenerational groupings of relatives built around a core group known as a *lineage.* Members of this group of "blood relatives" trace their descent from a common male ancestor through a line of males in some societies, such as the Yoruba of Nigeria, or from a female ancestor through a line of females, in societies such as the Ashanti of Ghana (see Figures 2.1 and 2.2). Those lineages that trace descent through the father line are termed *patrilineages,* and those that trace descent through the mother line are termed *matrilineages.*

Because lineage members were and are prohibited from marrying one another, they must take their spouses from other lineages. In this way, extended families are created. The adult members of an extended family consist of the lineage members who form the core group and their spouses, who "marry in" from different lineages. According to whether the rule of descent is patrilineal or matrilineal, the children (both male and female) are considered to be born into the lineage of their father (in patrilineal societies such as the Yoruba) or their mother (in matrilineal societies such as the Ashanti).

Traditionally, extended families lived together in residential units we term *compounds.* In the countryside, a compound might be a collection of small, conically shaped, one-room mud-brick (that is, adobe) houses facing inward around a large circular courtyard. To visualize a compound within a town,

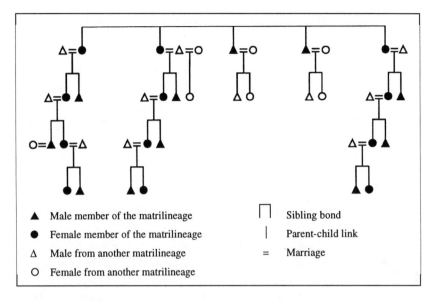

Figure 2.1. Schematic View of a Matrilineage
SOURCE: Adapted from Sudarkasa (1980).

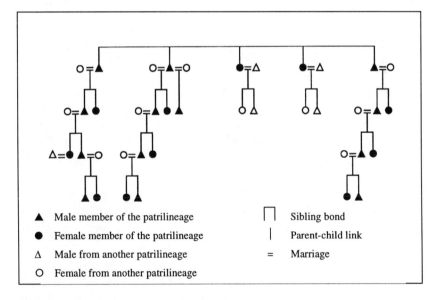

Figure 2.2. Schematic View of a Patrilineage
SOURCE: Adapted from Sudarkasa (1980).

imagine a series of one-story or two-story houses built adjacent to one another and enclosed by a large fence or wall. Alternatively, a compound could take the form of a one-story structure built around a large inner courtyard. Each side of this square-shaped building would be divided up into adjacent rooms facing a veranda or corridor that opens onto the courtyard. Members living in the compound might use the courtyard for recreation, outdoor cooking, meetings, and so forth. The back walls of such compounds would have small, highly situated windows, forming a continuous barrier to the outside. One would enter the compound through centrally located gates or large, heavy doors (see Figure 2.3).

Many families were (and are) so large that their compounds consisted of not just one but several such square buildings, and the entire cluster of dwellings might be enclosed by a wall. A compound might house 30 or 40 people, or its residents could number in the hundreds. Royal compounds might have thousands of members. Each compound, whether made up of one large dwelling or several such dwellings, was named after the lineage that formed the core of the extended family occupying the compound. The land on which a compound was built was collectively owned by a lineage, and lineage members built and owned the houses themselves. The oldest member of the lineage was its head, and all important decisions concerning the lineage or the compound were made or approved by the lineage head and the other elders.

From this brief description of the living patterns of West African extended families, it may be deduced that each extended family occupying a compound could be looked at from two perspectives. From the perspective of the lineage, the extended family consisted of its own lineage members, as one component, and in-marrying spouses as the other component (see Figure 2.3). Lineage members were related by "blood" ties conceived as existing in perpetuity. Spouses were "in-laws" whose relations could be broken "by law," and hence they were portrayed as an "outsider group" on certain ceremonial occasions (Marshall 1968; Sudarkasa 1980).

From the perspective of the individual families created by marriage, the extended family in a compound could be viewed as a group of related conjugal families (see Figure 2.3). Each of these conjugal families would consist of a man and his wife or wives and their children. These conjugally based families differed from typical "nuclear families" in several respects (Sudarkasa 1981, 1988). First, even when a man had only one wife, the possibility of plural wives was always there. Second, because of the lineage

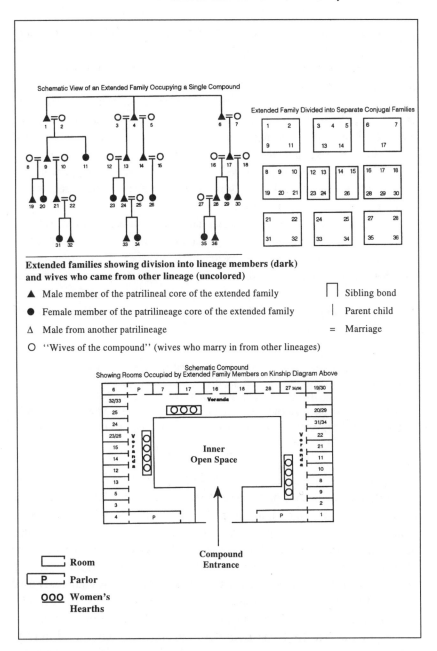

Figure 2.3. An Extended Family Occupying a Single Compound
SOURCE: Adapted from Sudarkasa (1980).

principle that linked members of the various conjugal families, children in the same generation grew up more or less like sisters and brothers, rather than strictly separating themselves into siblings versus cousins. In some languages, such as that of the Yoruba, there was and is no word equivalent to the English word *cousin,* only words for *older sibling* and *younger sibling* (*egbon* and *aburo,* respectively), used for both males and females. Thus the strength of the lineage principle made the boundaries of African conjugal families far less rigid than those that delineate nuclear families. For example, "uncles" might raise their "nephews" as their "sons" without any mechanism such as formal adoption. Usually, only in legal matters would questions of precise kinship relationships arise.

In describing what happened to African family structure when Africans were captured and enslaved in America, we must acknowledge that the family structures on plantations, as reconstructed from written records and oral history, cannot be viewed as examples of direct institutional transfer from Africa to America, but rather as examples of institutional transformation that took place from Africa to America (Sudarkasa 1981, p. 39). As I have stated previously:

> The extended family networks that were formed during slavery by Africans and their descendants were based on the institutional heritage which the Africans had brought with them to this continent, and the specific forms [these families] took reflected the influence of European-derived institutions as well as the political and economic circumstances in which the enslaved population found itself. (Sudarkasa 1981, p. 45)

The conditions of slavery did not allow the enslaved Africans to replicate or re-create the compounds and extended families they had left behind on the African continent. Yet, even in cramped quarters, one could find multigenerational families comprising couples, their children, some grandchildren, other relatives, and even nonkin. The influence of European norms as well as the demographics of the plantations meant that marriage was usually monogamous. Yet several historians have noted instances of polygamy (the commonly used term) where wives lived in separate houses (Gutman 1977, pp. 59, 158; Blassingame 1972, p. 171; Perdue, Barden, and Phillips 1980, p. 209).

Despite the fact that Africans enslaved in America were forced to compartmentalize their extended families, the importance of their kinship networks on the plantations and across plantations has been noted by many historians. Moreover, the continuing strength of the lineage principle was manifest through the strong sense of obligation to consanguineal ("blood") relatives. Gutman (1977) puts it this way: "The pull between ties to an immediate family and to an enlarged kin network sometimes strained husbands and wives" (p. 202) (see also Frazier [1939] 1966, part 2).

After slavery, wherever African Americans had access to large parcels of land, they re-created kin networks that resembled African extended families and compounds. Parents and their married children lived in houses built in close proximity to one another, and three and four generations of kin typically resided together in these houses. Two of my former students, Dr. Mary Faith Mitchell and Mr. Bamidele Agbasegbe Demerson, studied such compounds in the Sea Islands off the coast of South Carolina in the early 1970s (Demerson 1991).

Even where relatives did not live in spatial proximity, the extended family ties linked people across households and even across states, so that relatives could turn to one another for assistance, not only in child rearing but also in caring for the sick and the aged, in providing accommodations for those who migrated from one state to another, and in rendering financial support in times of need. Such patterns of transresidential extended family cooperation and support have been reported by contemporary writers (for example, Stack 1974; Aschenbrenner 1975; Billingsley 1992) as well as by many historians and sociologists writing about earlier periods.

To summarize, enslaved Africans living on plantations could not replicate African compounds, but their households were often "extended" beyond the nuclear family. Most important, they maintained transresidential kinship networks with many of the features of extended families that had resided together in single compounds in West Africa. When we speak of extended families among African Americans, we must always recognize that these are kin groups that transcend individual households. Billingsley (1968, 1992) uses the term *extended family* to refer to households in which family members such as grandparents reside with nuclear families. Such households do not in and of themselves constitute entire extended families. African American extended families embrace many households, some with two generations, some with three or more, and some of these households are headed by women, some by men, and some by both.

Household Formation Among African Americans

Several points concerning household formation among African Americans must be made before I present an examination of recent trends in Black family organization. The first and most general observation is that family and household are not the same thing. Indeed, in all societies, the notion of family embraces more than a single household. In the contemporary United States, however, there is a tendency to treat the concepts of family and household as if they are one and the same. This tendency stems from the fact that the majority culture in the United States views the nuclear family formed at marriage as the most important family (some would say the "real" family, in comparison to other relatives), and one that ideally should occupy a household separate and apart from that of others. Thus, in many instances, the words *family* and *household* are used interchangeably. For example, the concepts of "two-parent families" and "two-parent households" tend to be used interchangeably. So, too, are the concepts of "single-parent families" and "single-parent households."

Historically, among African Americans it has always been important to recognize that the term *family* refers not only to family members resident in particular households but to extended family members living in other households as well. Because of the strength of consanguineal ties, particularly those between mother and children, but sometimes also among siblings, one cannot conclude that the nuclear family built around the marital relationship is conceived of as "the" primary family. For many African Americans, marriage does not mean that the husband-wife relationship will "replace" the mother-daughter or mother-son relationship as the primary relationship in the newly married person's life. In the best of circumstances, these relationships become complementary; in the worst of circumstances, as Gutman (1977) points out, the consanguineal ties may place a "strain" on the husband-wife relationship. In any case, where these consanguineal ties are very strong, in order to understand the form and functioning of the "immediate" family among African Americans, one would have to study a cluster of related households, not simply any single isolated nuclear family household.

A second general observation to be made concerning household formation among African Americans is that, historically, although female-headed households were a minority of the households in the Black community, they were an accepted form of household organization. In fact, because of the general acceptance of female-headed households during slavery and afterward, some writers erroneously proclaimed this to be the typical or normative form of the African American family. Frazier's ([1939] 1966) characterization of *some* Black families as "matriarchal" was generalized by others to refer to "most" Black families.

The publication of Herbert Gutman's monumental book *The Black Family in Slavery and Freedom, 1750–1925* (1977) dispelled the myth of the Black family as predominantly "matriarchal" (or "matrifocal," which was the newer and more descriptive characterization). Gutman reported that from the mid-1700s through the mid-1920s, less than one-fourth of African American households were headed by single women. As recently as 1960, only 22% of African American families were female-headed (Jewell 1988, p. 17; Billingsley 1992, p. 36). Thus the incidence of female-headed households did not change much in 200 years. These data show that, contrary to popular belief, historically, African American women, like their African foremothers, typically gave birth to children within the context of marriage.

The point must be made, however, that a rate of 20% to 25% female-headed households within the African American population was still high compared with that of the Euro-American population. Billingsley (1968, p. 14) reports that in 1960 only 6% of White families with children were headed by women. To understand why a larger percentage of African American women were single heads of household, one must take into consideration a number of cultural, demographic, and economic factors.

First, it must be understood that, historically, African American women, like their African ancestors, placed a very high value on having children, and most of them wanted to have their own children even if they adopted or reared others (Sudarkasa 1975). Although this has changed somewhat under the influence of "radical feminism," even today very few African American women want to be childless throughout their lives.

Second, it has to be understood that because polygamy (or, more accurately, polygyny—the term for plural wives) was not and is not a legal form of marriage in the United States, unequal gender ratios among African Americans living in many areas meant that not all marriageable women would be able to find husbands during their prime childbearing years. Some of the factors that contributed (and still contribute) to the preponderance of African American women over African American men in many localities included the death or incarceration of males in their prime reproductive years; the migration of males in search of work; high male unemployment rates, which reduced the number of men available for, or interested in, the responsibilities of marriage; the overall higher birthrate of females; and the shorter life span of males. Given these factors and the high value placed on children, it is not surprising that historically nearly one-fourth of all African American families were headed by single women (Sudarkasa 1993).

This does not mean that the incidence of female-headed households was or is solely due to the birth of children out of wedlock. Some of the same factors mentioned above as contributing to the gender imbalance between males and females in some localities also contributed to a relatively high incidence of divorce, separation, and widowhood among African Americans. Thus, now and in the past, many mature, previously married women are among those heading single-parent households (Billingsley 1968, 1992; Jewell 1988; Sudarkasa 1993).

Turning from the issues surrounding the formation of female-headed households, the third point I want to make concerning household formation among African Americans relates to the notion of the "household head" itself. In the sociological literature and in the media in this country, considerable emphasis is placed on the question of who heads a household or family. In fact, the way the question is asked presumes that the position of household or family head is a straightforward, easily discernible status.

In the case of African American households, several points of caution need to be raised concerning the concept of household headship. First, the answer to the question of who heads a household may differ depending on whether the respondent is thinking about the primary decision maker or the primary provider. Second, key decision makers for a given household may not even reside in that household. This is especially true today, when households are headed by young single mothers who are dependent on other adults for advice and various forms of support. Third, in order to understand the functioning of a household, it is sometimes more important to understand who are the core adults in the household, rather than who "heads" it. Historically, this was particularly the case in multigenerational female-headed households. The oldest adults in the house (who might be two or three sisters, a sister and a brother, or an older woman and her mature daughters) might share the responsibilities of headship, in terms of both decision making and financial support.

The fourth and final point I wish to make concerning household formation among African Americans is that, historically, households headed by married couples (like those headed by women) typically included relatives other than parents and children (see, for example, Billingsley 1968; Stack 1974; Aschenbrenner 1975). Many of these two-parent households were multigenerational through the inclusion of grandchildren or a parent or parents of one of the spouses. Many of them were also "extended" laterally to include an uncle, aunt, cousin, niece, or nephew. In other words, even these two-parent families were not typical nuclear families. In the section that follows, I observe that the breakup of multigenerational households, headed by women and by married couples, subsumes and accounts for all the major trends that have been identified in Black family and household organization over the past few decades.

Recent Changes in African American Family and Household Organization

Without question, the major change that has occurred in Black family organization in the past three decades has been the rise in the number of female-headed households. The percentage has almost tripled in 30 years, a phenomenal increase that we are only now beginning to understand. Billingsley (1992) notes:

> The incidence of one of the alternatives to the traditional family, the female-headed single-parent family, has escalated enormously over the past generation. Consisting of a minority of 20 percent [actually 22 percent] of families with children in 1960, this family form had increased to 33 percent by 1970, to 49 percent by 1980, and to a whopping 57 percent by 1990. Over the same period single fathers bringing up their own children increased from 2 percent to 4 percent. (pp. 36-37)

He goes on to make the very interesting point that the change in household headship is mainly a reflection of changing marriage patterns rather than an indication of a diminishing commitment to family or to family living.

> The major observation here is that both black men and women have been avoiding or abandoning marriage in record numbers during recent years. *But this is more a shift in the marriage relation than in the family.* Marriage . . . is only one of several bases for family formation and endurance. The allegiance to families is still so strong that on any given day the overwhelming majority of African-American people will be found living in families of one type or another. In 1990, for example, 70 percent of the 10.5 million African-American households were family households with persons related by blood, marriage, or adoption. (p. 37; emphasis added)

This observation supports a point that cannot be overemphasized—namely, that marital stability and family stability are not one and the same. More than 20 years ago, I noted:

> Black families are not necessarily centered around conjugal unions, which are the sine qua non of the nuclear family. Among blacks, households centered around consanguineal relatives have as much legitimacy (and for most people, as much respectability) as family units as do households centered around conjugal unions. When this fact is understood, it becomes clear that the instability of conjugal relations cannot be taken as the sole measure of the instability of the family. That black families exhibit considerable stability over time and space is evidenced by the enduring linkages and bonds of mutual obligation found among networks of consanguineal kin. (Sudarkasa 1975, p. 238)

In the case of nuclear families, divorce signals the "breakdown" of at least one family, but where consanguineal relationships form the core of the family, the failure of a marriage or a companionate relationship does not necessarily have a disruptive effect on the unit, although it might have emotional effects on the individuals concerned.

As I stated earlier, in my view, the African American commitment to consanguineal relatives is traceable to Africa, where lineage ties based on descent, rather than marital ties based in law, provided the primary source of stability within extended families living together in compounds (Sudarkasa 1980, pp. 47-48; 1981, pp. 43-44). In the United States, the dependence on blood relatives as sources of support and stability in the family remained strong among African Americans, even in the face of the White American idea that the primary source of family stability is the marriage bond that forms the core of the nuclear family.

The strength and stability of consanguineal ties, as Gutman (1977) suggests, could be one cause of the fragility of marriage bonds noted among African Americans. Obligations to the extended family could be a source of dissension between spouses, particularly when these obligations appear to consume resources and time that could be devoted to their home and their nuclear family. Moreover, because the extended family is there as a source of support when a divorce or separation does occur, marital dissolution is less threatening and less traumatic for the partners involved (Sudarkasa 1981, pp. 49-50).

In the 1990s, we are facing a situation in which the great increase in the percentage of African American female-headed households, particularly among the working and nonworking poor (almost 70% of all African American households), means that these single parents must depend on their blood relatives for stability and support if there is to be any family stability at all. Yet one of the most alarming changes that has occurred since 1960 renders this support less readily available to them than it was in the past. I refer to the fact that many young single mothers are living alone with their children, whereas in the past most of them would have been living in households with other adult relatives who could provide economic assistance, emotional support, and, most important, advice and assistance in the rearing of their children.

It is very important to point out that the pattern of single mothers living alone with their children is a recent phenomenon among African Americans. As a teenager in the 1950s, I witnessed a relatively high dropout rate among girls in junior high school and high school, who left school because they became pregnant. These young women never set up households of their own. They lived with their mothers, with both parents, grandmothers, grandparents, or other senior relatives. And the younger the mother, the longer she probably would reside with other adults. Households headed by mature mothers and grandmothers were usually as stable as two-parent families in terms of their longevity and their ability to provide adequately for the needs of the adults and children within them.

Most of the discussion concerning the rise in the number of female-headed households among African Americans has focused on the breakdown of the nuclear family. In *Survival of the Black Family* (1988), Jewell is especially detailed in attributing the increase in divorce, separation, and births out of wedlock to welfare policies that started in the 1950s and began to show serious effects in the 1960s, 1970s, and 1980s. She also points out that from the 1950s onward, as more Black males shifted their occupations from farm worker to unskilled laborer, more of the Black elderly became eligible for social security benefits and therefore were less dependent on their children. With this came "the establishment of [more] independent living arrangements," as indicated by the decrease in the number of "subfamilies" living in the one household between 1950 and 1960 (p. 24).

Jewell (1988) summarizes the effects of social welfare policy on the structure of African American families as follows:

Although liberal social welfare legislation created economic independence for the elderly, conservative administration of social welfare programs, especially in the Aid to Families with Dependent Children program, promoted marital conflict, as welfare policies and practices required male absence as a condition for eligibility. Hence, through overt and covert practices, social welfare agencies, not black wives, forced men out of the home. Thus, the black female-headed household, created through separation, divorce, or nonmarriage, has been system-precipitated. Thus, one could expect an escalation in the dissolution of marriages among blacks and an increase in the number of black women with children who choose to permanently forego marriage. The trend in both of these areas was initiated in the 1950s and became firmly established by the 1980s. By excluding black males through the institution of the "man-in-the-house" policy in the 1950s and maintaining this policy in the 1960s and 1970s and by systematically entitling women, and not their husbands, to benefits, black two-parent families were undermined. (pp. 24-25)

Even though Billingsley and Jewell emphasize the "breakdown" in the nuclear family as a result of economic, demographic, and policy factors previously mentioned, the data presented by both authors demonstrate that another important trend is in evidence. I am referring to the breakup of multigenerational female-headed households, formerly the most common type of household headed by women. In the past, female-headed households usually included at least three generations, sometimes four. Women normally started having children at an early age (in their teens or early 20s) and might continue having them into their late 30s or 40s. Thus it was not uncommon for women to be rearing their own children while assisting their daughters with the upbringing of theirs.

Not only were these female-headed households extended lineally (that is, by including a woman, her children, grandchildren, and possibly great-grandchildren), but they often were also extended laterally to include never-married, widowed, or divorced sisters or brothers of the household head. For example, such households might include a woman, her adult sister or brother, her adult daughter(s), her adult unmarried son(s), and the dependent children of any or all of the women in the house, including any minor children the woman herself might have.

Today, owing to the effects of social welfare policies as delineated by Jewell (1988), and as a result of the skyrocketing unemployment of Black males since the late 1970s and 1980s, what might have been a single multi-generational female-headed household of the 1950s or early 1960s is likely to be several separate female-headed households. For example, a woman's unmarried daughters would probably be living alone with their dependent children, making three or four female-headed households where previously there would have been one.

After reflecting on the data presented by Billingsley, Jewell, and others, I have concluded that the major trend among African American families over the past 30 years has been the increasing *disaggregation of households*, whether headed by married couples or by women. In other words, we see more separate households in relation to population size than ever before. It is not surprising that the majority of those households are female-headed, given that many Black males are incarcerated, unemployed and "on the streets," unemployed and living in dependent relationships with their mothers or girlfriends, or otherwise unable to assume the responsibility of household headship.

The trend toward the disaggregation (and hence diminishing size) of households is evidenced not only by the proliferation of two-generational female-headed households, but by the increase in the number of elderly persons living alone or in couples, as noted by Jewell (1988), and by the substantial increase in the number and percentage of single persons living alone (Billingsley 1992, pp. 37-38, 47-48). As of 1990, 25% of all African American households were occupied by single adults, and most of these were single women.

Historically, for economic reasons as well as for reasons related to cultural traditions, unmarried African American adults lived with their parents or other relatives. In 1975, I cited this as one of the "fundamental structural differences" between Black families and traditional nuclear families:

> Adulthood for Black people does not necessarily entail the establishment of new households; therefore one finds many single adults living with married and unmarried relatives. In fact, in some places it is considered highly preferable for unmarried adults to live with relatives than to live alone or to live outside the family with "roommates." (Sudarkasa 1975, p. 238)

The rise in the number of households occupied by persons living alone represents a dramatic shift in patterns of residence over a 20-year period.

Implications of the Recent Changes

What are some of the consequences of the disaggregation of African American family households? In particular, does the proliferation of female-headed households signal a "crisis" in the Black family?

I have stressed above that most young single mothers used to live in multigenerational households that provided a wide range of mutual support. Such households were particularly important for the rearing of children—that is, looking after them on a day-to-day basis, sharing the expenses of their food and clothing, and providing for all their other needs. The breakup of these units has left many poor, inexperienced mothers alone to cope with child rearing, and this has created serious problems.

One of the often cited signs of "crisis" in the Black family is the inability of some single mothers to "control" their children, particularly their sons. When single mothers lived with their adult relatives, they could rely on these adults (male as well as female) to assist them in establishing and enforcing the rules by which children were brought up. The effect of a father's absence could be compensated for by the presence of a maternal grandfather, mother's brothers, and other male figures living in, or frequenting, a household. Today, even when these relatives play supporting roles in the life of a single mother and her children, the fact that they live in different residences, sometimes great distances apart, means that they cannot have the continuous influence on the children that they would have had in the past.

Adults as well as children are inevitably affected by the disaggregation of African American family households. On a very practical level, the economic support and sharing of resources that were features of the multigenerational households are unavailable to the same degree as in the past. In addition to gifts and in-kind services to one another, borrowing among relatives was a major feature of African American households of the past. Without other adults in the house today, single mothers have no one from whom to borrow small amounts of cash, personal items (such as toiletries, clothing, or jewelry), housewares, or food items. In the past, different members of the household would buy different appliances for the house, or they might all chip in to purchase what was needed. The loss of such material support cannot be underestimated, and it no doubt explains why single parents may "look the other way" when their children become involved in illegal activities that bring much-needed cash into the home.

The absence of the adult companionship provided by African American households of the past makes the life of the single mother today harder to bear. In the past, when a woman did not have a husband or "boyfriend," she could turn to her relatives in the household for companionship and support. Today, without the presence of adult relatives in the home, the burden of rearing children alone may be compounded by loneliness or, worse, by despair.

Even if we agree with Billingsley (1992) that "the so-called black family crisis is not of their own making" and that it is not "the worst crisis they ever faced and survived" (p. 79), we have to acknowledge that this is the first time since the breakup of families during slavery that external factors have had such a profound effect on African American family structure. To overcome what could become a crisis, it is necessary to consciously strengthen and augment the extended family networks that have been the key to the survival of Blacks in the United States and to which many people still turn for support (see, e.g., McAdoo 1978, 1983; Hatchett and Jackson 1993).

The changes discussed here have already sent an alarm through the African American community nationwide. Various initiatives to rekindle the commitment to kin and provide support to female-headed households are being undertaken by churches and other religious groups as well as by civic and service organizations, such as the National Council of Negro Women (NCNW), the Coalition of 100 Black Men, and national sororities and fraternities. Support is given to children and young adults in the form of tutoring, mentoring, and guided recreational activities, and help is also given directly to single mothers to enable them to better cope with their responsibilities. The NCNW's annual Black Family Reunion Day serves as an occasion to rededicate to familyhood and to demonstrate to the nation that the Black family is in much better condition than the media would have us believe.

In a recent paper on female-headed households, I have suggested that we also need to call for the building of public and private housing units that are large enough to accommodate multigenerational kinship and friendship groupings, which can provide single mothers with the help they need to be able to go to work to support themselves and their children. One way in which the government could assist welfare mothers to become working mothers would be through support to elderly women who now live alone, but who might be persuaded to live with or near young working mothers, helping them with their children, as African American grandmothers did in the past. In short, we need to strengthen and expand existing transresidential kinship and friendship networks and develop new types of extended residential arrangements in order to reverse the debilitating effects of the breakup of the multigenerational households of the past (Sudarkasa 1993, p. 89).

One thing is certain—we must be realistic about the trends we are seeing and about the best ways to respond to them. It is futile to think that the "salvation" of the Black family lies in the revival of the nuclear family, when the nuclear family per se has never been the dominant pattern in the African American community. It is true that most households were headed by married couples, but, as I have noted, at various phases in their domestic cycles they took in grandchildren, elderly parents, and other relatives. In other words, both two-parent and single-parent households among African Americans have usually been more inclusive than the typical nuclear family. It was such multigenerational households and the extended families that linked them together that enabled African Americans to survive and thrive in this country.

Rather than look to the nuclear family, with its ideology of isolationism and self-centeredness, as the building block for African American communities of the future, we need to look to the inclusive, mutually supportive household and family structures that proved their effectiveness in the past. We know that some of these households were successfully headed by women. As we seek to reconnect the disaggregated households that have become the reality of the 1990s, we need to accept the fact that in the twenty-first century many if not most of the African American households that will emerge will still be headed by women. As in the past, women will have to rely on male relatives and friends, wherever they reside, to play the supportive roles that will enable these households to thrive and succeed, just as they did in the past.

African American Family Values

If our families are to play the constructive roles they have in the past, rebuilding and redesigning their structures are only two of the tasks we must confront. Equally important are the tasks of rediscovering and instilling the values that made it possible for these families to persist and prevail in the past. The preceding sections of this chapter have demonstrated that the most fundamental of these values was the commitment to the family itself (Du Bois [1908] 1969; Frazier [1939] 1966; Herskovits [1941] 1958; Billingsley 1968, 1992; Hill 1971; Blassingame 1972; Stack 1974; Gutman 1977). This sense of commitment to kin and the values that were taught to children as a way of instilling and reinforcing this commitment were brought to America by the enslaved population, just as they brought memories of the African family structures they would seek to re-create in America.

Various writers have sought to delineate additional values that have been paramount in African American families. Drawing on the works of various scholars, Billingsley (1992) has developed a list of African American family values; these values include a commitment to education, a commitment to self-help, service to others, a strong religious orientation, and a strong work orientation (pp. 328-33). Few, if any, who have studied African American families would dispute this listing of values encouraged through these institutions.

Given the stereotypes that women on welfare "do not want to work" and that large numbers of Black males are unemployed because they are "lazy," I am sure that some would question whether a strong work orientation is indeed a value promoted within the Black family. Two points are relevant here. First, most women on welfare would work if they could earn enough to eke out a living and afford child care, transportation, and other job-related expenses. If they earn minimum wage, their disposable income would be no higher than what they receive from public assistance, and hence they cannot afford the additional cost that working represents. Those who earn more than the minimum wage risk losing their medical protection (Medicaid) if they earn around $10,000 annually (Jaynes and Williams 1989). Of note is the fact that recent programs to help welfare mothers join the workforce have begun to include provisions for day care and health care.

The second point concerns the stereotype that "Black men are lazy and do not want to work." Studies of employment trends in the African American community show that for more than 50 years the rate of unemployment for African American males has been more than twice that of White males (Jaynes and Williams 1989, p. 308). The actual rate of unemployment of Black males is even higher, because many of them are "defined" out of the workforce simply because they recognize the futility of looking for jobs. Anyone who skips one month of looking for work is classified as not in the labor force (Jaynes and Williams 1989, p. 301). Thus, through a statistical sleight of hand, actual unemployment statistics are underreported for many in the population, including Black males.

These high unemployment rates reflect a number of factors, notably the unavailability of opportunities for males looking for assembly-line work and other semiskilled jobs, which have declined dramatically over the last two decades. Even the menial jobs that Black males could depend on in the past may no longer be available to them as competition has increased from other groups seeking to make a living in difficult economic times. Thus the high rate of unemployment of Black males certainly cannot be attributed to their "laziness," nor can that unemployment be taken as a lack of commitment to the strong work ethic cited as a value in Black families by various scholars (Billingsley 1992, pp. 331, 332).

In my own effort to identify traditional values in African American families, I have taken a somewhat different approach from that of scholars who have sought to uncover the tenets that encourage achievement and upward mobility—commitment to education, work, self-help, service to others, and a strong religious orientation. All these I acknowledge as important values in Black family life, but I have been particularly interested in setting forth the basic precepts or values that have been taught to children and expected of adults in order to achieve the patterns of cooperation and self-help exemplified in the extended family.

As I read the historical accounts of African American family life during slavery and afterward, it was clear that the values taught and promoted in these families were very similar to those I had found in my reading and research on various societies in West Africa. In 1970, I first proposed that the principles of *respect, responsibility, restraint,* and *reciprocity* are four "cardinal values" undergirding African family life that had been retained in the family life of African Americans (Marshall 1970a, 1970b; Sudarkasa 1980, pp. 49-50). Over the years, as I continued to read and reflect on these values in African family life, it became clear that some key tenets of behavior were not covered by the "Four Rs." In an effort to incorporate into my teachings and writings these other principles, I added reverence, reason, and reconciliation, making a total of "Seven Rs."

The first five Rs seem clearly to have been carried over into African American family life. The last two, *reason* and *reconciliation,* which were important in African families and communities in settling disputes, may have diminished in importance in the United States because African Americans looked to America's legal system rather than their own authority structures for settling major disputes within their communities and even within their own families. Thus, reason and reconciliation were no longer key mechanisms in preserving social order as they had been in indigenous African societies. In setting forth the Seven Rs, I do not intend to suggest that these are the only values traditionally promoted in African families, nor do I mean to imply that these values are unique to Africa. Indeed, to some degree they are embraced by cultures in most, if not all, parts of the world. But the same can be said of the values contained in the doctrines of many of the world's religions. Thus it would not surprise me if people other than Africans identify some or all of the Seven Rs as values taught in their own families or communities.

My reason for discussing these values here is twofold. First, they provide an understanding of why the extended family structures described in the previous sections could be sustained in Africa, America, and other parts of the African diaspora over many centuries. It is my view that the African form of family organization was reinforced by precepts such as the ones enumerated here. These precepts or values were passed on through oral tradition and exemplified in the behavior of family members in their day-to-day relationships.

The second reason for focusing on these values is that they can be helpful to African American families coping with the troubled circumstances in which many find themselves today. In the face of poverty, homelessness, drugs, violence, crime, disease, and other problems that are threatening to destroy the family structures that have been the bedrock of African American survival, it is important to recognize these and other values that might help us rescue our families and save our communities.

It is understood, of course, that values alone are not sufficient to overcome the misery that poverty, crime, and disease create in too many African American communities. The long-term sustained improvement of these communities requires economic changes as well as social changes. To make these communities come alive with promise and hope, jobs must be created and local businesses must be established that will reinvest in these communities; schools and opportunities for higher education must be improved, and the people must be genuinely empowered through participation in the governance of their communities and ownership of some of the resources that sustain them. Nevertheless, values are also important because they instill the principles that guide the choices people make. I suggest, therefore, that we take another look at the family values that have enabled African Americans to persevere and prevail in the face of unbelievable obstacles in the past.

Respect is the first of the cardinal values that guided behavior within African families and communities. It governed the behavior of children not only toward their parents but also toward all elders with whom they came in contact. In fact, because seniority conferred rank and status within the African extended family, an individual owed respect and deference to all persons older than him- or herself. When Africans came to America, they retained respect as a fundamental precept on which their families and communities were built. Respect was shown through forms of address; older people were called by kinship terms such as *Uncle* or *Aunt* or by titles such as *Mister* or *Miss*. Respect was also shown in the way younger people treated their elders and through bows, curtsies, and other gestures that they learned early. Among Africans and African Americans, it was considered impolite for younger people to "look their elders dead in the eye." This emphasis on respect was widely reported from the period of slavery until as recently as 30 or 40 years ago.

Obviously, many of the specific ways in which respect was shown in the past would be considered old-fashioned and inappropriate today. Yet one way in which we can strengthen our families is through teaching respect. If our children are once again taught the importance of respecting others, they will be in a better position to demand and command respect for themselves.

Responsibility is the value that required members of African extended families to be their brothers' and sisters' keepers. Studies of African American families have shown that they, too, accept responsibility for a wide range of kin, if for no other reason than they consider it their duty to do so. Of course, in every society kinship imposes some responsibility, but societies differ in defining the limits of that responsibility.

Africans and African Americans traditionally accepted responsibility for a much wider network of kin than is typical of Americans with a nuclear family orientation, who consider "real" responsibility to kin to extend mainly to spouses, parents, and children. Among Americans committed to nuclear families and nuclear family values, even siblings can make only so many demands on one another. Individuals tend to help relatives outside of the nuclear families into which they have been born or that they have formed at marriage only if they do not have to put themselves out in order to do so. By contrast, African Americans have typically housed and fed distant relatives who migrated into their area looking for work, helped their sisters and brothers provide for their children, and cared for parents and other aging relatives who did not have children to look after them.

If African Americans are to prosper in the twenty-first century, particularly in the face of the large numbers of people who lack the education and the economic wherewithal to fend for themselves, we must once again be prepared to accept responsibility for the less fortunate in our extended families and our communities.

Reciprocity is the principle that compelled Africans and African Americans to give back to their families and communities in return for what had been given them. Entire treatises have been written on the principle of reciprocity in human societies (Mauss 1954; Sahlins 1972, chap. 5), and I do not claim that this is a value exclusive to Africans or African Americans. The point is that Africans placed a very high premium on mutual assistance, especially among relatives, and they expected that good deeds would be reciprocated either in the short run or in the distant future. Even if obligations were carried from one generation to the next, they should not be abrogated. The data on cooperation within the African American family indicate that the commitment to reciprocity has remained an important family value.

Today, many civic and service organizations as well as historically and predominantly Black colleges and universities are stressing the importance of "giving back to the community." It is a principle that will have to be reinforced within the family if self-help is to become once again the primary instrument of African American survival and success.

Restraint is probably the most difficult of African values to teach or accept in the highly individualistic and materialistic society of today's United States. Currently, "me and mine" usually takes precedence over "thee and thine." Everyone wants to do his or her "own thang." But within African families, when personal decisions had implications for the group as a whole (whether that was the immediate family, the lineage, or the extended family), a person had to give due consideration to the group when making those decisions. Of course, even the definition of what should be considered a "personal decision" was different in African and African American families of the past. Many such decisions were made by, or in consultation with, family elders. Restraint was manifest in many ways; parents went without so that their children might have; adult sons and daughters returned the sacrifice by putting the needs of their elderly parents before their own desires.

An often-cited example of the principle of restraint or sacrifice in African and African American communities is that of a sister or brother who did not go to school but instead worked to help pay for a sibling's education. This sacrifice was repaid when the educated sibling assumed responsibility for educating the brother's or sister's children. In this example, the principles of reciprocity, responsibility, and restraint are all manifest, but that of restraint (or sacrifice) is especially important to emphasize in an age in which everyone is taught to look out for "number one."

Reverence is the value manifested in the strong religious orientation of Africans and people of the African diaspora. Indeed, Africa's sons and daughters are known to be a spiritual people. In Africa, children were taught to revere the God of the Universe as well as lesser gods. They were also taught reverence for their ancestors as well as for many things in nature. Both

Christianity and Islam spread easily through Africa because of the people's predisposition to embrace religions that seemed to empower their adherents (Herskovits [1941] 1958). Among African Americans, after the family, the church has been the strongest institution and continues to be one of the anchors of African American communities today. Islam is also spreading among African Americans, who welcome its uplifting influence among many of the youth. It is no accident that, over the years, many of our most prominent national or community leaders have had a base in the church or, in a few notable instances, in the mosque.

The third stanza of the "Negro National Anthem," *Lift Ev'ry Voice and Sing*, by James Weldon Johnson, begins:

> God of our weary years, God of our silent tears,
> Thou who has brought us thus far on the way;
> Thou who has by Thy might, led us into the light,
> Keep us forever in the path, we pray.

Such unabashed, and some would say sentimental, spirituality may be too old-fashioned for many people today. Yet the appeal to a higher power, the reverence and respect for a high God, by whatever name, has been an indispensable part of the survival of Blacks in America. The belief in God has given hope in situations that otherwise would have been hopeless, and as the Reverend Jesse Jackson has said, today more than ever, African Americans need to "keep hope alive." If reverence for a higher power can continue to sustain African Americans in our fight for empowerment here on earth, it is one of those values that should be retained in our twenty-first century "survival kit."

Reason is a value that is often invoked in many African contexts. As African Americans, however, we are often portrayed (and portray ourselves) as emotional people, characterized by spontaneity and expressiveness. We see ourselves as a people with rhythm. Indeed, as a people we have all these attributes, but historically reason was more important than all of them in maintaining social order in African communities. I saw the importance placed on reason in human affairs when I was conducting anthropological research in the towns and villages of Nigeria and Ghana in the 1960s.

I was always impressed by the premium that Africans placed on reason-ableness in the settling of disputes within the family and within the wider community. When a dispute broke out, elders appealed to reason, not to emotion, to settle the matter. In the small Yoruba town in Nigeria where I lived in the early 1960s, most disputes and breaches of the law were settled by elders within the compounds or by the traditional chiefs in the town. In Ghana, where I studied Yoruba traders in the late 1960s, the Yoruba town unions, known as Parapos, tried to settle all matters that arose within the Yoruba communities throughout Ghana, without going to court.

When elders convened to adjudicate matters brought before them, they took as much time as necessary to persuade the parties concerned to come to a reasonable settlement. Sometimes I was amazed at how much people were willing to compromise to reach agreement on a fair and reasonable settlement. I often thought that Americans, including African Americans, would have done far less.

The art of reason and compromise can be taught, and it seems to me that efforts should be made in our families, as well as through the churches, mosques, schools, and other institutions, to teach the importance of taking a reasoned approach to settling differences.

Reconciliation is a value that was also essential to the maintenance of social order in African extended families and in the wider communities. When I reflect on what I have seen in the decades that I have been in and out of West Africa, I realize that one of the most important lessons taught through the family is the importance of forgiveness and reconciliation. The ultimate sign of respect among the Yoruba is for a woman to kneel or for a man to prostrate himself before another person. Inevitably, when a person goes before another to "beg" forgiveness, he or she will prostrate or kneel, as required. It is virtually unthinkable that anyone would be so hard-hearted as to ignore or rebuff such a gesture. It is considered uncultured to fail to reconcile with a relative or friend, or even an adversary, who begs to put the matter to rest. One often hears people say, when asked about disputes or dissension within the family or the community, "We have settled the matter." After that, nothing more needs to be said.

Although the art of reconciliation appears to have been lost or cast aside in the evolution of African families transplanted and transformed in America, it is a value that should be reclaimed as we seek to strengthen our domestic institutions. Through an emphasis on the importance of reconciliation, hostilities can be diffused and quarrels de-escalated. The more easily this can be accomplished, the more likely it is that households and families will be able to focus on the larger goals they wish to achieve.

These Seven Rs—respect, responsibility, restraint, reciprocity, reverence, reason, and reconciliation—represent African family values that have supported kinship structures (lineages, compounds, and extended families) that have lasted for hundreds, even thousands, of years. The strength of these values is indicated by the fact that most of them were retained and passed on in America, thereby enabling African Americans to create and maintain extended family networks that sustained them here, just as their prototypes had sustained their ancestors on the African continent. Today, in the face of circumstances that threaten the existence of these extended family structures, a revival of the values that allowed them to persist could strengthen the family and community structures on which African Americans must depend in the twenty-first century.

Conclusion

There have been profound changes in African American household and family organization over the past three decades. The four most significant of these have been the decline in the number of two-parent households, the proliferation of female-headed households, the increase in the percentage of single persons living alone, and the increase in the number of elderly persons living alone or as couples apart from any other relatives. Together these changes add up to an overall trend toward the breakup or disaggregation of the large multigenerational households in which most African Americans used to live. The most serious consequence of this trend is that now we see many single mothers living alone with their children (that is, in two-generational households), whereas in the past most of them would have been in households with their mothers and other kin who could provide assistance with the upbringing of their children and with other aspects of their lives.

Recognizing that demographic, social, and economic realities make it likely that these female-headed households are here to stay, in one form or another, I suggest that we undertake an all-out effort to rebuild extended family support systems for these single mothers rather than hold out the unrealistic expectation that two-parent families will reemerge as the predominant household structure in the Black community. In the past, African American households that were organized around core groups of consanguineal kin could be just as stable as those organized around married couples. A similar flexibility in household structures will be required if we are to build strong family networks for the future.

In the meantime, as African American scholars, we must not be seduced by the myth that female-headed households are the cause of the deplorable social conditions that exist in the poverty-stricken communities in which most of these households are found. Unemployment, dilapidated schools, drug infestation, and the incidence of violent crime have increased at the same time female-headed households have tripled, but that does not mean there is a one-way causal relationship between family organization and the social pathologies with which they have to cope.

This is not to say that family structures and relationships have no effect on the behavior of those within them. The question is whether changing family structure will make as much difference in the lives of people as would intervention to change the deplorable conditions in which they live. There is no evidence that two-parent families living in drug- and crime-infested neighborhoods are significantly better off than single-parent families in those same neighborhoods. The available evidence indicates that by expanding opportunities for the poor (providing them with jobs, access to better schools, and caring and concerned role models who can help young people on the road to a better life), we go a long way toward changing behavior that has been alleged to be caused by family structure. To address the root cause of the violence and despair we see among the youth in many of our inner cities, we must advocate a genuine "war on poverty," one that will eliminate rather than mask unemployment, and one that will make an all-out assault on drug abuse.

Finally, as African American scholars, we must remind our communities and inform the wider society of the roles that our families have played in our survival in America. We cannot blame others for the perpetuation of stereotyped notions about African American families when we ourselves assume them to be inferior simply because they differ from family structures handed down from Europe. In form, African American families have been some of the most flexible, adaptable, and inclusive kinship institutions in America. In function, they have been among the most accepting and nurturing of children and the most supportive of adults. These are institutions for which we should be grateful rather than apologetic.

References

Aschenbrenner, J. 1975. *Lifelines: Black Families in Chicago.* New York: Holt, Rinehart & Winston.

Billingsley, A. 1968. *Black Families in White America.* Englewood Cliffs, NJ: Prentice Hall.
———. 1992. *Climbing Jacob's Ladder.* New York: Simon & Schuster.
Blassingame, J. W. 1972. *The Slave Community.* New York: Oxford University Press.
Demerson, B. A. 1991. "Family Life on Wadmalaw Island." In *Sea Island Roots,* edited by M. S. Twining and K. Baird. Trenton, NJ: Africa World Press.
Du Bois, W. E. B. [1908] 1969. *The Negro American Family.* New York: New American Library.
Frazier, E. F. [1939] 1966. *The Negro Family in the United States.* Chicago: University of Chicago Press.
Gutman, H. 1977. *The Black Family in Slavery and Freedom, 1750–1925.* New York: Vintage.
Hatchett, S. and J. S. Jackson. 1993. "African American Extended Kin Systems." In *Family Ethnicity: Strength in Diversity,* edited by H. P. McAdoo. Newbury Park, CA: Sage.
Herskovits, M. J. [1941] 1958. *The Myth of the Negro Past.* Boston: Beacon.
Hill, R. 1971. *The Strengths of Black Families.* New York: Emerson Hall.
Jaynes, G. D. and R. M. Williams, Jr., eds. 1989. *A Common Destiny: Blacks and American Society.* Washington, DC: National Academy Press.
Jewell, K. S. 1988. *Survival of the Black Family: The Institutional Impact of U.S. Social Policy.* New York: Praeger.
Marshall, G. A. [Niara Sudarkasa]. 1968. "Marriage: Comparative Analysis." Pp. 8-19 in *International Encyclopedia of the Social Sciences,* vol. 9. New York: Macmillan.
———. 1970a. "Integrative Elements in African Social Life." In *Black Perspectives in the Social Sciences,* video lecture series. Kent, OH: Kent State University, Institute for African American Affairs.
———. 1970b. "Interpersonal and Institutional Relationships in African Society." In *Black Perspectives in the Social Sciences,* video lecture series. Kent, OH: Kent State University, Institute for African American Affairs.
Mauss, M. 1954. *The Gift.* London: Longman.
McAdoo, H. P. 1978. "Factors Related to Stability in Upwardly Mobile Black Families." *Journal of Marriage and the Family* 40(4):761-76.
———. 1983. *Extended Family Support of Single Black Mothers.* DHSS Research Report No. NIMH 5701, MH32159. Washington, DC: Government Printing Office.
Moynihan, D. P. 1965. *The Negro Family: The Case for National Action.* Washington, DC: U.S. Department of Labor, Office of Policy Planning and Research.
Perdue, C. L., Jr., T. E. Barden, and R. K. Phillips. 1980. *Weevils in the Wheat: Interviews With Virginia Ex-Slaves.* Bloomington: Indiana University Press.
Sahlins, M. 1972. *Stone Age Economics.* Chicago: University of Chicago Press.
Stack, C. B. 1974. *All Our Kin: Strategies for Survival in a Black Community.* New York: Harper & Row.
Sudarkasa, N. 1975. "An Exposition on the Value Premises Underlying Black Family Studies." *Journal of the National Medical Association* 67(May):235-39.
———. 1980. "African and Afro-American Family Structure." *Black Scholar* 11(8):37-60.
———. 1981. "Interpreting the African Heritage in Afro-American Family Organization." In *Black Families,* edited by H. P. McAdoo. Beverly Hills, CA: Sage.
———. 1988. "Interpreting the African Heritage in Afro-American Family Organization." Pp. 27-43 in *Black Families,* 2nd ed., edited by H. P. McAdoo. Newbury Park, CA: Sage.
———. 1993. "Female-Headed African American Households: Some Neglected Dimensions." In *Family Ethnicity: Strength in Diversity,* edited by H. P. McAdoo. Newbury Park, CA: Sage.
Wilson, W. J. 1987. *The Truly Disadvantaged: The Inner City, the Underclass, and Public Policy.* Chicago: University of Chicago Press.

Old-Time Religion

Benches Can't Say "Amen"

WILLIAM HARRISON PIPES

Preaching and churches have traditionally been a mainstay of Black families. Among Blacks in the United States today, old-time preaching (the uneducated Black man's emotional type of preaching that came from slavery) is still a vital element. The fundamental reason why the Black man clings to the old-time religion is that he has been without a means of normal outward expression, due to his domination by powers beyond his control—in Africa, under colonial control; in America before the Civil War, the institution of slavery; in America today (especially in the "Black Belt" and to a lesser degree in other parts of the United States), the plantation system and/or "divine white right." In Africa and in America many Blacks have made their adjustment to an "impossible world" by means of an emotional escape—the frenzy and shouting of old-time religion.

To explain the preaching of this old-time religion, the author (a) investigated the African and slavery time characteristics of this type of preaching,

AUTHOR'S NOTE: This chapter is condensed and adapted from William Harrison Pipes, *Say Amen, Brother!* (New York: William-Frederick Press, 1951). Copyright by William Harrison Pipes. Used by permission.

and (b) compared and contrasted these findings with the characteristics of the preaching that was recorded in Macon County, Georgia.

Besides the religious motive, the chief purpose of old-time Black preaching appears to be to "stir up," to excite the emotions of the audience and the minister as a means for their escape from an "impossible world." The old-time purpose of persuading people to come to Jesus is still present in varying degrees, but the emphasis here seems to be a secondary one.

Early American and African Heritages

It cannot be overstressed that the "real" old-time Black preaching—undiluted by education and freedom—existed in America only during the days of slavers. Preaching in Macon County is merely its most immediate descendant. The rhythmical preaching of some sermons is illustrative. Indeed, it should be, for the preacher is a living example of the sudden crossing of two religious cultures.

This section seeks to show that the mixing of American and African backgrounds of religious practices produced old-time Black preaching. This was done by (a) considering the very earliest American background and the coming of enslaved Africans, (b) considering the African religious background of the slaves, (c) showing the actual mixing of the cultures, and (d) observing actual preaching of the Black church.

The American Heritage

It appears that there was Christian civilization in America, on the island of Greenland, as early as the twelfth century (O'Gorman 1895). But America had little pulpit eloquence until the sixteenth century, although it is said that Columbus's first act, in 1492, of kneeling to thank God for a safe journey might be considered preaching of a sort. It is known that, on returning to America in 1494, Columbus brought with him 12 priests. In the sixteenth century, Spanish Catholic priests wrote America's first real chapter in preaching, a chapter of humble missionary teaching.

It was the seventeenth century that marked the significant period in the development of the American heritage of preaching, especially as it was to influence Black preaching. Africans were first brought to America in large numbers in 1619 (Bacon 1898). In this century there were two centers of preaching in America: Virginia and New England. Preaching activities in Jamestown, Virginia (settled in 1607), are very important, because this state fell within the "Black Belt" section, where there were many newly arrived enslaved Africans. " 'About the last of August (1619),' says John Rolfe in John Smith's *Generall Historie,* 'came a Dutch man of warre, that sold us twenty Negars.' These Blacks were sold into servitude, and Virginia . . . ; and thus slavery gained a firm place in the oldest of the colonies" (Brawley 1921).

The Black slave faced a severe type of colonial religion in the beginning. But he had his own African religious heritage. The author is not unaware of Frazier's (1939) insistence that "African traditions and practices did not take root and survive in the United States" (pp. 7-8). Frazier attempted to destroy the contentions that Black religious practices in the United States may be attributed to African sources, but his attempts are feeble. For example, he stated:

> Of the same nature is the claim of Herskovits (1935, pp. 256-57) that the practice of baptism among Negroes is related to the great importance of the river-cults in West Africa, particularly in view of the fact that, as has been observed, river-cult priests were sold into slavery in great numbers. It needs simply to be stated that about a third of the rural Negroes in the United States are Methodists and only in exceptional cases practice baptism.

Frazier's refutation is fallacious for two reasons. First, he simply made a statement about the proportion of Blacks who are Methodists, without proof or documentation. The author knew from experience that some Methodists do baptize; but even if one accepted Frazier's unsupported implication that a third of the Blacks in the rural South do not practice baptism, Herskovits's contention that the American Black man's practice of baptism is related to the river-cults in West Africa may still stand. Over a period of 320 years, without contact with African religious practices, the American Blacks naturally have lost much of the African traditions and heritage. It is possible that they could have lost entirely the practice of baptism, but it is also possible that the continuity still remains. Frazier ignored these lines of reasoning, and labeled as "uncritical" and "absurd" the assertions of Herskovits, Woodson (1936), and others. Even if Africans were not allowed to bring actual religious practices to America, they certainly did bring with them their religious memories and their temperaments. As Park (1919) concluded, the tradition may have been American, but the temperament was African.

Contrary to John Hope Franklin (1947), Turner (1949), in an examination of the extent of Africanisms in the Gullah dialect, uncovered the use of 4,000 African words, names, and numbers used by Blacks in the United States today. Good (1926) spoke even more specifically:

> Negroes have not lived in this country long enough to destroy the customs of the race developed in Africa. They hand down from generation to generation many of the customs and superstitions of the race, though most of them are greatly modified by life in the United States.

Du Bois (1903) pointed out very definitely that the American Black's religion was influenced by African practices:

> It [the Negro church] was not at first by any means a Christian Church, but a mere adaptation of those heathen rites which we roughly designate by the term Obe Worship, or "Voodooism." Association and missionary effort soon gave these rites a veneer of Christianity, and gradually, after two centuries, the Church became Christian . . . , but with many of the old customs still clinging to the services. It is this historic fact that the Negro Church of today bases itself upon the sole surviving social institution of the African fatherland, that accounts for its extraordinary growth and vitality.

It is significant that Herskovits (1930) said that the African influence in America was strongest in the South and especially in Georgia.

It does seem reasonable that these Africans who were brought to America retained something of their African background. It cannot be denied that time and American influences modified and even eliminated some of this background. But it is inconceivable that a people could suddenly lose all of their religious practices. As Park (1919) said, "It is in connection with his [the Black man's] religion that we may expect to find, if anywhere, the indications of a distinctive Afro-American culture."

A Study of Black Preaching

This study was concerned with the preaching of the Black church, furthermore, because this phase of the creations of the American Black has not been studied extensively. As James Weldon Johnson (1932) pointed out, "A good deal has been written on the folk creations of the American Negro: his music, sacred and secular; his plantation tales, and his dances; but that there are folk sermons, as well, is a fact that has passed unnoticed." Since Johnson made this statement, some interest has been shown in old-fashioned preaching. The moving picture industry, newspapers, and radio have given attention to the subject. However, in almost every instance, the Black man's religion is used for entertainment; it is not considered seriously.

The fact that Black preaching has not been studied thoroughly in this field might not justify this investigation if it were not also true that for Black families within the Black man's most important institution (the church), the preacher (and his preaching, of course) is most important. "The Negro ministry is still the largest factor in the life of this [the Black] race" (Woodson 1921). W. E. B. Du Bois (1903), the eminent sociologist, evaluated the Black minister in these terms:

> The preacher is the most unique personality developed by the Negro on American soil. A leader, a politician, an orator, a "boss," an intriguer, an idealist—all these he is, and ever, too, the center of a group of men, now twenty, now a thousand in number.

It should be stressed here that the old-fashioned (old-time) Black is the unique personality referred to, for the more educated, unemotional Black ministers preach much the same as ministers of other races. But the

> old-time Black preacher has not yet been given the niche in which he properly belongs. He has been portrayed only as a semi-comic figure. He had, it is true, his comic aspects, but on the whole he was an important figure, and at bottom a vital factor. . . . It was also he who instilled into the Negro the narcotic doctrine epitomized in the Spiritual, "You May Have All Dis World, But Give Me Jesus." This power of the old-time preacher, somewhat lessened and changed in his successors, is still a vital force; in fact, *it is still the greatest single influence among the colored people of the United States.* The Negro today is, perhaps, the most priest-governed group in the country. (Johnson 1932)

Study Approach

The purpose of this work was to make an interpretive study of old-time Black preaching as it was reflected during the late 1930s and early 1940s in Macon County, Georgia, using the recordings of several sermons.

Old-time Black preaching is important without a doubt, but James Weldon Johnson declared, "The old-time Negro preacher is rapidly passing." And this fact leads to the distinctive nature of this project: the recording of the sermons. Although the type of preaching under consideration is passing out of existence, students of American homiletics, of Black dialect, of public speaking, social sciences, and the general public may use the recordings made for this study as a basis for further study and understanding.

Without taking cognizance of the recording machine, Johnson (1932) declared of Black sermons: "There is, of course, no way of recreating the atmosphere—the fervor of the congregation, the amens and hallelujahs, the undertone of singing which was often a soft accompaniment to parts of the sermon." The recordings, even though they are unable to capture all of these aspects, go a long way toward a true presentation of these characteristics.

Choice of Macon County

Throughout, the study had been confined to Macon County because conclusive proof had been given by Arthur Raper, an able sociologist, that among Blacks the closest parallel to pre-Civil War days (during which time old-fashioned Black preaching flourished on the big slave plantations) was to be found in the "Black Belt." The "Black Belt" is the name given to some 200 counties that stretch, crescentlike, from Virginia to Texas. The name has no reference to the color of the many Blacks who live in this section of the country, but to the rich, black soil of these counties. During slavery days, the large slave plantations, on which were found most of the Blacks in the United States, were to be found in the Black Belt (Raper 1936).

It became a formidable task to record representative Black sermons, which are delivered in almost every part of the country. Because the vast majority of Blacks live in the South, the problem became one of finding a typical Southern locality.

Since Reconstruction, and up to the present time, the Black Christian has become more and more like the white man; former beliefs in the sinfulness of dancing and card playing, for example, are being discarded. The author knew this to be true from actual experience as a member of a Black family in the Black Belt. In the course of this work, he often drew upon this experience, but only when there was no better source of information available. His grandfather, Harrison Shaffer, a former slave, furnished much information concerning the days of slavery in the Black Belt.

Only in the Black Belt do we still have situations that are very close to the Black man's slavery days: the slave plantations with master and slaves become plantations with landlord and croppers; here alone have the Black man's earliest (old-time) religious practices been kept almost intact (Powdermaker 1939). Macon County is typical of that part of the Black Belt that has clung most to the conditions of the old days. Macon County was acceptable as the "Middletown" of Black society.

These churches usually "hold services" (with preaching) on one regular Sunday in each month—every first Sunday, for example. This situation exists because one church alone is unable to pay a preacher a full salary. Consequently, a minister usually pastors four churches and preaches one Sunday a month at each church.

Methodology

The initial survey uncovered much interesting information on the Black man and many allusions to Black preaching; but, more significant to the investigator, it revealed that no detailed study with recordings had been made of genuine old-fashioned preaching among Blacks. From the beginning, it was felt that only by means of the recording machine could these sermons be put down accurately. Shorthand could not be depended upon. Yet the sermons had to be taken down as delivered because this type of minister does not (often cannot) write his sermon. It was agreed, then, that the recording machine had to be used.

The following plan was followed:

1. Study literature pertaining to the folkways, religion, beliefs, etc. of the audiences in the Black churches in Macon County.
2. Attend church services to (a) record a representative number of sermons, (b) observe the practices of each preacher as to gestures, etc.
3. Confer with each preacher and some of his members to learn the minister's training, preparation for a particular sermon, etc.
4. Make the interpretation of Black preaching on the basis of accumulated data.

The original plan of procedure was followed closely, despite many difficulties. The Fort Valley State College purchased a Victor recording machine, and the college president kindly made the equipment available for recording Black sermons over a period of 3 months.

Fortunately, Macon County is only a few miles from Fort Valley State College, where the author, during the summer of the recordings, was teaching a class in the summer school's English Workshop. The students in this group were teachers from the high schools and grade schools of Georgia, and many of them came from Macon County. They knew where the churches were located, whether or not the churches had electricity, when preaching was "held," the denominations of the various churches, the ministers' names, and other information. This was very important, but even more important was the fact that these summer school teachers were known in the various communities in Macon County. Having them as members of the visiting party made it less likely to destroy the normalcy of the preaching situation. Rural teachers in Georgia often attend church services regularly; therefore, these teachers from Macon County were a part of the church audiences and were not considered strangers or outsiders.

Caution along this line was most important. An outsider has a difficult time learning anything about the inner thoughts and beliefs of Blacks in the Black Belt. They smile and act "nice," and the outsider thinks he has the facts. But the truth is often concealed. There are numerous sociological "investigations" that are supposed to reveal facts about the Black man; many of them only confuse the facts. As a Black who was born on a cotton plantation in the heart of the Black Belt and who grew up picking cotton and plowing as a typical Black Belt Black before leaving for Tuskegee Institute, the author knew this to be true from experience. It would be all but impossible for a white man to record sermons in Macon County without destroying the normalcy of the situation. (To make a successful study of the county, Raper, a white man, had to live in the county for the greater part of a year.) It was fortunate for this study that the author was able to joke with the people before church, talk their language in church and Sunday school, sing and pray, and, in general, become one of them.

The English Workshop Group and the author's wife, Anna Howard Russell Pipes, became the planning board for the recordings; Black preaching in Macon County became their project. First, it was agreed that, since of the 130 or more Black churches in Macon County, 78 were Missionary Baptist, 20 were Primitive Baptist, and 15 or 20 were Methodist, the six sermons to be recorded might be three Missionary Baptist, two Primitive Baptist, and one Methodist. We became known as the "Preaching Group."

The group left Fort Valley early on Sunday mornings and journeyed to the chosen church in time for Sunday school. Usually the investigator had to teach Sunday school (not a new experience for him) and the other members of the Preaching Group mixed with the church people and made friends. After these preliminaries, it was generally an easy matter to obtain permission to make the recording. Then the apparatus was set up outdoors and out of sight; only the microphone was visible to the audience during the recording. When there was a minister's study near the pulpit, it was used to house the apparatus; when it rained, the apparatus was set up inside the group's automobile, which was parked close to the rear of the church.

The greatest difficulties in carrying out the recording project were due to the war and were beyond the power of this board: (a) Recording discs (because of their rubber base) became almost unobtainable—the regular price doubled and tripled, and then they were not obtainable at any price; and (b) gasoline rationing had come to Georgia. The four gallons allowed per week would hardly take the group to some places in Macon County and back to Fort Valley. One student in the group was a minister himself and had an "X" card; thus he saved the project.

After the sermon was recorded, invariably the recorder was asked to play back the services and the sermon. The minister and the audience (now no longer religiously emotional) laughed and enjoyed hearing themselves. Frequently someone remarked, "Dat's jest whut he sed!" Others considered it "wonderful" that a member of their race could make records.

It is not likely that the recording tended to destroy the normalcy of the preaching situation to any great degree. Once or twice there was some artificiality at first, but the ministers and the audiences always accepted us or forgot about our presence when the "spirit" touched them. The recordings caught the spontaneity of the preaching and the reaction of the audience.

Sermons[1]

Sermon III: "John the Baptist—A Voice Crying in the Wilderness"

It's very pleasant to be present here with you all today. Short service if possible. Got me kinda run-up; Communion at Smith Chapel, to preach Anniversary Sermon. Not feeling good. Ben on road, two weeks of service. Journeyed all night to git home. Don't feel good; got headache. You all peach-struck[2] you all tired; been "gwine to it." Since you been "gwine to it" and am tired and I been "gwine to it" and am tired, don't 'spect too much.

Omitted Sunday school. Kinda late; hafta bear with you 'cause I know you ti'ed. *(Reads from the bible in such a manner that one hardly can understand a word.)*

"In those days came John Baptist, preaching in the wilderness—*(of Judea).*[3] And saying, Repent ye; for the kingdom of heaven is at hand. For this is he that was spoken of by the prophet Esaias, saying, *The voice of one crying in the wilderness, Prepare* ye the way of the Lord, make his paths straight . . . (Matthew 3:1-17).

"Then was Jesus led up of the spirit into the wilderness to be tempted of the devil. And when he had fasted forty days and forty nights, he was afterward an hungered. And when the tempter came to him, he said, If thou be the Son of God, command that these stones be made bread. But he answered and said, It is written, Man shall not live by bread alone, but by every word that proceedeth out of the mouth of God"[4] (Matthew 4:1-4).

John was a preacher, baptizing folks. John the Baptist *(Loud cry of a baby in the audience.)*—and he was preaching to folks telling them about repentance of sin. Men don't lack you to tell them that.

Revival meeting about here. Been helping a man who gwine to help us. Gave me swell time down there. Only one thing: didn't have the spirit you got. *(Amens.)* I knocked 'round there. He will help us. We don't want to treat him no way but royal. If you want to be helped, have to help somebody. We wont to put him on a good revival. He got a home right there at home next to mine. If he don't treat me right, he's right there where I can hear what he say. *(Chuckles.)* We start now to make our aim. Five dollars or eight dollars ain't gwine to speak to no good preacher. Ten dollars ain't gwine to speak to no preacher. He gwine to preach! Every time I bring a man here, he better preacher'n me. *("No, he ain't," from the audience.)*

John was a preacher; preach 'pentance of sins, I *(have taken in a)* number of devils since I been here. Whether they converted or not, I don't know. I like that they sit down. But you'll do. Talk to me now. *(Asking for audience response.)* Them little black places dere ain't no good if you can just sit down. *(Humor; refers to the black faces of the audience.)* Consecrate myself now. *(Get serious.)* Get fair with you. I ain't got no need to come here; no one's a Christian here. Benches can't say, "Amen." You all can hear, can't yer? But John was a preacher and he went down there by himself. Wasn't no crowd down dere when he got dere.

Jesus said, "Lift Me up from the earth and I draw all men unto Me. And I draw all men unto Me." In the life you live—some us lives mighty—lift him up. We live it while we at the church, in the church, in your songs, your moans, and your groans. Lift him up. Let's see—er—John went down there and lift Him up. Jesus came to him and talked to him and when the Tempter came to Him, "If Thou the Son of Man, turn these rocks to bread."

He answered, "Man shall not live by bread alone." Testing Jesus, showing Him all the good things, calling Him in question. Ef he done got hungry, "Then make bread outta them stones lying around the mountain, jest like yer see 'em. Look at 'em!"

Then He got hungry, and they say to Him, "If Thou be the Son of God, command that these stones be made bread." Ain't that what he say? Preach it out there with me. I know what I'm talkin' 'bout; you too!

They thought that a fast change Him and carry Him their way. Some folks, if dey carry you their way, it's all right; ain't got nothin' to do for you if dey can't. After done been to wilderness, fast and pray. "Fast" mean don't eat, don't drink. After that, at a certain time, He got hungry. He thought *(The Tempter did.)* dat a fine time, fine time, fine chance to change Him—change His idea, change His mind—and he didn't stay 'way! You know, some folks belong to the church; long's dey can't carry you dey way, dey have nothing' for you to do. Ain't dat right? Now dat's de Lawd's turf! But as long as dey git you to do what dey want, dey wid you.

After he'd taken Him on the pinacke of dat temple, then He got hungry. He got—let me tell you, he don't eat, don't drink—after that, at a certain time, He got hungry, see? He got hungry. Then he[5] say that "this is my time." We're on our way. "Hungry; got nothing to eat, but He says He's the Son of God." He said, "If you Christ, you outta prove it! You talk and don't prove it. Doing! He said that He God's Son; he always been with His Father; He hungry; got nothing' to eat and got no money and, quite natural, He'll yield to it." (You know, sometimes a fellow take things off people he wouldn't do it, but it's conditions.) Conditions make you do things that you wouldn't do. If conditions didn't have us so "tight," have us going, don't you know you wouldn't work all day and all night Saturday? *(Amens.)*[6] Our conditions! Conditions! You look right at yer God sometime folks. God! Jesus look right at that rock. Rocks! Rock's something hard; something you can't bite; danger to swallow. (Conditions make you do things that you wouldn't do, don't you know.) Rock's hard; bust fellow's brains out. "Turn to bread; make bread out of these." . . .

John, forerunner of Jesus Christ, born of Elisha, come before Jesus Christ advertising Jesus Christ. One hundred years before His coming, Ezekiel—David say likewise. Daniel says he saw Him as a stone tore out of a mountain. "I'll give him all power." Ezekiel saw Him as a wheel; Ezekiel saw Him as a wheel comin' from—teeming. One Ezekiel saw Him; kept spying things—spectacle of force. Wheel in a wheel, little in big, Matthew—Luke—John—He's coming. John then grew up; maturity come up.

Don't know how much done in a run of a day. Lotta cussin' done in a run of a day; lotta disaster done in a run of a day; so much disaster done in a run of a day; no end to lying in the run of a day. Here's a day; another day. Grow—one day—days seem—. John Baptist preached in wilderness; say he go there by himself, holding up Jesus. Preached only one text. I'm got to git 'nother text every time I come here. Give up world; give 'self to God. Then you see Him, shall find the kingdom of Heaven at hand. He talk about Jesus; he talk about Jesus.

I know what I's telling you 'bout. "The Rose of Sharon, Knight of the Mornin' Star, come down to be ruler of the day. Kingdom of Heaven is at hand; Jesus not far off; always there to come to your need." That was spoke about by the prophet, the one crying in the wilderness: "Prepare ye the way of the Lord; make His paths straight; prepare the way for Him." Oh, brother, we ought to walk in such a life that somebody else ought to be prepare' through you for the Kingdom of God, the Kingdom of Heaven.

Heaven! I feel like it's a very splendid place. Heaven! I feel like it's the best place ever I have known. Wharever you at—in your state, in your field—when dat spirit of God hit you, you feel like you in Heaven right dare. You—ain't you never got happy? By yourself? You just done forgot everything and—and God knows you just feel like you in Heaven right then and there. *(Amens.)* Heaven is a spiritual place, spirit place. And Heaven make His paths straight—er—first why—.

* * *

Some folks say, "I'm a straight man myself; I'm a straight woman." Oh-oh-oh-oh, just follow on down the line; you just go her way; you'll find out whether she's straight or no. You'll find out whether she's straight or no, brother. You just deal with a man; you'll find out; you'll find out he's crooked as can be. Don't make 'em no crookeder'n him. He—. A straight man or woman don't care what time, when or where they are, they want to do right, want to walk out-right, plain before the world. Not ashamed of their lives; "I'm living straight." I ain't talking about walking straight and calmly, but your life! Straight! Straight! I ain't talking. . . .

Forty days, forty nights—I told yo' what fasting mean. They got hungry. Bible said they tempted them. They—call Son of God, commanded stone be made bread. Testing—Jesus said, "Man, man shall not live by bread alone." Ain't dat true, man? *(The audience chants: "Man shall not live by bread alone.")* Man, God's word good. Hungry soul, hear somebody sing and pray. Certain, man can't get filled till he harken.

Uncle Sam calling for me; mighty war on calling for me. Dis last remark to you. Sit on a high hill, sit on a high hill—East and West—Lilly of the Valley—. Things of the world, things of the world, things of the world. This world—. Yes—oh, Jesus! Oh, Jesus! Sundown—. Pinackle of temple—. Lily of the Valley—. Beautiful things. "All this is mine, all this is mine. It is mine, it is mine, it is mine." Oh, Lord! "I tell you what you do now, if you just fall down and worship me."

"Get behind!" My Lord! God got His eyes on you. See all you do. Midnight! Save Jesus.[7] Save Jesus. Died on Calvary Hill. Save Jesus, save Jesus, save Jesus. Hint to the wise. Save Jesus. Get free. Save Jesus. Leper—save Jesus—take up your bed and go home. Save Jesus. Writing on the ground. Save Jesus. Man to depend on when trouble come. Put truth to him *(Devil)* and he go away. Truth breaks down things; truth washes down things. Last day—disciples—this Friday—took Him this night, took Him this night—all night long—now before Pilate. Judas, as he betrayed—little money—Judas as he betrayed, told 'em with a kiss, (Kiss ain't so good.) Judas, as he betrayed Jesus, betrayed with a kiss. Mighty man.

Hold it *(the spirit),* hold it! Sometimes makes you cry, sometimes makes you cry, sometimes makes you pray, sometimes makes you moan, sometimes makes you right-living. If it makes you cry, I'll be with you, will not forsake you. Mother cry. Father fine. Everybody thinks you git it. Hold it. *(Moaning.)* Go with you to graveyard. He makes you your dying bed. Mercy! Hold it. *(Sings.)* I been had hold Him a long time; he ain't never let me down.

'Tis on cross, Friday evening. Lord! Right there Sunday morning soon, Sunday morning soon *(Christ)* rose out of the grave. Soon, soon *(Sings it),* soon *(Shouting in the audience—climax begins);* watches 'round grave; felt like dead man on to himself. Oh—oh, knocked off dying smile; put back in one corner of grave. Angel sitting on Heavenly grave holding God's hand.

Sat right there; nobody in the grave; saw it standing gaping open. He not there; somebody done stole Him away. I see Him go back. John go down to grave, do down to grave, go down to grave, go down to grave. Look-a-yonder, look-a-yonder; who do you see? Who you see? Jesus! Jesus! "I looked for Jesus, but shook and tremble." Jesus! Rocks began to roar. Jesus! "Got to tell my brother." Jesus! "I'm going before day."

Ahhhhhhh! Ahhhhhhh! *(Climax! General confusion.)*

Got my *(Pause.)* . . . in your soul. got to cry sometime. Know I been born again. Git off by 'self and cry. My soul *(Audience moans, "My soul.")*. My soul have Savior. Have trouble and tribulation; sometimes afflicted; have to crawl into your home. Farewell; Farewell! *(Uniformed ushers come to administer to the shouting ladies.)* For motherless child, nowhere to go, nobody to go to. Fatherless child . . . *(Leaves pulpit and comes down to the audience.)* My! My! Don't you feel lonely sometime in world by yourself? Give me your hand. *(Picks up a tune on "Give me your hand." Audience joins in singing.)* Lord, give me your hand. Won't He lead you? *(Talking now.)* Won't he take care of you, chillun? Be consolation for you? My, my Lord! I done tried! I know He *do* care of you, preserve your soul, and den what I like about You, carry you home. Here rain wouldn't fall on you. Beautiful land. Gwine to sing and open de doors of the church.

Old-Time Preaching

People listen attentively to a speaker if they feel that his message vitally concerns them. Are the speaker's ideas worthy of their sincere considerations? If they are, the speaker may be assured of their interest and goodwill. The emotions and the basic beliefs—friendship, duty, honor, fear, shame, emulation, patriotism, compassion—are the stuff of which emotional or pathetic appeal is made. These are the elements of emotional proof. Stripped of the unparalleled emphasis upon this appeal, old-time Black preaching is not unique. But, as James Weldon Johnson (1932) declared, the old-time Black preacher "had the power to sweep his hearers before him; and so himself was often swept away." This was the original old-time Black preacher. Do the original elements of pathetic proof appear in Macon County sermons? What is the nature of the new influence?

This question suggests the role of pathetic (emotional) appeal with the old-time Black audience. Blacks keep this emotional light burning within themselves constantly—in their moans, in their spirituals, and in their prayers; as they work the fields or walk the roads; as they shy down the streets of the country town or bow into some country store (always fearful of the Lords of the South and of Judge Lynch). They come to church with this emotional spark already within them; they only want the minister to fan it into a flame—to encourage them to let this light set them on fire with shouts and groans. This is their emotional escape from an impossible world; this action of shouting and moaning and laughing and crying relieves them. Therefore, a consideration of pathetic appeal with such people resolves itself into a determination of the methods the Black minister employs to fan these emotional sparks into flames. The audience's knowledge of the Bible (the chief source of information) equals that of the speaker; the congregation and the minister share the same religious ideas. Therefore, this is not an intellectual occasion; this is not a time for thinking. The problem becomes one of arousing the emotions, of helping the tired, subdued Black man to associate his trials, sorrows, and joys with those of the biblical characters.

The genuine old-time preacher knows that his mission in part is to fan emotions into flames. He accomplishes this by leading the audience to concentrate upon "getting happy" by suggestion (directly or indirectly) through action, by the audience and by the minister (delivery). This initial action suggests the climactic emotional state that the audience and the minister seek.

The old-time Black preacher, although a master hypnotist, follows in the footsteps of great orators when he appeals to his audience's basic beliefs—biblical ideas that have been adjusted to fit the descendants of Africans and of American slaves. The conception of God is at the center of these beliefs; to the Black man, God is mysterious and all-powerful. The Black man's attitude toward God makes the congregation susceptible to certain emotional appeals. This preacher appeals to his audience's great *admiration* and *joy* over the power of God. Revealing how vital to them is their subject, ministers dwell on the audience's *love* for God and their *hope* for a new life to come.

The *fear* of God is another emotion to which the old-time Black preacher appeals:

"My Lord! God got His eyes on you! See all you do."
"Have mercy now; oh, Jesus, have mercy now."

Fear has consistently dogged the footsteps of the Black man—as an African, as an American slave, and now as a second-class citizen. Observe how a minister produces shouting by appealing to *fear* of God:

> "Yonder He come. . . . God Almighty. . . . Thunder, your conscience; lightening in Your hand. . . . Everybody is gwine ter pray now!" *(Audience shouts wildly.)*

There is suggestion too in the last statement:

> "You may be too proud *(Suggests the preacher)* to pray now; too proud to shout now, but you *will* shout and pray when God comes, so why not now?"

The people agree, and they do shout and pray. The audience's *fear* of God often approaches *awe* under the spell of the preacher's description of God's work.

But unadulterated *fear of death* is the emotion to which a minister appeals. The minister, even when not striking directly at fear-producing descriptions of death, likes to talk about things with which *death* has some connection. Any mention of the grave or of death serves the purpose—to produce shouting. Jesus' triumph over the great mystery, *death,* is most effective. The biblical story of the strange death of Almighty God's Son is used frequently:

> Christ "kept on dying *(on the cross).* He never stopped dying."

The preacher often stimulated the emotions of his audience by telling of his "call" to preach. In all instances, when the members of the audience are excited and open to the mildest suggestion, they are thinking of their own trials, joys, and sorrows, and their emotional condition is heightened by the rhythmical delivery and their own actions. For example, when the minister, after telling the biblical story of Joseph the Dreamer, says:

> "I seed Him . . . , a shield over here one Sunday mornin'. He was takin' on board. . . . And I *dream, chillun.*" *(Sings the last two words; the audience joins in. Shouting.)*

He unlocks the door of his audience's world with the words "*dream, chillun,*" as did Martin Luther King in his "I Had a Dream" sermon. They too had trials and problems (like Joseph); they too were *dreaming* and hoping for a better day to come. When the preacher says "dream, chillun," he stimulates thoughts and emotions within the audience that lie too deep for words. The people understand; they shout. "How long" is the unlocking key to the door of frustration when a minister moans:

"How long? How long must I work in the vineyard?"

The words "how long" suggest to the Black his apparently endless chain of trials. How often he has wondered *how long* the Lord would permit his chosen servant to be mistreated in this world below. *"How long."* Pent up emotions overflow. Shouting.

When It Comes Our Time to Die[8]

The Black man's old-time religious prayer is not confined to the church. Outside the church, it keeps the emotional flame alive. It replaces the sermon at home, at the sickbed, and at wakes. Blacks in the Black Belt still observe the old custom of sitting up all night with the dead. Friends and relatives visit the house of the deceased on the night of the wake; the body is in plain view, and the night is spent in talking of death, of the dead person (especially, how the "end"—death—came), and in drinking coffee or something stronger.

This prayer given at a wake in the Black Belt is not unusual—and demonstrates too the new influences, which fight against the prayer's old-time emotional appeal:

"Oh, Gawd, we come this evenin' beared down wid the sorrows of this worl'. We come as paupers to Thy th'one o' grace. We been down in the valley o' the shadder, an' our hearts is heavy this evenin,' Lord. Thou's done thundered fo'th Thy will. Thou's done took from out our mist one o' Yo' lambs. Thou's done took a good brother who's done lived his 'lotted time an' died, Gawd, lie we all mus' die. Ummmmmmmmmmmmm. Thou's done come into this house o' sons an' wid Yo' own han', Yo' own grat han', Gawd—Ummmmmmmmmmmmmm— Thou's done dashed down the vessel outta what Yo' po'ed life into them. Thou's done took a father an' a gran'-father. Thou's done beared down hearts. Thou's done put burdens on 'em. Thou's done whupped 'em wid stripes. 'Member dese hearts, great Lawd. Relieve 'em. you know when t'suns's been a-shinin' too long an' the earth's all parched an' barren, You sen's Yo' rain, Lord. You relieve the earth. When wars rage, like the one ragin' now, an' mens dies an' makes widders an' orfins, den, in Yo' own good time, Gawd—Yo' precious time Ummmmmm—You sen's peace. You takes the burden off'n the hearts o' nations. An' You promise', Father, by the sweetflowin' blood o' Jesus, to rescue the perishin', suckle the needy, give health to the ailin' . . ."

(He did not pause at a piercing scream from Jamie. *She is shouting.* His extended fingers worked spasmodically, as if each had a life, independent of him.)

"An' sen' balm to the hearts o' sufferin'. Sen' it now, Lord. Let it flow like the healin' waters o' Gilead, an' ease the burden o' dese hearts broken by the fulfillin' o' Yo' almighty will. Amen."

(The preacher opened his eyes and looked around as he lowered his arms, shooting his cuffs as he did so. The three brothers stared at spots about six inches beyond their toes. One corner of his thick mouth drawn in a hard snarl, Paul lifted the pitcher *(of whiskey)* from the table and drank. In the other room there was a general snuffling and loosening of throats. Walter was the first to recover.)

"That was a fine prayer, Rev'ren'," he said. "Mighty fine."

"Thank you, brother."

. . . "That's fine. That's jus' fine," the preacher said pompously. "Uncle Henry's *(Refers to the dead man.)* goin, a smile up there wid Gawd tomorrer. I'm aimin' to do him proud."

With that, he went back into the other room. Neely closed the door.

"He can lay a pow'ful prayer." (Redding 1942)

The prayer, like the sermon, appeals to the emotions of gratitude to God, compassion, fear of death, fear of God, sorrow, shame; it, too, employs suggestion.

Like the prayer, the singing is important in stimulating the emotions. The hymn (like the spiritual) is really a blending of emotions. The words themselves are unintelligible unless they are "lined." That is, someone states a line or two before the audience sings them; the audience sings and pauses while additional lines are stated; the singing continues in this manner until the end; the audience is seated part of the time and stands part of the time. Even after the song is "lined," the words are so run together in the long-meter fashion that they are not distinguishable. Such singing is an emotional experience, like an instrumental rendition. Spirituals carry the same emotional charge. The singing is so important in setting the stage emotionally that the sermon is almost inconceivable without it.

Du Bois (1903) said that "three things characterize the religion" of the Black man: the preacher, the music, and the frenzy.

The music is that plaintive rhythmic melody, which is touching in minor cadences, which, despite caricature and defilement, still remains the most original and beautiful expression of human life and longing yet born on American soil. Sprung from the African forests, where its counterpart can still be heard, it was adapted, changed, and intensified by the tragic soul-life of the slave, until, under the stress of law and whip, it became the one true expression of a people's sorrow, despair, and hope.

The old-time Black man is indeed a master of this art of emotional appeal. Even the order of services builds toward the desired emotional climax of shouting. Observe the order of services for the sermon, "Thou Shalt Love the Lord Thy God:"

1. *Song:* "My Faith Looks Up to Thee."
2. *Prayer:* A deacon thanks the Lord for having permitted *death* to leave them in the world "a little longer." *(The minister did not ordain the use of these exact words, but he knows the content of the average Negro old-time prayer.)*
3. *Song:* "I Love Jesus." *(A perfect selection.)*
4. *Song:* "Come, Thou Fount of Every Blessing."
5. *Hymn:* "Father, I Stretch My Hands to Thee."
6. *Responsive reading from the Bible.*
7. *Song:* More of "Father, I Stretch My Hands to Thee."
8. *Prayer:* A preacher thanks the Lord for sparing them. The goodness of God is stressed.
9. *Song:* "Where He Leads Me I Will Follow."
10. *Scripture reading:* "Thou Shalt Love the Lord Thy God."

In the order of services a prominent place is given to the prayer. Much can be said of the importance of prayer in emotional appeal. The prayer (or prayers) precedes the sermon and, using many of the same appeals to the emotions that are to be found in the sermons, serves to prepare the way, to set the mood, for the ultimate emotional frenzy caused by the sermon. The following prayer reveals the importance of the prayer for pathetic appeal:

(The congregation, bowed, hums the last verse of "My Faith Looks Up to Thee" as the deacon moves searchingly and rhythmically into his prayer.) "Dear Lawd, we come befo' Thee and ask Thee ter stand by us. Thank Thee for ev'ry

thing Thou's did for us. Christ, essemble between these four walls; git in the hearts uv men and women, boys and girls, Thou art God an' God alone.

"since the last time we's bowed, we's done things that we ought not uv done, an' we's left things undone what we ought uv done. Rule over Heav'n and earth; rule over these people down here, the sick an' afflicted and weary. And bind us one to another.

"Now, Lawd, when it come our time to *die,* pray You receive us into Thy kingdom an' give us souls a resting place. Amen."

This prayer, given by another minister from the pulpit, revealed the effectiveness of prayers in emotional appeal: They "warm up" the emotions of the audience for the sermon.

The Preacher: Man of God

Some Blacks declared that the magnetism and power of the preacher solely are responsible for a "good meetin'," that the minister's ability to affect the emotions of the audience accounted for the shouting and the frenzy. Few observers accepted logical argument as an important element in old-time Black preaching.

The audience's conception of the Black minister as a "Man of God" is obviously a persuasive element. Even before the preacher speaks, his listeners are in a receptive mood, for the old-time Black preacher does not "just go to school" and then begin preaching; he is "called of God to preach." But what forces and influences develop this "man of God"? What is the nature of being "called"? What character qualities of the preacher make him persuasive? How does the "Man of God" differ from other Christians?

The preparation of the "man of God" often begins before birth, with the dedication of the child to God by a pregnant mother. Others are called after living a life of sin. There are "good" Negroes and "bad" Negroes who become ministers. The background of the "bad" Negro gives him ethical appeal because of the contrast between his new life and his old, "sinful" life. The people reason, "As bad as old Henry was, he surely must have been 'called' or he never would have become a preacher." Both types of preachers are "called" and both have appeal because of what they are.

Booker T. Washington (1924) implied that the Negro preacher is not always sincere in his claim that he has been called to preach. He tells the story of the Negro who, working along in the cotton field one day, suddenly stopped and cried in a pulpit voice:

De sun am so hot and dis Nigger am so tired, bless my soul, I believe I done been called to preach! Glory!!

A common joke among Blacks is that such-and-such a preacher thought God said, "Go *preach,*" when what He really said was, "Go *plow!*"

The character of Black preachers persuades their audiences—despite the moral weakness of some of them. The old-time Black preacher is "a good man." Blacks stress this point: The preacher must not dance, play cards, or drink. Yet some preachers are "the biggest devils" in the church. Members of the church can name the "sweethearts" of such pastors. Occasionally, a "sister's" husband or lover takes a knife or a razor and "cuts up" the minister. Almost every Black knows "dirty jokes" about the minister's lack of morals; it is a common saying that preachers love three things: money, women, and chicken. Yet the old-time Black preacher is respected and honored. (The author knows there are many upright and moral Black ministers. His intention here is not to disparage such ministers or their profession.) His being a "Man of God" is not the full answer. Other elements of his character are important to the understanding of this paradoxical situation.

Perhaps, above all, the old-time Black preacher was superior to his people in intelligence. As James Weldon Johnson (1932) said:

The old-time preacher was generally a man far above the average in intelligence; he was, not infrequently, a man of positive genius. The earliest of these preachers must have virtually committed many parts of the Bible to memory through hearing the scripture read or preached from.

Native intelligence gave him leadership, for the old-time preacher lacked education to give him prestige.

The Black preacher's small income meant that well-educated men did not pastor these churches. This introduced other characteristics of these ministers. "Pastoring" three churches, the typical minister received an average of $546.60 a year. He spent about one-sixth for traveling expenses. Even this small amount was not paid as salary. It was charity. The minister had to "take up collection." This explained two other characteristics of the preacher: first, why he was extremely money conscious and, second, why he must please the audience. Only a burning desire to be a leader could compensate for this situation.

This *desire to lead* is an important element in the preacher's character; it often accompanied natural leadership. Perhaps "leadership" is not the proper word, but certainly these old-time preachers tackled any problem. James W. Johnson tells of an old Black minister who opened his Bible one Sunday and read from a rather cryptic passage. He did not understand a word of it, but (always the leader) he removed his eyeglasses, slammed the Bible shut, stared down at his respectful and expectant congregation, and said: "Brothers and sisters, this morning—I intend to explain the unexplainable—find out the undefinable—ponder over the impossible—and unscrew the inscrutable." Intelligence, leadership ability, and the "man of God" conception serve the Macon County preacher well.

Summary

The methods of persuasion of the Macon County preaching demonstrate that emotional appeal remains dominant; appeal through the character of the preacher (the "Man of God") runs a close second. Logical argument is not entirely absent. Especially in the sermons of the more highly educated ministers, there appear evidences of both inductive and deductive reasoning (at the less emotional points of the sermon). The method of instructing the audience unemotionally is being ushered in by the more highly educated Black ministers. Another modern influence seems to be the underlying purpose of soliciting money.

The style of Macon County preaching is basically simple: short words that are familiar to the audience (with a long word thrown in occasionally for effect). Sentences are often elliptical (without complete subject and predicate). Such sentences, however, are joined by conjunctions, to help maintain the speaker's rhythmical flow of words. Slang and Black dialect (the language of the audience) form the level of expression. But the style is figurative, with the use of metaphor, based on the experiences of the audience or drawn from the Bible, taking the lead. The style is narrative—for the listener rather than for the reader. The amount of poetic, biblical prose is decreasing, perhaps because education (newspapers, magazines, radio) is bringing in new expressions—a condition that is unlike the original complete dependency upon the Bible.

The delivery of the Macon County sermon is most characteristic of earlier old-time Black preaching. Entirely impromptu, it is rhythmical—which helps to heighten the emotions of the minister and the audience. It gains effect by the change from conversational to rhythmical speaking. The delivery is also made more effective by the preacher's appearance, his sincerity, his bombastic gestures, and his many movements in the pulpit. Possibly most important, the preacher's delivery is aided by his masterful modulation and control of his excellent voice. The recorded Macon County sermons indicate that old-time Black preaching today is still a vital part of the Black man's existence. Preaching is still the soul of a frustrated people.

The background of this study of American Blacks, a people in bondage (from Africa, to American slavery, and to present-day second-class citizenship), explains old-time Black preaching partly as an escape mechanism for a frustrated people. This study also points up two conclusions: (a) The Black race in the United States has made unparalleled progress in normal adjustment (against odds), but the Black man should not expect to exercise first-class American citizenship immediately—unless America herself decides (probably beginning with a Supreme Court decision) to practice true democracy *for all people,* to remove from the American scene the half-century-old concept (based on a ruling of the U.S. Supreme Court) of "separate but equal"; and (b) the crying need of the Black race in the United States is for improved leadership, regardless of the timetable of democracy—first-class citizenship for the Black man *now* as his American right.

First-class citizenship for the Black man now. If the masses of U.S. Blacks are to have their frustration-producing condition eliminated permanently in the near future, America must somehow come to realize the menace to the nation of racial prejudice in a nuclear age; she must realize in deed as well as in word that it is the American creed and law that no man deserves second-class citizenship because of race, color, or previous condition of servitude; she must realize that the best *preparation* for the Black man's wise use of first-class citizenship is to be found in the Black man's *practice* of first-class citizenship.

Long-range first-class citizenship will come to the Black man mainly through the unity of effort on the part of Blacks themselves; this unity of effort must be used to prepare members of the race to exercise wisely their rights as citizens and to prepare the minds of southern white people to permit such democracy. If the Black man is frustrated because of persecution, the mind of the white man is warped because of the un-American practices of enslaving and degrading the Black man; Booker T. Washington stated it in this manner: "You cannot hold a man down in a ditch without remaining there yourself."

Freedom for the Black man through unity of effort on the part of Blacks themselves? Is this not the blind leading the blind? Certainly, united action on the part of the Black Belt Blacks is in the distant future, for the Black man (due to his background of bondage) is far from belonging to a race that has solidarity. Old-time Black ministers often declare, "Negroes just won't stick together." As Gunnar Myrdal (1944) shows, however, the masses of a people *must* have education and some degree of economic security before they can unite to improve themselves permanently in a social, economic, and political way. Blacks as a group are still a semi-illiterate proletariat, and hence cannot be expected to unite to improve the masses of their people until a sizable group of Blacks are both more highly educated and more economically secure. The Black man himself cannot make this a fact within the near future, nor is the white man likely to clear his mind of prejudice voluntarily within the near future. American democracy never had a greater command—for when the Black man is denied first-class citizenship, American democracy as a whole is debased.

Undoubtedly, the old-time Black preacher is *the* Black leader today; it is to him that the great majority of Blacks in this country look for guidance. The degreed and trained Black educators, ministers, writers, et al. should not delude themselves into thinking that they are the true Black leaders. The masses of Blacks seldom get to know these "leaders" and even when the opportunity does bring the highly trained leader into contact with the average Black the latter either does not understand the "highbrow" leader or distrusts his motives—and not always unjustly. But the old-time preacher is "one of the flock." He is trusted, listened to, and understood. Therefore, the crying need in improving the Black masses (whether first-class citizenship comes immediately or in the distant future) is for improved Black leadership.

As Richardson (1947) pointed out in his study, improvement of the Black ministry can do much to improve the condition of the Black masses, but the author is dubious of the leadership of any Black who is economically dependent on the goodwill of prejudiced white persons (which eliminates many college presidents and teachers) or who is economically dependent upon the masses of Blacks (which seems to minimize the effectiveness of the leadership of (the average Black minister, who is dependent upon Blacks for his income).

Without a feeling of despair or pessimism (but trying to read the timetable correctly, which is essential for the Black race in making the journey to first-class citizenship), the author does not conceive of Blacks possessing within the immediate future the educational and economic improvement necessary to wrest first-class citizenship from a reluctant country—and the country will be reluctant for some time to come. Will the greatest democracy on earth meet the challenge? Will the "Land of the Free" return to *her* old-time religion, *freedom for all people:* "All men are created equal and from that equal creation they derive rights inherent and unalienable, among which are the preservation of life and liberty and the pursuit of happiness"?

If America really wants to return to her old-time religion of freedom for all people, then let her say in deed—"Amen, Brother!" ("Benches can't say 'Amen.' You all can hear, can't yer?")

Notes

1. Complete transcriptions of each of the sermons may be found in *Say Amen, Brother!* (Pipes 1951).

2. It was peach-packing season in Georgia and most of the audience had worked until very late Saturday night, really until Sunday morning.

3. These words, like many others in this passage, he omitted. He often mumbled. It was discovered later that he could not read very well.

4. It appeared that the minister read on and on until he struck something in the Bible that appealed to him, something that would serve as his subject; entirely extemporaneous.

5. The Tempter.

6. He means the sermon, the emotional part, is getting under way.

7. Observe how "Save Jesus" becomes a refrain.

8. The minister, closing Sermon IV: "May the Lord bless us, may He help us, and may He save us when it comes our time to die. Amen."

9. Sermon III.

References

Bacon, L. W. 1898. *A History of American Christianity.* New York: Scribner's.

Brawley, B. 1921. *A Short History of the American Negro.* New York: Macmillan.

Du Bois, W. E. B. 1903. *The Souls of Black Folk: Essays and Sketches.* Chicago: McClurg.

Franklin, J. H. 1947. *From Slavery to Freedom.* New York: Knopf.

Frazier, E. F. 1939. *The Negro Family in the United States.* Chicago: University of Chicago Press.

Good, A. 1926. *Sociology and Education.* New York: Harper.

Herskovits, M. 1930. "The Negro in the New World." *American Anthropologist* 32(November).

Johnson, J. W. 1932. *God's Trombone: Seven Negro Sermons in Verse.* New York: Viking.

Myrdal, G., with R. Sterner and A. Rose. 1944. *An American Dilemma: The Negro Problem and Modern Democracy.* New York: Harper & Row.

O'Gorman, T. 1895. *A History of the Roman Catholic Church in the United States.* New York: Christian Literature.

Park, R. 1919. "The Conflict and Fusion of Cultures With Special Reference to the Negro. *Journal of Negro History* 4(April).

Pipes, W. H. 1951. *Say Amen, Brother!* New York: William-Frederick.

Powdermaker, H. 1939. *After Freedom: The Portrait of a Negro Community in the Deep South.* New York: Viking.

Raper, A. A. 1936. *Preface to Peasantry: A Tale of Two Black Belt Counties.* Chapel Hill: University of North Carolina Press.

Redding, J. S. 1942. *No Day of Triumph.* New York: Harper.

Richardson, H. 1947. *Dark Glory.* New York: Friendship.

Turner, L. D. 1949. *Africanisms in the Gullah Dialect.* Chicago: University of Chicago Press.

Washington, B. T. 1924. *Up From Slavery.* Garden City, NY: Doubleday.

Woodson, C. 1921. *The History of the Negro Church.* Washington, DC: Associated Publishers.

———. 1925. *Negro Orators and Their Orations.* Washington, DC: Associated Publishers.

———. 1936. *The African Background Outlined.* Washington, DC: Associated Publishers.

Conceptualizations of African American Families

JUALYNNE ELIZABETH DODSON

Contrasting Approaches

Few would argue that research on African American families in the United States is filled with complex and often controversial issues. Much of the controversy is linked to the nation's history of institutional racism and the way that racism has informed the investigation and analysis of family life in this community. No small amount of the controversy is attributed to linkages between U.S. social policy and biases of the research. Similarly, a body of investigations that attempt to challenge the biases and/or social policy also draws impetus from the context of U.S. racism. One way of sorting out the myriad studies and their significance is to focus on the conceptual assumptions of the investigators and their findings. These assumptions can be divided into two basic schools of thought: ethnocentrism and cultural relativism.

The ethnocentric school is grounded in the assimilationist ideology that informed much of life in the United States up through the time of the civil rights movement in the 1960s. This approach has presumed that everyone who would be a citizen wanted and would take on values, attitudes, and behaviors of middle-class Anglo-Saxon Protestants. That ethnic group was presumed to represent the norm of U.S. life, and all others would want to adhere to that norm.

In this ethnocentric context, African American family life, from its beginning up to the present, has not adhered to the norm. Research based on this perspective has labeled black families as pathological and dysfunctional because of their variation from the expected norm. The work of E. Franklin Frazier (1939) and Daniel P. Moynihan (1965) served as the foundation of this school of thought and research. Further complexity has been added to this issue as the works of these scholars has culminated in social policies predicated on the assumption that the African American family is unstable, disorganized, and unable to provide its members with the social and psychological support and development they need to assimilate fully into U.S. society.

The second school of thought that has undergirded much of the research is that of cultural relativism. Researchers from this school begin with the assumption that African American family patterns possess a degree of cultural integrity that is neither related to nor modeled on white American norms. Most scholars of this school trace the origins of these cultural distinctions back to black Americans' African cultural heritage, and all tend to focus on the "strengths" of African American families rather than their weaknesses.

The cultural relativistic view, developed primarily as a reaction to assumptions of deficit and pathology, maintains that the African American family is a functional entity. This conceptual perspective is designed to challenge theories and social policies that have emanated from the ethnocentric approach.

Underlying the theoretical and empirical arguments of the two schools is the common assumption that African American families and European American families are qualitatively different, culturally. The schools diverge, however, in their interpretation and explanation of the causes of cultural differences. The cultural ethnocentric school, operating on the assumption that the United States is culturally homogeneous and has a single set of universal norms for citizens' cultural behavior to which all groups must conform, accounts for the differences by pointing to certain presumed inadequacies in African American people. Supporters of this school of thought also place a negative value judgment on the fact that African American families deviate from the presumed norm.

The cultural relativism school, in contrast, assumes that the United States is a society whose members come from a variety of cultural backgrounds.

Adherents of this view conclude that differences in African American family life are largely accounted for by variation in the cultural backgrounds and experiences of African Americans and European Americans.

The assumption that black and white families are qualitatively different culturally is not shared by all who study African American family life. A third body of research can be said to fall outside both schools noted above. Researchers in this group emphasize the role of social class in determining family patterns and characteristics. They maintain that when one controls for social class, no appreciable differences are found between African American and European American families. In-depth discussions of each of the two major approaches to the study of African American family life follow. I then consider some of the limitations of using social class as a variable in analyzing African American family structure and functioning.

The Ethnocentric School

E. Franklin Frazier (1894–1962) was the leading twentieth-century exponent of the cultural ethnocentric school. He and W. E. B. Du Bois pioneered in the study of the African American family as a social phenomenon, but, unlike Du Bois, Frazier was concerned with understanding the process through which the African American family became culturally assimilated into American life. It is important to note that Frazier's works, as Lyman (1972) points out, were influenced by his determination (a) to refute the argument advanced by Melville Herskovits (and Du Bois) that much of black life is a continuation of African cultural forms and (b) to demonstrate empirically Robert E. Park's race relations cycle. Frazier believed that black American marriage and family patterns, customs, and structures were the consequence of slavery and American culture, not African cultural transfers. He did not accept Herskovits's conclusion that African American family structure, marital customs, and sexual practices were derived from African cultures. Rather, for example, Frazier (1939) interpreted "indiscriminate" and extramarital sexual behavior among blacks as a product of slavery and unrelated to customs and practices in traditional polygamous African cultures.

Researchers attempting to discover possible African cultural transferences to the New World focused on the slavery period. At the time Frazier began his work, leading authorities on the history of American Negro slavery shared Frazier's rather than Herskovits's position. Frazier's (1939) assertion that as "a result of the manner in which the Negro was enslaved, the Negro's African cultural heritage has had practically no effect on the evolution of his family in the United States" (p. 66) reflected the views of both U. B. Phillips (1929) and, subsequently, Stanley Elkins (1959). Both concluded that although significant African cultural traits, such as names and folklore, did survive initially, they were eventually lost or distorted. Accordingly, for example, Uncle Remus stories were altered to reflect the new animals and surroundings of the storytellers (Phillips 1929, p. 195). If the culture of the African slaves was destroyed, then it is unreasonable to expect that the evolution of the African American family was influenced by that culture. So begins the logic of the ethnocentric school.

The stability of the African American family during slavery was controlled, these scholars maintain, by the plantation owners. If a family arrangement failed to produce offspring, some slave owners matched members of the couple, or usually at least the woman, with other mates. In addition, slave families were frequently broken up, and members sold individually. In spite of the slaves' unstable formal or legal marital and familial life, researchers of this school believe that blacks accepted and attempted to conform to the social norms of the majority society.

Frazier viewed African Americans as an assimilation-oriented minority following the race-relations cycle predicted and outlined by Ezra Parks (1926–1950). Indeed, Frazier saw the black family's assimilation toward the dominant U.S. norms as part of the process by which it evolved from slavery and servitude toward freedom. In his study of African Americans living in Chicago, Frazier (1939) found that as they moved outward from the inner city, these families appeared more culturally and physically assimilated, based on the proportion of interracial marriages. It was his faithfulness to Parks's race relations cycle that seemingly motivated Frazier to interpret black masses as assimilative and to ignore evidence to the contrary. Although the race relations cycle has yet to be validated empirically, Frazier earnestly attempted to do so. It is, in a sense, a tragic conclusion to his intellectual career that he was forced to observe on the last page of one of his last books, *Black Bourgeoisie: The Rise of a New Middle Class in the United States* (1957), that when blacks achieve "middle-class status their lives generally lose both content and significance" (p. 238).

The line of research pursued by Frazier (1932, 1939, 1949a, 1949b) was followed by a number of investigators and culminated in proposals for social policy. In 1965, the Office of Policy Planning and Research of the U.S. Department of Labor issued a 78-page document prepared by the assistant secretary, Daniel P. Moynihan, under the title *The Negro Family: The Case for National Action.* This report repeatedly cited Frazier as support for its conclusions that the African American community was characterized by broken families, illegitimacy, matriarchy, economic dependency, failure to pass armed forces entrance tests, delinquency, and crime. Moynihan placed the blame for these problems on a supposedly broken and unstable African American family. Following his trend-making step, other investigators began to concentrate on the pathologies of African American families.

In 1967, Elliot Liebow published his participant-observation study of 24 "street corner" African American men. He concluded that the men had internalized the American norms for family roles but that the oppressive conditions of their societal environment prevented their fulfilling these expectations. Lee Rainwater (1968), examining the matrifocal character of black American and Caribbean families, concluded that matriarchal families are pathological and detrimental to the personality development of African American children. He also suggested that such families interfere with the ability of African American males to develop normal heterosexual roles.

Jessie Bernard (1966) traced the evolution of the African American family's stability from 1880 to 1963 and reported that the decrease in the proportion of African American infants born out of wedlock was related to two distinct lifestyles independent of social class. One lifestyle was oriented toward the pursuit of pleasure and material consumption, and the other adhered to a firm belief in and acceptance of the Protestant ethic. This hedonistic orientation accounts for the decline in legitimate births among blacks. Having failed to internalize the marital norms of U.S. society, this line of research suggests, this subgroup ignores its responsibility when adherence becomes too difficult. The matrifocal family is seen as an outgrowth of the failure of African American men to fulfill their paternal roles.

Parker and Kleiner (1966) contrasted the adjustment and attitudes of mothers in broken and intact families and examined the possible impact of these characteristics on their children. They found that mothers in broken-family situations had poorer psychological adjustment and were less concerned about goals for their children than were other mothers. These findings suggest that children raised in female-headed households would not have the psychological support of their mothers. Such research advances the argument that matriarchy and female-headed households are pathological and undermine male-female relationships in the family (Blood and Wolfe 1969; Duncan and Duncan 1969; Bracey, Meier, and Rudwick 1971; Parker and Kleiner 1966).

Other investigators have reported that the data supporting Moynihan's matriarchal concept are conclusive (Hyman and Reed 1969). Investigators who have focused on the validity of the female role in the African American family have generally concluded that matrifocal families are not produced by values of the African American community, but by structural factors in the society that necessitate that males frequently abandon their roles (Yancey 1972; Staples 1974). Tenhouten (1970) was unable to substantiate the dominant role attributed to African American mothers as implied in the Moynihan report. Furthermore, King (1967, 1969) found that black fathers were not perceived by their children as passive in decision making, and black mothers were perceived as less dominant than had been reported in earlier studies. Delores Mack (1971) examined social class and racial differences in the distribution of power attributable to race, and Heiss (1972) found that instability in the African American family does not necessarily lead to instability in future generations.

Studies that have concentrated on the dysfunctional and disorganized aspects of African American family life have deduced that the typical family is fatherless, on welfare, thriftless, and overpopulated with illegitimate children. Inevitably, they have recommended economic reforms for "saving" black families from their own pathology (see, for example, Moynihan 1965; Rainwater 1965; Rodman 1968). However, Andrew Billingsley (1968) has challenged these stereotypes, pointing out that two-thirds of African American families living in metropolitan areas are headed by husbands with their wives; half have managed to pull themselves into the middle class, and nine-tenths are self-supporting.

There remains, then, considerable controversy among researchers concerning the ability of nonwhite Americans to establish and maintain viable marital and familial relations. Particularly, there are a large number of studies that underscore the dysfunctionality of African American families. Implicit in the dichotomous conceptualization of functional versus dysfunctional capacities is an assumption regarding normative model families. The belief that a statistical model of the American family can be identified and used to ascertain the character of the families of all U.S. cultural groups is based in myth at best. Furthermore, such an assumption contradicts the ideals of a democratic society and the realities of a culturally plural one.

The Cultural Relativism School

Researchers of the cultural relativism school, which arose primarily in reaction to the ethnocentric view, assert that the African American family is a functional entity. This conceptualization is largely advanced and supported by Andrew Billingsley (1968), Virginia Young (1970), Robert Hill (1971), Wade Nobles (1974), and others. The perspective has been buttressed by old and new investigations that see black Americans' culture as different from that of whites (Valentine 1968; Young 1974) and possibly related to their African heritage (Herskovits 1941; Nobles 1974; Dodson 1975, 1977). Although not all proponents of the cultural relativism school agree on the degree to which African culture has influenced the culture of black Americans, they do concur that black Americans' cultural orientation encourages family patterns that are instrumental in combating the oppressive racial conditions of U.S. society.

U.S. studies of the African American family, and of blacks in general, have long ignored the works of Melville Herskovits (1885–1963), one of the first scholars to recognize similarities between African cultural patterns and those of African descendants living in the United States, the West Indies, and Brazil. Herskovits found what he considered to be authentic African cultural patterns reflected in language, music, art, house structure, dance, traditional religion, and healing practices. To many students of the African American family, Herskovits's research raises the possibility that other aspects of "Africana" could have influenced the nature of the African American family in the United States. Herskovits's work deals only in a limited way with such possible relations, but one of his major contributions is a true conceptualization of family life in traditional African societies, where the family is characterized by unity, stability, and security (Herskovits, 1938).

Other writers have since reexamined the unity and stability of African families to refute any assertion that chaos and problems of African families parallel the problems of contemporary black American families. From such studies, Billingsley (1968) concludes:

Thus the men and women who were taken as slaves to the New World came from societies every bit as civilized and "respectable" as those of the Old World settlers who mastered them. But the two were very different types of society for the African family was much more closely integrated with the wider levels of kinship and society. (p. 48)

In examining the American black family, proponents of cultural relativism in North America point out that slavery did not totally destroy the traditional African base of African American family functioning (Blassingame 1972; Nobles 1974; Turnbull 1976). To these scholars, the African American family represents a continuing fountain of strength and endurance built on, and issuing from, its African cultural heritage.

The field research of Young (1970) reflects that blacks are not merely versions of white Americans impoverished by lack of access to many of the rewards of American culture. She found that southern rural African American families were culturally distinct from European American families and demonstrated retention of African forms. Her findings closely parallel Herskovits's (1941) contentions; they are especially supportive in the areas of interpersonal behavior and deep-level communication.

Similar to Charles Johnson (1934) and Hortense Powdermaker (1939), but contrary to Frazier (1939) and Moynihan (1965), Young (1970) did not find African American families disorganized or dysfunctional. She observed patterns of high illegitimacy rates and frequent marital dissolutions, which are usually associated with disorganization, but she interpreted these patterns as natural to the emotional underpinnings of the family system and, thus, functional.

Nobles (1974; Nobles et al. 1976) has indicated that the African American community is oriented primarily toward extended families, in that most involve a system of kinship ties. This idea has been supported by Hayes and Mendel (1973), Billingsley (1968), Hill (1971), Stack (1974), and others. The extended family system is assumed to provide support for family members, as assistance either for protection or for mobility. It is argued that the extended family in the African American community consists not only of conjugal and blood relatives but of nonrelatives as well. In addition, the prevalence of extended families, compared with nuclear families, is held as another cultural pattern that distinguishes whites and blacks. However, the extent to which such families are characteristic of the African American community has not been adequately substantiated.

Hayes and Mendel (1973) have demonstrated that the extended family is a more prominent structure for African American families and that blacks differ from whites in intensity and extent of family interaction. Their study of midwestern urban families, however, included a sample of only 25 complete and incomplete black and white families. The findings show that, with the exception of parents, blacks in the sample interacted with more of their kin than did the whites. The African American families also received more help from kin and had a greater number and more diversified types of relatives living with them than did the European American families. Hayes and Mendel suggest that minority status in a hostile society strengthens kinship ties.

In a related study, Dubey (1971) examined the relationship between self-alienation and extended family, using black, white, and Puerto Rican subjects. His data support the hypothesis that subjects with a high degree of powerlessness are significantly more oriented toward the extended family. Dubey's study raises the question of whether the extended family is used as a buffer between oppression of the dominant society and the unmet needs of the family. Stack (1974) proposes that the extended family is, in part, a strategy for meeting physical, emotional, and economic needs of African American families and involves a reciprocal network of sharing to counter the lack of economic resources. McAdoo (1978) found that reciprocal extended family help patterns transcend economic groups and continue to be practiced even when families move from poverty to the middle income level.

Nobles (1974) believes that the African American kinship pattern is derived from African cultures not destroyed in the "Middle Passage" or in slavery; this suggests that perhaps the survival of "Africana" among black American families is not as remote as Elkins (1959) and Frazier (1939) have argued. Blassingame (1972) states that not only did African cultural patterns survive American slavery, but new cultural patterns unique to black Americans were created. Even Frazier (1963) has noted indisputable non-Western religious practices in the black church. A more recent advocate of this view, Colin Turnbull (1976), sums it up succinctly: "The slaves who were exported to the Americas were Africans before they were slaves and Africans afterwards, and their descendants are still Africans today" (p. 242).

As Turnbull notes, it is interesting that in some cases African cultural patterns were developed and preserved in the Western Hemisphere while they were lost in Africa. A case in point is Surinam (South America), where slaves escaped and recovered their independence. Although some of the Surinam ethnic cultures (comprising six "tribal" groups) resemble original African cultures, Turnbull cautions that these cultures could not have remained totally in isolation. With the exception of clearly identifiable African cultural patterns in islands along the Georgia coast, the splintering of ethnic clans during slavery, along with enforced acceptance of language and Western values, did much to repress African cultures in the United States.

A model that may prove useful for further understanding of the New World "Africana" culture and black American families has been developed by Smith (1962). Equally important to the clarification of these issues is Nobles's work currently being conducted on African orientations in American families. However, we must await further research findings from the cultural relativism perspective before we can determine the cultural origins of black family life.

Social Class:
An Issue From Both Schools

Research on racial differences in African American family structure and function has been contaminated by methodological problems that make it difficult to conceptualize clear differences within and between groups. Social class has been widely employed as a variable in social science research. It is primarily used for classifying individuals into categories above or below one another on some scale of inferiority and superiority. The scale is intended to denote position in terms of social and economic prestige and/or power.

The most popular measure of social class in the United States is an occupation-scaled measure that is commonly used to reflect prestige. Other types of class measurement consist of single variables, such as education, income, and possessions. A number of multiple indices also exist. It has been questioned whether such measures can be applied equitably to all groups in an oppressive, pluralistic, and fluid society such as exists in the United States. This is especially critical because most measures of social class have been developed by and for whites, and there is little convincing evidence that they accurately measure social class for black Americans.

A number of investigators, among them Drake (1965) and Jencks (1972), have demonstrated that education and income are less related for blacks, compared with whites, than may be expected. It has been shown that blacks are more frequently underemployed, in that they often have more education, training, or skills than their jobs require. Consequently, they receive salaries and wages disproportionate to their preparation. Because an underemployed African American has a lower income than a European American with equivalent years of education, the former cannot afford the same standard of living as the latter. This lower standard of living requires the African American to adopt a different lifestyle than his or her status, as measured by education, would indicate.

Neither does occupation tend to indicate the same social classification for blacks as for whites. The owner of a small business in a black shopping area, for example, might not have nearly the same income as the owner of a similar business located in a white shopping area. According to the occupation categories of the Hollingshead-Redlich scale, however, both persons would fall into a middle-income social classification (see Hollingshead and Redlich 1968). Another problem with occupational ranking is that disparities exist within occupations as well as between them.

Jencks (1972) contends that one limitation to the definition of occupation as indicator of social class is that it refers only to occupations, not to specific jobs within them. Some jobs are more attractive and rewarding than others, even though they are classified together under a single occupation category.

Billingsley's (1968, p. 123) assertion that current indicators of social class are relatively more reliable when used for European American ethnic groups than when used unmodified with African American groups has never been adequately refuted. He believes that such indicators have resulted in an overestimation of the number of lower-class blacks, and that this obscures rather than clarifies the varieties of social classes and behavior among black Americans. Although Billingsley accepts the utility of social class as an indicator, he claims that current measures are mostly applicable to economic and social positions in the wider white community, not accurate descriptions of which blacks associate with whom and why.

It should be pointed out that social classification depends primarily on the degree to which an individual or individuals are held in esteem by their fellow group members. Social class, therefore, depends on the cultural values of the group. Deference is awarded according to what the group cherishes as noble or worthy. Hence social class may be based on such characteristics as age, wisdom, heredity, or economic power, and it may vary from one cultural group to another. Given that the cultural distinctiveness of black Americans still warrants investigation, measures of social class also await clearer determination. The extent to which blacks possess different values regarding what is worthy in an individual determines their different orientations to family, to their community, and to the wider white community.

Cultural relativism becomes an important, yet complicated, factor when one attempts to make social class comparisons of heterogeneous groups within a single society. It appears logical to assume that different ethnic groups within the same society can be compared using the same social class criteria, but this is not the empirical reality for the United States. The logical but incorrect assumption that, because both peoples live within the same societal geography (nation), black and white communities perceive social class the same way is misleading.

I concur with Billingsley's observation that the importance of social class is that the higher the social class of an individual, the greater will be his or her ability to survive with integrity in a hostile society. For a historically subjugated group such as black Americans, survival and dignity may be invaluable social qualities. Furthermore, given the nature of the historical and material experiences of, and relationship between, blacks and whites in North America, the extent to which they can be compared using similar social indicators is dubious. To ignore these fundamentally different realities and classify them into common social classes is to commit serious historical, methodological, and theoretical errors.

Toward Reflective Analysis

I have undertaken this examination of major schools of thought in studies of the African American family in the United States to help direct thinking regarding prerequisite components of a "reflective analysis." Admittedly, this has been a limited review. For example, I have not addressed here the individual roles of family members. These are seen primarily as intertwined with the sociocultural patterns of marriage and family in contemporary African American communities. For those who desire a more thorough and complete review of the literature, there are at least three substantive sources: Allen (1978), Staples (1974, 1978), and Peters (1978). The particular approach I have taken has emphasized the ideological assumptions undergirding researchers' definitions of and approaches to research on African American family life. I have used this perspective because I have assumed that the ideological debate has indeed created the current impasse in African American family research. Given this review of the debate, Walter Allen's conclusions about the status of studies on African American family life is accurate:

> The literature on black families is characterized by inconsistent findings, poor problem conceptualization, overly simplistic research designs, questionable inferences from data, and general disagreement over the relative appropriateness of competing perspectives of black family life. The question to be addressed now is: How might researchers go about the business of reconciling some of these problems and in the process strengthening the literature? To begin, theory construction/codification activities should be intensified. . . .
>
> The area of African American family studies would also benefit from a change in focus of empirical research. (personal communication 1976)

Any attempt to bring theoretical clarity to human phenomena must be informed by an understanding of the sociocultural, economic, and political contexts in which the phenomena occur. This axiom applies especially to the exploration of questions related to contemporary African American family life in the United States.

In recommending the following components for a reflective analysis of African American family life, my conceptualizations have been developed in concert with Ruth Dennis, Harriette McAdoo, Art Mathis, and Howard Dodson. This group of black scholars and researchers met and worked together from 1974 through 1977 to develop work aimed toward a reflective analysis of African American family life.

Drawing from the strengths and weaknesses of previous studies, a reflective analysis would, at minimum,

1. focus on socialization of black families as the process that brings together individual, cultural group(s), and society in a dynamic interactive process;
2. account for the effects—positive and/or negative—of the relative unavailability of maximum social, economic, and political societal resources to black families; and
3. account for the environmental reality that black families are forced to use relatively minimal resources to effect a socialization process and product that allows individuals to function in two social realities of the United States—a nonblack world of consistent, sufficient social support and a black world of fluctuating scarcity of resources.

Using these minimal components as a guide, a schema for evaluating African American family socialization can be suggested. Positive evaluations can be placed on socialized behavior that allows the individual to interact with any segment of the society and maintain a sense of self-worth. However, because the realities of African American family life are often contradictory, socialized behavior that may be evaluated as positive within one level of social functioning may be evaluated as negative within another. African American families must be able to socialize individuals who are able to participate in the larger society and yet protect themselves from negative social attitudes and actions that impinge on self-esteem, feelings of self-worth, and human evolutionary development.

References

Allen, W. R. 1978. "The Search for Applicable Theories of Black Family Life." *Journal of Marriage and the Family* 40(1):111-29.

Bernard, J. 1966. *Marriage and Family Among Negroes*. Englewood Cliffs, NJ: Prentice Hall.

Billingsley, A. 1968. *Black Families in White America*. Englewood Cliffs, NJ: Prentice Hall.

Blassingame, J. W. 1972. *The Slave Community: Plantation Life in the Antebellum South*. New York: Oxford.

Blood, R. O. and D. M. Wolfe. 1969. "Negro-White Differences in Blue-Collar Marriages in a Northern Metropolis." *Social Forces* 38(1):59-64.

Bracey, J. H., A. Meier, and E. Rudwick, eds. 1971. *Black Matriarchy: Myth or Reality*. Belmont, CA: Wadsworth.

Dodson, J. 1975. *Black Stylization and Implications for Child Welfare*. Final Report, No. OCDCB-422-C2. Washington, DC: Office of Child Development.

———. 1977. *Afro American Culture: Expressive Behaviors*. Atlanta, GA: Atlanta University.

Drake, S. C. 1965. "The Social and Economic Status of the Negro in the United States." In *The Negro American*, edited by T. Parsons and K. B. Clark. Boston: Beacon.

Dubey, S. N. 1971. "Powerlessness and Orientation Toward Family and Children: A Study in Deviance." *Indian Journal of Social Work* 32:35-43.

Duncan, B. and O. D. Duncan. 1969. "Family Stability and Occupational Success." *Social Problems* 16:273-85.

Elkins, S. W. 1959. *Slavery*. Chicago: University of Chicago Press.

Frazier, E. F. 1932. *The Negro Family in Chicago*. Chicago: University of Chicago Press.

———. 1939. *The Negro Family in the United States*. Chicago: University of Chicago Press.

———. 1949a. "The Negro family in America." In *The Family: Its Function and Destiny*, edited by R. W. Anshen. New York: Harper & Row.

———. 1949b. *The Negro in the United States*. New York: Macmillan.

———. 1957. *Black Bourgeoisie: The Rise of a New Middle Class in the United States*. New York: Free Press.

———. 1963. *The Negro Church in America*. New York: Schocken.

Hayes, W. and Mendel, C. H. 1973. "Extended Kinship in Black and White Families." *Journal of Marriage and the Family* 35(1):51-57.

Heiss, J. 1972. "On the Transmission of Marital Instability in Black Families." *American Sociological Review* 37(1):82-92.

Herskovits, M. J. 1938. *Dahomey: An Ancient African Kingdom.* New York: J. J. Augustin.

———. 1941. *The Myth of the Negro Past.* New York: Harper & Row.

Hill, R. B. 1971. *The Strengths of Black Families.* New York: Emerson-Hall.

Hollingshead, A. B. and F. C. Redlich. 1968. *Social Class and Mental Illness.* New York: John Wiley.

Hyman, H. H. and J. S. Reed. 1969. "Black Matriarchy Reconsidered: Evidence From Secondary Analysis of Sample Survey." *Public Opinion Quarterly* 33:346-54.

Jencks, C. 1972. *Inequality.* New York: Basic Books.

Johnson, C. S. 1934. *Shadow of the Plantation.* Chicago: University of Chicago Press.

King, K. 1967. "A Comparison of the Negro and White Family Power Structure in Low-Income Families." *Child and Family* 6:65-74.

———. 1969. "Adolescent Perception of Power Structure in the Negro Family." *Journal of Marriage and the Family* 31(4):751-55.

Liebow, E. 1967. *Tally's Corner: A Study of Negro Street Corner Men.* Boston: Little, Brown.

Lyman, S. M. 1972. *The Black American in Sociological Thought.* New York: Capricorn.

Mack, D. E. 1971. "Where the Black-Matriarchy Theorists Went Wrong." *Psychology Today,* January, pp. 24, 86-87.

McAdoo, H. P. 1978. "Factors Related to Stability in Upwardly Mobile Black Families." *Journal of Marriage and the Family* 40(4):761-76.

Moynihan, D. P. 1965. *The Negro Family: The Case for National Action.* Washington, DC: U.S. Department of Labor, Office of Policy Planning and Research.

Nobles, W. W. 1974. "Africanity: Its Role in Black Families." *Black Scholar* 5(June):10-17.

Nobles, W. W., et al. 1976. *A Formulative and Empirical Study of Black Families.* DHEW Publication OCD-90-C-255. Washington, DC: Government Printing Office.

Park, R. E. 1939. "The Nature of Race Relations." In *Race Relations and the Race Problem,* edited by E. T. Thompson. Durham, NC: Duke University Press.

Parker, S. and R. Kleiner. 1966. "Characteristics of Negro Mothers in Single-Headed Households." *Journal of Marriage and the Family* 28(4):507-13.

Peters, M. F., ed. 1978. [Special issue]. *Journal of Marriage and the Family* 40(November).

Phillips, U. B. 1929. *Life and Labor in the Old South.* Boston: Little, Brown.

Powdermaker, H. 1939. *After Freedom: The Portrait of a Negro Community in the Deep South.* New York: Viking.

Rainwater, L. 1965. *Family Design.* Chicago: AVC.

———. 1968. "Crucible of Identity: The Negro Lower-Class Family." *Daedalus* 95:258-64.

Rodman, H. 1968. "Family and Social Pathology in the Ghetto." *Science* 161:756-62.

Smith, M. G. 1962. *West Indian Family Structure.* Seattle: University of Washington Press.

Stack, C. B. 1974. *All Our Kin: Strategies for Survival in a Black Community.* New York: Harper & Row.

Staples, R. E. 1974. "The Black Family Revisited: A Review and a Preview." *Journal of Social and Behavioral Sciences* 20(Spring):65-78.

———, ed. 1978. *The Black Family: Essays and Studies.* Belmont, CA: Wadsworth.

Tenhouten, W. 1970. "The Black Family: Myth and Reality." *Psychiatry* 33:145-73.

Turnbull, C. M. 1976. *Man in Africa.* Garden City, NY: Doubleday.

Valentine, C. A. 1968. *Culture and Poverty.* Chicago: University of Chicago Press.

Yancey, W. 1972. "Going Down Home: Family Structure and the Urban Trap." *Social Science Quarterly* 52:893-906.

Young, V. H. 1970. "Family and Childhood in a Southern Negro Community." *American Anthropologist* 72:269-88.

———. 1974. "A Black American Socialization Pattern." *American Ethnologist* 1:405-13.

African American Family Life

An Instrument of Culture

WADE W. NOBLES

Given the critical importance of child-rearing practices and orientation in shaping the personalities, behaviors, and values of future citizens in any society, the parent-child relationship should be viewed as one of the major points at which the family's obligation to the state and the state's obligation to the family are crystallized. Unfortunately, a clear understanding of African American parent-child relationships and their subsequent importance in our understanding of the African American family's obligation to the state and the state's obligation to the African American family has been clouded by racism.

A proper understanding of the strengths of African American families, the difficulties they face, and the ways in which they are affected by public policy is confused and clouded by several commingling issues, among which the most prominent is racism. The issue of racism totally masks the understanding of African American culture itself, to say nothing of the family as an instrument of culture.

It has been racism, primarily, that has allowed the guiding assumption of the "innate" inferiority of African people to go almost completely unchallenged in more than 200 years of research and scientific investigation. It has been primarily the research guided by this assumption that has resulted in the examiners of African American family life consistently offering evidence, information, theory, and analyses that focus solely on the so-called problems inherent in African American family systems. Blinded by this racist assumption, these researchers have created what is the overwhelming historical character of the field; that the African American family system was (is) an organization inherently laden with problems and inadequacies.

Similarly, though far more subtle and sophisticated, the new thrust toward highlighting and examining only the African American middle-class, well-to-do family creates the false image that the socioeconomic gap between African Americans and white Americans has closed, that African Americans are no longer victims of poverty and racism, and that all African American people have benefited from the civil rights struggle. The basis of this false image is just as racist as the false image that all African American families are on welfare.

In a very sophisticated way, by overprojecting the image that there is nothing "wrong" with the African American family, contemporary scientific researchers have participated in a scheme to take away the gains of the 1960s and simultaneously misdirect the blame for the concrete condition of African American family life. The actuality is that generally there has been a perpetual state of disadvantage for most African American families, yet the literature and available data define the condition of the African American family as progressively more advantaged.

One need simply recognize that the United States is still a racist country (ergo, the continued popularity of KKK and Nazi parties) and that to be African American in a white racist society is problematic by definition. Consequently, the family life of African American people would be and is characterized by real and definite problems and conditions associated with racism and oppression.

Although a great deal of research has been done, the gap in useful, usable knowledge remains just as wide. In fact, the legacy of white-dominated research and racist scientific investigations has totally prevented us from understanding the nature of African American family life; consequently, as a result of racist research, the understanding of African American family life has been, in a very real way, held hostage by the intellectual instrument of the socioeconomic, political establishment.

Discrimination or Scientific Colonialism: African American Family Life Held Hostage by White-Dominated Thinking

To see the pervasive and insidious nature of the phenomena that negatively affect African American families, one must understand two concepts. First, one must recognize that discrimination is an act designed to separate individuals or people for the purpose of allowing one group to receive preferential treatment and/or advantage. Second, one must understand that in a system characterized by racism and oppression, almost every element or process managed by the racist system is designed primarily to continue and secure the status of the advantaged by guaranteeing in all arenas their preferential treatment.

It is not difficult to equate a racist system with the act of holding a thing or a person hostage. The latter is an act designed to keep under control the person or thing held in order that the hostage can be used to bargain with or in exchange for one's own safety, benefit, or freedom. Combined, the almost total misrepresentation of African American family life and the almost absolute control of the scientific understanding of African American family life by non-African thinkers suggests that the African American family has been and is being held hostage by white-dominated research and scientific studies. Some would argue that African American families are not being held hostage physically; if anything, it is the understanding of African American family life that is being held hostage. Given the concrete condition of African American family life, this distinction is debatable.

Given that the first Africans came to these shores as enslaved captives in the mid-1700s, we could legitimately say that African American families have been held hostage for more than 89,000 days. From this historical perspective, we can see that exploitation, domination, and control of African people in this country have been its most constant features. Hence it is fair to say that the state of African American family life has been held hostage while other segments benefited from the disadvantage experienced by African people.

If, for example, one simply notes that white researchers from the early 1700s have consistently argued for and supported (without proof) the notion of African American family inferiority (see Von Linnaes 1735; Burmeister 1835; Galton 1969; Spencer 1884; Hall 1904; Thorndike 1940; Terman 1916), then one is compelled to ask why. Given the prevalence of institutionalized racism in all areas of American life—politics, job opportunities, and education are three of the most noted areas—such a concerted effort suggests that science also was (is) being used as a tool of oppression and control and that indeed the creation of these findings were (are) beneficial, if no more than psychologically, to non-African people in this country. Of course, such information placed African American people at a decided disadvantage. The African American family as an area of investigation, for instance, has been examined from almost every conceivable orientation, and in almost every case it has been found to be less than viable (see Frazier 1932; Bernard 1966; Jeffers 1967; Chilman 1966; Willie 1970; Scanzoni 1971). One cannot, in this regard, dismiss the relationship between the "results" of this line of research and the treatment of African American families in the society at large. It is in fact the case that, guided by the assumption that blackness is intrinsically inferior, racist models, theories, and/or orientations coupled with unsophisticated scientific treatments and analyses of African American family life have not only led to mass confusion and an unusable body of knowledge, they have also translated to the direct maltreatment of African American families (for example, forced sterilization).

Unfortunately, as long as this country remains racist, the need to hold African American families hostage will exist and, with it, the continued uncritical adoption of non-African interpretations and/or analytic frameworks, which will invariably result in both misdirected analyses of African American life and blind acceptance of erroneous assumptions and "meanings" that "define" the reality of African American family life.

This, in effect, is the legacy we bring to the analysis of African American life, and this is the legacy from which we must free ourselves as we go forward with the study and understanding of African American family life.

Parent-Child Relationships Held Hostage

The analogy of African American families being held hostage is, of course, designed to refocus our attention on the real condition of African American life in the United States and on the fact that, like those who were earnestly concerned about the Americans who were held hostage in Iran, we know very little about what happened to them. The knowledge gap we face is extremely wide, even though huge amounts of data have been accumulated over the years. The major gap is in studies that honestly reflect the conditions of

African American family life and are not guided by various racist assumptions of African inferiority and negativity. The lack of a substantial body of studies (of all types) that, from conceptualization to methods, from procedures to analyses, and from conclusions to interpretations, respect and reflect the cultural integrity of African American family dynamics is the major gap in the field.

Despite this dilemma, there exist several classical contributions (Billingsley 1968; Staples 1976; Hill 1971) that have addressed the mandate to answer the question, What are the strengths of the African American family? Though none focuses on the more narrow issue of parent-child relationships exclusively, the important works of Robert Hill, Andrew Billingsley, and Robert Staples have served as cornerstones for the understanding of African American family strengths. However, one must keep in mind, as these authors have, that to talk only about the strength of the African American family without simultaneously recognizing that, without this dogged strength and resilience, African American families would have been shattered and torn apart long ago is tantamount to closing one's eyes to the full complexity of the problem at hand. Given the continued and historical concrete conditions of racism and oppression, it is, in fact, a testimony to our humanity and a miracle of the human spirit that we even have an African American family left to talk about.

Strengths and Interpersonal Relationships

The benchmark work on African American family strength is Hill's classic *The Strength of African American Families.* The focus of this discussion is interpersonal relationships, particularly those between parents and their children, and the associated family strength found in that arena.

Traditionally, analyses of parent-child relationships have centered on understanding how parents instill in their children particular behavior repertoires, attitudes, and beliefs in their childhood training, child-rearing practices, and socialization strategies. Seldom has attention turned to an examination of strengths implicit in the parent-child relationship. Though some researchers have examined the psychological dispositions and/or behavioral or personality styles that emerge from parent-child interaction, seldom have they turned their attention to an examination of the strengths and support implicit in the interpersonal relationships (parent-child and others) found in the family.

In a study of the African American family system, Shimkin, Louie, and Frate (1978) isolated five critical elements of African American family life that distinguish it from the family structure of other ethnic/racial groups. They note that the traditional African American family is a unique cultural form enjoying its own inherent resources. It comprises several individual households, with the channels of authority reaching beyond the household units that compose it. In periods of crises and at times of ceremony, the extended family is most visible and provides needed emotional support for its members. The family may (and often does) perform many ritual, social (and psychological) functions, including the education of the family's young and the adjudication of internal conflicts. Even though some features of the African American family can be explained "situationally" (that is, are adaptive responses to certain pressures of the moment) or through "borrowing," the underlying structure of the African American extended family is ultimately traceable to Africa.

Almost 10 years prior to Shimkin et al.'s work, Billingsley (1968) pointed out that the African American family unit is itself an element embedded in a larger network of mutually interdependent relationships with the African American community and the wider (white) society. Billingsley went on to point out that, even though the African American family system is one institution in a complex of various American institutions, the African American family cannot be totally understood or interpreted from a general (white) analytic framework. The limits of using a general analytic framework can be seen through an earlier study conducted by my colleagues and I in which we found that a critical aspect of the parent-child relationship in African American families is that parents prepare their children to deal with racism (Nobles et al., 1976). In fact, the unique child-rearing techniques found in African American families seem to be geared to prepare children for a *particular kind* of existence in a hostile racist environment. Children are in effect prepared to take on appropriate sex and age roles as well as the racial role.

Consistent with Billingsley's conception of interlocking systems, Staples's (1976) work offers valuable insight into the relation between African American families and the wider society. Staples suggests that the African American family has been a sanctuary that protects individuals from the pervasiveness of white racism and provides needed support systems that are unavailable in other majority group institutions. Consequently, the processes in the African American family promote and maintain the emotional well-being of its individual members in spite of the wider society.

In the study leading to *A Formulative and Empirical Study of Black Families* (Nobles et al., 1976), we found that African American parent-child interactions are characterized by an "atmosphere" or attitude that emphasizes strong family ties or orientations, unconditional love, respect for self and others, and the assumed natural goodness of the child. Child-rearing techniques associated with the parent-child bond centered on the unconditional expression of love. That is, parents seldom make their love for their children a reinforcement contingency. The interpersonal relationship between parent and child could, therefore, be characterized by parent anger, punishment, and disappointment as well as the child's mistakes, failures, and misbehavior without canceling out the love associated with the parent-child bond.

A family strength, like the support network or system in which it operates, is any process or network of interactions that aids or helps individuals in anticipating, addressing, interpreting, managing, or otherwise successfully responding to their concrete conditions or situations. Within this definition, the kinds of elements or features mentioned above are African American families' strengths. Upon further analyses of the interpersonal dynamics of African American family styles and mental health support systems (see Nobles et al., 1979), five additional strengths of African American families have been identified, classified, and defined: legitimation of beingness, provision of a family code, elasticity of boundaries, the provision of information/knowledge, and mediation of concrete conditions.

Legitimation of beingness. Through the parent-child, sibling, and other familial relationships, the family provides its members with a source of connection, attachment, validation, worth, recognition, respect, and legitimacy. If one is secure in one's own personal meaning, then one is more capable of addressing and responding to complex, vague, and unfamiliar experiences confronted outside the home.

Provision of a family code. By providing its members with a "family code" (guidelines for behaving in novel and/or confusing situations), the family, through interpersonal relations, aids its members in interpreting, managing, and responding to both known and undefined situations.

Elasticity of boundaries. Legitimation of beingness and the provision of a family code produce an elasticity in African American family interpersonal relationships. The unbreakable bond and associated rules of conduct give

African American family members the latitude and opportunity they need to stretch out and develop their own sense of "specialness" without fear of violating the familyhood. In a sense, the phrase or label *elasticity of boundaries* is indeed a literal interpretation of this phenomenon, in that family boundaries stretch to accommodate various expressions of individual styles, personalities, and/or conditions. The sense of almost unconditional permanence or undeniable belonging strengthens family members' ability to respond to their unique concrete condition in ways that satisfy or are peculiar to their individual and personal needs.

Provision of information/knowledge. By providing family members the benefit of shared insights and experiences, African American families strengthen their abilities to interpret and understand the events and happenings that affect their lives. The transgenerational mutual sharing of knowledge and experience heightens individual members' (young and old) abilities to address, manage, and respond to the rapidly changing as well as constant conditions in their reality.

Mediation of concrete conditions. The family's ability to mediate the conflicts and other concrete conditions affecting its members provides a strength or support so obvious that it barely warrants explication. Clearly, the abilities to provide family members with concrete aid and pragmatic help and to engage in interpersonal relations around problem solving and decision making (in response to both external and internal issues) while constantly buffering and repairing the damage resulting from racism and oppression directed at family members constitute a critical strength of African American families.

African American Family Parent-Child Relationships and Our Obligation to the State

Given that African American children must become adults during a period in which racism, discrimination, and oppression will change disguises and not simply go away, the family parent-child relationship must center on the creation and maintenance of three senses: the sense of history, the sense of family, and the sense of the ultimate supreme power (God).

The sense of history will tell African American children that they are first and foremost Africans and that we are Africans because of our common cultural orientation, which gives us the same sense of the natural universe and human condition that characterizes all African peoples, and we have a common history of racial oppression that has resulted in shared victimization. The sense of history will help African American children to recognize that as Africans they must and will continue to struggle for the liberation of the human condition from oppression and racism. The sense of history will help them understand that the natural human condition is one of freedom and growth, and that any person, people, or invention that denies their freedom and potential to grow should be opposed and fought against. History will tell them that to resist and struggle against such a force is the only natural human response. To do otherwise is to conspire in their own dehumanization. The sense of history will also tell them that "the struggle" is by definition a human struggle and not an individual, personalized battle. Finally, the sense of history will tell African American children that the enemies of human growth and freedom, wherever they are found in the world, are easily recognized by their behavior and attitudes. History will show them that the historical enemy of our people is still our enemy today and that until that enemy changes its basic response to other human beings, it will always remain our enemy.

The sense of family is really the specific application of the sense of history previously defined. The sense of family will explicitly give African American children the understanding that their identity and being are in the family—that, unlike the families of other groups, our family is a source of strength. It is not a burden to individual aspirations. In fact, in understanding the sense of family, African American children will also understand that they will expand in personal strength as the family expands in size. The sense of family will give them the security of knowing that no matter what happens, the family love and protection will be unconditional and ever present. The sense of family will help them realize that in their people (and not necessarily things) they will find a common meaning (definition) and a common ground.

The final sense that should emerge from the parent-child interaction is a sense of a supreme being (God). The importance of formalized religion is in its ritual, which helps to replenish the necessity and the belief in the supreme force. It is important that African American children engage in religious ritual. It is even more important that African American children understand, respect, and obey the supreme spirit that makes them human. The sense of the supreme being will help African American children realize that there is a power and a will that is greater than all else. The sense of the force will tell them that the power is in us all and that its natural laws must be obeyed.

Knowing that the force is in them will help them realize that in being the manifestation of the supreme force, they have no limitations—as long as they obey the natural (God's) laws of the universe. The sense of the supreme being will help them realize that just as the natural path of living plants is to grow toward the sun, our natural path is to grow (in understanding) toward the supreme force.

Ultimately, the parent-child relationship in the African American family must become the focal point for the crystallization of the African American family's obligation to the state and the state's obligation to the African American family. For human beings, especially those who are being oppressed and discriminated against, the parent-child relationship should make clear that the state's obligation to every family within its domain and jurisdiction is to guarantee each and every family a level of existence or a quality of life that ensures and guarantees the family's ability to advance and affirm the life and well-being of its members. In turn, and in tandem with the state's obligation, the human family's obligation to the state is to support the state in its correctness (in deed and action) and never to allow the state as the agent and instrument of the people to infringe upon or allow to continue in any form the dehumanization and degradation of its citizenry or in any way diminish, discriminate against, or disallow the growth of the human potential.

References

Bernard, J. 1966. *Marriage and Family Among Negroes.* Englewood Cliffs, NJ: Prentice Hall.

Billingsley, A. 1968. *Black Families in White America.* Englewood Cliffs, NJ: Prentice Hall.

Burmeister, H. 1953. *The Black Man: The Comparative Anatomy and Psychology of the African Negro.* New York: W. C. Bryant.

Chilman, C. 1966. *Growing Up Poor.* DHEW Publication No. 13. Washington, DC: Government Printing Office.

Frazier, E. F. 1932. *The Negro Family in Chicago.* Chicago: University of Chicago Press.

Galton, F. 1969. *Hereditary Genius.* London: Macmillan.

Hall, G. S. 1904. *Adolescence.* New York: Appleton-Century-Crofts.

Hill, R. 1971. *The Strength of Black Families.* New York: Emerson Hall.

Jeffers, C. 1967. *Living Poor.* Ann Arbor, MI: Ann Arbor.

Nobles, W. W., et al. 1976. *A Formulative and Empirical Study of Black Families.* DHEW Publication OCD-90-C-255. Washington, DC: Government Printing Office.

———. 1979. *Mental Health Support Systems in Black Families.* DHEW Publication. Washington, DC: Government Printing Office.

Scanzoni, J. 1971. *The Black Family in Modern Society.* Boston: Allyn & Bacon.

Shimkin, D. B., G. J. Louie, and D. A. Frate. 1978. "The Black Extended Family: A Basic Rural Institution and a Mechanism of Urban Adaptation." In *The Extended Family in Black Cities,* edited by D. B. Shimkin, E. M. Shimkin, and D. A. Frate. The Hague: Mouton.

Spencer, H. 1884. *The Man Versus the State.* Baltimore: Penguin.

Staples, R. E. 1976. *Introduction to Black Sociology.* New York: McGraw-Hill.

Terman, L. M. 1916. *The Measurement of Intelligence: An Explanation of and a Complete Guide for the Use of the Stanford Revision and Extension of the Binet-Simon Intelligence Scale.* Boston: Houghton Mifflin.

Thorndike, E. L. 1940. *Human Nature and the Social Order.* New York: Macmillan.

Von Linnaes, C. 1735. *Systema Natural.* Luyduni: Butavurum.

Willie, C. 1970. *The Family Life of Black People.* Columbus, OH: Charles E. Merrill.

Three Decades of Black Family Empirical Research

Challenges for the 21st Century

LEANOR BOULIN JOHNSON

In August 1993, contrasting perspectives on Black families appeared on the cover of two national magazines. *Newsweek* drew attention of the world to the endangered Black family. Featured were absent fathers, fathers who provided for their family by hustling on the streets, hopeless children and frustrated teenage mothers. In contrast, *Ebony* magazine celebrated Black families by focusing on their determination, strength and diversity. How can both portrayals be accurate? The answer lies in the choice of perspectives. Guided by different perspectives while using the same data, Black and White social scientists often differ on the nature of Black family life and the direction social policies should take. Contrasting portrayals have had a long history. For example, the works of Moynihan (1965) and Hill (1972) demonstrate the critical link between data and interpretive frameworks (see Johnson 1978). Although both analyzed the same U.S. Census data, they

AUTHOR'S NOTE: I am indebted to Tony Haynes of Florida State University, whose original conceptualization contributed greatly to this chapter.

employed different theoretical perspectives and arrived at divergent conclusions. Moynihan reported a deteriorating Black family and recommended social policies that would encourage changes in the Black family's structure and values. Hill observed the resilience of Black families and recommended social policies that could build on the strengths of Black family values and structure. Without arguing the validity of either conclusion, the importance of studying perspectives governing Black family research should be evident. Yet too often, when trying to create a fit between scientific data and social needs, researchers argue over apparent discrepancies in the data or debate the merit of various statistical methods while ignoring another possible culprit—the subjective frame of reference (Gouldner 1970; van den Berghe 1967; Mills 1959; Mannheim 1936; Adams 1985).

Recognizing both the limitations of scientific objectivity, particularly when racial groups are the target of analysis, and the tendency for policymakers to use social science research to guide policies on Black families, Staples (1974), Allen (1978), and Allen and Stokes (1981) identified major theoretical and value frameworks that either impede or facilitate a fuller understanding of Black families and the social policies that govern their lives. Notwithstanding these researchers' valuable contributions, they failed to document empirically the frequency of these frameworks and their occurrence over time. Furthermore, their methodology prevents a systematic identification of changing perspectives in empirical Black family research. Thus in this chapter I propose to extend Staples's and Allen's studies by identifying journals that have fostered empirical Black family studies to determine the frequency of their frameworks over time and to identify topics studied within each framework.

Theoretical Perspectives

The more than 500 journal articles on the Black family that appeared in the 1960s and 1970s represent five times more such literature than was produced during the preceding century (Staples and Mirande 1980). With the exception of Allen (1978) and Staples (1974), social scientists have not categorized the various frameworks represented in this growing body of literature. Allen identifies three theoretical perspectives or value orientations: "cultural deviant" (CD), "cultural equivalent" (CE), and "cultural variant" (CV). The first framework views Black families as pathological, the second depicts Black families as legitimate when they adopt the lifestyle and norms of middle-class White families, and the third views Black families as different but functional family forms.

Using a time typology, Staples identifies four eras through which Black family research has progressed: the "poverty/acculturation" period, the era of researchers as "pathologists," the "reactive" era, and the period of "Black Nationalist family studies." According to Staples, studies focusing on the pathological nature of Black families appeared during the 1930s, 1940s, and 1960s (that is, during the poverty/acculturation and pathologists' eras). During the poverty/acculturation period of the 1930s and 1940s, Du Bois, Frazier, and others believed that the solution to Black family disorganization and poverty was conformity to White family norms. The pathologists, who emerged in the 1960s, differed from this approach, and their views had significant effects on public policy. Most of these scholars were White, and they blamed the family for Blacks' inferior social position. Studies reacting to this negative image of Black families emerged during the reactive era (approximately 1966–1977). Most recently, Black Nationalist family studies have depicted Black families as unique and functional.

Common to both Allen's and Staples's categorizations are basic value orientations (see Table 6.1). The cultural deviant perspective recognizes qualities that differentiate Black and White families and gives negative meaning to—that is, sees pathological or dysfunctional attributes in—Black family traits. Both the poverty/acculturation and pathologists' eras manifest orientations similar to the cultural deviant perspective. During the poverty/ acculturation era (early 1900s), the massive Black migration from the agrarian setting to the cities uprooted a significant group in the Black community. Du Bois (1908) and Frazier (1932, 1939) focused on the rates of illegitimacy and the number of female-headed households among this unstable Black group; both concluded that conformity to White middle-class family norms would eliminate family disorganization. Approximately 60 years later, the pathologists extended this thesis by blaming Black families for the deterioration of the Black community. The 1965 Moynihan report characterized this period.

The reactive era extended from approximately 1966 to 1971, during which time White and Black behavioral scientists reacted to Moynihan's "blame the victim" conclusions. By arguing that economic and racial discrimination victimized Blacks, they concluded that, given the same economic conditions,

TABLE 6.1   Theoretical Frameworks Used in Studying Typologies of Black Families

Framework	Examples
Poverty-acculturated	Frazier 1932, 1939; Du Bois 1908
Cultural deviant	Frazier 1939; Moynihan 1965
Pathologist	Moynihan 1965; Aldous 1969
Reactive	Liebow 1967; Billingsley 1968
Cultural equivalent	Frazier 1939; Scanzoni 1971
Black Nationalist	Cates 1977; Hill 1972
Cultural variant	Rodman et al. 1969; Ladner 1971

Black and White families are equivalent. Thus the views of this era parallel Allen's cultural equivalent perspective, although Allen includes Frazier's writings of the 1930s, which describe Black families as "Black Puritans" when they adopt White morals, along with authors of the late 1960s and early 1970s (such as Scanzoni 1971; Bernard 1966). It must be remembered that although within this framework the Black family was not being blamed for the problems it faced, little or no positive value was attributed to the unique traits of Black family structure.

The cultural variant perspective acknowledges certain family functions as universal, but recognizes that various constraints may produce culturally distinct structures and dynamics. Thus the importance of cultural relativity is stressed. Although differences between Black and White families are noted, unique aspects of Black family life are not necessarily taken as reflections of pathologies (Allen 1978). Consistent with this approach is the perspective used during the era of Black Nationalist research, which first began to delineate the strengths of Black families. According to Staples (1974), the reactive researchers challenged the pathologists' position but failed to attach positive value to the unique aspects of Black family life, whereas Black Nationalists contend that if social scientists desire to report on the behavior of a culture other than their own, they must not use their own cultural framework and definitions to explain that behavior. Consequently, Black values cannot be used to explain White cultural patterns, nor can White values be used to explain Black cultural patterns (Johnson 1978).

Methodology

In the following analysis of the treatment of Black families in the research literature of the 1965–1978 period, I make use of Allen's trichotomized typology, which is free from a time sequence idea yet captures the orientations underlying the stages presented by Staples. When my focus is on trends, however, Staples's stages are the referent.

In some cases in which more than one perspective appeared to be represented, an effort was made to label according to the most dominant theme. Given that a clear distinction was not always possible, the reader may disagree with a particular interpretation. For the reader's benefit, each article is labeled by perspective in the bibliography at the end of this chapter.

Articles were classified according to three criteria. They are labeled *cultural deviant* (CD) if emphasis is given to White middle-class norms as the referent to which Black families are compared and if deviation from these norms by Black families is explicitly or implicitly interpreted as pathological (Aldous 1969). The label *cultural equivalent* (CE) is used if emphasis is given to White middle-class family norms as the referent to which Black families are compared and if similarities between the two groups are explicitly or implicitly interpreted as support for shared cultural values (see, e.g., Scanzoni 1971). The *cultural variant* (CV) label is applied if White middle-class norms are not the primary referent and Black cultural patterns are primarily explained by use of Black values and experiences (Jackson 1971). The reliability of this content analysis was maintained through the consistent application of these classification criteria (see Lantz, Schmitt, Britton, and Snyder 1968).

The table of contents in each periodical was carefully scanned for titles and abstracts related to aspects of Black family life (the unit of analysis). If, from a reading of the first few and the last paragraphs, the article appeared relevant, the entire article was examined and the appropriate classification made. In order to minimize sampling error, the list of articles was randomly checked against articles cited in the *International Bibliography of Research in Marriage and the Family,* volume 2.

Journals from two fields were selected: sociology, because of its focus on social institutions and relationships, and social work, for its traditional concern with the welfare of families. From sociology, five journals were selected; two specialized in family research and three were among the most widely circulated. From social work, the five most widely circulated journals were chosen. The following list displays the titles of the journals reviewed as well as abbreviations used in the text.

- Sociology
  Journal of Marriage and the Family (JMF)
  Journal of Comparative Family Studies (JCFS)
  American Journal of Sociology (AJS)
  American Sociological Review (ASR)
  Social Forces

- Social Work
  Child Welfare
  Social Casework
  Social Service Review
  Public Welfare
  Social Work

To assure representation from "established" Black periodicals, that is, journals in circulation for at least 10 years, three of these were added: *Black Scholar, Journal of Social and Behavioral Sciences (JSBS)*, and *Phylon*. Only those empirical articles that explicitly discussed some aspect of Black families were selected.

Findings

Although Moynihan's 1965 attack on Black families stimulated a plethora of articles, the journals reflect few empirical studies. Of the 7,017 articles published during the 13-year period, 3,547 (51%) were empirical family studies, but empirical articles on Black families represented .01% (92) of all articles and .03% (107) of all empirical studies. The *JMF* special issue on Black families, edited by a Black scholar, and the Black journals accounted for 38% of all Black articles. Considering only the nonspecialized journals (that is, excluding *JMF* and *JCFS*), the Black journals contributed 57% of the empirical Black family studies. Although *JSBS* did not specialize in family articles, it devoted a slightly higher percentage of its articles to Black families than did *JMF* (6% versus 4.9%). Obviously, special issues and Black

TABLE 6.2 Black Family Studies by Periodical and Year

Periodical	Publication Year														
	1965	1966	1967	1968	1969	1970	1971	1972	1973	1974	1975	1976	1977	1978	Total
Journal of Marriage and the Family	1	3	2	3	6	2	0	5	2	2	4	2	3	11	46
Journal of Social and Behavioral Sciences[a]	0	0	0	3	2	1	1	1	0	5	0	0	0	0	13
American Sociological Review	0	0	0	0	0	0	2	3	1	0	0	0	0	0	6
Phylon[a]	1	0	0	0	0	0	0	10	0	0	1	5	1	9	27
American Journal of Sociology	0	0	0	0	1	1	1	0	2	2	0	0	0	0	6
Social Forces	1	0	0	0	1	1	0	0	0	1	0	0	0	0	4
Journal of Comparative Family Studies	—b	—b	—b	—b	—b	0	1	0	0	0	2	1	0	0	4
Black Scholar[a]	—b	—b	—b	—b	0	1	10	0	0	0	0	0	0	2	13
Social Casework	0	0	0	0	1	0	0	0	0	0	0	0	0	0	1
Social Work	0	0	0	0	0	0	0	0	0	0	0	1	0	0	1
Total	3	3	2	6	11	5	6	10	5	10	6	5	8	12	92

a. Black journal.
b. Journal was not published in this year.

journals have played an important role in publicizing the data from Black family research (see Table 6.2).

In the 1960s, 60% of the Black family studies were published by *JMF*, and the remainder appeared in five other journals. In contrast, during the first 5 years of 1970, *JMF* published only 31% of the articles; the others were distributed among seven other journals, including two new journals: *Black Scholar* and *JCFS*. Even when we exclude the new journals, *JMF* published only 33% of the articles. Although *JMF*'s monopoly was weakened during this period, its 1978 special issue on Black families supplied 92% of the 12 articles published that year.

Given social work's traditional concern with family welfare, it is surprising that not only did *Social Casework* and *Social Work* each publish only one article in the 13-year survey period, but no empirical articles appeared in the other three selected social work journals. These three, however, did publish a few nonempirical Black family studies.

A greater percentage of articles was published between 1969 and 1972 (35%) than in the previous or following 4 years; 15% and 28%, respectively. Although these 3 years represented the zenith for empirical articles, the social work journals produced their articles prior to and after this period.

The frequency with which each of the theoretical perspectives appeared in the periodicals is shown in Table 6.3. Most journals contained studies that interpreted their data through a cultural equivalent framework. The cultural deviant perspective was absent from 6 of the 10 journals. Although *JMF* gave preference to cultural equivalence, cultural deviance was represented in one-fourth of its articles. If *JMF*'s 1978 special issue on Black families is excluded, the representation of cultural deviance in *JMF* increases to one-third and the cultural variant approach decreases from one-third to less than 12%. It should be noted that 69% of the cultural variant articles appeared in Black-edited journals. Black editors were generally more likely than non-Black editors to publish studies that used the cultural variant perspective, and they were least likely to publish articles that used the cultural deviant perspective.

In tabulating Table 6.3, the three perspectives were evenly distributed among the six articles appearing in *ASR,* whereas all articles appearing in *Social Forces, JCFS,* and *Social Casework* used the cultural equivalent perspective.

The unilinear evolutionary typology developed by Staples implies that each era will lead to and culminate in the next: the poverty/acculturation era

TABLE 6.3   Black Family Studies by Periodical and Theoretical Perspective, 1965–1978

Periodical	Total Reports	Theoretical Perspective		
		CD	CE	CV
Journal of Marriage and the Family	46	11	21	14
Journal of Social and Behavioral Sciences	13	1	8	4
American Sociological Review	6	2	2	2
Phylon	9	0	5	4
American Journal of Sociology	6	2	2	2
Social Forces	4	0	4	0
Journal of Comparative Family Studies	4	0	4	0
Black Scholar	2	0	0	2
Social Casework	1	0	1	0
Social Work	1	0	0	1
Total	92	15	48	29

NOTE: CD = cultural deviant; CE = cultural equivalent; CV = cultural variant.

to the pathologists' era (both equivalent to a cultural deviant framework), to the reactive era (cultural equivalent), to the Black Nationalist era (cultural variant). Although the cultural deviant perspective was present throughout the 1960s and early 1970s, it disappeared after 1974. Throughout the 13-year period, cultural equivalence tended to dominate the literature, which no doubt reflects America's long-standing commitment to various forms of Anglo-conformity. The cultural variant perspective emerged in 1968, when Edwards, a Black researcher, published his *JMF* article "Black Muslim and Negro Christian Relationships." Throughout the 1960s and continuing through 1976, this perspective maintained a low profile; its most recent 2-year prominence resulted primarily from the *JMF* special issue.

Most writings of the 1960s referenced Frazier, not Moynihan. The first major response to Moynihan appeared in 1968, when Geismar and Gerhart published their *JMF* article "Social Class, Ethnicity, and Family Functioning: Exploring Some Issues Raised by the Moynihan Report." This article and the one by Aldous (1969) represent the most policy-oriented research of

TABLE 6.4 Area Studied, by Theoretical Perspective

Area Studied	Total Reports	CD	CE	CV
		Theoretical Perspective		
Family roles	27	7	11	9
Family structure	18	3	8	7
Family functions	18	8	9	1
Mate selection and premarital sex patterns	12	0	8	4
Fertility	8	1	4	3
Marital stability	7	1	5	1
Housing	2	0	1	1
Total	92	20	46	26

NOTE: CD = cultural deviant; CE = cultural equivalent; CV = cultural variant.

the 1960s. Although both articles appeared within the reactive era noted by Staples, the response to Moynihan appeared throughout the 1970s (for example, Bould 1977; Balkwell, Balewick, and Balkwell 1978).

The conceptual framework of the areas studied is shown in Table 6.4. The cultural variant perspective was used in interpreting one-third of the family roles and structure articles, and approximately two-fifths and one-fifth were interpreted through the cultural equivalent and cultural deviant frameworks, respectively. A total of 44% of the data on family roles, structure, and function were interpreted through the cultural equivalent perspective. In contrast, family roles, structure, and function represented 29% and 27% of the cultural deviant and cultural variant perspectives, respectively. The cultural variant framework was absent in family function studies, and the cultural deviant perspective did not appear in studies on housing and mate selection or in those on premarital sexual patterns.

Although a vast amount of literature on minority families and housing appears in economic journals, housing issues and their sociopsychological effects on minority families received insignificant attention in the selected journals. Only two studies (2% of all reports) were published on this topic in the 13-year survey period.

Half the studies focused on family structure and roles, for example, role aspiration, attitude, and performance. Although not shown in Table 6.4, nearly two-fifths of these studies were published in the 1960s. More important, these two areas represent 75% of the studies published in that decade. During the next 9 years, the diversity of areas increased—the other five areas represented 55% of the articles during 1970–1975, and thereafter their representation increased an average of 1% each year. In the two categories of "Marital Selection or Premarital Sexual Pattern" and "Fertility," only one study appeared in each category during the 1960s. By the end of 1978, another 10 articles (5 from a special issue) had appeared in the former category and 7 in the latter.

Conclusion: Challenges for the 21st Century

During the period from 1965 to 1978, empirical articles on Black families represented less than 1% of all empirical family studies. Surprisingly, such articles were virtually absent from the social work journals. Although a disproportionate number of these studies were published in Black-edited journals, *JMF* was the major source of Black articles, particularly during the sixties. Furthermore, since 1978 this journal has shown an upward trend in the number of articles devoted to Black families (ranging from 6% to 26% during the 1979-1987 period). And the 1979 Black family special issue edited by Marie Peters continued to account for the highest proportion of Black family articles (Demos, 1990).

Our analysis revealed variations in theoretical perspective by journals and across time. While most journals interpreted their data within the cultural equivalent perspective, the cultural deviant perspective was least likely and the cultural variant perspective was most likely to emerge in journals edited by Black scholars (e.g., the 1979 *JMF* special issue). Generally, the cultural deviant and cultural variant perspectives followed Staples's typology. However, with the exception of 1978, the cultural equivalent framework was strong throughout the 13-year period, and reactions to the Moynihan Report continued throughout the seventies. The golden years for empirical studies were 1969 to 1972, during which virtually every journal published at least one article.

In reviewing the three perspectives, we note that Black-White comparisons have been an inherent bias of the cultural equivalent and deviant approaches. Too often these comparisons depict Blacks as deviant or problematic when statistical differences emerge. For those studies of the 1980s that compared Blacks and Whites, this depiction continued (Bryant and Coleman, 1988; Demos 1990). As the cultural deviant perspective has become less prominent and the cultural variant frame of reference has gained greater recognition, there has been some decline in such biases. Unfortunately, other sources of bias threaten to negate the advantages of these changes. For example, Demos (1990) notes that with increased government funding for studies dealing with social problems, family researchers will be more inclined to focus on problematic Black families. This inclination is made more likely by the decline in life expectancy for Blacks and the growing poverty rate among Black children, a rate that is higher now than at any time since 1967 (Hildebrand, et al., 1996 and Staples and Johnson, 1993). Thus, our growing knowledge of the rich, diverse, and complex nature of Black families runs the danger of reverting back to viewing the Black family as pathological and monolithic. In fact, recent surveys of college textbooks reveal that while there is a slow movement towards greater ethnic inclusion, the cultural deviant model has not been eradicated (Bryant and Coleman, 1988).

During the 13-year survey period, a preoccupation with certain topics made for a narrow agenda. This was particularly true for the sixties. Housing received the least attention (both publications appeared in the seventies), while considerable emphases was given to roles and structure. This perhaps reflects the preoccupation with stability of the Black family and its presumed inability to fulfill societal prerequisites (e.g., the socialization of children). This concern, sparked by Frazier and revisited by Moynihan, has not only resulted in a narrow agenda but also spotlights the negative.

Studies of the post-1978 era continue to reflect a narrow agenda. The literature overplays teenage unwed mothers and the one quarter of young Black males who are in jail or have police records. Consequently, the idea that the majority of Black adolescents are principled is unthinkable. Considering the limited economic and social environment in which many Black youth grow up, the fact that 75% of young Black males and a higher percentage of females are not in trouble begs studies on Black adolescent competency. Empirical information is needed on Black youth's coping behavior, motivation, personality identity, attitude formation, cognitive, emotional, and moral development, family relationship with parents and siblings, and the selection of significant others—issues about which there is an established or growing literature on White youth (Staples and Johnson, 1993; Taylor, 1987; Taylor, Chatters, Tucker, and Lewis, 1990).

Relative to the general population, the Black community has traditionally had a higher proportion of youth, child adoptions, large families, multi-earners within families, low-income families, single parents, and blended families. Yet, the 1965-1978 and post-1978 periods showed few studies on childrearing patterns, sibling relationships, dating and courtship, dual-job families, and the role of housing policies in the support of single-parents and extended families. These areas provide a rich field of investigation for the 1990s.

Equally important to the youth are the elderly. They are the fastest growing segment of the Black population. An increasing number are serving as parent surrogates for their grandchildren. Family scientists must address the implications these demographics have for family housing, custody issues, social policies, health care, child care/socialization, work-family interaction, leisure, retirement, and so forth.

Greater attention should be given to stable Black couples. Emphasis on high rates of fertility, particularly among teenagers, diverts attention from the relatively high rate of involuntary "childlessness" among married Black couples. In addition, stable Black couples of all classes have a high risk of experiencing economic strains that can weaken their marriages. Focus is needed on factors that strengthen their marital bonds and enhance their individual growth and self-actualization. Furthermore, Black men's role as fathers within the family has been ignored in favor of the absent father. Research efforts are needed for understanding the Black father's childrearing practices with regard to emotional, social, and academic success.

Finally, given the growing number of Blacks who come from diverse countries and cultures, studies in the 21st century must stretch the definition of what it means to be an African American. Particular attention must be drawn to the early and recent influx of Black immigrants (e.g., West Indies, Central and South American, Africa) whose families are challenged by intergenerational conflicts stemming from differential acculturation of young and old members. While all people of color share degrees of racial prejudice and discrimination, they differ from each other in fertility rates, upward mobility, marital stability, residential living arrangements, and family rituals. No longer should it be acceptable to lump all minorities ("non-White") together as if their differences have no consequences for family outcome measures (Billingsley 1992; Mindel, Habenstein, and Wright 1988).

By 2056, the average U.S. resident will trace his or her descent to Africa, Asia, the Hispanic world, Arabia, or almost anywhere except White Europe (Henry 1990; U.S. Bureau of the Census 1996). Given these changing demographics, it is critical that we replace deviant pathological models with culturally sensitive frameworks. While the cultural variant perspective shows the most promise, it is clear that the reality of any people's experience is too complex to capture with any one perspective.

Thus, the greatest challenge for family scholars in general, and Black family scholars in particular, is to maintain an intellectual posture of openness to the many shades of family life.

References

Adams, B. N. 1985. "The Family: Problems and Solutions." *Journal of Marriage and the Family* 47(3):525-29.

Aldous, J. 1969. "Wives' Employment Status and Lower-Class Men as Husbands-Fathers: Support for the Moynihan Thesis." *Journal of Marriage and the Family* 31(3):469-76.

Allen, W. 1977, October. "The Effects of Government Policies on Black Families." Division on Education and Research: Public Education, The Ford Foundation.

———. 1978. "The Search for Applicable Theories of Black Family Life." *Journal of Marriage and the Family* 40(1):111-29.

Allen, W. and S. Stokes. 1981. "Black Family Life Styles and Mental Health of Black Americans." In *Perspectives on Minority Group Mental Health*, edited by R. Endo and F. Munoz. Chicago: Charter House.

Balkwell, C., J. Balewick, and J. W. Balkwell. 1978. "On Black and White Family Patterns in America: Their Impact on the Expressive Aspect of Sex-Role Socialization." *Journal of Marriage and the Family* 40(4):743-47.

Bernard, J. 1966. "Note on Educational Homography in Negro-White and White-Negro Marriage, 1960." *Journal of Marriage and the Family* 28(3):274-76.

Billingsley, A. 1968. *Black Families in White America.* Englewood Cliffs, NJ: Prentice Hall.

———. 1992. *Climbing Jacob's Ladder: The Enduring Legacy of African-American Families.* New York: Schuster.

Bould, S. 1977. "Female-Headed Families: Personal Fate Control and the Provider Role." *Journal of Marriage and the Family* 39(2):339-49.

Bryant, L. Z., and M. Coleman. 1988. "The Black Family as Portrayed in Introductory Marriage and Family Textbooks." *Family Relations* 37(3):255-259.

Cates, W. 1977. "Legal Abortion: Are American Women Healthier Because of It?" *Phylon* 38(3):267-81.

Demos, V. 1990. "Black Family Studies in the *Journal of Marriage and the Family* and the Issue of Distortion: A Trend Analysis." *Journal of Marriage and the Family,* 52(3):603-612.

Du Bois, W. E. B. 1908. *The Negro American Family.* Atlanta, GA: Atlanta University Press.

Edwards, H. 1968. "Black Muslim and Negro Christian Relationships." *Journal of Marriage and the Family* 30(4):604-11.

Frazier, E. F. 1932. *The Negro Family in Chicago.* Chicago: University of Chicago Press.

————. 1939. *The Negro Family in the United States.* Chicago: University of Chicago Press.

Geismar, L. L. and U. C. Gerhart. 1968. "Social Class, Ethnicity, and Family Functioning: Exploring Some Issues Raised by the Moynihan Report." *Journal of Marriage and the Family* 30(3):480-87.

Gouldner, A. 1970. *The Coming Crisis of Western Sociology.* New York: Avon.

Henry, William A., III. 1990, April 9. "Beyond the Melting Pot." *Time Magazine,* pp. 28-31.

Hildebrand, V., Phenice, L. A., Gray, M. M., and Hines. R. P. 1996. *Knowing and Serving Diverse Families.* Englewood Cliffs, NJ: Prentice Hall.

Hill, R. 1972. *The Strength of Black Families.* New York: Emerson Hall.

Jackson, J. 1971. "But Where Are the Men?" *Black Scholar* 3(4):34-41.

Johnson, L. 1978. "The Search for Values in Black Family Research." Pp. 26-34 in *The Black Family: Essays and Studies,* edited by R. E. Staples. Belmont, CA: Wadsworth.

Jones, M. 1976, Fall. "Scientific method, value judgments, and the Black predicament in the U.S." *Review of Black Political Economy,* 7(1).

Ladner, J. 1971. *Tomorrow's Tomorrow: The Black Woman.* Garden City, NY: Doubleday.

Lantz, H., R. Schmitt, M. Britton, and E. Snyder. 1968. "Pre-industrial Patterns in the Colonial Family in America: A Content Analysis of Colonial Magazines." *American Sociological Review* 33(3):413-26.

Liebow, E. 1967. *Tally's Corner: A Study of Negro Street Corner Men.* Boston: Little, Brown.

Mannheim, K. 1936. *Ideology and Utopia.* London: Routledge & Kegan Paul.

Mindel, C. H., R. W. Habenstein and R. Wright, Jr. 1988. *Ethnic Families in America: Patterns and Variations.* New York: Elsevier.

Mills, C. W. 1959. *The Sociological Imagination.* New York: Grove.

Moynihan, D. P. 1965. *The Negro Family: The Case for National Action.* Washington, DC: U.S. Department of Labor, Office of Policy Planning and Research.

Nobles, Wade W. 1978, November. "Toward an Empirical and Theoretical Framework for Defining Black Families." *Journal of Marriage and the Family,* 40:679-688.

Rodman, H., F. H. Nichols, and P. Voydanoff. 1969. "Lower Class Attitudes Toward 'Deviant' Family Patterns: A Cross-Cultural Study." *Journal of Marriage and the Family* 31(2):315-21.

Scanzoni, J. 1971. *The Black Family in Modern Society.* Boston: Allyn & Bacon.

Staples, R., and L. B. Johnson. 1993. *Black Families at the Crossroads: Challenges and Prospects.* San Francisco: Jossey-Bass.

Staples, R. E. 1974. "The Black Family Revisited: A Review and a Preview." *Journal of Social and Behavioral Sciences* 20(Spring):65-78.

Staples, R. E. and A. Mirande. 1980. "Racial and Cultural Variations Among American Families: A Decennial Review of the Literature on Minority Families." *Journal of Marriage and the Family* 42(4):887-903.

Taylor, R. J., L. M. Chatters, M. B. Tucker, and E. Lewis. 1990. "Developments in Research on Black Families: A Decade Review." *Journal of Marriage and the Family,* 54(4):993-1014.

Taylor, R. L. 1987. "Psychosocial Development." In *Black Adolescence: Topical Summaries and Annotated Bibliographies of Research.* The Consortium for Research on Black Adolescence, University of Connecticut.

Ulrich's International Periodical Directory. 1978. New York: R. R. Bowker.

U.S. Bureau of the Census. 1996, February. *Population Projections of the United States, by Age, Sex, Race, and Hispanic Origin: 1995-2050.* CPR Series P-25-1130.

van den Berghe, P. 1967. *Race and Racism: A Comparative Perspective.* New York: John Wiley.

Bibliography of Selected Research Reports
and Assigned Classifications

NOTE: In the parentheses following each citation, the first designation refers to the area studied and the second to the theoretical perspective: CD = cultural deviant, CE = cultural equivalent, CV = cultural variant.

American Journal of Sociology

Epstein, C. F. 1973. "Positive Effects of the Multiple Negative Explaining the Success of Black Professional Women." 78(4):151-73. (Role: CV)

Goldschieder, C. and P. R. Uhlenberg. 1969. "Minority Group Status and Fertility." 84(4):361-72. (Fertility: CE)

Kandel, D. B. 1971. "Race, Maternal Authority, and Adolescent Aspiration." 76(6):999-1020. (Family functions: CE)

Lopata, H. A. 1973. "Social Relations of Black and White Widowed Women in a Northern Metropolis." 78(4):241-48. (Role: CE)

Roberts, R. E. and E. S. Lee. 1974. "Minority Group Status and Fertility Revisited." 80(2):503-23. (Fertility: CD)

Udry, J. R., K. E. Bauman, and C. Chase 1971. "Skin Color, Status, and Mate Selection." 76(4):722-33. (Mate selection: CV)

American Sociological Review

Centers, R., B. H. Raven, and A. Rodrigues. 1971. "Conjugal Power Structure: A Re-Examination." 36(1):1-17. (Role: CD)

Heiss, J. 1972. "On the Transmission of Marital Instability in Black Families." 37(1):82-92. (Marital stability: CV)

Hermes, G. 1972. "The Process of Entry Into First Marriage." 37(2):173-82. (Mate selection: CE)

Reynolds, F. and A. I. Hermalin. 1971. "Family Stability: A Comparison of Trends Between Blacks and Whites." 36(1):1-17. (Marital stability: CD)

Roland, J. and J. E. Marble. 1972. "Family Disruption and Delinquent Conduct: Multiple Measures and the Effect of Subclassification." 37(1):93-99. (Family functions: CE)

Sampson, W. A. and P. H. Rossi. 1975. "Race and Family Social Standing." 40(2):201-14. (Role: CV)

Black Scholar

Jackson, J. 1971. "But Where Are the Men?" 3(4):34-41. (Mate selection: CV)

Reed, J. 1970. "Marriage and Fertility in Black Female Teachers." 1(3-4):22-28. (Fertility: CV)

Journal of Comparative Family Studies

Jackson, R. N. 1975. "Some Aspirations of Lower Class Black Mothers." 6(2):171-81. (Family functioning: CE)

Monahan, T. P. 1971. "Interracial Marriage and Divorce in Kansas and the Question of Instability of Mixed Marriages." 2(1):107-20. (Mate selection: CE)
———. 1976. "The Occupational Class of Couples Entering Into Interracial Marriages." 7(2):176-92. (Mate selection: CE)
Tobin, P. L., W. B. Clifford, R. D. Mustian, and S. C. Davis. 1975. "Value of Children and Fertility Behavior in a Triracial Rural County." 6(1):46-53. (Fertility: CE)

Journal of Marriage and the Family

Agresti, B. F. 1978. "The First Decades of Freedom: Black Families in a Southern County, 1870 and 1885." 40(4):697-706. (Family structure: CV)
Aldous, J. 1969. "Wives' Employment Status and Lower-Class Men as Husbands-Fathers: Support for the Moynihan Thesis." 31(3):469-76. (Role: CD)
———. 1972. "Children's Perception of Adult Role Assignment: Father Absent, Class, Race, and Sex Influences." 34(1):55-65. (Role: CD)
Axelson, L. J. 1970. "The Working Wife: Differences in Perception Among Negro and White Males." 32(3):457-64. (Role: CE)
Balkwell, C., J. Balewick, and J. W. Balkwell. 1978. "On Black and White Family Patterns in America: Their Impact on the Expressive Aspect of Sex-Role Socialization." 40(4):743-47 (Role: CV)
Bartz, K. W., and E. S. Levine. 1978. "Childrearing by Black Parents: A Description and Comparison to Anglo and Chicano Parents." 40(4):709-19. (Family functions: CV)
Bauman, K. E. and J. R. Udry. 1972. "Powerlessness and Regularity of Contraception in an Urban Negro Male Sample: A Research Note." 34(1):112-14. (Role: CE)
Bernard, J. 1966. "Note on Educational Homogamy in Negro-White and White-Negro Marriage, 1960." 28(3):274-76. (Mate selection: CE)
Bould, S. 1977. "Female-Headed Families: Personal Fate Control and the Provider Role." 39(2):339-49. (Family structure: CE)
Broderick, C. 1965. "Social Heterosexual Development Among Urban Negroes and Whites." 27(2):200-12. (Role: CE)
Brown, P., L. Perry, and E. Harburg. 1977. "Sex Role Attitudes and Psychological Outcomes for Black and White Women Experiencing Marital Dissolution." 39(4):549-61. (Role: CE)
Christensen, H. T. and L. B. Johnson. 1978. "Premarital Coitus and the Southern Black: A Comparative View." 40(4):721-32. (Premarital sexual patterns: CV)
Cromwell, V. L. and R. E. Cromwell. 1978. "Perceived Dominance in Decision Making and Conflict Resolution Among Anglo, Black, and Chicano Couples." 40(4):749-59. (Family functions: CV)
Dickinson, G. E. 1975. "Dating Behavior of Black and White Adolescents Before and After Desegregation." 37(3):602-08. (Mate selection: CE)
Dietrick, K. T. 1975. "A Reexamination of the Myth of Black Matriarchy." 37(2):367-74. (Role: CE)
Edwards, H. 1968. "Black Muslim and Negro Christian Relationships." 30(4):604-11. (Role: CV)
Fischer, A., J. D. Beasley, and C. L. Harter. 1968. "The Occurrence of the Extended Family at the Origin of the Family of Procreation: A Developmental Approach to Negro Family Structure." 30(2):290-300. (Family structure: CD)
Geismar, L. L. and U. C. Gerhart. 1968. "Social Class, Ethnicity, and Family Functioning: Exploring Some Issues Raised by the Moynihan Report." 30(3):480-87. (Family functions: CE)

Haney, C. A., R. Michielutte, C. M. Cochrane, and C. E. Vincent. 1975. "Some Consequences of Illegitimacy in a Sample of Black Women." 37(2):359-66. (Role: CE)

Harrison, A. O. and J. H. Minor. 1978. "Interrole Conflict, Coping Strategies, and Satisfaction Among Black Working Wives." 40(4):799-805. (Role: CV)

Heer, D. M. 1966. "Negro-White Marriage in the U.S." 28(3):262-73. (Mate selection: CE)

————. 1974. "The Prevalence of Black-White Marriage in the U.S., 1960 and 1970." 36(2):246-58. (Mate selection: CE)

Hobbs, D. F. and J. M. Wimbish. 1977. "Transition to Parenthood by Black Couples." 39(4):677-89. (Family functions: CE)

Kami, C. and N. L. Radin. 1967. "Class Difference in the Socialization Practice of Negro Mothers." 29(2):302-10. (Role: CD)

King, C. A., T. J. Abernathy, and A. H. Chapman. 1976. "Black Adolescents' Views of Maternal Employment as a Threat to the Marital Relationship: 1963–1973." 38(4):733-37. (Role: CE)

King, K. 1969. "Adolescent Perception of Power Structure in the Negro Family." 31(4):751-55. (Role: CD)

Kuvlesky, W. and A. Obordo. 1972. "A Racial Comparison of Teen-age Girls' Projections for Marriage and Procreation." 34(1):75-84. (Role: CD)

Lammermeier, P. J. 1973. "Urban Black Family of the Nineteenth Century: A Study of Black Family Structure in the Ohio Valley, 1850–1880." 35(3):440-56. (Family structure: CE)

Landry, B. and M. P. Jendick. 1978. "Employment of Wives in Middle Class Black Families." 40(4):787-97. (Family functions: CV)

McAdoo, H. P. 1978. "Factors Related to Stability in Upwardly Mobile Black Families." 40(4):761-76. (Family functions: CV)

Melton, W. and D. L. Thomas. 1976. "Instrumental and Expressive Values in Mate Selection of Black and White College Students." 38(3):509-17. (Mate selection: CE)

Mercer, C. V. 1967. "Interrelations Among Family Stability, Family Composition, Residence, and Race." 29(3):456-60. (Family structure: CD)

Miao, G. 1974. "Marital Instability and Unemployment Among Whites and Nonwhites: The Moynihan Report Revisited—Again." 36(1):77-86. (Marital stability: CE)

Nolle, D. 1972. "Changes in Black Sons and Daughters: A Panel Analysis of Black Adolescents' Orientations Toward Their Parents." 34(3):443-47. (Family functions: CE)

Parker, S. and R. J. Kleiner. 1966. "Characteristics of Negro Mothers in Single-Headed Households." 28(4):507-13. (Family structure: CD)

————. 1969. "Social and Psychological Dimensions of the Family Role Performance of the Negro Male." 31(3):500-11. (Role: CE)

Pope, H. 1969. "Negro-White Differences in Decisions Regarding Illegitimate Children." 31(4):756-64. (Family structure: CV)

Reed, F. W., J. R. Udry, and M. Ruppert. 1975. "Relative Incomes and Fertility." 37(4):799-805. (Fertility: CE)

Rodman, H., F. H. Nichols, and P. Voydanoff. 1969. "Lower Class Attitudes Toward 'Deviant' Family Patterns: A Cross-Cultural Study." 31(2):315-21. (Family structure: CV)

Savage, J. E., A. V. Adai, and P. Friedman. 1978. "Community-Social Variables Related to Black Parent-Absent Families." 40(4):779-85. (Family structure: CV)

Scanzoni, J. 1975. "Sex Roles, Economic Factors, and Marital Solidarity in Black and White Marriages." 37(1):130-44. (Marital stability: CE)

Staples, R. E. 1978. "Race, Liberalism, Conservatism and Premarital Sexual Permissiveness: A Bi-racial Comparison." 40(4):733-42. (Premarital sexual patterns: CV)

Vincent, C. E., C. A. Haney, and C. M. Cochrane. 1969. "Familial and Generational Patterns of Illegitimacy." 30(4):659-67. (Family structure: CD)

Williams, J. A. and R. Stockton. 1973. "Black Family Structure and Functions: An Empirical Examination of Some Suggestions Made by Billingsley." 35(1):39-49. (Family structure: CV)

Willie, C. V. and S. L. Greenblat. 1978. "Four 'Classic' Studies of Power Relationships in Black Families: A Review and Look to the Future." 40(4):691-94. (Family functions: CE)

Journal of Social and Behavioral Sciences

Billingsley, A. and M. G. Greene. 1974. "Family Life Among the Free Black Population in the 18th Century." 20(2):1-18. (Family structure: CV)

Epps, E. G. 1968. "Parent Social Status and Personality Characteristics of Negro High School Students." 13(2):27-33. (Role: CE)

Harrison, A. E. 1974. "Dilemma of Growing Up Black and Female." 20(2):28-40. (Role: CV)

Jackson, J. J. 1970. "Kinship Relations Among Older Negro Americans." 16(1-2):5-17. (Family Structure: CE)

————.1974. "Ordinary Black Husbands: The Truly Hidden Man." 20(2):19-27. (Role: CE)

Kennedy, E. J. 1968. "The Relationship of Maternal Emotionality to Obstetric Complications and Childbirth Abnormalities." 13(2):3-8. (Family functions: CE)

Kreptal, E. R. and E. G. Epps. 1968. "The 'Father Absence' Effect on Aspirations: Myth or Reality." 13(3):9-17. (Family roles: CE)

Kutner, N. G. 1974. "Differential Adaptation Among Lower-Class Black Homemakers in a Rural Urban Community." 20(3):55-65. (Role: CE)

Ladner, J. 1974. "Black Women in Poverty." 20(2):41-50. (Role: CV)

Rhodes, E. C. 1969. "Family Structure and the Achievement Syndrome Among Students at Tennessee A&I State University." 14(1):55-59. (Family functions: CD)

Sherman, E. G. 1969. "Urbanization and the Negro Family: A Case Study in Florida." 14(1):36-41. (Family structure: CE)

Smith, R. 1971. "Family Life and Environment in the Lincoln Neighborhood Community." 18(1):80-89. (Housing: CV)

Staples, R. E. 1972. "The Influence of Race on Reactions to a Hypothetical Premarital Pregnancy." 18(3):32-35. (Premarital sexual patterns: CE)

Phylon

Anderson, J. E. 1977. "Planning of Births: Difference Between Black and White in U.S." 38(3):323-96. (Family structure: CE)

Babchuck, N. and J. A. Ballweg. 1972. "Black Family Structure and Primary Relations." 33(4):334-47. (Family structure: CE)

Cates, W. 1977. "Legal Abortion: Are American Women Healthier Because of It?" 38(3):267-81. (Fertility: CV)

Hawkins, H. C. 1976. "Urban Housing and the Black Family." 37(1):73-84. (Housing: CE)

Kovar, M. G. 1977. "Mortality of Black Infants in the U.S." 38(4):378-97. (Fertility: CV)

Lee, A. S. 1977. "Maternal Mortality in the United States." 38(3):259-66. (Fertility: CV)

Schwartz, M. 1965. "The Northern U.S. Negro Matriarchy: Status vs. Authority." 26(1):18-24. (Family structure: CE)

Simon, R. 1978. "Black Attitudes Towards Transracial Adoption." 39(2):135-42. (Family functions: CV)

Stokes, C. S., K. W. Croker, and J. C. Smith. 1977. "Race, Education, and Fertility: A Comparison of Black-White Reproductive Behavior." 38(2):160-69. (Fertility: CE)

Sweet, J. A. and L. L. Bumpass. 1970. "Differentials in Marital Instability of the Black Population: 1970." 34(4):323-31. (Marital stability: CE)

Social Casework

Billingsley, A. 1969. "Family Functioning in the Low-Income Black Community." 50(1):563-72. (Family structure: CE)

Social Forces

Bacon, L. 1974. "Early Motherhood, Accelerated Transition, and Social Pathologies." 52(3):333-41. (Marital stability: CE)
Bell, R. R. 1965. "Lower Class Negro Mothers' Aspirations for Their Children." 43(4):493-500. (Family functions: CE)
Blood, R. O. and D. M. Wolfe. 1969. "Negro-White Differences in Blue-Collar Marriages in a Northern Metropolis." 38(1):59-64. (Role: CE)
Monahan, T. P. 1970. "Are Interracial Marriages Really Less Stable?" 48(4):461-73. (Marital stability: CE)

Social Work

Beckett, J. O. 1976. "Working Wives: A Racial Comparison." 21(5):463-71. (Role: CV)

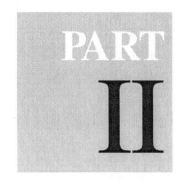

Family Patterns

Economics and Social Mobility

Poverty has been and continues to be the lot of most Blacks, as Paul C. Glick shows in his chapter in this section on demographic characteristics and as Robert B. Hill and Marion Wright Edelman point out in their chapters on social policy and advocacy in Part V. Despite severe economic and occupational isolation and lack of role models for many of the children, some Black families and individuals have managed to master the necessary skills, education, and jobs to achieve comparatively more secure situations. Yet their situations are tenuous because there is so little inherited wealth among Black families, and because they tend to depend totally on wages earned in service fields. This means that in each generation a Black family must re-create the effort needed to climb the mobility ladder, whereas in majority families the status of the father can be transferred to his children and future generations. The major contributions Black families have traditionally been able to make to their children have been the drive to succeed and the motivation to achieve within the school setting.

The goal of many Blacks has been to move from poverty to more secure economic status, as the authors of several chapters in this volume point out

115

strongly. Paul C. Glick notes this in Chapter 7, on the demographic characteristics of African American family life; Harriette Pipes McAdoo addresses
it in Chapter 8, on transgenerational mobility; and Robert B. Hill and Marion
Wright Edelman deal with it in their respective chapters on social policy and
advocacy.

The increase in the numbers of upwardly mobile Blacks and the decrease
in the lower socioeconomic group is discussed here in light of the changes
occurring within the Black community. No longer are we able to speak of
"the" Black family or even a "bifurcated" family. We must recognize that
Blacks have taken on many mobility patterns over the years. Just as we
cannot simplify the lives of Whites or Chinese into one or two patterns, it is
increasingly evident that the economic and social lives of Blacks are complex. This complexity becomes even more obvious when the social and
economic connotations of skin color, hair type, and absence or presence of
Negroid facial features are discussed. Economic and geographic mobility are
also examined here in light of the changes that have occurred.

Paul Glick documents the changes that have occurred in Black family life
in Chapter 7, which is packed with demographic data that effectively pull
together multiple sources and should prove of great value to other writers in
the field. Glick's clear presentation helps to point up the complexity of the
mass of information he covers. He reviews the most current analyses and
portrayals of the Black family one might ever find. He reemphasizes the
reality that there is no such thing as "the" Black family, for different forms
exist at different levels and among different classes. Glick covers three areas
in detail: family composition, marriage and divorce, and employment and
income. He points to the following facts in his review: that Black families
tend to have more young children; that there is short joint survival of the unit
after the children leave the home; that half of all Black children now live
only with their mothers; and that Black men tend to be less educated than
their wives, although the level of education as a whole is increasing. Other
trends he highlights are that the number of children in one-parent homes
among Blacks has grown at a slower rate than in non-Black homes, and that
more adult children now remain in the Black family because of their inability
to maintain separate households. He notes that the notorious imbalanced sex
ratio among Blacks is predicted to decline by the mid-1990s. Glick recognizes the centrality of children in Black families and predicts a decrease in
the differences between Black and other families in the future, if there is less
stratification by race.

The transgenerational mobility patterns of African American families are examined by Harriette Pipes McAdoo in a theoretical discussion of the role the extended family plays in assisting Blacks to avoid the kind of destructive cycle outlined by John U. Ogbu in Chapter 13 of this volume. McAdoo finds that educational achievements are the result of personal perseverance as well as strong support and often sacrifice by other family members. Blacks do not have to cut themselves off from the reciprocal obligations of the kin support network in order to be mobile. This network is not only a coping strategy for those in poverty, it has evolved into a cultural pattern that tends to transcend social class. The barriers to mobility are so great that it takes more than one generation for a Black family to move from abject poverty to middle-class status. One mobility pattern McAdoo examines is that of families who appear to be operating with a minimum amount of stress and who have attained the highest educational, occupational, and economic rewards after three generations of struggle. She shows that the members of such families remain in their supportive networks for cultural and family reasons even after they have achieved higher socioeconomic status. She also notes that those in the middle class tend not to remain there, but gradually slip back through succeeding generations, falling victim to their own lowered academic attainments and discrimination within the labor market.

Demographic Pictures of African American Families

PAUL C. GLICK

Among the many well-recognized differences between Black families and families of other races in the United States, some have been converging, some diverging, and others simply persisting. These differences are important but can be overemphasized, because all families tend to share in the periodic changes that occur in economic opportunities and in other aspects of the cultural environment, even though the sharing is not always equal. During periods of economic expansion, Black families have tended to improve their relative position, but during recessions they have tended to lose some of their gains. Also, in recent decades, Black families have been sharing in certain benefits, such as those resulting from the decreasing burden of large families and from an especially rapid increase in the educational level of their young adults, but they have had more than their share of the deprivation associated with the rise in the number of one-parent families.

This chapter examines recent changes in the United States concerning the diversity of Black family patterns and those of all races combined. The presentation will confirm that "the" Black family is itself a fiction; "different family forms prevail at different class and income levels throughout our society" (Willie 1970, p. v). The chapter is organized around three major demographic areas: family composition; marriage and divorce; and education, employment, and income. The concluding section explores some implications of the outstanding features of Black family life.

Family Composition

According to the traditional norm, families are formed through marriage, and couples who marry remain married until one spouse dies. The extent to which current marital behavior differs from the norm will be examined in this section, along with some of the implications for the living arrangements of children, for young adults leaving home and establishing new families, and for the composition of households as distinct from families.

Variety of Family Types

Most of the families in the United States consist of a married couple or one parent and one or more of the parent's own young children. Fully 80% of Black families in 1992 were one of these types, compared with 90% for all U.S. families (see Table 7.1). The proportion of families not of either type was twice as high among Black families compared with all others (20% versus 10%). In the less common category are families that consist of relatives, such as grandparents and their grandchildren, brothers and sisters, and others, including neither a married couple nor a lone parent and young children.

A continuing feature of Black families is that they are more likely than other families to have young children among their members. By 1992, 57% of Black families compared with 49% of all families included one or more son or daughter under 18 years of age in the home. This reflects, among other things, the higher birthrate among Black women and the shorter survival of Black marriages after the children leave home (Norton and Glick 1986). There has been a decline since 1980 in the proportion of Black married-couple families with young children present, but little change in the quite high proportion of lone parents with children present.

Among the 57% of Black families in 1992 with young children in the home, more were one-parent families (33%) than married-couple families (25%). In stark contrast, among the families of all races with young children,

TABLE 7.1 Families by Type, Race, and Presence of Own Children Under Age 18: United States, 1992, 1980, and 1970

Type of Family and Presence of Own Children Under 18	All Races			Black			% Black
	1992	1980	1970	1992	1980	1970	1992
All families (000s)	67,173	58,426	51,586	7,716	6,042	4,887	12
Percentage	100	100	100	100	100	100	—
With own children	49	52	56	57	62	61	14
No own children	51	48	44	43	38	39	10
Married-couple families	78	83	87	47	55	68	7
With own children	36	42	50	25	31	41	8
No own children	42	21	37	22	24	27	6
Parent-child families	12	10	6	33	31	20	20
Mother and own children	10	9	5	31	29	18	33
Father and own children	2	1	1	2	2	2	14
Other families	10	7	7	20	14	12	25
Female householder	7	5	5	16	11	10	27
Male householder	3	2	2	4	3	2	18

SOURCE: U.S. Bureau of the Census (1971, 1981a, 1993).

only 12% were one-parent families, and 36% included married couples. As far back as 1950, the one-parent family was twice as prevalent among Blacks (9% versus 4%), so this is one feature of family life in which the gap between Blacks and families of all races has been growing.

Living Arrangements of Children

Some of the sharpest differences between the family lives of Blacks and those of other races can be found in the living arrangements of young children. For example, of all children under age 18 in 1992, 16% were Black, but only 8% of those living with two parents were Black, and 36% of those living with a lone mother were Black (see Table 7.2). The most extreme contrast is found among children living with a mother who has never been married; in 1992 three of every five (59%) of these children had a Black mother. In fact, more Black children were living with a never-married parent than with a divorced or separated parent (31% and 21%, respectively). By comparison, about two-thirds as many children of all races were living with a never-married parent as with a divorced or separated parent (8% versus 13%).

TABLE 7.2 Living Arrangements of Noninstitutional Children Under Age 18 by Race: United States, 1992, 1980, and 1970

	All Races			Black			% Black
Living Arrangements	1992	1980	1970	1992	1980	1970	1992
All children under 18 (000s)	65,965	61,744	69,162	10,427	9,290	9,406	16
Percentage	100	100	100	100	100	100	—
Living with							
Two parents	71	76	85	36	42	58	8
One parent	26	20	12	57	46	33	34
Mother only	23	18	11	54	44	30	36
Divorced	8	7	3	10	11	5	19
Married	6	6	5	12	16	15	32
Separated	5	5	3	11	15	13	34
Widowed	1	2	2	2	4	4	23
Never married	8	3	1	31	13	6	59
Father only	3	2	1	3	2	3	15
Divorced	1	1	—[a]	1	1	—[a]	10
Married	1	1	1	1	1	2	15
Separated	1	—[a]	—[a]	1	1	1	16
Widowed	—	—[a]	—[a]	—	—[a]	1	23
Never married	1	—[a]	—[a]	1	—[a]	—[a]	21
Other relatives only	2	3	2	6	11	7	47
Nonrelatives only	1	1	1	1	1	2	37

SOURCE: U.S. Bureau of the Census (1972, 1981b, 1992a).
a. Base of fewer than 75,000.

Nearly all the racial differences that can be demonstrated from the data in Table 7.2 present a picture of much greater family disorganization in the living arrangements of Black children than of other young children. Even though there was a downturn of about one-third between 1980 and 1992 in the proportion of Black children living with a separated or widowed mother, the proportion living with a never-married mother more than doubled (from 13% to 31%). There also was more than a doubling for children of all races living with a never-married mother, but the proportion rose only from 3% to 8%; the latter was about the figure for Black children 15 years earlier, in 1970. A continuing small proportion of children live with a lone father (3% in 1992).

The rapid growth in the number of young children living with a never-married mother is closely related to the sharp upturn in births to unwed mothers. Between 1970 and 1990 such births rose from 35% to 67% among

Blacks, compared with an increase of "only" 6% to 28% for all races. Although the rate of increase was not great among Blacks, the level was still more than twice as high as that for all races (67% versus 28%).

As recently as 1960, more young children lived with a widowed than a divorced parent, but now far more live with a divorced parent than with a widowed parent. This shift has resulted from both a declining mortality rate for young mothers and a vast increase in the divorce rate.

A continuing larger proportion of Black than other children under age 18 live apart from either parent. According to the 1980 U.S. Census, the figures were 4.5% for all races and 11% for Blacks. About two-thirds of the children resided with relatives, the rest with foster parents or in institutions, and about two-thirds of the relatives were grandparents. In many cases, the children were left in the care of older relatives while the mothers—being younger, better educated, and more employable—went elsewhere to increase the opportunity to earn a living.

As a noteworthy sidelight, census data show that young boys are more likely than young girls to be living in homes where fathers are present. In 1992, there were 110 boys for every 100 girls under 18 years of age in Black families maintained by a father and mother; the corresponding ratio for families with a lone mother was only 102 to 100, whereas that for lone fathers was 134 to 100. In families of divorced mothers, the ratio was only 98 boys to 100 girls. (Corresponding data for families of divorced fathers are not shown because of the small numbers involved.) The results are similar for children in families of all races combined. Evidently, marriages are more likely to remain intact if boys are present, and divorced mothers are more likely to be willing to remarry (or are more likely to be asked to remarry) if they have custody of sons rather than daughters. Studies show that boys tend to be harder to rear than girls, and at least for that reason divorced mothers of young sons usually have a special need to remarry, just as married mothers of young sons have a need to remain married.

A rapidly increasing but still small proportion of Black children live in the suburbs of metropolitan cities. Between 1980 and 1992 the number of suburbanites increased nearly twice as fast for the Black population as for persons of all races (64% versus 35%). In 1992, however, only 30% of the Black population, compared with 49% of the entire U.S. population, lived in metropolitan suburbs.

The median age of Black children under age 18 decreased by about 1 year between 1980 and 1992, as more women were marrying later and having children they had delayed until after they gained some work experience.

Young Adults Leaving Home

The departure of young adults from the parental home generally occurs during the late teens or early 20s and is a critical period for all concerned. In 1940, just at the end of the Great Depression, 32% of the Black population aged 18 to 29 still lived in the parental home or had returned there. In 1960, near the end of the baby boom, 31% of Black youths lived with their parents. But in the next decade, the trend turned upward and has continued to rise. In 1970 the figure increased to 40%, and by 1992 it stood at 41%, well above the proportion of 36% for all races. The trend toward late departure from (or return to) the parental home has occurred among young adults of all races and is attributed, among other things, to relatively high rates of unemployment, divorce, and unmarried parenthood, as well as to delayed marriage while young people attend the rapidly growing number of community colleges near their homes (Glick and Lin 1986).

Childbearing and Childlessness

After young adults leave home, most of them eventually marry, establish their own homes, and begin childbearing. Historically, Black families have had more children than other families, but there are signs that the average number of children born to mothers in the two groups may be converging. This assertion is based in part on answers received by the U.S. Census Bureau from women about how many children they had already borne and how many more they expected to have. In 1987, among women 18 to 34 years of age, regardless of marital status, Black women had given birth to an average of 1.4 children, 27% higher than the average of 1.1 children for women of all races combined, but the average "lifetime births expected" by Black women was 2.0 children, or 5% lower than the average of 2.1 for all women. Incidentally, an average of 2.1 children per woman will reproduce the population from one generation to the next, aside from any net immigration.

Other evidence of a somewhat larger decline in the fertility of Black women than other women is found in the results for women whose childbearing is nearly completed. Thus between 1969 and 1987, the average number of children ever born to Black women age 35 to 44 declined by 1.2 children, from 3.8 to 2.6 children, whereas for women of all races the decline was 1.0 child, from 3.1 to 2.1 children. These findings indicate that the overall rate of childbearing among this age group in 1987 was about enough to replace the population, regardless of race.

Poorly educated Black women tend to have more children than do their counterparts of other races, but highly educated Black women have about as few children as those of other races. In 1987, for example, Black women aged 35 to 44 with fewer than 12 years of schooling had borne 3.6 children, on the average, compared with 2.9 children for comparable women of all races; for college graduates the figures were 1.8 children for Black women and 1.6 for all women. Thus, at the higher educational level, the average family size for the two groups has almost completely converged.

Childlessness, another measure of fertility, generally varies conversely with the birthrate, and it has declined sharply in the United States during the last quarter of a century. In 1960, among women 35 to 44 years old, who thus had borne most of their children before the baby boom, fully 22% of the Black women had given birth to no children; for women of all races the figure was 13%. By 1987 the childlessness rate for this age group had declined dramatically, to only 11% for Black women and 16% for women of all races. These women had been at the crest of their childbearing during the transition from the baby boom to the baby bust. Viewing childlessness from another angle, when women 18 to 34 years of age in 1982 were asked by the U.S. Census Bureau how many children they had borne and how many more they anticipated, 10.1% of Black women reported that they expected no more, slightly higher than the 9.6% for women of all races. Therefore, with respect to childlessness to date and expected in the future, some trends for the two groups not only have converged but also appear to be crossing over.

Family and Nonfamily Households

A family household is maintained by a head who shares the living quarters with at least one relative. A nonfamily household contains no relatives. The numbers of nonfamily households have been growing much more rapidly than have the numbers of family households because of such factors as delayed marriage, which postpones the establishment of married-couple households; more women surviving their husbands and living alone; divorce that results in one-person households; and cohabitation (Glick and Spanier 1980; Glick 1984).

About 3 of every 10 households in 1992, regardless of race, were of the nonfamily type. The vast majority consisted of people who lived alone and these were divided about evenly among never-married, separated or divorced, and widowed persons. Nearly all the rest were informally cohabiting couples.

Between 1970 and 1985, the number of unmarried couples of all races increased from 0.5 million to 2.0 million; it reached 3.3 million in 1992. These unmarried couples are termed POSSLQs by the U.S. Census Bureau, that is, "persons of the opposite sex sharing living quarters." According to the 1980 census, among the nation's 1.8 million cohabiting couples, roughly one-third (0.6 million) were households maintained by Black adults (U.S. Bureau of the Census 1985). Among all couples (married and unmarried combined), 7.7% were unmarried Blacks, compared with 3.4% of unmarried couples of all races. Another way of showing the relatively heavy concentration of this living arrangement in the Black population is to point out that 16.5% of all unmarried couples in 1980 constituted households maintained by Black adults, far higher than the figure of 6.8% for all married Black couples.

In 1980, the proportion of interracial unions was especially large among cohabiting couples. In couples with a Black man and White woman, 27% were not married to each other; for couples with a White man and Black woman, the corresponding figure was 21%.

Because of the sharp increase during recent decades in households with one parent, one person, or an unmarried couple, only 43% of the Black population in the United States lives in households maintained by married couples; the corresponding fraction for persons of all races is significantly higher, about two-thirds. The most common living arrangement in the United States is a household containing a married couple and one or more children under age 18; one of every three Black persons, compared with three of every five persons of all races, was living in this type of home in 1992.

Marriage and Divorce

Changes in marriage and divorce are reflected in marital status trends, and each marital status category is dominated by a particular age range. Consequently, the following treatment focuses on the most relevant age group in each category.

Delay of Marriage

Young adult Blacks consistently postpone marriage longer than young adults of all races. A sharp increase occurred between 1970 and 1992, as shown in Table 7.3, in the percentage of persons in their 20s who had never married. The median age at first marriage for both men and women falls in these years. From 1970 to 1992, the proportion of those never married increased by three-fifths for young men in their 20s and doubled for young women, regardless of race. By 1992, 76% of Black men in their 20s and 70% of the Black women in that age group had never married. The figures for young adults of all races were distinctly lower, 63% and 49%, respectively. Contributing factors include continued high unemployment rates, especially among Blacks seeking their first permanent jobs; more time devoted to education; more persons opting for cohabitation; and the effects of a phenomenon called a "marriage squeeze" (Glick and Norton 1979).

The first marriage squeeze resulted from the upturn in births during the late 1940s and 1950s and the tendency for young men to be 2 or 3 years older than the women they marry. Thus a woman born in 1947, when the birthrate had risen, was likely to marry a man born in 1944 or 1945, when the birthrate was still low. Accordingly, about 20 or 25 years later, there was an excess of women of marriageable age, and this situation persisted for those born throughout the baby boom. Here, the marriageable age for men is considered to be 18 to 27 years; for women, 16 to 25 years. In 1970, only 74% of Black men compared with Black women fell in these age groups. By 1980, the ratio had risen to 80 and by 1990 to 98. Those born during the baby bust are currently experiencing a reversal of the marriage squeeze; by 1995 there were 102 Black men for every 100 Black women in this age range. Whereas the earlier marriage squeeze made it difficult for Black women to marry, the future marriage squeeze will make it harder for Black men. The ratios for young adults of all races are considerably higher because a smaller percentage of Black births are boys and because young Black men are undercounted to a greater extent than are other men in censuses and surveys.

Separation and Divorce

Since 1970, there has been not only a delay of marriage but also an acceleration in the extent of marital disruption, defined as separation or divorce. As seen in Table 7.3, the level of disruption is much higher for Black women than for Black men. In fact, more women than men of all races are reported as separated, although the numbers should be the same. One likely reason for this is that many women who have had births and who have never married incorrectly report themselves as separated. Separation has been increasing less rapidly than divorce, however, apparently because more

TABLE 7.3 Marital Status of the Noninstitutional Population in Selected Age Groups by Race and Sex: United States, 1992, 1980, and 1970

Marital Status, Age, and Race	Men			Women		
	1992	*1980*	*1970*	*1992*	*1980*	*1970*
Percentage never married, 20-29 years old						
All races	63	51	39	49	37	25
Black	76	62	44	70	53	34
Percentage separated or divorced, 25-34 years old						
All races	9	9	5	14	14	8
Black	10	13	9	17	28	20
Percentage in intact marriage, 35-44 years old						
All races	70	81	84	69	84	79
Black	52	61	69	41	49	58
Percentage widowed, 55 years old and older						
All races	10	9	11	36	37	38
Black	18	14	16	43	45	44

SOURCE: U.S. Bureau of the Census (1972, 1981b, 1992a).

separated persons have been dissolving their marriages by divorce so that they can remarry or at least "make a clean break."

The "divorce ratio" shows how many divorced persons there are for every 100 people in intact marriages. In 1992, there were 31% as many Black divorced persons as Black married persons: 23% for men and 39% for women. These ratios are extremely high, far above those for all races: 13% for men and 18% for women.

The likelihood of divorce is negatively correlated with income for men and positively correlated for women, regardless of race. Evidently, relatively affluent men not only are less likely to become divorced but also, if they do, are more likely to remarry rather quickly. In contrast, relatively affluent divorced women tend to be more deliberate about remarrying, and when they want to remarry they are likely to find that most of the desirable men are already married or remarried.

Women with incomplete college educations are more likely than those in any other education group to be divorced before they reach middle age. Many of these women started toward the goal of a full college education but, because of adverse circumstances, did not achieve it. Those with graduate school training also have a rather high probability of divorce. Women with advanced college degrees are most often absorbed in career interests that compete with the desire to maintain a permanent marriage.

Intact Marriages

As marital disruption has become more frequent, the proportion of persons with intact marriages at midlife has declined. Both this trend and racial differentials accelerated during the 1980s, as is evident from the data in Table 7.3 for persons 35 to 44 years old. Regardless of the trend, men with high income levels are more likely to continue in their first marriages. This phenomenon is strongest at the lower end of the income distribution, apparently implying that marital permanence for men depends less on their being well-to-do than it does on their not being poor. Among men in 1980 who had both the highest educational level and the highest income level, there was no significant racial difference with respect to the proportion still in their first marriage at the age of 45-54 years.

The pattern for women is different. Those with high earnings are generally less likely, regardless of race, to be in an intact first marriage by middle age. Married women with high incomes may find that the demands of work interfere with their marital adjustment, and the situation may be the worst for that one-sixth of wives who earn more than their husbands, although there is evidence that men are becoming increasingly tolerant of their wives' having the higher income.

The extent to which marital stability has been affected by changes in the proportion widowed after the mid-50s is very slight (Table 7.3). At that period in life, widowhood continues to be much more prevalent among women than among men, largely because of lower death rates for women and higher remarriage rates for men, regardless of race.

Remarriage

Black persons who remarry after divorce are less likely than persons of all races to do so at the usual age, that is, between 25 and 44. According to the 1980 census, Black persons with a partial high school education are the most unlikely to remarry. Specifically, among Blacks who had ever been married and were high school dropouts, only 14% of men and women age 25 to 44 years had remarried. This compares to figures for all races of 21% for men and 25% for women. These data are consistent with the findings of Eckhardt, Grady, and Hendershot (1980) that the proportion of divorced persons who remarry is lower among Blacks than Whites at each age interval after divorce.

Teenage marriage, regardless of race, is much more likely than marriage at a more mature age to be associated with divorce followed by remarriage within 5 to 10 years after the first marriage. In fact, the likelihood is twice as great. Here, "a more mature age" refers to 20-24 years for women and 25-29 years for men. These ages include the period when college graduates are most likely to marry.

One 1980 study demonstrated that remarriage is more likely to be followed by redivorce among Black women age 35 to 44 than among women of all races of the same age (Glick 1980). It also showed that Black women this age with no young children were more likely to become redivorced than were those with children, especially preschoolers. This may reflect the greater ease with which childless women, compared with mothers, can be self-sustaining.

Interracial Marriage

At the time of the 1980 census, 1,012,000 interracial couples were reported in which both the husband and the wife were in their first marriage. This was three times as many as the 330,000 reported in 1970 and six times as many as in 1960. Some of this phenomenal increase may have resulted from more willingness to report accurately, but it also may reflect a growing acceptance by young adults of interracial marriage as a tolerable lifestyle, especially among the better educated. The 121,000 Black-White couples in 1980 (both married once) were almost twice the 65,000 in 1970. Three-fourths (78%) of these couples in 1980 involved a Black husband and a White wife, compared with two-thirds (63%) in 1970. Although the Black-White married couples in 1980 represented 3.4% of all Black couples, they represented only 0.3% of all White couples. Incidentally, intermarriage was much higher for other racial groups than for Blacks: Half of Native American first marriages were mixed; for Japanese wives the figure was 40%; for Chinese, 10%; and for Filipinos, 23%.

Interracial married couples have a greater probability of disruption than do same-race couples, whether Black or White. Heer (1974) analyzed 1970 census data for first marriages contracted in the 1950s that were still intact in 1970. The results showed that 90% of the White-White couples and 78%

of the Black-Black couples were still together. Much smaller proportions of the interracial couples had continuing marriages: 63% of the couples with a Black husband and a White wife, and only 47% of the couples with a White husband and a Black wife. Comparable figures from the 1980 census on first marriages during the 1960s that were still intact in 1980 show the same pattern, but the proportions are smaller: White-White 79%, Black-Black 68%, Black-White 58%, and White-Black 44%. Evidently, Black-White couples account for more and longer interracial marriages than do White-Black couples.

Education, Employment, and Income

In this final major section, I present information about education in terms of children and the extent of their parents' schooling. Data about employment focus on wives and mothers. Regarding income, the units examined are primarily families, by type.

Education of Parents

The great majority of young children live with parents who are less than 45 years old. Moreover, nine-tenths of Black families maintained by adults of this age have children under age 18 in the home. It may come as a surprise that in 1992, 33% of these children had a parent with at least one year of college training (see Table 7.4), a far higher figure than in 1970 and half again as high as in 1980.

For Black children under age 18 in one-parent families, it is significant to note that the proportion of parents who had not completed high school declined by nearly one-fifth between 1980 and 1992. The proportion of parents who had finished at least some college education increased at a much higher rate, by about one-half. Therefore, it is correct to infer that Black children live with parents who are much better educated than just a few years ago, and the rate of improvement in the parents' education has been much higher than that of other parents. Nevertheless, the average educational level of Black parents is still substantially lower than that of parents of all races combined. The gap has been narrowing, but differences still persist.

Another area of racial difference is found in the gap between the educational attainment of husbands and wives. Specifically, Black women are

TABLE 7.4 Years of School Completed by Parents Under Age 45 of
Noninstitutional Children Under Age 18 by Type of Family and Race:
United States, 1992 and 1980

Family Type and Parent's Education[a]	*All Races*			*Black*		
	1992	*1980*	*% Change 1980–1992*	*1992*	*1980*	*% Change 1980–1992*
All children in families						
Total under 18 (000s)	51,310	46,102	—	7,418	6,369	—
Percentage	100	100	11	100	100	17
Parents' education						
0-8 years	5	9	–34	3	11	–70
9-11 years	12	15	–10	22	28	–10
12 years	37	40	3	43	41	20
13-15 years	25	17	62	23	15	86
16 or more	21	19	20	10	5	110
Children in families of lone mothers						
Total under 18 (000s)	11,448	8,624	—	4,177	3,344	—
Percentage	100	100	33	100	100	25
Mother's education						
0-8 years	7	12	–25	3	12	–68
9-11 years	23	26	13	28	33	5
12 years	38	41	25	44	39	40
13-15 years	24	15	119	21	13	107
16 or more	8	6	76	4	3	78

SOURCE: U.S. Bureau of the Census (1981a, 1993).
a. Years of school completed by fathers under age 45 in families with a male householder and by mothers under age 45 in families with a female householder.

more likely than other women to be married to men with less education than
the wife. This situation is exaggerated among women in their second and
subsequent marriages (Spanier and Glick 1980) and is related to the much
smaller proportion of Black husbands than other husbands who are college
educated. Again, this differential has been decreasing.

Working Wives and Mothers

Most Black husbands as well as husbands of other races are in the labor
force, but an increasing proportion of men have been retiring at earlier ages.
Thus 84% of Black husbands were in the labor force in 1970, but the figure

was 77% in 1992 (U.S. Bureau of the Census 1973a, 1993). For husbands of all races the rate dropped from 86% in 1970 to 78% in 1992.

The labor force participation rate for wives of all races has been increasing, with that for Black wives continuing to be especially high. Between 1969 and 1993, the rate for Black wives rose from 51% to 66%, compared with a rise from 40% to 59% for wives of all races. The worker rate for divorced women remained higher than for married women, but the 70% for Black women in 1984 was not quite as high as the 74% for women of all races. The growth in the proportion of women in the labor market reflects many social and economic changes, including the decline in the birthrate, the improved educational level and therefore employability of women, and more opportunities for clerical and professional employees.

Wives with no children under age 18 have continued to account for a high and increasing percentage in the labor force. In 1984, childless Black wives had a participation rate of 54%, a few points above the 47% for childless women of all races. Likewise, Black married mothers had a higher worker rate than all married mothers, 70% versus 59%, but childless divorced women had the highest rates of all, 80% for Black divorcees and 85% for divorcees of all races. Meanwhile, the unemployment rate for Black fathers in 1984 was much higher than for fathers of all races, 13% compared with 9%. The especially high jobless rate and the relatively low average educational level of Black fathers no doubt discourage many from even looking for work.

Family Income

Changes in family income by race during recent years have been profoundly affected by the shift in family types as well as by the higher proportion of wives in the labor force. This generalization can be verified through examination of the rows at the bottom of Table 7.5. The median income of Black families in 1991 was 60% as large as that for families of all races, still quite low and even lower than the 64% in 1969 (U.S. Bureau of the Census 1970, 1992b). For three of the four types of families shown in the table headings, however, there was an appreciable improvement between 1969 and 1991 for Blacks compared with all families. One of the greatest improvements since 1969 has occurred for Black families with the wife in the paid labor force; in 1991 the median income of these families was 86% as large as that for families of all races, compared with 79% in 1969.

TABLE 7.5 Median Family Income by Type of Family and Race for Selected
Years (income in 1991 dollars)

Year and Race	All Families	Married Couple, Wife in Paid Labor Force	Families, Wife Not in Paid Labor Force	Male Householder, No Wife Present	Female Householder, No Husband Present
All races (percentages)					
1992	100	47	32	4	17
1980	100	40	42	3	15
1970	100	34	53	2	11
Black (percentages)					
1992	100	32	16	6	46
1980	100	33	23	4	40
1970	100	36	32	4	28
Median annual family income ($)					
All races					
1991	35,939	48,169	30,075	28,351	16,692
1979	36,051	45,758	32,589	30,936	18,185
1969[a]	32,608	40,200	30,693	28,830	16,669
Black					
1991	21,548	41,353	20,288	24,508	11,414
1979[a]	21,302	37,775	21,303	22,850	12,635
1969[a]	20,945	31,575	19,400	21,512	11,549
Black as % of all races					
1991	60.0	85.8	67.5	86.4	68.4
1979	59.1	82.6	65.4	73.9	69.5
1969	64.2	78.5	63.2	74.6	69.3

SOURCE: U.S. Bureau of the Census (1973, 1980a, 1992b, 1993) and unpublished Current Population Survey data.

An important factor to note is that a much larger proportion of Black wives than wives of all races work year-round and full-time (48% versus 32% in 1984). Moreover, the median income of these Black women in 1984 ($14,700) was almost as high as that for all wives ($15,100). Perhaps surprisingly, the median income of all Black wives in 1984 was actually 14% higher than that of all wives regardless of race ($8,500 compared with $6,600). In contrast, Black men were less likely to work full-time and had lower average wages than other men. These are among the reasons the median income of families with the wife in the paid labor force in 1991 was "only" 86% as high for Black families as for families of all races in 1979.

Incidentally, according to census data for 1979, Black wives had incomes the same as or greater than those of their husbands in 25% of the families, compared with 15% for wives of all races (U.S. Bureau of the Census 1980a). By 1984, the latter figure was 18% (U.S. Bureau of the Census 1986d).

The net effect has been a substantial increase in the relative income position of Black families of most types since 1969, despite a moderate decrease in the position of Black families as a whole. Nonetheless, the income level for Black families remains comparatively low for each family type. A much fuller exposition of this situation is presented in U.S. Bureau of the Census (1980b, chap. 9).

The poverty rate for Black families in 1990 was 32%, somewhat above the 28% rate in 1973. During the same period, the poverty rate for all families increased from 9% to 12% (U.S. Bureau of the Census 1992c). Accordingly, the poverty rate has continued to be about two or three times as high for Black families as for all families. Again, a prime reason is the higher poverty rate for the increasing proportion of Black families maintained by a woman with no husband in the home. Even though the poverty rate for Black families has been quite high during the past two decades, it was much higher in 1959: 48% for Black families of all types combined and 65% for families maintained by Black women. Comparable rates for families of all races were much lower—19% and 43%, respectively.

Per capita income is a measure that assesses the relative income standing of different population groups at least partially independent of the type of family structure. Information for 1991 shows that the average income per Black person in the noninstitutional population was $8,912, compared with $14,474 for all races, making per capita income for the Black population 62% of that for persons of all races. In 1970, the corresponding figure was 60%, implying little change in the gap by race for this measure.

Child support and alimony are also important aspects of family income in an era when a large proportion of women are divorced and three of every eight of them have children under age 18 in the home. In 1989 only 35% of the Black women who had sole custody, compared with 58% for similar women of all races, were awarded child support payments, and a smaller proportion of the Black women granted such payments actually received them (two-thirds compared with nearly three-fourths). For custodial mothers regardless of race, the amount of child support received constituted about 25% of their total income, and those who received payments averaged a larger total income than those who received none. This fact is no doubt related to the husbands' income level and the effectiveness of mothers in obtaining the payments awarded to them. Only about 11% of Black women in 1989 were awarded alimony at the time of divorce, and about four-tenths of them actually received it.

Discussion

This chapter represents an attempt to add to the growing number of "works on Black families that tend to view them from a positive rather than a negative perspective" (Wilkinson 1978, p. 707). From a balanced viewpoint, Black families are regarded as "an important subculture of American society, different in many ways from White families, but possessing a value system, patterns of behavior, and institutions which can be described, understood, and appreciated for their own strengths and characteristics" (Peters 1978, p. 655).

A strength, as well as a liability, prominent among Black families is "the centrality of children," to borrow an apt expression from Cazenave (1980). As Table 7.1 demonstrates, a larger proportion of Black families than families of other races include young children among their members. Another distinguishing feature of Black families is the large and continually growing proportion maintained by women. These characteristics have been interpreted, in part, as adaptations to the special circumstances in which many Black persons find themselves and, in part, as preferences for certain values that often differ from those of members of other races. Yet Black families vary widely in the personal and social characteristics of their members; moreover, because of differing circumstances or matters of choice, Black family members tend to be concentrated in selected parts of the range of these characteristics relative to family members of other races.

Some of the apparent differences between Black and other families are probably the result of unequal amounts of misreporting in censuses and surveys on such subjects as the presence of the husband in the household. Most likely, many poor couples, regardless of race, yield to the temptation to report that the husband is absent if they believe that doing so will improve their chances of receiving welfare benefits; if such reporting is more likely to occur among Black families, at least part of the reason is that so many

Black families are poor. Also, Black husbands are more likely than other husbands to live apart from their wives due to serving in the armed forces or because of incarceration.

Some signs of diminishing differences between Black and other families also deserve attention. For example, even though a larger proportion of Black children live in one-parent families, the rate of increase has been less rapid since 1970 than among children of other races. Therefore, this gap has been narrowing. Other tendencies toward convergence since 1970 include the more rapid increase in the average educational level of Black women compared with other women who maintain homes and the more rapid increase in the (generally lower) median incomes of Black families compared with other families of three of the four types shown in Table 7.5. In some respects these developments are evidence that Blacks have "managed to sustain their families under pressures that are now being shared by a growing number of non-Black families" (McAdoo 1978, p. 776).

Many of the racial differences in family characteristics persist but are demonstrably smaller within socioeconomic levels than they are for all levels combined. If racial differences in socioeconomic stratification should diminish during coming years, one might reasonably expect that more of the residual differences in family characteristics will become matters of choice to fulfill aspirations rather than necessary to cope with unique problems of adjustment.

References

Cazenave, N. A. 1980. "Alternate Intimacy, Marriage, and Family Lifestyles Among Low-Income Black Americans." *Alternative Lifestyles* 3(November):425-44.

Eckhardt, K. W., W. R. Grady, and G. E. Hendershot. 1980. "Expectations and Probabilities of Remarriage: Findings From the National Survey of Family Growth, Cycle 11." Unpublished manuscript.

Glick, P. C. 1980. "Remarriage: Some Recent Changes and Variations." *Journal of Family Issues* 1(4):455-78.

———. 1984. "American Household Structure in Transition." *Family Planning Perspectives* 16(September/October):205-11.

Glick, P. C. and S. L. Lin. 1986. "More Young Adults Are Living With Their Parents: Who Are They?" *Journal of Marriage and the Family* 48(1):107-12.

Glick, P. C. and A. J. Norton. 1979. "Marrying, Divorcing, and Living Together in the U.S. Today." *Population Bulletin* (February):1-41.

Glick, P. C. and G. B. Spanier. 1980. "Married and Unmarried Cohabitation in the United States." *Journal of Marriage and the Family* 42(1):19-30.

Heer, D. M. 1974. "The Prevalence of Black-White Marriage in the United States, 1960 and 1970." *Journal of Marriage and the Family* 36(2):246-58.

McAdoo, H. P. 1978. "Factors Related to Stability in Upwardly Mobile Black Families." *Journal of Marriage and the Family* 40(4):761-76.

Norton, A. J. and P. C. Glick. 1986. "One-Parent Families: A Social and Economic Profile." *Family Relations* 35(1):9-17.

Peters, M. F. 1978. "Black Families: Notes From the Guest Editor." *Journal of Marriage and the Family* 40(4):655-58.

Spanier, G. B. and P. C. Glick. 1980. "Paths to Remarriage." *Journal of Divorce* (Spring):283-98.

U.S. Bureau of the Census. 1970. "Income in 1969 of Families and Persons in the United States." *Current Population Reports,* Series P-60, No. 75. Washington, DC: Government Printing Office.

———. 1971. "Household and Family Characteristics: 1970." *Current Population Reports,* Series P-20, No. 218. Washington, DC: Government Printing Office.

———. 1972. "Marital Status." In *1970 Census,* 11:4C. Washington, DC: Government Printing Office.

———. 1973a. "Employment and Work Experience." In *1970 Census,* 11:6A. Washington, DC: Government Printing Office.

———. 1973b. "Persons by Family Characteristics." In *1970 Census,* 11:4B. Washington, DC: Government Printing Office.

———. 1980a. "Money Income and Poverty Status of Families and Persons in the United States: 1979." *Current Population Reports,* Series P-60, No. 125. Washington, DC: Government Printing Office.

———. 1980b. *Social Indicators III.* Washington, DC: Government Printing Office.

———. 1981a. "Household and Family Characteristics: March 1980." *Current Population Reports,* Series P-20, No. 366. Washington, DC: Government Printing Office.

———. 1981b. "Marital Status and Living Arrangements: March 1980." *Current Population Reports,* Series P-20, No. 365. Washington, DC: Government Printing Office.

———. 1984. *Statistical Abstract of the United States: 1985.* Washington, DC: Government Printing Office.

———. 1985. "Living Arrangements of Children and Adults." In *1980 Census,* IIB. Washington, DC: Government Printing Office.

———. 1986a. "Child Support and Alimony: 1983." *Current Population Reports,* Series P-23, No. 148. Washington, DC: Government Printing Office.

———. 1986b. "Household and Family Characteristics: March 1985." *Current Population Reports,* Series P-20, No. 411. Washington, DC: Government Printing Office.

———. 1986c. "Marital Status and Living Arrangements: March 1985." *Current Population Reports,* Series P-20, No. 410. Washington, DC: Government Printing Office.

———. 1986d. "Money Income of Households, Families, and Persons in the United States: 1984." *Current Population Reports,"* Series P-60, No. 151. Washington, DC: Government Printing Office.

———. 1992a. "Marital Status and Living Arrangements: March 1992." *Current Population Reports,* Series P-20, No. 468. Washington, DC: Government Printing Office.

———. 1992b. "Money Income of Households, Families, and Persons in the United States: 1991." *Current Population Reports,"* Series P-60, No. 180. Washington, DC: Government Printing Office.

————. 1992c. *Statistical Abstract of the United States: 1992.* Washington, DC: Government Printing Office.

————. 1993. "Household and Family Characteristics: March 1992." *Current Population Reports,* Series P-20, No. 467. Washington, DC: Government Printing Office.

U.S. Bureau of Labor Statistics. 1984. "Working Mothers Reach Record Number in 1984." *Monthly Labor Review* (December).

Wilkinson, D. Y. 1978. "Toward a Positive Frame of Reference for Analysis of Black Families: A Selected Bibliography." *Journal of Marriage and the Family* 40(4):707-8.

Willie, C. V. 1970. *The Family Life of Black People.* Columbus, OH: Charles E. Merrill.

Upward Mobility Across Generations in African American Families

HARRIETTE PIPES McADOO

The challenge of being of African descent and attempting to reach and maintain a comfortable middle-class existence has affected family life for many generations. Scholars who earlier examined these families include W. E. B. Du Bois (1903), E. Franklin Frazier (1939), and Gunnar Myrdal (1944). Though small in number, middle-class African American families have existed for many generations. They have existed since the skilled craftsmen and -women who were freedmen were able to save enough from their own industry to buy their own businesses and homes. They also existed during enslavement when individuals were able to work and save money to buy their freedom and then establish a traditional family life. They existed among the children who were born of the union of White male and African female, who were raised in the "big house" rather than in the plantation fields, and who became a control level of individuals who existed between the White and the enslaved individuals.

Although it is true that many African Americans have achieved the education and financial security of middle-class status within the past few decades, there are middle-class families now extending into the sixth or seventh generation. They have served as role models within the African American community, and many members of these families have experienced tremendous achievement. Their influence has been widespread within self-contained residentially segregated communities. We cannot overlook these families as we view families who have come from a variety of economic backgrounds. Yet there continues to be a public perception that African Americans who are now of middle-class status are the first generation to go to college.

This chapter examines the mobility patterns of 128 African American families. Some were newly mobile based on their own efforts and the help of their extended families, others have been middle-class for two generations, and yet others have had this status for three or more generations. I will compare the similarities and differences among these families with different mobility patterns, look at the consequences of the head starts some of them had, and examine the circumstances of others that allowed them to make phenomenal progress.

Theoretical Considerations

Three theoretical considerations must be taken into account in focusing on mobility within Black families. The first relates to the disagreement within the field of Black family studies about the relative merits of African-linked cultural patterns. Some writers believe that no such links exist and that any deviations from the mainstream are the results of class, race, and poverty (Heiss 1975; Hill 1981). Existing African American family forms are thus seen as adaptations of individuals within poverty status to mainstream family structures and organization (Shimkin, Shimkin, and Frate 1978; Aschenbrenner 1973). This view is also supported by the belief that nonpoor Black families are indistinguishable from nonpoor non-Black families (Heiss 1975).

Some writers prefer to use ethnicity as a way to focus on Black families, combining class level and castelike status (Scanzoni 1971; Ogbu 1974). Others have posited that to look at class only within some cultural framework is to view the families within a vacuum, even when extensive assimilation has occurred (Herskovits 1941; Nobles et al. 1976; Sudarkasa 1980, 1993).

This last group emphasizes the cultural continuity of Black family patterns. The positions adopted by particular writers are often reflections of their academic disciplines; sociologists rely more on income and class data, and anthropologists, along with some psychologists, lean toward cultural data.

The second theoretical consideration is whether kin support networks help or hinder upward mobility. Some writers have stressed the draining aspect of such mutual aid because of the lack of support from community institutions (Pleck 1979; McQueen 1971). Most have indicated that mutual aid is essential, however, in that it extends the economic reach of all the family members (Billingsley 1992; Boyd-Franklin 1989; Hill 1971; Stack 1974; McAdoo 1978). The inherent reciprocity of the obligation requires family members to keep their resources fluid and open to the emergencies of those within the extended circle. Although this prevents individuals from focusing their resources only on the family of procreation, the assurance of available help is deemed to far outweigh the negative aspects of involvement within the kin insurance network.

The third theoretical consideration concerns whether or not extended family patterns exist only because of sheer poverty. The lack of resources for poor Blacks requires a continuation of kin helping patterns as a coping strategy. Researchers who take this point of view would expect that extended kin patterns would no longer exist for families above the poverty level. Also, they would assert that there is no basis in fact for the belief that there is some continuity between present African American families and distant African family patterns, which were lost during and after enslavement. (All of these varying views are discussed in detail in other chapters in this volume.)

Support made available to some Black families during enslavement and the decades immediately afterward resulted in certain families being given advantages or head starts over other families. Many of these same families have been able to consolidate their gains and achievements and have maintained these advantages to the present time. These were the families whose adults received or earned their freedom early, who were taught to read during enslavement (an illegal activity), who developed skills, or who acquired land or other valuable assets or attributes that gave them advantages over other families. They often were able to obtain apprenticeships, normal school education, and advanced college and graduate degrees while the vast majority of freedmen were still in rural poverty. The children and grandchildren of many of these families went on to become the leading educators, religious and civil rights leaders, and medical and scientific front-runners of the twentieth century.

Many of these skills and acquisitions were the results of the special talents and intelligence, fortunate circumstances, and intense hard work of the individuals themselves. Some advancement came from the collective efforts of entire families, who "invested" in the most talented of their youth. These extended family efforts were often the important ingredient allowing them to be upwardly mobile (McAdoo 1978; Martin and Martin 1978; Wilkinson 1987).

Other early advancements resulted from assistance provided by non-Blacks. For example, some help came from missionaries who went South to set up freedmen's schools and from persons who provided college tuition for gifted students (Haley 1976). In other instances, help was provided by White relatives who openly funded the education of their offspring or who quietly facilitated the entrance of close relatives into historically Black colleges or northern White schools. This latter group was a remnant of the miscegenation that occurred during and after enslavement.

Whatever the source of support that provided "screens of opportunity" to some families, the resulting advantages often persisted for generations (Billingsley 1968; Horton and Horton 1979; Pleck 1979). Other families had greater obstacles to overcome. They often took more than one generation to move from poverty to solid working-class status and then, in the third or fourth generation, into comfortable middle-class status (McAdoo 1978).

The transgenerational mobility patterns of African American families have ebbed and flowed along with the country's economic circumstances. Blacks as a group have made important mobility changes from the point of their arrival on the continent into this century. Significant improvements were made during the 1940s through the 1970s. Many families were able to be upwardly mobile and to enable their children to have greater opportunities. The progress toward the American dream of improved circumstances peaked and then declined during the 1980s. The 1990s brought inflation and job retrenchment that threatened the stability of all middle-class families. As we enter the twenty-first century, there are many improvements that still need to be made. Persons in the mainstream are growing fewer and older, while persons of color are becoming the dominant workers of the future (McAdoo 1995), yet their economic status is threatened (U.S. Bureau of the Census 1993).

The overall impression presented in the public media is that a growing number of Black families have become middle-class through the opportunities provided by higher education and affirmative action. Some now believe that affirmative action programs are no longer needed and that Blacks have received greater economic rewards than they deserve. In fact, the number of Black middle-class families has declined since the mid-1970s. A steady erosion has occurred in the proportion of Blacks preparing for and being employed by the traditional professions. The recessions of the mid-1970s dealt serious blows to the progress of the Black middle class while intensifying the decline in all other groups. The economic decline continued through the 1980s. College attendance decreased for Blacks, especially males. The increase in the need for technological skills, even in entry-level jobs, will make it more difficult for Black individuals and families to maintain themselves at levels of self-sufficiency and will preclude mobility into more secure status.

Patterns of Mobility in the Larger Society

Economic Mobility

The economic upward mobility of Black families has been reflected more in the attainment of family units in which two parents are present and both are in the workforce. Substantial improvements occurred during the 1960s and early 1970s in the income level, educational attainment, school enrollment, and home ownership of Black married couples. Between 1971 and 1981, the number of Black owner-occupied housing units increased 45% (U.S. Bureau of the Census 1983). This progress occurred while other groups (unmarried mothers, youth, elderly) were experiencing marked decline in this area.

Upward mobility is extremely difficult for family units composed only of women and children, regardless of race. The special stresses of single mothers are shown in the low level of professional occupations among them, probably reflecting their difficulty in obtaining advanced education and training. Earning power per family unit has decreased for Black families in relation to all other families in the United States (U.S. Bureau of the Census 1993). More people are being forced to "double up" with other family members as a result of the high unemployment rate and rising inflation. The growing underclass entrapment of Blacks, including the working poor, prevents any consideration of upward mobility (Glasgow 1980).

One Black subgroup has reached economic parity with non-Blacks of the same age group—the "golden cohort" of young male and female professionals, ages 25 to 35, who delayed childbearing and are concentrating their energies on their careers (Malveaux 1981). Those in this group are college graduates employed at salary levels equal to those of Whites. This new element has led some writers to believe that race is no longer an important element in employment for these select people who have obtained advanced education (Wilson 1978). Though racial differences are minimal now in this younger professional group, no data have yet emerged on the differential changes that may occur as the two racial groups mature and attempt to climb the occupational ladder. Initial employment and salary increases may be on a par while employees are in their early career stages, but with time, race and solidarity preference patterns are expected to become more evident as promotions, salary increases, and transfers into managerial positions are unequally distributed and continue to reinforce the older patterns built on racial group membership.

Another factor that has been proposed as a barrier to mobility of very poor families is the bifurcation of Black families into poorer and more affluent groups, with the latter moving into predominantly White urban and suburban communities (Wilson 1987). The rigidly segregated communities of the pre-1960s were closed to Blacks who had the resources to move into more affluent housing, and thus poor and wealthy Blacks lived in the same neighborhoods, attended the same schools and churches, and participated in the same Black institutions. Although their social lives were strictly segregated along economic lines, Black professionals provided resident role models for poorer individuals. Now, African American professionals, as have Whites, have moved outward from central-city areas as schools, jobs, and new residences have been developed (O'Hare and Frey 1992).

The concentration of poor Blacks within urban centers, the intensification of the impoverishment of single mothers, and the lack of exposure to persons who are attempting to be upwardly mobile contribute to the decline in middle-class families. Yet one must be careful to avoid blaming upwardly mobile Blacks for the conditions of the remaining poor. External pressures, discrimination, and changes in government policies are the forces that sap the initiative of the poor who have aspirations of upward mobility. When one examines income mobility, factors other than simple ability are obviously at play. Blacks receive a lower dollar return for their education in general and in proportion to the number of years spent in school (Schwartz and Williams 1977). Regardless of similarities in test scores, backgrounds, and amount of advanced education between Blacks and Whites, the data clearly show that employers hire and promote on the basis of race, regardless of which factors are controlled in statistical calculations (Corcoran 1977). Blacks unfailingly become victims of the job ceiling (see Ogbu, Chapter 13, this volume).

Blacks with higher levels of education and the enthusiasm of youth do not represent the vast majority of Blacks, who do not have those resources. The elimination of affirmative action programs will also truncate the career mobility of those who are fully qualified but lack opportunities to realize their full potential. Only time will tell the precise effects of such limitation.

The increasing number of single mothers has had a definite effect on the ability of Black families to move into or even to remain in the middle class. The earnings of two adults who are sharing parenting and financial support are needed for families to maintain their economic level and garner the resources needed to move into higher status. Black families have historically been more vulnerable to the external economic and policy environments and have been affected earlier than have other groups.

Marriage is becoming a minority lifestyle for many African Americans. They are delaying marriage until their late 20s and early 30s. Marriage rates have declined: Only 44% of Black adults were married in 1991, compared with 64% in 1970, according to the U.S. Bureau of the Census (1991). One major reason for the decline in marriage, first noted by Du Bois (1903) and consistently noted ever since, is the imbalance in the sex ratio. There simply are not enough men for the available women to marry (Tucker and Mitchell-Kernan 1991). This makes it difficult to form couples who can bring in the dual incomes often necessary to maintain a middle-class lifestyle. There are many reasons Blacks find it difficult to establish and maintain marital relationships in which children can be loved and encouraged to achieve (Chapman 1994).

Even when Black families have been able to achieve middle-class status, changes in government policies, technological advances, and restrictions caused by the growing national deficit have contributed to a decline in the numbers of families who are able to be upwardly mobile. The help provided by extended family and other networks of support is expected to be even more important in the near future than it has been in the past.

Educational Attainment

Educational attainment has been a traditional source of pride for African Americans. In the past, financial success often was not possible, even when high educational status was obtained. A proverb often passed on to young children is, "Education is the one thing you can have that cannot be taken away." Jobs and money may be lost, but what you learn is always in your head. Family histories are repeated of persons who escaped from enslavement and eventually, through the Underground Railroad, made their way North, where they worked at near slavery-level wages to put themselves through college and graduate school. After emancipation, they returned and opened schools or hospitals to help those who were not as fortunate. Others left their families as early as the sixth grade, for there were no classes higher than that for Negroes in many southern states, and went to the schools, such as Tuskegee Institute, that prepared them for college. They worked hard at an early age, paid for every cent of their own education, and received excellent instruction that allowed them to enroll in graduate or medical schools in the North.

Other screens of opportunity were provided by White fathers, sometimes quietly and sometimes openly, who sent their children to the Negro colleges of Fisk and Howard. White colleges such as Oberlin in Ohio and Berea College in Kentucky were open to both Blacks and Whites until the Jim Crow laws came into being. The role that the Negro colleges played in Black families' attainment of higher status cannot be overstated. Even today, more African American students are enrolled in White colleges, but more of them graduate from colleges that have always been predominantly Black.

Despite the effects of discrimination and the pall of poverty that lies over so many Black families, some have managed to acquire the needed education, skills, and achievement to become economically secure. This security is tenuous and depends, for the most part, on the good health and employment of wage earners. Successful Blacks have had to overcome the adaptive reaction to the castelike status of Blacks, which can lead to the expectation and realization of lowered school achievement, which inhibits mobility (Ogbu 1974).

Few Black families have wealth to pass on to their children. Each generation thus must re-create the mobility cycle and generate the effort necessary to succeed and move upward again. The greatest gifts Black families have been able to bestow upon their children are the motivation and the skills necessary to succeed in school.

Only through their achievements, with the support of the wider community and extended family, have individual Blacks been able to obtain the advanced education needed to move into higher-status jobs and professions. Although there are proclaimed "self-made" persons who earn high incomes, a close examination usually reveals that they had access to screens of opportunity (Billingsley 1968, 1992)—special help from relatives, teachers in segregated school systems, community groups, or mentors (Franklin 1979; Hill 1971; Martin and Martin 1978; McAdoo 1978; see also Manns, Chapter 11, this volume).

Although education for the next generation has been valued, it has often been difficult for young Black people to obtain. Life circumstances, the educational programs available, and socialization practices within Black families often make educational achievement very difficult. The coping strategies necessary for living in poor urban communities may be the very ones that interfere with a child's ability to take advantage of the opportunities within school systems (McAdoo 1981). This dissonance is particularly salient for young Black males, who often are unable to make the proper "match" between their own characteristics and the attributes that would facilitate their success in relationships with teachers and the educational system. The subtle, and sometimes not so subtle, denigration of young Black males tends to stifle their academic pursuits and channel them into sports (Rasberry 1987; McAdoo 1993). It therefore becomes more difficult for them to meet their own mobility goals. As a result, fewer Black males are now attending college than are Black females.

The difficulty that many urban Black children have in school also has been attributed to the conscious and unconscious attempts children make to maintain their identity and the acceptance of their peers, who may not be oriented toward educational attainment. Fordham and Ogbu (1986) have clearly demonstrated that in order to be accepted, bright Black children often behave in ways that ensure they are not perceived, by their peers or their teachers, as achievers. They do this to maintain their perceptions of what it is to be "Black," to avoid "acting White" or being seen as "brainiacs." Their experiences have been referred to as "cultural inversion"; that is, they give verbal support to academic achievement but avoid actual achievement behavior. These cultural frames of reference continue even when children are reared in middle-class Black homes. Often young people do not take advantage of educational and occupational opportunities owing to an unconscious fear of a loss of cultural identity. Ogbu (1986) further explains the difficulties that Blacks have in being upwardly mobile by referring to the social context of subordination they experience. This limits access to the most valued and most highly remunerative occupational positions and thus restricts mobility.

The cultural dimensions and the devaluation of the individual of color that exist in educational institutions contribute to the difficulties that Blacks encounter when they attempt academic mobility. But the greatest deterrent to college enrollment and completion, overshadowing all other factors, continues to be the socioeconomic situation of so many Black families. The continuing segregation and financial differentiation of the public schooling of Black children are only manifestations of socioeconomic pressures.

College enrollment does not give the total picture, for many Blacks are in junior colleges that do not provide the degrees and skills that allow them to be upwardly mobile. The shift in financial aid for higher education from grants to loans makes it more difficult for students to obtain advanced degrees. As noted earlier, more Blacks are enrolled in White institutions, but more of those attending Black colleges receive their degrees. More also go on to obtain professional degrees when they have earned their undergraduate degrees at Black colleges.

Geographic Mobility

Blacks have traditionally sought better economic conditions by moving from the rural South to southern cities, from the South to the industrial North, and from the mid-Atlantic and southern coastal regions to the Northeast. The present pattern appears to include the return of older workers to their native South in search of a slower pace and the movement of young workers from depressed northern cities to the Sunbelt for immediate employment. Northern urban patterns have often consisted of an urban-to-inner-suburban-to-outer-suburban movement as families search for a perceived better life and education for their children. Each wave of migrants hopes that a better economy will provide greater resources for family members. Not all are successful, but enough have been able to improve their conditions to fuel the continual search for a better place.

Moving in order to take advantage of perceived increased opportunities has continued into the present generation. Movements to new areas have often been within the sponsorship of the broader extended family. These chain migrations of geographic mobility often operate when one person moves to a new site and becomes established. This person, in turn, sponsors other relatives, friends, and church members as they relocate to the same area (Pleck 1979; Horton and Horton 1979; Boyd-Franklin 1989). Such support chains may result in the relocation of virtually entire youth cohorts of particular communities. The chain ensures that a person who moves to an area is not totally isolated and has a supportive network that can offer him or her assistance until the individual finds a niche.

Patterns of Mobility Within Black Communities

Sources of Status

E. Franklin Frazier (1939) made two divisions within the Black middle class. The first mobile group was composed of more established, well-educated, puritanical, quiet persons closely tied to the Black community. The second wave, rich as a result of industrial growth or the war economy, became the notorious "Black bourgeoisie" who believed in conspicuous consumption and placed less emphasis on education. These two groups have blended in the present-day younger and middle-aged groups, along with the newly mobile who fit neither of the earlier categories. The two older groups, however, are clearly evident in the older society of most urban centers.

The media have portrayed the African American middle class as being mostly made up of the Black bourgeoisie, but some writers believe that Frazier's views are distorted and that Black society is much more complicated than Frazier depicted it (Lawrence-Lightfoot 1994). Several forms of status demarcation have long existed within the Black community. These include the standard differentiation that comes with advanced economic, educational, and occupational status. In addition, high status is afforded those in the public entertainment and athletic fields who have recognition and high income but not necessarily the education or security of other mobile groups. Status also comes from political and community influence, such as that of elected officials. Status is sometimes given to wealthy individuals who live at the outer limits of legal activities. There are those within the community who, independent of their jobs, wield tremendous influence through leadership in church or social organizations. The Black church has provided leadership and sources of status for generations. Among both Whites and Blacks, upper-middle-class life is fraught with external trappings and status symbols (Lawrence-Lightfoot 1994). Blacks often face contradictions and divided loyalties, and they often maintain contact with family members who are from many social-economic groupings.

Skin Color Differentiations

One form of status differentiation unique to Blacks is based upon skin color, hair type, and the absence or presence of Negroid or Caucasoid facial features. This is the direct result of the internalization of mainstream society's preference for European characteristics to the denigration of African physical characteristics. It is a remnant of the period of exploitative miscegenation during enslavement and reflects the continuing sexual vulnerability of females of African descent within this century.

Groups to whom these distinctions were important became middle-class families in the same manner and at about the same time that many White families also moved into this status. Some of the families had the same appearance as African Americans who remained impoverished, but in other families miscegenation set them apart. This group often assimilated ideas about the alleged racial inferiority of the purer Africans and attempted to maintain their light skin color differentiation for generations. Yet, because of the mass miscegenation that occurred during and after enslavement, there are few African American individuals who are not a mixture of African, Native American, and European ancestry. Unfortunately, some mainstream African American families have adhered to the ancient values of racial superiority and have continued to make life more difficult for other families attempting to maintain financial security.

In the past, one route to upward mobility within Black communities was to marry a person lighter in color, for skin color was often an attribute used to establish attractiveness. This motive in mate selection was most obvious in the choice of wives by Black males who had "moved up." Skin color now is not as important a component of status, but nevertheless, some light-skinned Blacks continue to intermarry, feel superior, and prefer to socialize with those of similar appearance. Others who are very dark continue to harbor feelings of group-imposed inferiority or insecurity. This can lead to certain levels of antagonism between light- and dark-skinned Blacks (Russell, Wilson, and Hall 1992). Though diminished in importance, skin color differentiation can still be a viable, but usually unspoken, criterion of status.

Although not totally reflective of a "self-hatred" philosophy (McAdoo 1977; Cross 1987), color preference is an external representation of the castelike status of African Americans within U.S. society (Ogbu 1986). It reflects the continuing preferences of the wider society for White over Black.

A major contribution of the civil rights and Black consciousness movements was a decrease in the importance of physical appearance as an attribute of social status and upward mobility. For a time following these movements, individuals in some younger groups expressed a preference for darker over lighter skin. Within recent generations, skin color advantages have lessened as Blacks, regardless of socioeconomic status or skin color, have been able to obtain some of the benefits of higher education in a variety of settings and locations. Other than to mark a person permanently within a racial caste in our society, physical appearance is not as important a mobility criterion now as is individual achievement.

Ideally, skin color should be irrelevant to status or mobility. Despite color variations, all African Americans are met with the same devaluation and economic isolation, which can only be attributed to their African heritage.

An Empirical Examination of Upward Mobility and Extended Family Interactions in Black Families

In examining mobility patterns in a representative sample of African Americans, we looked at whether some of the traditional "strengths" of Black families actually do exist and can be empirically observed. This study also focused on whether involvement within the extended family support network is a help or a hindrance to upward mobility. Theories related to the value of support networks as a coping strategy of poverty and not of culture were directly addressed.

The primary purpose of the study was to obtain good descriptive data on upwardly mobile African American families. The secondary purpose was to test the hypothesis that certain family cultural patterns are a viable element within African American family life and remain as families move upward. One pattern selected for observation was that of extended family support networks, operationally defined as close and frequent interactions among kin and the frequent exchange of emotional support, goods, and services.

The second hypothesis tested was that active extended family support is found in all mobility patterns and is similar regardless of the length of time the family has been at its economic level, either newly mobile or middle-class for two or more generations. It was assumed that the help of the extended family is more than a mechanism for coping with poverty, and that individuals retain their cultural pattern of close involvement with kin and fictive kin when they are no longer poor.

In order to test these hypotheses and to examine some of the mobility patterns of Blacks, we selected a group of currently middle-class persons and traced with them the geographic, educational, and occupational mobility their families had followed over the past three generations. This study was designed to answer the following questions:

1. What are the characteristics and mobility patterns of upwardly mobile Black families?
2. Are currently middle-class Black families involved in extended family support patterns?
3. Are the family support patterns for those who were born poor different from those who were born middle-class?
4. Is the reciprocity inherent in support networks felt to be excessive?
5. Are family characteristics different in the three mobility patterns?

Methods

The data used to answer the preceding questions were obtained from surveys of an urban and suburban sample of middle-income Black families with school-aged children; the parents had some college education and were above the age of 25. Suburban families were randomly selected, with replacement, from a list of all Blacks living in the area. Once they were interviewed, their educational and occupational levels were matched with a comparative sample from a nearby mid-Atlantic city.

Families were interviewed for about 5 hours each. Attempts were made to control as many external variables as possible. The interviewing was done only after the questions had been field-tested twice and extensively modified to be sensitive to the race-related and personal topics covered. Each parent was interviewed by a Black, college-educated adult, the fathers by males and the mothers by females.

Because of the rigid segregation of Black communities in the past and because of the duality of Black existence, some criteria of socioeconomic status (SES) apply that are identical to those of the majority society, but unique criteria are also applied within the Black community to differentiate between higher and lower status. The stereotypical view that Blacks have only one status, low, does not recognize the diversity within the Black community.

To avoid the difficulties of applying standardized SES scales to Blacks, five different procedures were used: the modified scoring of the Hollingshead-Redlich scale, self-ratings of social class status, educational rankings, occupational rankings, and the standard Hollingshead-Redlich scale. For this report, only the modified SES, in which education is given a higher factor loading than occupation, is used. Income was obtained but not used in SES classifications because of the lower incomes of Blacks regardless of their occupations.

Results

Family Descriptions

Data were obtained from 178 domestic units with 305 parents—131 fathers and 174 mothers. Although no control was made for family type (one- or two-parent families), 28% were one-parent homes. In 93% of the families there was a nuclear structure including either one or two parents. Only 6% were extended in structure, whereas 2% were augmented—that is, non-relatives lived in the home. The average number of children per family was 2.37, consistent with the low number of children traditionally born to middle-income families. The parents' mean ages were 41 years for fathers and 37 years for mothers.

Geographic mobility was low among these parents: 85% had moved only once or never. Almost half had been born in the mid-Atlantic area, and one-fourth had been born in the South and moved North. They were the children of southern migrants to the area and had remained geographically close to their kin.

Religion continued to play an important role in the lives of only half the parents, in direct contrast to the important role of the church in the lives of their parents and grandparents. One-fourth indicated that religion had no role in their lives. There was a definite move across the three generations from the fundamentalist denominations as income increased. For example, Baptists were the largest group in all three generations, but membership declined from more than 60% in the grandparents' generation to 32% in the subjects' generation. Meanwhile, Catholic membership doubled (from 7% to 15%), and Episcopal membership tripled (from 3% to 9%).

The fathers' occupational status was high but still not commensurate with their very high educational achievement, as shown by the SES differences when the two status codings were made. The occupations of the employed mothers had much lower status than would be expected based on their education. The mobility or financial stability of these families was clearly tied to the occupation and income of the father. The maternal occupation dominance stereotype was not supported for these families. Although mothers had jobs of generally lower status than the fathers, in earlier generations the mothers' families had higher-status jobs for both male and female. The males' fathers were skilled workers, and the females' fathers held higher clerical positions.

The stereotype of the woman being better educated did not hold in the present sample. In the two-parent homes, the fathers were significantly better educated than the mothers (χ^2 [12] = 29.90, $p < .003$). When their education was compared by their status at birth, no educational difference was found between the fathers who were born middle-class and those who were born working-class. Mothers who were born working-class, however, had significantly higher educational levels than did those born into middle-class families (χ^2 [4] = 15.69, $p < .001$). In earlier generations, the mother tended to be better educated than the male. Over three generations, it appears that education of the parents peaked at the point of mobility into the middle class. Education was maintained in the second generation and began to decline in the third generation of middle-class status.

Support Network Involvement

The hypothesis that families would continue to be involved in the kin help exchange network after obtaining middle-class status was supported. Parents indicated an extensive and intensive involvement with the network. The majority tended to live within 30 miles of their family members, which facilitated interaction. They felt that it was relatively easy for them to stay in contact with their kin.

Family members were seen as the most important source of outside help. Overall, 80% of the families had reciprocal involvement with their kin. They gave and received help with child care, financial aid, and emotional support. The reciprocal obligations of the support network were not felt to be excessive and were considered part of everyday life. The pressure on the newly mobile to help kin who were less fortunate was significantly stronger than for those who were born middle-class. This was not perceived as a burden by the newly mobile, but simply as the way things are done in the family. Many mentioned that their advanced education was possible only because of family help.

When the three mobility patterns were combined into those who were born working-class versus those born middle-class, no significant differences appeared between the two social classes of origin with regard to the amount or kind of help given to or received from family members or in the attitudes about the reciprocity. The hypothesis that extended family involvement continues beyond the point of mobility was supported. Families could not maintain their status without family support, even into the third generation.

Cross-Generational Mobility Patterns

Four generations of SES were computerized for 128 of the families, going from the children of the subjects (all born middle-class) back to the subjects' grandparents. The three possible points of mobility were the three oldest generations. The mobility patterns revealed, surprisingly, that no one was able to move from abject poverty into middle-income status in just one generation. Several subjects said that they went from being poor to where they are now, but a closer examination of the data indicated that although their parents had low incomes, they had higher educational levels than expected. They would not be considered part of the permanent underclass but, rather, solid working-class but poor individuals. The original nine mobility patterns were condensed into the four shown in Table 8.1.

Pattern I: Born working-class, newly mobile. Families in the largest group represented the typical Black middle-class status. The parents were born into solid working-class families—poor but self-supporting and independent of government assistance. They were able to achieve their status through the acquisition of professional degrees that allowed them to move into higher-status jobs. Some 79% had college or professional training. As the first

TABLE 8.1 Patterns of Three Generations of Mobility

Patterns	Grandparents	Parents	Subjects	Percentage
I	working-class	working-class	middle-class[a]	62
II	lower-class[a]	working-class[a]	middle-class[a]	23
III	working-class	middle-class[a]	middle-class	6
IV	middle-class	middle-class	middle-class	9
Total				100

(Patterns III and IV bracketed together: 15)

a. Point of upward mobility.

generation to move up, they have relatives who are much poorer but with whom they keep in frequent contact.

Their parents usually had grade school or less than high school education. Their mothers tended to be better educated than their fathers. Their grandparents had grade school education, although 17% of them did attend some college. As a group, the grandparents and the parents had just a little more education than the average Black, and they were able to get solid, respectable working-class jobs.

Pattern II: Upwardly mobile in each generation. Over three generations, these families had been at three different levels. The grandparents were reared in lower-class families, and the parents in this group had the highest academic training—almost all had college or advanced degrees. Their fathers had high school and their grandparents had junior high or grade school education. Again, their mothers were better educated than their fathers: 14% had college degrees and 24% had some college training. The mobility in the second generation may have been helped a great deal by the education of the mother. Among all four patterns, this one had the highest educational, occupational, and income levels and the lowest level of stress.

Pattern III: Upwardly mobile in parents' generation. These subjects had all been born into middle-class status, whereas their grandparents had been born into working-class families. The mobility occurred in the second generation, and educational achievement had decreased in the present generation. Only 29% had graduate or professional training, compared with 63% of the fathers and 50% of the mothers in the previous generation. This group's second generation was better educated than in any of the other four patterns. In the paternal grandparents' generation, one-third of each sex had high school training. In the maternal line, the males had completed grade school, the females had finished high school, and 14% of the maternal grandmothers had graduated from college. Education clearly was a goal within these families. The small cell size for which we have three generations of information, however, limits the implications that can be drawn from this group.

Pattern IV: Middle-class over three generations. For these families, the subjects' grandparents had been middle-class, and this status had been maintained into the subjects' generation. In all, 9% of the families were in this group. A subset of this pattern, 3% of all families, had parents and grandparents who were at a higher level than they had reached. This was usually because the subjects had received less education and were earning much lower salaries than had the past two generations. Because these subjects were clearly still middle-class, they are included in this group.

An interesting finding for the three-generation middle-class group was that it had the lowest level of education—33% had college and only 9% had advanced professional degrees. The parent generation had the same level of achievement as the subjects (father, 42%; mother, 25%). They had maintained their accomplishments but had not moved beyond their parents. Grandfathers (born in the late 1800s) on both sides, however, were very well educated, even by today's standards. They were clearly upper-middle-class. In all, 60% of the paternal grandfathers and 20% of the maternal grandfathers had college and advanced degrees. A definite decline in overall status was noted for this group, for the first two generations tended to be upper-middle-class and the present only middle-class.

The Role of Dual Incomes in Mobility

Overall mobility was dependent on the education and income of the father. Because of pay inequities, however, the cross-generational data indicate that the point of mobility for the family coincided with employment outside the home of both mother and father. Mobility would not have been possible without two incomes and could not be maintained without the continued employment of both parents.

Although the level of maternal employment was high in all patterns, there were some indications that the present level of maternal employment was related to the father's ability to maintain the middle-class lifestyle on one income. More mothers worked when income tended to be low, and fewer worked when the father's income, education, and occupational status were high. When a choice was feasible, more tended not to work and to concentrate on the home and the family.

The role model provided by an employed grandmother was not a factor, for only 30% of the grandmothers worked in all of the patterns. The role model of a working mother may be a salient point for the fathers, however. For the mobility pattern in which almost all the mothers now work, the male subjects' mothers worked outside the home.

Sons born to families in which the mothers had higher-level occupations than the men currently are the highest achievers. Their motivation may be attributed, in part, to the drive of the employed mother with limited education who was able to move to a position higher than that of the subject's father.

The most important factor for the mother in deciding to work was economic necessity and the precariousness of Black middle-class families, who, because of the dearth of inherited wealth and unearned income are only one paycheck away from poverty. Despite their high educational level, Blacks' lower pay has meant they have little surplus income to invest and use to augment their earnings. Middle-class Black families are where they are because of their own efforts, not because the financial surplus of earlier generations has been passed on, as is frequently the case in non-Black middle-class populations.

Discussion

Middle-Class Decline

When the educational levels of each mobility pattern were reviewed over the generations, it was obvious that the level of education peaked at the point of mobility. The level was maintained in the second and definitely declined in the third generation of middle-class status. These families seem to pass on the major benefits achieved from one generation to the next only when they are upwardly mobile. Once mobility occurs, it is difficult to maintain the higher status. The highest levels of education, occupation, and income were found in the pattern that had been upwardly mobile for each of the three generations.

There are many explanations for this decline. First, it could be a function of a regression toward the mean in education and achievement. Second, it could be that the comparative security these families experience as the children are growing up tends to sap the motivation of youth. Third, as members of the younger generation do not feel the need to select jobs for basic survival, they may choose occupations on the basis of interest rather than financial security. Fourth, with both parents deeply involved in their jobs, they may not give their children the guidance and structure they need in order to match the academic excellence of their parents. An indulgent lifestyle may be the middle-class "dream" the parents worked so hard to give their children, but this may be the type of environment that does not reinforce the drive toward achievement. As society is not supportive of the maintenance of Black upward mobility, unless the drive to achieve remains active and sacrifices are made, status will decline, especially in the absence of inherited wealth.

Familial Social Support and Mobility

This examination of upwardly mobile patterns in Black families indicates that the education and achievement of middle-class individuals often is impossible without the support of extended family. Upward mobility, the result of professional training that leads to high-paying jobs, appears to require intensive effort by family members, and without perseverance there is a tendency for status to decline. The employment of both parents is required for initiation and maintenance of upward mobility, but maternal employment appears to lessen if the husband is able to support the family adequately on his salary. Families with only one parent are at a distinct disadvantage and find it difficult to maintain their hard-earned status. The positions held by many of the parents in the study sample were not as high as would be expected given their educations, and the racial "job ceiling" effect was evident even within the professions and for people with special talents.

The continuation of the extended family support system reflects cultural patterns that are retained after achievement of middle-class status and helps cushion the vulnerability of the African American middle class. Both factors operate within all the mobility patterns studied. The kin support network is as essential now as it was in earlier generations, for it involves cultural patterns created and retained from earlier times that are still functional and supportive of Black family life.

The combination of dual employment of both parents, support of the wider family, high achievement against many odds, and the application of the adage that "Blacks have to work twice as hard as Whites to be seen as doing normal work" seem to be the major factors in Black families' reaching middle-class status. Constant striving to provide a better life for themselves and for their children has contributed to transgenerational upward mobility among Blacks.

References

Aschenbrenner, J. 1973. "Extended Families Among Black Americans." *Journal of Comparative Family Studies* 4:257-68.

Billingsley, A. 1968. *Black Families in White America.* Englewood Cliffs, NJ: Prentice Hall.

———. 1992. *Climbing Jacob's Ladder.* New York: Simon & Schuster.

Boyd-Franklin, N. 1989. *Black Families in Therapy: A Multisystems Approach.* New York: Guilford.

Chapman, A. 1994. *Too Good Loving: The Black Male-Female Battle for Love and Power.* New York: Henry Holt.

Corcoran, M. 1977. "Who Gets Ahead: A Summary." In *Who Gets Ahead? The Determinants of Economic Success in America,* edited by C. Jencks. New York: Basic Books.

Cross, W. 1987. "A Two-Factor Theory of Black Identity: Implications for the Study of Identity Development in Minority Children. In *Children's Ethnic Socialization, Pluralism, and Development,* edited by J. Phinney and M. Rotherman. Newbury Park, CA: Sage.

Du Bois, W. E. B. 1903. *The Souls of Black Folk: Essays and Sketches.* Chicago: McClurg.

Fordham, S. and J. Ogbu. 1986. "Black Students' School Success: Coping With the Burden of Acting 'White.' " *Urban Review* 36(3).

Franklin, V. 1979. *The Education of Black Philadelphia: The Social and Educational History of a Minority Community, 1900–1950.* Philadelphia: University of Pennsylvania Press.

Frazier, E. F. 1939. *The Negro Family in the United States.* Chicago: University of Chicago Press.

Glasgow, D. 1980. *The Black Underclass: Poverty, Unemployment and Entrapment of Ghetto Youth.* San Francisco: Jossey-Bass.

Haley, A. 1976. *Roots: The Saga of an American Family.* Garden City, NY: Doubleday.

Heiss, J. 1975. *The Case of the Black Family: A Sociological Inquiry.* New York: Columbia University Press.

Herskovits, M. 1941. *The Myth of the Negro Past.* New York: Harper & Row.

Hill, R. B. 1971. *The Strengths of Black Families.* New York: Emerson-Hall.

———. 1981. "The Black Family and National Policy." Paper presented during Black History Week, University of Wisconsin.

Horton, J. and L. Horton. 1979. *Black Bostonians: Family Life and Community Struggle in the Antebellum North.* New York: Holmes & Meier.

Lawrence-Lightfoot, S. 1994. *I've Known Rivers: Lives of Less and Liberation.* New York: Merloyd Lawrence/Addison-Wesley.

Malveaux, J. 1981. "Shifts in the Occupational and Employment Status of Black Women: Current Trends and Future Implications." Paper presented at the Conference on Black Working Women, University of California, Berkeley, May 21.

Martin, E. and J. Martin. 1978. *The Black Extended Family.* Chicago: University of Chicago Press.

McAdoo, H. P. 1977. "The Development of Self-Concept and Race Attitudes of Young Black Children Over Time." Pp. 46-82 in *Empirical Research in Black Psychology,* vol. 3, edited by W. Cross. Washington, DC: U.S. Department of Health, Education and Welfare, National Institute of Education.

————. 1978. "Factors Related to Stability in Upwardly Mobile Black Families." *Journal of Marriage and the Family* 40(4):761-76.

————. 1981. "Youth, School, and the Family in Transition." *Urban Education* 16(3):261-77.

————. 1995. "African American Families and Children." *Challenge: Journal of Research on African American Men* 5(2).

McAdoo, J. 1993. "The Role of African American Fathers: Families in Society." *Journal of Contemporary Human Services* 7(1):28-35.

McQueen, A. 1971. "Incipient Social Mobility Among Poor Black Urban Families." Paper presented at the Howard University Research Seminar, Spring.

Myrdal, G., with R. Sterner and A. Rose. 1944. *An American Dilemma: The Negro Problem and Modern Democracy.* New York: Harper & Row.

Nobles, W. W., et al. 1976. *A Formulative and Empirical Study of Black Families.* DHEW Publication OCD-90-C-255. Washington, DC: Government Printing Office.

Ogbu, J. 1974. *The Next Generation: An Ethnography of Education in an Urban Neighborhood.* New York: Academic Press.

————. 1986. "The Consequences of the American Caste System." In *The School Achievement of Minority Children: New Perspectives,* edited by U. Neisser. Hillsdale, NJ: Lawrence Erlbaum.

O'Hare, W. and W. Frey. 1992. "Booming, Suburban and Black." *American Demographics* (September):30-38.

Pleck, E. 1979. *Black Migration and Poverty, Boston 1986–1900.* New York: Academic Press.

Rasberry, W. 1987. "Missing: Black Men on Campus." *Washington Post,* July 21, p. A15.

Russell, K., M. Wilson, and R. Hall. 1992. *The Color Complex: The Politics of Skin Color Among African Americans.* Garden City, NY: Anchor.

Scanzoni, J. 1971. *The Black Family in Modern Society.* Chicago: University of Chicago Press.

Schwartz, J. and J. Williams. 1977. "The Effects of Race on Earnings." In *Who Gets Ahead? The Determinants of Economic Success in America,* edited by C. Jencks. New York: Basic Books.

Shimkin, D., E. Shimkin, and D. Frate, eds. 1978. *The Extended Family in Black Societies.* The Hague: Mouton.

Stack, C. B. 1974. *All Our Kin: Strategies for Survival in a Black Community.* New York: Harper & Row.

Sudarkasa, N. 1980. "African and Afro-American Family Structure." *Black Scholar* 11(8):37-60.

————. 1993. "Female-Headed African American Households: Some Neglected Dimensions." In *Family Ethnicity: Strength in Diversity,* edited by H. P. McAdoo. Newbury Park, CA: Sage.

Tucker, B. and C. Mitchell-Kernan, eds. 1991. *The Decline of Marriage Among African-Americans: Causes, Consequences, and Policy Implications.* New York: Russell Sage.

U.S. Bureau of the Census. 1983. *America's Black Population: 1970 to 1982, A Statistical View.* Special Publication, P10/POP-83-1, July. Washington, DC: Government Printing Office.

———. 1991. "Marital Status and Living Arrangements." *Current Population Reports,* Series P-20, No. 461, March. Washington, DC: Government Printing Office.

———. 1993. *Census of Population and Housing: 1990.* Public Use Microdata Sample. Washington, DC: Government Printing Office.

Wilkinson, D. 1987. "Ethnicity." Pp. 182-210 in *Handbook of Marriage and the Family,* edited by M. Sussman and S. Steinmetz. New York: Plenum.

Wilson, W. J. 1978. *The Declining Significance of Race: Blacks and Changing American Institutions.* Chicago: University of Chicago Press.

———. 1987. *The Truly Disadvantaged: The Inner City, the Underclass, and Public Policy.* Chicago: University of Chicago Press.

Socialization Within
African American Families

Marie Ferguson Peters begins this section with a historical overview of the Black family socialization literature. She shows how early works in this field were descriptive and used a comparative deficit-oriented approach, and how more recent work has finally become more value-free in the ecological approach. In her excellent review, she points out the major contributions made by various studies and critiques the weaknesses of several noted ones. For instance, many family studies have not mentioned race; others have focused only on the mother-child relationship or have used simplistic correlation and excluded possible influences of other factors. Peters also offers critiques of different intervention methods and of the questionable research methodologies used in earlier studies. She details several key variables: protectiveness, discipline, idiosyncratic child-rearing practices, and changes in parental values. Peters's examination brings light to some of the dim concepts commonly held about socialization; she also addresses the blurring of sex-typed roles in family tasks and child-care practices of both parents and children. There have been changes in the values of parents in upwardly mobile families and in those who prepare their children for mobility through "anticipatory socialization." Peters presents the differences that do exist in

Black lifestyles within the context of the family's attempt to shield the child from a hostile environment as long as possible.

In Chapter 10, John McAdoo describes the limited literature available on Black fathers' involvement in their children's development. He provides an extensive review of stereotypes of Black fathers, the differential roles of fathers, fathers' influence on mothers, fathers' involvement in child-related decision making, interaction patterns of fathers and their children, and the expectations fathers hold for their children. He notes that the exclusive reliance on fathers' instrumental role found in the past has changed to one of greater involvement. Fathers themselves rate their companionship with their children as primary, not their instrumental role. As fathers gain more economic security, they tend to become more involved with their children. Decision making has moved from the dominance of fathers to more egalitarian sharing between fathers and mothers. McAdoo delineates authoritarian and authoritative fathering and shows that the father-child interactions of African Americans have tended to be more supportive for the achievement and independence of girls compared with boys. He also notes that the parent-child interaction is not unidirectional, but circular. McAdoo observes that the Black father's role is still not clearly understood. Fathers of all races have similar expectations for their children, but they may use different approaches to child rearing. Few ethnic differences have been found in actual parenting styles. As McAdoo points out, the reciprocal relationship between father and child has yet to be researched adequately.

Wilhelmina Manns discusses in Chapter 11 the roles played by significant others in the lives of Black families. She defines *significant others* as the persons by whom one would like to be held in high esteem and who are influential in one's life. Such significant others have been found to be components of extended family support networks, both kin and nonkin, who enable families to survive under continuing adversity. Nonrelatives are often as influential as relatives, a fact that highlights the elasticity of the extended family. Those of lower status and with few financial resources have been found to have a greater number of significant others to offset their negative life experiences. Manns notes that Black parents are important in relation to their children's achievement—lower-income parents mandate achievement, and middle-income parents provide achievement-oriented family atmosphere—but are not extensively involved in teaching as a component of their support. Parental influence lasts throughout the life cycle, with more Blacks than whites reporting having parents who are significant in these dimensions well into adulthood. Other relatives who are supportive tend to serve as models, whereas nonkin members of the support network tend to be members of structured institutions, such as the church or a community center.

In Chapter 12, Beverly Daniel Tatum addresses the situation of African Americans who live in predominantly white suburbs, who find themselves caught between the Black community and their suburban surroundings. The "assimilation blues," as described by Tatum in her 1987 book of that name, occur when Black parents decide to take their families to live in the suburbs because of the education systems and pleasant environment there. Their children are often cut off from those who value their uniqueness and who would provide them with support. Some Black suburban parents are concerned that their residential choices will lead their children to reject their African and African American heritage.

In Chapter 13, John Ogbu offers an explanation for why the educational levels of young Blacks are low, an explanation that is counter to some well-accepted theories. His main thesis is that Black youth and their educators and parents are all locked into a system based on Blacks' castelike status, a system from which there is no exit. Ogbu's work shows the futility of a nature/nurture argument for lower Black school achievement by clearly articulating the effects of being a member of a castelike minority. Black youth, upon receiving education that is often deliberately inferior to that received by whites, correctly perceive the lack of comparable payoff of advanced education and are molded by both Blacks and whites to enter and remain in lower-status positions.

Ogbu rejects as faulty the four major excuses that have been put forward for the lack of academic achievement among Blacks: home environment, school environment, genetics, and different cultural values that reinforce skills different from those utilized in school. Ogbu asserts that those who put forth these reasons have not adequately compared data and do not perceive the role that racial discrimination plays in African Americans' situation. Most theories offered to explain poor achievement, and the policies that are implemented to overcome the differences, are color-blind; they see the life experiences of Blacks and non-Blacks as alike. This is a false assumption, for Blacks and other poor minorities are unable ever to escape their castelike position. Ogbu compares the achievement of Blacks with that of other "immigrant minorities" and explains the differences that exist in their perceptions of job opportunities and thus their different motivations to prepare themselves for jobs.

Ogbu points to the collective historical experience of discrimination, the structural barriers that have a reciprocal influence on employers and on students' perceptions of their ability to get jobs. This circular interaction of perceptions and actual barriers results in a job ceiling that is obvious to youth, who then stop attempting to move out of their castes. Schools play their part in reinforcing children in the directions that will ensure they remain in their current status, making them the victims of the "double stratification of class and race caste." Ogbu's analysis is refreshing, and his arguments are free of the customary defensiveness and negative explanations that often appear in discussions of African American schooling. As a Nigerian who has been trained as an anthropologist, Ogbu may have the objectivity that many Americans lack, allowing him to analyze clearly the downward spiral within which Black youth in the United States find themselves caught.

James Jackson, Wayne McCullough, and Gerald Gurin examine in Chapter 14 the role of the family in the formation of identity and socialization among African Americans, especially in the development of children's group identity and consciousness. The family forms a buffer within the home that protects the children, gradually introduces them into the heterogeneous and often hostile society, and remains a refuge for them, as Peters also points out in Chapter 9. Jackson and his colleagues provide an extensive review of the differences between pre-civil rights and post-civil rights literature on this subject. Earlier studies related negative effects of Black identification, and all accepted the premise of self-hatred, yet they did not measure racial attitude and self-concept variables separately. Research conducted after the civil rights era has looked at the positive psychological effects of strong Black identification and has gone beyond simple measures of association. Researchers now feel that racial homogeneity within the home aids children in their personal identification of race, helps children in the compartmentalization of their private and public selves, and filters the effects of a nonsupportive environment outside the home. Children are then able to go out into the heterogeneous world and be successful. The family is seen as the mediating link between the individual's self-concept and the racial group. Jackson, McCullough, and Gurin call for the refinement of group identity theories.

Historical Note

Parenting of Young Children
in Black Families

MARIE FERGUSON PETERS

Most Black parents, like most parents in every society, socialize their children to become self-sufficient, competent adults as defined by the society in which they live. For Black families in the United States, socialization occurs within the ambiguities of a cultural heritage that is both Afro-American and Euro-American and a social system that espouses both democratic equality for all citizens and castelike status for its Black citizens. Although social scientists have appreciated the uniqueness of Blacks, research on Black children and their families has generally been simplistic and often pejorative in approach (Allen 1978; Mathis 1978).

Today, many social scientists are moving beyond the comparative, pathological approach of much of the research of the 1960s and early 1970s and are beginning to study Black families from a perspective that recognizes the cultural variations, functionality, and validity of Black family lifestyles. This research has begun to provide basic information about parenting in Black families. My purposes in this chapter are to describe briefly the history of research on the behaviors and attitudes of Black parents and to summarize the major findings concerning child rearing and the parent-child relation-ships that many families with young Black children share.

Because the topics social scientists choose to investigate and the scientific research methodologies they use reflect the prevailing philosophies and concerns of the time, research that has focused on Black mothers and fathers has changed through the years. Early research was descriptive. It was then generally replaced by comparative deficit-oriented research. Currently, much research on Black parenting and parent-child interaction employs ecologically oriented and culturally relevant approaches.

Critique of Research Approaches

For those interested in parent-child relationships in Black or other minor-ity families, a search of the literature reveals a number of methodological weaknesses and problems in many of the available studies. The most preva-lent shortcomings include the following:

1. Many studies do not specify the race of the participants. Culture-specific influences are thus ignored.

2. Research is often unidirectional: The focus is typically on mother's influence on child and does not observe child's influence on mother.

3. When the research population involves both Black and white parents, the research design, typically, compares Blacks with whites and comparative statistics are used. Rarely is the research ethnomethodological and descrip-tive.

4. Simplistic correlations often exclude the possible influences of other envi-ronmental forces. For example, in Radin and Kamii's 1965 study, it was assumed that if a child identified with a warm mother, the child's intellectual development would be positive. Yet teacher warmth was not measured, nor was the child's relationship with other adults in the family considered. The influence of kin in the lives of Black children has been well documented (McAdoo 1978; Nobles 1978; Stack 1974).

5. Researchers tend to view Black families as monolithic. Few studies incorpo-rate both lower-class and middle-class Black families in the study population. Consequently, the accessibility of lower-class families in welfare agencies or urban schools (and their concomitant absence in college communities) gen-erally influences researchers to use the all-inclusive category of race as a monolithic variable.

6. When Blacks are studied, so-called problem populations are often the focus of research—single parents; parents of emotionally disturbed, mentally retarded, or academically nonachieving or delinquent children, and/or youths; or low-income families. The majority of Blacks are ordinary American citizens not in special trouble categories, but they are typically not included in these research studies.

7. The research design used to study an all-Black population often differs from that used to study whites. When a white population is used, an investigation may be concerned with process, examining how various influences affect the subjects in the study. This central concern shifts subtly to one of intervention when a Black population is involved. The focus of research becomes *changing* the target subject to conform to the abilities and behaviors of white parents and children, and investigators are concerned with the achievement or nonachievement of this goal.

8. Studies that examine parent-child interaction and include Blacks in their samples are often conducted in unfamiliar, intimidating experiment rooms. Data are often correlated with IQ or socioeconomic status and are typically based on but one or two observations. We know that rates of parent-child interaction are much higher in laboratory settings than in the natural setting of the home.

9. The presence of an outside "expert" is often an unmeasured influence. Studies have shown that when a research study or intervention program requires visiting homes with a bag of toys and books and observing or recording parent-child interaction with these special toys/books only, mothers talk to their children more than they normally do every day.

10. The research methodology may incorporate subjective measures of the quality of home environments—based on the researcher's personal unarticulated values, such as organization versus disorganization or "quiet" home environment believed to be conducive to study versus high noise level and activity, presumed to be distracting and confusing to a child.

Descriptive Approaches

Systematic research on Black families was first approached within a descriptive framework that recognized the pressures, demands, and extreme constraints of the environment in which Blacks lived. This research essentially provided facts about Blacks and described aspects of the lives of Black families. Publishing the first sociological study of Black families in America in 1908, W. E. B. Du Bois described the social conditions of Afro-American families living in Philadelphia at the beginning of this century. He accounted for the influences of Africa and of slavery on the development of Black people. However, Du Bois said little about child rearing. Some years later, social scientist Charles S. Johnson, in his books *Shadow of the Plantation* (1934) and *Growing Up in the Black Belt* (1941), provided insightful descriptions of family life among Blacks in the South, including child rearing and socialization practices. The publications of social scientists before World War II, such as the works of historian Carter G. Woodson, together with the slave narratives collected during the 1930s, have provided a rich source of descriptive data essential to understanding Black family life today. However, during and after World War II, descriptive approaches to research on the Black family began to be eclipsed by more sophisticated research methodologies patterned after the physical sciences (see Lewin 1935). This approach reflected changing perspectives in this country regarding race.

Comparative Deficit Approaches

During the 1940s and 1950s, research was highly stimulated by the assimilation theories of two outstanding sociologists, Robert Park of the University of Chicago and Gunnar Myrdal, author of *An American Dilemma* (1944). The theories of Park and the writings of Myrdal, in assuming that assimilation of Blacks into American society was possible and probable, helped to provide a scientific basis for research that investigated why Blacks were not assimilating into American society (Lyman 1972). They articulated a rationale for comparative deficit approaches that assume Blacks are culturally deprived and view differences found between white mainstream Americans and Black Americans as deficits. Behaviors, abilities, or attitudes observed in Black mothers, it was assumed, "needed to be changed" (see Mathis 1978).

The perspectives of sociologists studying Black families, in shifting from descriptive research to comparative deficit approaches, reported findings about Black families within a Black/white comparative framework. For example, Davis and Dollard (1940), two of the first researchers to describe in detail the socialization of Black children, analyzed Black families according to class, structure, and parental roles. Comparing Black families to white families, they reported that Black mothers were more restrictive than white mothers in toilet training and more likely to employ physical punishment in disciplining their young children. In a study published 25 years later, Radin and Kamii (1965), whose innovative methodology has served as a model for much parent-child observational research, similarly provide an example of this approach. In Radin and Kamii's study, a small group (45) of "culturally deprived" Black mothers, more than half of whom received public assistance, and a small group (50) of middle-class white mothers were observed in a laboratory playroom. Their behaviors in interacting with their preschool children were compared. The finding that Black mothers often shielded their children from problems was interpreted by these researchers as "overprotective." Neither the importance of varying influences of environmental differences in the home situations nor the differential effects of the laboratory observations on the mothers were acknowledged in this interpretation of the research findings.

In many similar studies, if white mothers participated, Black mothers were compared with whites directly; if white mothers were not part of the study, the Black mothers were compared with whites indirectly and by assumption. In either case, the Black mothers were viewed negatively, as generally inferior and as unable to fulfill their responsibilities adequately.

Frazier's classic study *The Negro Family in the United States* (1939), a major source of information about Black families, provides a dramatic illustration of the comparative deficit approach. In this and other works, Frazier (1933, 1950) accurately reported findings descriptive of Black families, but interpreted the behaviors of Blacks pejoratively. He supplied a model for the study of Blacks that emphasized family disorganization and dysfunction—an approach that directly influenced subsequent research of the 1960s and early 1970s. The influential government-sponsored Moynihan report (1965) viewed Blacks' differences from whites as deficits and identified Black "matriarchal" mothers as responsible for the "breakdown" and "pathology" of Black families (which, Moynihan claimed, were responsible for high rates of illegitimacy, delinquency, and unemployment). The deficit perspective found in Moynihan's work spawned more than a decade of research that focused on improving the child-rearing practices of Black mothers, and it influenced many of the programs and policies subsequently developed for Black children and their parents.

In response to the government's "War on Poverty" efforts, a number of sociologists and psychologists turned their research interests to low-income Black families who received public assistance and who lived in public housing or in inner-city ghettos. Their findings on low-income families, although about a minority of the Black population, became generally accepted as descriptive of the family life of all Blacks in America (Hannerz 1969; Liebow 1967; Rainwater 1965; Schulz 1969). In much research Black families were viewed as monolithic and were conceptually linked to data regarding low-income families. Socioeconomic differences were often assumed to be the same as Black/white differences. This methodological weakness made it difficult, if not impossible, to unravel the "packaged variable" of class and race in much of this research (Whiting 1973). The comparative deficit perspective of most Black parent-Black child studies of this period influenced family sociology textbooks, which similarly incorporated the cultural deprivation deficit approach (Peters 1974).

Ecological Approaches

Perhaps in reaction to the negativism of the comparative deficit approach and the criticisms of many social scientists of this research emphasis (Richardson 1981), in the 1980s much research on parenting in Black families shifted to an ecological approach. Similar to the earlier descriptive research, but incorporating the more sophisticated social science theories, methodologies, and techniques of the present, researchers taking the ecological approach observe parental and child behavior within the environment in which it occurs and analyze behavior according to the value system of a family's indigenous culture or subculture.

By providing a theoretical framework for ecologically oriented research, the writings of Lewin (1935) and Kuhn (1962) had an important influence on many researchers concerned with understanding the sociological and psychological factors involved. Black families and parent-child interaction were now examined from a culture-specific or functional perspective, and the Black family's socialization of its children was considered in terms of the values and realities of its Afro-American culture.

Research findings of ecologically oriented studies have dramatically changed the picture of parenting and child behaviors of Blacks and are providing interesting, myth-destroying information. It is assumed that Black families encourage the development of the skills, abilities, and behaviors necessary to survive as competent adults in a racially oppressive society (Willie 1976), and a number of studies have investigated the characteristic, often culture-specific, child-rearing behaviors and survival mechanisms that enable Black parents to cope with everyday exigencies or with crisis situations (Gutman 1976; Hill 1971; Stack 1974).

In general, Black families are reported to be strong, functional, and flexible (Aschenbrenner 1973; Billingsley 1968; Hill 1971; Martin and Martin 1978; Scanzoni 1971, 1975; Stack 1974). They provide a home environment that is culturally different from that of Euro-American families in a number of ways (Abrahams 1970; Gay 1975; Ladner 1971; Lewis 1975; Nobles 1974a, 1974b; Young 1970). The environment of Black children is described as including not only the special stress of poverty or of discrimination but the ambiguity and marginality of living simultaneously in two worlds—the world of the Black community and the world of mainstream society, a phenomenon unique to Blacks (Willie 1976). From this perspective, Black children are seen as socialized into a dual but normal existence of being both Afro-American and Euro-American, and many ambiguities and inconsistencies are reconciled without surprise or conflict (Dixon 1971).

Approach to Discipline

Discipline techniques of Black parents have often been noted by observers of Black parent-child interaction. Although definitive studies of discipline in Black families have yet to be done, many researchers have described the Black parent's more direct, physical form of discipline, which differs from the psychologically oriented approach preferred by mainstream families, such as withdrawal of love or making approval or affection contingent on the child's behavior or accomplishment. The strict, no-nonsense discipline of Black parents—often characterized as "harsh" or "rigid" or "egocentrically motivated" by mainstream-oriented observers (Chilman 1966)—has been shown to be functional, appropriate discipline administered by caring parents (Peters 1976; Young 1970).

A recent study of discipline techniques in a sample of working-class Black families reported that mothers became more dynamic in their disciplining as their young children began to understand the appropriate behavior parents expected. Most parents emphasized obedience. However, obedience was not viewed negatively; it was an important issue, often of special significance to a parent. Parents said that they believed obedience "will make life easier for my child," "means respect," "is equated with my love," or "is necessary if my child is to achieve in school" (Peters 1981).

Socialization Toward Encouragement
of Noncompetitive Individualism

A number of researchers have commented on the high value placed on personal uniqueness in Afro-American culture. Young (1970), who studied parental behavior and child-rearing practices of Black families in a southern community during the late 1960s, noted the highly idiosyncratic interactions of mothers in the preparation of food, feeding, and toilet training of young children. Others (such as Lewis 1975; Lewis 1955) have described individualism within great interpersonal involvement of infants, children, and adults with one another. This individualism is often expressed in the way Black men and women as well as young Black boys and girls have been observed to interact with and respond to the infants and young children in the family (Lewis 1975; Young 1970).

Sex/Age Roles

Within many Black families more importance is attached to getting a job done than to the sex of the child for a task. Children's behaviors are viewed more in terms of the child's competence and age than of the child's gender. The firstborn, for example, whether boy or girl, is expected to become nurse-child to younger children in many Black families (Young 1970), and a high positive value is placed on "mothering," whether the person doing so is male or female (Lewis 1975).

Comparative Relevant Approaches

Concomitant with ecologically oriented research, comparative relevant studies have examined the child-rearing patterns of both Black and white parents with young children. This research perspective espouses cultural pluralism and uses the nonevaluative cultural variant model (Allen 1978). The comparative relevant approach observes differences in behaviors but attempts to avoid ethnocentric judgments by focusing on process and through empirical research that attempts to link parental behaviors with child outcomes. Ethnicity, race, education, and social class indicators are typically controlled.

Parent-Child Communication

There have been many studies of parent-child communication patterns of Black and white parents and of differences in the verbalization of Black children compared with white children. Investigators have analyzed the grammar and language patterns of Black and white parents and their children. Although it has been found that Black parents talk to young children less than do white parents, the significance placed on race may be misleading. Schacter's (1979) review of this literature emphasizes the importance of social class. Studies show verbal stimulation to be a major factor in distinguishing between the environments of young children from economically advantaged and economically disadvantaged homes. However, Schacter reports that "differences in total verbal production are related to maternal educational level and not to race. . . . Black mothers with educational and economic advantages speak just as much to their toddlers as do whites with similar advantages" (p. 155).

Parental Teaching Styles

Black mothers, according to Hess et al. (1968), appear to prefer two types of teaching styles, both of which have an influence on the cognitive competence of 4-year-old Black children (see also Hess 1970). One style, which Hess et al. describe as the "personal-subjective" style, is responsive to the child—his or her needs, preferences, interests, moods, stage of development. The mothers who employ this style are concerned about the orientation and preparation their children need in new situations and try to make tasks rewarding to their children. A second style is identified by Hess et al. as the "status-normative" teaching style. Mothers using this style tend to teach their children tasks or insist on certain behaviors because it is the "correct" way or because it conforms to a rule or regulation. These mothers do not generally consider the children's preferences. The differences between these two parenting styles appear to be quite similar to the differences between authoritative and authoritarian parenting styles identified by Baumrind (1972).

Hess's findings have been supported by other studies. For example, Schacter (1979) reports that educated mothers "appear to adopt a responsive communication style" (p. 65). Similarly, Carew (1976) found that the intellectual quality of the play activities created or encouraged by the mothers of toddlers correlated with their children's IQs at age 3. Clarke-Stewart's (1973) study of Black and white working-class children ages 9-18 months also found that a relationship existed between parental behaviors and children's academic abilities. The quantity of a mother's verbalization and the responsiveness, warmth, and stimulation of her interactions with her young child significantly affected the child's intellectual development and linguistic performance.

In a study of Black infants and preschool children, Andrews, Blumenthal, Bache, and Wiener (1975) found that parents differed in their interactions with their children and that their children's subsequent social and cognitive behaviors reflected these differences. A series of studies conducted by Bradley and Caldwell (1976a, 1976b, 1978) and Elardo, Bradley, and Caldwell (1975, 1977) found that measures of children's home learning environments predicted IQ scores significantly better than did the socioeconomic status variables typically used in studies of achievement or IQ. Slaughter (1978) examined linkages between parental teaching styles and children's cognitive development and play behaviors. Her findings, supporting the observations of Hess, Carew, Clarke-Stewart, and others, show a relationship between specific maternal behaviors and children's abilities and behavioral styles. Mothers in Slaughter's study were supportive and nondirective with their children. White, Kaban, Shapiro, and Attanmucci (1977) found that 1- and 2-year-old children whose caregivers talked to them a lot were developing better than children raised in less verbal environments. Zegiob and Forehand (1975) investigated interactions of mothers and their children, ages 4 to 6 years, in an experiment room equipped with toys. They found that the most significant factor in determining maternal interactive behavior was the socioeconomic status of the family. Other studies have reported similar findings.

Parental Attitudes

Zegiob and Forehand (1975) observed that many Black parents in their sample were in the process of changing their values and attitudes. As they became upwardly mobile, many began to adopt middle-class values concerning child rearing. Scanzoni (1971) has described how lower-class Black families prepare their children to be upwardly mobile via "anticipatory socialization." Thus parenting behavioral styles among Blacks may be in a state of flux. Many identify with middle-class value systems, especially when their own families are upwardly mobile.

The above-noted studies of parent-child interactions in their natural home environments provide the most reliable information available about childhood socialization in Black families. Although this research can involve only small samples, the rich descriptive data, often facilitated by audiovisual recordings, can enable us to view socialization processes in families with young children—to see what parents do, to understand why they do it, and to see the behavioral outcomes in their children.

The Impact of Race on Parenting

An inescapable aspect of the socialization of Black children in the United States is that it prepares them for survival in an environment that is hostile, racist, and discriminatory against Blacks (Bernard 1966). According to Harvard psychiatrist C. Pierce (1969), Black Americans live in a unique but mundane extreme environment of subtle to overt racism. Oppressive environmental forces influence how Black families live and raise their children (Peters 1980). Research on the socialization of Black children supports these observations.

Daniel (1975), in a study of 25 Black fathers of preschool sons, found that 19 of the fathers mentioned specifically that race had an impact on their fathering. Renne (1970) found that in Black families of all income levels, racial identity had a strong impact on the amount of protection a Black parent could provide a child. Even families with adequate income could not protect their children completely from the "irrational restrictions, insults, and degradation black people encounter in this society" (p. 62). Renne further suggests that rearing children in a white-dominated society places special pressures on the Black parent. However, as Harrison-Ross and Wyden (1973) note in their manual on child rearing for Black parents, Black parents want "to bring their children up to be comfortable with their blackness, to be secure, to be proud, to be able to love. . . . [They] want their children to grow up being and feeling equal, comfortable, responsible, effective, and at home in the world they live in" (pp. xx-xxi).

Peters and Massey (1988) describe how Black families have developed coping behaviors that enable them to deal with the racism they and their children may encounter. Black parents recognize that their children must be accepted in the Black community in order to have friends, and they must be accepted in the white community in order to survive. Parents understand the stress placed on their children when they are forced to perform better than whites in order to be recognized. Black parents "have internally developed patterns of coping with racial oppression, strategies proven to be effective in the past that are incorporated into their own socialization process" (Peters and Massey 1988, p. 3).

In her study of Black mothers of young children, Richardson (1981) found that most of the parents believed "this society places more limitations on Blacks' life chances and opportunities than on any other group of people within the society" because of racism. They agreed that "being black in this country full of anti-black feelings and/or actions (racism) presents real problems" (pp. 154-64). Their own experiences influence their decisions about how they will raise their children. In preparation for expected encounters with racism, the mothers in Richardson's study felt that it was necessary to develop high self-esteem and self-confidence in their children. Other studies of Black parenting have also reported the high priority Black parents give to developing self-esteem in their children (Peters 1976; Peters and Massey, 1988).

A number of Black parents decide not to discuss racism or discrimination with their children because they do not want them to feel bitter, resentful, or prejudiced against others (Lewis 1955). These protective parents expect that their children will discover institutional or individual racism someday, and they are prepared to help their children cope with this reality as necessary (Peters 1976, 1981). Black parents provide a buffer for the negative messages that may be transmitted to their children by a society that perpetuates stereotypical images of Black people (Ogbu 1978; Scanzoni 1971).

Summary

Researchers are beginning to learn about the socialization of young Black children and to explore how they grow and develop to become self-sufficient, competent adults in the face of the real constraints American society places on Black Americans. The lives of Black parents and their child-rearing approaches are embedded in the racial, cultural, and economic situations of Blacks in the United States. Research on parenting in Black families must reflect this reality.

Research on Black families overwhelmingly shows that the behaviors and lifestyles of Black people are different from those of whites. Their child-rearing priorities, attitudes, and patterns of behavior have developed out of the exigencies of the unique economic, cultural, and racial circumstances in which they have lived. However, because of the pervasive belief that Blacks can and should eventually assimilate into mainstream society once they learn the "ways" of white mainstream Americans, social scientists often have not recognized or been interested in the validity and functionality of the parenting behaviors Black families have developed based on the realities of survival in an environment that continues to be hostile. Instead, social scientists have frequently viewed the adaptations of Black families to the circumstances of poverty and discrimination and the subtle behavioral aspects that reflect their African heritage, where they differed from the behaviors and living patterns of whites, as the source of "their problem." Research priorities, therefore, have often emphasized educating Blacks to conform to the values and behaviors of mainstream white Americans.

Recently, however, researchers have begun describing the child-rearing patterns and socialization practices of Black parents from the perspective of their effectiveness as relevant, supportive, or practical strategies appropriate to the social realities Black people face. Mainstream America and its social scientists are becoming aware of a reality in American life that Blacks cannot, for long, forget—that this is a culturally pluralistic country and the historical roots of its multiethnic peoples are varying, valuable, and strong. As Richardson (1981) has observed, the cultural styles and child-rearing approaches unique to Black families have enabled them "to provide supportive and effective environments for the development of black children" (pp. 100-101). Research into the parenting and socialization of Black children promises to provide rich data essential for the development of social and educational policies by local, state, or federal governing agencies that determine and support programs directed at Black families and Black children.

References

Abrahams, R. D. 1970. *Deep Down in the Jungle*. Chicago: AVC.

Allen, W. R. 1978. "The Search for Applicable Theories in Black Family Life." *Journal of Marriage and the Family* 40(1):117-29.

Andrews, S., J. Blumenthal, W. Bache, and G. Wiener. 1975. "Parents as Early Childhood Educators: The New Orleans Model." Paper presented at the annual meeting of the Society for Research for Child Development, Denver, CO.

Aschenbrenner, J. 1973. *Lifelines: Black Families in Chicago.* New York: Holt, Rinehart & Winston.

Baumrind, D. 1972. "An Exploratory Study of Socialization Effects on Black Children: Some Black-White Comparisons." *Child Development* 43:261-67.

Bernard, J. 1966. *Marriage and Family Among Negroes.* Englewood Cliffs, NJ: Prentice Hall.

Billingsley, A. 1968. *Black Families in White America.* Englewood Cliffs, NJ: Prentice Hall.

Bradley, R. and B. Caldwell. 1976a. "Early Home Environment and Changes in Mental Test Performance in Children From 6 to 36 months." *Developmental Psychology* 12:93-97.

———. 1976b. "The Relation of Infants' Home Environments to Mental Test Performance at 54 Months: A Follow-Up Study." *Child Development* 47:1172-74.

———. 1978. "Home Environment, Social Status, and Mental Test Performance." Unpublished manuscript.

Carew, J. V. with I. Chan and C. Halfar. 1976. *Observing Intelligence in Young Children.* Englewood Cliffs, NJ: Prentice Hall.

Chilman, C. 1966. *Growing Up Poor.* DHEW Publication No. 13. Washington, DC: Government Printing Office.

Clarke-Stewart, K. A. 1973. "Interactions Between Mothers and Their Young Children: Characteristics and Consequences." *Monographs of the Society for Research in Child Development* 38(6-7, Serial No. 153).

Daniel, J. 1975. "A Definition of Fatherhood as Expressed by Black Fathers." Ph.D. dissertation, University of Pittsburgh.

Davis, A. and J. Dollard. 1940. *Children of Bondage.* New York: Harper & Row.

Dixon, V. 1971. "Two Approaches to Black-White Relations." In *Beyond Black or White: An Alternate America,* edited by V. J. Dixon and B. G. Foster. Boston: Little, Brown.

Du Bois, W. E. B. 1908. *The Negro American Family.* Atlanta, GA: Atlanta University Press.

Elardo, R., R. Bradley, and B. Caldwell. 1975. "The Relations of Infants' Home Environments to Mental Test Performance From Six to Thirty-Six Months: A Longitudinal Analysis." *Child Development* 46:68-74.

———. 1977. "A Longitudinal Study of the Relation of Infants' Home Environments to Language Development at Age Three." *Child Development* 48:595-603.

Frazier, E. F. 1933. "Children in Black and Mulatto Families." *American Journal of Sociology* 39:12-29.

———. 1939. *The Negro Family in the United States.* Chicago: University of Chicago Press.

———. 1950. "Problems and Needs of Negro Children and Youth Resulting From Family Disorganization." *Journal of Negro Education* 19:269-77.

Gay, G. 1975. "Cultural Differences Important in Education of Black Children." *Momentum* (October):30-33.

Gutman, H. G. 1976. *The Black Family in Slavery and Freedom, 1750-1925.* New York: Pantheon.

Hannerz, U. 1969. *Soulside: Inquiries Into Ghetto Culture and Community.* New York: Columbia University Press.

Harrison-Ross, P. and B. Wyden. 1973. *The Black Child: A Parents' Guide.* New York: Peter H. Wyden.

Hess, R. D. 1970. "Social Class and Ethnic Influences on Socialization." In *Carmichael's Manual of Child Psychology,* edited by P. Mussen. New York: John Wiley.

Hess, R. D., et al. 1968. *The Cognitive Environments of Urban Preschool Children.* Report to the Children's Bureau, U.S. Department of Health, Education and Welfare. Washington, DC: Government Printing Office.

Hill, R. B. 1971. *The Strengths of Black Families*. New York: Emerson-Hall.

Johnson, C. S. 1934. *Shadow of the Plantation*. Chicago: University of Chicago Press.

————. 1941. *Growing Up in the Black Belt*. Washington, DC: American Council on Education.

Kuhn, T. S. 1962. *The Structure of Scientific Revolutions*. Chicago: University of Chicago Press.

Ladner, J. 1971. *Tomorrow's Tomorrow: The Black Woman*. Garden City, NY: Doubleday.

Lewin, K. 1935. *A Dynamic Theory of Personality*. New York: McGraw-Hill.

Lewis, D. 1975. "The Black Family: Socialization and Sex Roles." *Phylon* 26(Fall):471-80.

Lewis, H. 1955. *Blackways of Kent*. Chapel Hill: University of North Carolina Press.

Liebow, E. (1967). *Tally's Corner: A Study of Negro Street Corner Men*. Boston: Little, Brown.

Lyman, S. M. 1972. *The Black American in Sociological Thought*. New York: Capricorn.

Martin, E. P. and J. M. Martin. 1978. *The Black Extended Family*. Chicago: University of Chicago Press.

Mathis, A. 1978. "Contrasting Approaches to the Study of Black Families." *Journal of Marriage and the Family* 40(4):667-78.

McAdoo, H. P. 1978. "Factors Related to Stability in Upwardly Mobile Black Families." *Journal of Marriage and the Family* 40(4):761-76.

Moynihan, D. P. 1965. *The Negro Family: The Case for National Action*. Washington, DC: U.S. Department of Labor, Office of Policy Planning and Research.

Myrdal, G., with R. Sterner and A. Rose. 1944. *An American Dilemma: The Negro Problem and Modern Democracy*. New York: Harper & Row.

Nobles, W. W. 1974a. "African Root and American Fruit: The Black Family." *Journal of Social and Behavioral Sciences* 20(Spring):66-77.

————. 1974b. "Africanity: Its Role in Black Families." *Black Scholar* 5(June):10-17.

————. 1978. "Toward an Empirical and Theoretical Framework for Defining Black Families." *Journal of Marriage and the Family* 40(4):679-90.

Ogbu, J. 1978. *Minority Education and Caste: The American System in Cross-Cultural Perspective*. New York: Academic Press.

Peters, M. F. 1974. "The Black Family: Perpetuating the Myths—An Analysis of Family Sociology Textbook Treatment of Black Families." *Family Coordinator* 23(October):349-57.

————. 1976. "Nine Black Families: A Study of Household Management and Childrearing in Black Families With Working Mothers." Ph.D. dissertation, Harvard University.

————. 1980. "Childrearing in Black Families: Potential Continuities and Discontinuities Between Home and School." Paper presented at the annual meeting of the National Council on Family Relations, Portland, OR, October.

————. 1981. "Childrearing Patterns in a Sample of Black Parents of Children Age 1 to 3." Paper presented at the annual meeting of the Society for Research in Child Development.

Peters, M. F. and G. C. Massey. 1988. "Chronic vs. Mundane Stress in Family Stress Theories: The Case of Black Families in White America." Unpublished manuscript.

Pierce, C. 1969. "The Effects of Racism." Paper presented at the 15th Annual Conference of State Mental Health Representatives, American Medical Association, Chicago.

Radin, N. and C. Kamii. 1965. "The Child-Rearing Attitudes of Disadvantaged Negro Mothers and Some Educational Implications." *Journal of Negro Education* 34(2):138-46.

Rainwater, L. 1965. "Crucible of Identity: The Negro Lower-Class Family." Pp. 160-204 in *The Negro American*, edited by T. Parsons and K. B. Clark. Boston: Beacon.

Renne, K. R. 1970. "Correlates of Dissatisfaction in Marriage." *Journal of Marriage and the Family* 32(1):54-67.

Richardson, B. B. 1981. "Racism and Child-Rearing: A Study of Black Mothers." Ph.D. dissertation, Claremont Graduate School.

Scanzoni, J. 1971. *The Black Family in Modern Society.* Boston: Allyn & Bacon.

———. 1975. "Sex Roles, Economic Factors, and Marital Solidarity in Black and White Marriages." *Journal of Marriage and the Family* 37(1):130-44.

Schacter, F. F. 1979. *Everyday Mother Talk to Toddlers: Early Intervention.* New York: Academic Press.

Schulz, D. 1969. *Coming Up Black: Patterns of Ghetto Socialization.* Englewood Cliffs, NJ: Prentice Hall.

Slaughter, D. 1978. *Modernization Through Education of Mother-Child Dyads.* Final Report 1 to the National Institute of Child Health and Human Development. Evanston, IL: Northwestern University.

Stack, C. B. 1974. *All Our Kin: Strategies for Survival in a Black Community.* New York: Harper & Row.

White, B. L., B. Kaban, B. Shapiro, and J. Attanmucci. 1977. "Competence and Experience." In *The Structuring of Experience,* edited by I. C. Uzgiris and F. Weizman. New York: Plenum.

Whiting, B. 1973. "The Problem of the Packaged Variable." Paper presented at the Biennial International Conference on Behavioral Development, Ann Arbor, MI, August.

Willie, C. V. 1976. *A New Look at Black Families.* New Bayside, NY: General Hall.

Young, V. 1970. "Family and Childhood in a Southern Negro Community." *American Anthropologist* 72(April):269-88.

Zegiob, L. and R. Forehand. 1975. "Maternal Interactive Behavior as a Function of Race: Socioeconomic Status and Sex of the Child." *Child Development* 46:564-68.

The Roles of African American Fathers in the Socialization of Their Children

JOHN L. MCADOO

Sociological and psychological research related to the socialization of the child in the United States has been described as matricentric in character (Lamb 1976a; Rapaport, Rapaport, and Strelitz 1977). Rapaport et al. (1977) have even suggested that the matrifocal paradigm for parenting in our society is in need of revision, and most researchers feel that the role of the father in the socialization of their children is only beginning to be understood (Lamb 1976a; Biller 1972). The exploration of the Black father's role in the socialization of his children is almost nonexistent in the social science literature. From the matricentric researcher's point of view, the Black father is usually seen as an invisible man who is not active in and has no power, control, or interest in the socialization of his children (McAdoo 1979). There is a need, then, to describe some of the research findings related to Black fatherhood.

The objectives of this chapter are to present some of the literature related to the parenting styles of Black fathers in the socialization of their children, to examine some of the trends in father-child research, and to indicate some of the implications of these trends for the stereotyping of the Black father's role in the socialization of his children. The chapter examines a variety of roles: that of provider; the father's influence in decisions related to child rearing, nurturing, and control functions; the father's expectations of his children; and interaction patterns between father and child.

Provider Role

Most of the sociological literature relating to the provider role of the father follows Parsons and Bales's (1955) description of the instrumental and expressive modes of family process. The father has generally been described as playing only an instrumental role. That is, he has been seen as primarily a provider who both protects the family from the outside world and acts as the conduit of information and resources between the family and the outside world. The mother-child relationship has been seen as the key expressive relationship until the child has passed the preschool stage. Although Parsons and Bales's theories have served as a theoretical model in early family socialization literature, the literature does not provide clear-cut support for their thesis. At least one researcher has provided evidence suggesting that fathers are engaged in expressive socialization functions (Cazenave 1979).

Price-Bonham and Skeen (1979) note that the effectiveness of the Black father in his role as a provider is viewed as dependent on his abilities to aid in supporting his family and to share the provider role with his wife, thus legitimating his authority within the family and allowing him to serve as a model of responsible behavior to his children. Tausch (1952) found that Black fathers and fathers of other racial and ethnic groups saw themselves as more than just economic providers to their families, and that they valued companionship with their children more than the provider role. The role of provider for these fathers may have presented a dilemma for them, given that the amount of time the fathers spent with their children was partially controlled by employment pressures.

In analyzing the research of Maxwell (1976) and others (Cafritz 1974; Fasteneau 1976), Cazenave (1979) found that they overemphasized the provider role as a parenting style in focusing exclusively on the lack of paternal participation, involvement, and expressiveness in white middle- and upper-middle-income classes. In his research with middle-income Black fathers, Cazenave found that the greater the economic security, the more active the father became in the child-rearing function. His findings on 54 mailmen seem to support this conclusion, as these fathers were found to be more active in child-rearing activities than their fathers had been.

In summary, although many researchers appear to use Parsons and Bales's theory as a guide, it now appears evident from Cazenave's and others' data relating to paternal nurturance (McAdoo 1979; Radin 1972; Radin and Epstein 1975) that Parsons and Bales may have overemphasized the instrumental or provider role of the father. It is safe to assume that the American father plays many roles in the family—provider, decision maker, nurturer, husband, and father. Research that isolates or focuses on any one of these roles may provide misinformation about fathers' role in the nurturing of their children. Although in this chapter each of the roles of fathers is discussed separately, it is important to recognize the interrelationship of the roles fathers play and the reciprocity of father/mother and sibling/child roles in the socialization process.

Decision Making

Several authors have described the Black family as egalitarian in decision-making patterns (Dietrich 1975; Hill 1971; Lewis 1975; Reuben 1978; Staples 1976; Tenhouten 1970; Willie and Greenblatt 1978). Much of this literature has been written in reaction to social scientists' assertions that the Black family is matriarchal in structure (Moynihan 1965). Willie and Greenblatt (1978), in reviewing the power relationship literature, found that Black families appear to be more egalitarian than white families, with the middle-class Black family being more egalitarian than any other type. McDonald (1980), in an extensive review of the family power literature, suggests that because of theoretical and methodological problems inherent in family power research, we have not moved much beyond the original finding of Blood and Wolfe (1960) on this issue.

Blood and Wolfe (1960) and others have demonstrated that American fathers are moving toward an egalitarian relationship with mothers in the decision-making and power relationship in the home. Jackson (1976) found that lower-class Black fathers tended to be more patriarchal in their decision-making patterns than lower-class white fathers and Black and white middle-income fathers. In her review of selected literature on Black and white families, she noted that wife-dominant families (matriarchal) were more characteristic of white professional families with unemployed wives. Mack (1978) found that regardless of race or class, fathers perceived themselves as the dominant decision makers.

The studies related to child-rearing decision making in Black and white families indicate that the predominant pattern is egalitarian. That is, fathers share equally in decisions about their children's needs (McAdoo 1980). In my own previous work, I found that middle-income Black fathers shared equally with their wives in decisions on child-rearing activities (McAdoo 1979). However, Cromwell and Cromwell's (1978) analysis of husbands' and wives' reports of dominance on child-rearing decision making revealed conflicts in Black and Chicano homes on this issue. This points up the need to develop theoretical and methodological frameworks that allow researchers to look at both process and outcomes of decision making in child-rearing practices. Reports by father, mother, or both about the father's role in this process may be limited without some actual observational data collected in conflictual and nonconflictual situations (McDonald 1980).

We may conclude, given the preceding assertions, that both Black and white middle-income fathers' involvement in decision making regarding child-rearing practices appears to be changing in the same general pattern found by Bronfenbrenner (1958) in his analysis of the literature 23 years ago. He found the predominant child-rearing decision-making pattern to be egalitarian and attributed the change to the influence of professional child development practitioners. These changes perhaps were also due to the increased numbers of mothers in the workforce and the use of television in getting child development practitioners' messages to more people.

More systematic study is needed on the impact that sharing of the provider's role has on child-rearing decision making within Black and other families. The sharing of the provider's role has led in most cases to greater economic and educational resources in Black families, but there is also some need to understand what this change has meant for other family processes and functioning in addition to decision-making processes. Questions may be raised as to the impact on paternal attitudes and parenting style.

Parenting Style

A review of the literature reveals that there are very few studies available relating to fathers' expectations and parenting styles. Bartz and Levine (1978), in a study of 455 parents of different ethnic groups, found that fathers of all socioeconomic classes shared similar expectations of their children's behavior. Ethnic differences in fathers' expectations of their children's behavior were a matter of degree and not kind. Working-class fathers of all ethnic groups and races believed that children should help formulate rules and have the right to express their own ideas within the family. Black fathers and fathers belonging to other ethnic groups thought that parents earn the respect of their children by being fair, not by imposing parental will or authority.

Whereas Bartz and Levine's data seem to suggest that Black fathers in lower socioeconomic groups may be changing their traditional values to meet new demands for socialization in society, it is clear from the work of other researchers (Staples 1978; Taylor 1978; Coles 1978; Schulz 1978) that many of them retain and support the values common to those within their socioeconomic status. These men see themselves as the head of the family, and they believe they are expected to punish their children for transgressing externally imposed rules and regulations. They describe themselves as strict, using physical as opposed to verbal punishment liberally. The child's punishment is related to the transgression's consequences rather than the intent of the child's actions.

Cazenave (1979), who reviewed the changes in child-rearing activities in two generations of Black fathers, found that middle-income fathers reported being more actively involved than their fathers in child-care activities. This sample was more actively involved in changing their children's diapers, in baby-sitting, and in playing with their children than their fathers had been. They reported spending more time with their children and claimed to punish their children physically less often than their fathers had punished them.

Black middle-income fathers in one of my own studies resembled those in Cazenave's study, in that they were equally involved in making child-rearing decisions (McAdoo 1979). Most of these fathers could be described as traditional (Duvall 1946) in their values toward child rearing. They expected their child to respond immediately to their commands, would almost never allow their children to display anger or throw temper tantrums, and perceived themselves and their attitudes toward child rearing as moderate to very strict. These fathers expected good behavior from their children, as opposed to assertive and independent behavior. They were more likely to tell their children that they approved of their good behavior than to show approval through hugging and kissing. Their attitudes appeared to be like those of Baumrind's (1968) authoritarian fathers.

Baumrind (1966, 1967, 1973), in a series of research studies, has described three parenting styles that cut across all ethnic groups: permissive, authoritarian, and authoritative. Each of these kinds of parents has different child-rearing values and different expectations for their own role behaviors. The permissive father is described as the father who responds to his child's impulses, desires, and actions in a nonpunitive, accepting, and affirmative manner. This father makes very few demands on his child for orderly behavior or doing household chores. He sees himself as a consultant to be used as the child desires and not as an agent responsible for shaping the child's ongoing or future behavior.

In contrast, the authoritarian father attempts to shape, control, and evaluate his child's behavior and attitudes in accordance with a set standard of conduct. He values and expects obedience as a virtue and believes in punitive, forceful measures to control the child's behavior when it is in conflict with what the father believes is right. There are few give-and-take discussions between father and child, and the child is expected to accept the father's view of what is right.

The authoritative father seems to be a composite of the best points of the authoritarian and permissive fathers. This parent, according to Baumrind, attempts to direct the child's activities, but in a rational, issue-oriented manner. The authoritative father is able to encourage give-and-take discussions and gives reasons for his rules and expectations. The authoritative father tends to value both expressive and instrumental attributes, both autonomous self-will and disciplined authority. This father provides firm control with explanations when the child violates family policy; he believes in the use of reasoning as well as power in achieving his objectives with the child.

Baumrind's (1971) series of observational studies demonstrated that authoritative fathers promoted purposive and dominant behavior in boys and girls. Authoritative paternal control was associated with the development of social responsibility in boys and with achievement (but not friendly, cooperative behavior) in girls. Fathers who were either authoritarian or permissive in their child-rearing styles had children who were either markedly high or markedly low on overall competence.

In a comparative exploratory study observing Black and white fathers and their preschool children, Baumrind (1973) found sex differences in the fathers' expectations and the behavior of the children. There were few significant differences in Black and white fathers' expectations of their sons' behavior. Black sons were expected to behave in a mature fashion, and the fathers were likely to encourage independent behavior in their sons. Although no significant differences were observed in the behavior of the children, Black boys appeared to be less achievement oriented and more aggressive than white boys. Fathers of Black girls appeared to be significantly different from fathers of white girls in their parenting styles and child-rearing practices. Black fathers did not encourage individuality and independence or provide enrichment of their daughters' environment. Black fathers did not promote nonconformity in their daughters and were authoritarian in their practices. The conclusion drawn by Baumrind is that socialization practices that would characterize Black families as authoritarian by white social science standards, and therefore in need of change, actually benefit Black daughters. In comparing Black and white girls, Baumrind found that Black daughters of authoritarian parents were exceptionally independent and at ease in the nursery school setting where the observations took place. Thus this study provides an interesting observation that needs to be verified and clarified in future research.

Black authoritarian fathers and families differ significantly from white authoritarian families in the degree to which they adhere to rigid standards. White fathers who were found to be authoritarian in Baumrind's studies were more likely to be seen as having an authoritarian personality syndrome (Adorno, Frenkel-Brunswick, Levinson, and Sanford 1950)—that is, dogmatic and intolerant attitudes motivated by repressed anger, emotional coldness, and a sense of impotence.

To summarize, it would appear that Black fathers socialize their children differently than do white fathers, and the impact of that process may lead to the development of high competence in girls. There appears to be a need for more research related to Black fathers' attitudes toward child rearing, some observational validation of their behavior in relationship to their expressed values, and some validation through data gathering from significant others in Black families. There is a need to evaluate the three types of parenting styles in more depth to determine whether cultural, ethnic, or racial differences influence Black fathers' particular parenting style and its relationship to child outcome variables. Finally, there is a need to determine how the particular parenting style a father adopts influences his relationship to his sons and/or daughters.

Parent-Child Relationships

Walters and his associates have done the most consistent reviews of the research related to parent-child relationship issues (Walters and Stinnett 1971; Walters and Walters 1980). Their latest work focused on the emerging research trends of physiological influences, parent-infant relationships, divorce, fathering, stepparenting, child abuse and neglect, values of the child, methodological issues, and intervention strategies. Among their conclusions is that patterns of parent-child relationships are influenced by parenting models that fathers and mothers provide to each other. To understand the concurrent contributions of parents to each other and to their children, researchers should focus on the mother-father-child relationship and on the mother-father-sibling-child relationship rather than on the father-child or mother-child relationship.

Walters believes that a clearer picture or conceptualization is emerging from the research literature on the reciprocal effects of relationships between parents and children. Family researchers are moving away from a unidirectional model, in which the relationship is seen as going from parent to child, toward one that emphasizes the reciprocal nature of the relationship between parent and child. Children not only influence their parents' behavior but are also important determiners of their own behavior patterns (Walters and Walters 1980).

Although Walters emphasizes the need for research on parent-child interactions and reciprocal relationships, he also makes clear, as do others (Lamb 1976b; Price-Bonham and Skeen 1979), that the role of the father in the parent-child relationship is not well understood. Studies of father-child relationships tend to emphasize the relationship between fathers and sons and leave the impact of fathers on daughters virtually unexplored (Walters and Stinnett 1971). Further, as Staples (1970) notes, the role of the Black father in these studies is not explored very well. Staples concludes that the

Black male may be more difficult to reach, the implication being that social science researchers tend to select other sources for their information on Black fathers.

Price-Bonham and Skeen (1979), in their review of the literature, agree with Staples's assessment and suggest that studies of Black father-child relationships suffer from the same deficiencies as do studies of other ethnic groups. Most researchers doing family relationship studies generally collect data on fathers from mothers and/or wives (Walters and Stinnett 1971; McAdoo 1979), neglect to control for social class (Busse and Busse 1972), and focus on the impact of absent fathers.

In summary, what seems lacking from the various literature reviews is a theory that describes how these relationships differ over the span of the child's development within the family. This theory should address racial, ethnic, and social class differences within the father-child relationship. More descriptive research methodologies need to be developed using both questionnaire and observational techniques to generate databases related to the general concept of parent-child relationships and to particular aspects of that relationship. For Black father-child relationships, given socioeconomic class and other variables, there is a need to develop the boundaries, quality, and quantity of the parent-child relationship over time.

Once the relationships between fathers and children are identified, more sophisticated research designs can be used to determine the impact of mothers, siblings, and the kin network system on the development of and changes in the parent-child relationship process. This would suggest the use of multitrait and multimethod approaches with more complex research designs (Walters and Walters 1980). Using such approaches, researchers could begin to measure the impact of the child on the relationship and move away from linear models to curvilinear or other models that are appropriate.

Father-Child Interaction

Observations of father-child interaction patterns and their effects on the preschool child's social and cognitive growth are relatively new phenomena for social science researchers. The two most studied interaction patterns are nurturance and control. *Nurturance* may be defined as the expression of warmth and positive feelings of the father toward the attitudes and behaviors of his child.

Several researchers (Radin 1972; Radin and Epstein 1975; Baumrind 1971) have suggested that maternal warmth (nurturance) facilitates the child's identification with the mother, particularly the female child. Radin (1972) has suggested that paternal nurturance facilitates the male child's identification with the father. Identification with either parent should lead to an incorporation by the child of the parent's ideas, attitudes, beliefs, and feelings about the child. The parent communicates to the child a positive acceptance of the child as a person. Nurturance is one of the patterns of interaction that is important in the development of social competence in preschool children.

Nurturance is used most by parents who recognize and respond to their children's needs, who communicate acceptance, and who are available for interaction, in contrast to parents who are inaccessible and insensitive. Warmth is seen as a characteristic of both parent roles (Newman and Newman 1978). Newman and Newman (1978) note that warmth is usually expressed in praise or approval; in nonverbal interactions such as patting, touching, stroking, hugging, kissing; and in playful activities. Rodman (cited in Newman and Newman 1978) presents evidence that warmth and rejection can be observed across a variety of cultural groups.

Parental control is another dimension of father-child interaction patterns. *Control* refers to the parent's insistence that the child carry out important directions and adhere to rules that the parent feels are important. Control and nurturance are seen as necessary ingredients in authoritative parents' socialization patterns (Baumrind 1973). Authoritarian fathers usually use restrictive control interaction patterns in socializing their children. These fathers' verbal interaction patterns with their preschool children are described in the literature as restrictive, rather cold, unfeeling, and aloof, and therefore represent an expression of the authoritarian father's negative feelings toward his child's attitudes and behavior within the family (Radin 1972).

Parental restrictiveness does not facilitate positive communication and identification (Radin 1972) between child and parent. Restrictive behaviors are those behaviors that are not warm, loving, and supportive of the child. Nonsupporting behaviors usually take the form of criticism or expressed disapproval and may also include grabbing, pushing, or restraining the child from some event or activity without explanation. Such behaviors may be viewed as negative reactions by the parent to the child's attitude, behavior, and beliefs. Nonsupport may also lead the parent to handle the symptoms of the problem and not the needs of the child, or to control behavior and cut off the usual patterns of identification and communication of the child. Restrictiveness in parents may lead children to develop negative images of themselves and their worth as human beings, as well as to have negative feelings about those around them.

Radin and her associates observed white lower- and middle-income fathers interacting with their preschool children (Radin 1972; Radin and Epstein 1975; Jordan, Radin, and Epstein 1975). They found the predominant pattern of interaction to be nurturance. The fathers were warm and loving toward their children. The researchers hypothesized that children of nurturant fathers would do well on cognitive tasks in kindergarten. They were able to support the hypothesis for boys of middle-income fathers, but not for boys of lower-class fathers. Radin and her colleagues also found that the relationship between paternal nurturance and the child's intellectual functioning was higher for boys than for girls. Radin and Epstein (1975) have suggested that the fathers of girls may be sending mixed messages to their daughters, and that this may lead to a reduction in intellectual performance.

In a study published in 1979, I partially replicated Radin's work with Black middle-income fathers. I hypothesized that the predominant pattern of verbal interaction between Black fathers and their sons and daughters would be nurturance, and that hypothesis was supported: 75% of the Black middle-income fathers in the sample were found to be nurturant toward their children (McAdoo 1979). Fathers were equally nurturant toward their sons and daughters. One unanticipated finding was that children of restrictive parents initiated the interaction between themselves and their fathers significantly more often than did children of nurturant parents. This finding supports Walters and Walters's (1980) suggestion that there needs to be an examination of the impact of the reciprocal nature of the pattern of interaction between parent and child.

I was not able to find any relationship between a father's interaction patterns and his sons' and daughters' self-esteem. The children's positive self-esteem led me to suggest that the relationship between father-child interaction and self-esteem may be indirect (McAdoo 1979). Walters and Stinnett (1971), in their decade review of parent-child relationships, note that the research results converge in suggesting that parental acceptance, warmth, and support are positively related to favorable emotional, social, and intellectual development of children. They further note that extreme restrictiveness, authoritarianism, and punitiveness without acceptance, warmth, and love tend to be negatively related to a child's positive self-concept and emotional and social development. The studies they reviewed also indicate that parental attitudes and behaviors vary according to sex and behavior of the child.

Mackey and Day (1979), in one of the most comprehensive cross-cultural observational studies conducted involving father figures in the United States, Ireland, Spain, Japan, and Mexico, found that American father figures did not interact much differently from father figures of other nations. They found that father figures interacted more nonverbally with younger children and were closer to them. American men were as nurturant to their children as were American women. No differences in intensity of interaction level between men and women were observed in American families.

Summary

I have reviewed here selected literature related to the roles Black fathers play in the socialization of their children. I have noted that when economic sufficiency rises within Black families, one may observe an increase in the active participation of Black fathers in the socialization of their children. Black fathers, like fathers in all ethnic groups, take an equal part in child-rearing decisions in the family. Their expectations for their children's behavior in the home also appear to be similar given socioeconomic status patterns. Unlike other fathers who may be classified as authoritarian, Black fathers who behave in authoritarian ways in relation to their daughters appear to be socializing their daughters to be more competent and independent at an early age. The predominant relationship and interaction pattern of Black fathers appears to be nurturant, warm, and loving toward their children. Finally, as Lamb (1976a) has suggested, the father's socialization role is defined by his position within the family system.

The implications of these findings appear to be that research should now move beyond the ethnocentric studies of the past that have focused on the most problematic, economically devastated Black families, sometimes inappropriately comparing them to families of college professors, and study the various roles Black fathers play in the socialization of their children. More studies are needed that describe fathers' attitudes, expectations, values, and beliefs about the roles they play in both problematic and nonproblematic situations and in both stressful and nonstressful conditions. There needs to be more observational research related to the kinds of socialization activities and interaction patterns that take place between Black fathers and their children in the home and community.

Theoretical frameworks and methodologies are needed that examine all the reciprocal socialization relationships of the total family system. We need to describe and evaluate reciprocal interaction and relationship patterns among father, mother, children, siblings, and kin. There is a need to go beyond dyadic models and linear relationships to a more dynamic interaction model that looks at family interaction processes in a developmental way and evaluate these processes in terms of social, emotional, and cognitive development of Black children and their families over time.

References

Adorno, T. W., E. Frenkel-Brunswick, D. J. Levinson, and R. N. Sanford. 1950. *The Authoritarian Personality.* New York: Harper & Row.

Bartz, K. W. and B. S. Levine. 1978. "Child Rearing by Black Parents: A Description and Comparison to Anglo and Chicano Parents." *Journal of Marriage and the Family* 40(4):709-20.

Baumrind, D. 1966. "Effects of Authoritative Parental Control on Child Behavior." *Child Development* 37(4):887-907.

———. 1967. "Child Care Practices Anteceding Three Patterns of Preschool Behavior." *Genetic Psychology Monographs* 75:43-88.

———. 1968. "An Exploratory Study of Socialization Effects on Black Children: Some Black-White Comparisons." *Child Development* 43:261-67.

———. 1971. "Current Patterns of Paternal Authority." *Developmental Psychology Monographs* 4(1):pt. 2.

———. 1973. "Authoritarian vs. Authoritative Parental Control." In *Socialization,* edited by M. Scarr-Salapatek and P. Salapatek. Columbus, OH: Charles E. Merrill.

Biller, H. B. 1972. *Parental Deprivation.* Lexington, MA: D. C. Heath.

Blood, R. O. and D. M. Wolfe. 1960. *Husbands and Wives.* New York: Free Press.

Bronfenbrenner, U. 1958. "Socialization Through Time and Space." In *Readings in Social Psychology,* edited by E. E. Maccoby, T. M. Newcomb, and E. L. Hartley. New York: Holt, Rinehart & Winston.

Busse, T. and P. Busse. 1972. "Negro Parental Behavior and Social Class Variables." *Journal of Genetic Psychology* 120:289-91.

Cafritz, J. S. 1974. *Masculine/Feminine or Human?* Itasca, IL: F. E. Peacock.

Cazenave, N. 1979. "Middle Income Black Fathers: An Analysis of the Provider's Role." *Family Coordinator* 28(November).

Coles, R. 1978. "Black Fathers." In *The Black Male in America,* edited by D. Wilkerson and R. Taylor. Chicago: Nelson-Hall.

Cromwell, V. L. and R. E. Cromwell. 1978. "Perceived Dominance and Conflict Resolution Among Anglo, Black and Chicano Couples." *Journal of Marriage and the Family* 40(4):749-59.

Dietrich, K. T. 1975. "A Reexamination of the Myth of Black Matriarchy." *Journal of Marriage and the Family* 37(2):367-74.

Duvall, E. 1946. "Conceptions of Parenthood." *Journal of Sociology* 52(November):193-203.

Fasteneau, M. 1976. *The Male Machine.* New York: Macmillan.

Hill, R. B. 1971. *The Strengths of Black Families.* New York: Emerson-Hall.

Jackson, J. 1976. "Ordinary Black Husbands: The Truly Hidden Men." Pp. 139-44 in *The Role of the Father in Child Development,* edited by M. E. Lamb. New York: John Wiley.

Jordan, B. E., N. Radin, and A. Epstein. 1975. "Paternal Behavior and Intellectual Functioning in Preschool Boys and Girls." *Developmental Psychology* 11:407-8.

Lamb, M. E. 1976a. "Interactions Between Eight-Month Old Children and Their Fathers and Mothers." In *The Role of the Father in Child Development,* edited by M. E. Lamb. New York: John Wiley.

———. 1976b. "The Role of the Father: An Overview." In *The Role of the Father in Child Development,* edited by M. E. Lamb. New York: John Wiley.

Lewis, D. K. 1975. "The Black Family: Socialization and Sex Roles." *Phylon* 36(Fall):221-37.

Mack, D. E. 1978. "Power Relationships in Black Families." *Journal of Personality and Social Psychology* 30(September):409-13.

Mackey, C. W. and R. O. Day. 1979. "Some Indicators of Fathering Behaviors in the United States: A Cross-Cultural Examination of Adult Male Interactions." *Journal of Marriage and the Family* 41(2):287-98.

Maxwell, J. 1976. "The Keeping of Fathers in America." *Family Coordinator* 25:387-92.

McAdoo, J. L. 1979. "A Study of Father-Child Interaction Patterns and Self-Esteem in Black Pre-School Children." *Young Children* 34(1):46-53.

———. 1980. *Socializing the Preschool Child.* NIMH Contract No. 1 R01 MH25838-01. Washington, DC: Government Printing Office.

McDonald, G. W. 1980. "Family Power: The Assessment of a Decade of Theory and Research 1970–1979." *Journal of Marriage and the Family* 42(4):881-54.

Moynihan, D. P. 1965. *The Negro Family: The Case for National Action.* Washington, DC: U.S. Department of Labor, Office of Policy Planning and Research.

Newman, B. M. and P. R. Newman. 1978. *Infancy and Childhood Development and Its Contents.* New York: John Wiley.

Parsons, T. and R. F. Bales. 1955. *Family Socialization and Interaction Process.* New York: Free Press.

Price-Bonham, S. and P. Skeen. 1979. "A Comparison of Black and White Fathers With Implications for Parents' Education." *Family Coordinator* 28(1):53-59.

Radin, N. 1972. "Father-Child Interaction and the Intellectual Functioning of Four-Year Old Boys." *Developmental Psychology* 8:369-76.

Radin, N. and A. Epstein. 1975. "Observed Paternal Behavior and Intellectual Functioning of Preschool Boys and Girls." Paper presented at the annual meeting of the Society for Research in Child Development, Denver, CO.

Rapaport, R., R. N. Rapaport, and Z. Strelitz. 1977. *Fathers, Mothers and Society.* New York: Basic Books.

Reuben, R. H. 1978. "Matriarchal Themes in Black Literature: Implications for Family Life Education." *Family Coordinator* 27(January):33-41.

Schulz, D. A. 1978. "Coming Up as a Boy in the Ghetto." Pp. 7-32 in *The Black Male in America,* edited by D. Y. Wilkerson and R. L. Taylor. Chicago: Nelson-Hall.

Staples, R. E. 1970. "Educating the Black Male at Various Class Levels for Marital Roles." *Family Coordinator* 20:164-67.

———. 1976. "The Black American Family." In *Ethnic Families in America,* edited by C. H. Mindell and R. W. Haberstein. New York: Elsevier.

———. 1978. "The Myth of the Black Matriarchy." In *The Black Male in America,* edited by D. Y. Wilkerson and R. L. Taylor. Chicago: Nelson-Hall.

Tausch, R. J. 1952. "The Role of the Father in the Family." *Journal of Experimental Education* 20:319-61.

Taylor, R. L. 1978. "Socialization to the Black Male Role." Pp. 1-7 in *The Black Male in America,* edited by D. Y. Wilkerson and R. L. Taylor. Chicago: Nelson-Hall.

Tenhouten, W. 1970. "The Black Family: Myth or Reality." *Psychiatry* 2(May):145-73.

Walters, J. and N. Stinnett. 1971. "Parent-Child Relationships: A Decade of Research." In *A Decade of Family Research and Action,* edited by C. B. Broderick. Minneapolis: National Council on Family Relations.

Walters, J. and L. H. Walters. 1980. "Parent-Child Relationships: A Review 1970–1979." *Journal of Marriage and the Family* 42(4):807-24.

Willie, C. V. and S. L. Greenblatt. 1978. "Four Classic Studies of Power Relationships in Black Families: A Review and Look to the Future." *Journal of Marriage and the Family* 40(4):691-96.

Supportive Roles of Significant Others in African American Families

WILHELMINA MANNS

Many persons, performing a variety of roles and functions within individual lives, contribute to the socialization processes of members of the family. Moreover, such persons are often significant others. Examining the influence of the significant other in the life of individual blacks, therefore, increases knowledge about selected aspects of the socialization processes within the black family.

The concept of the significant other developed from the formulations of Cooley ([1902] 1964) and later Mead ([1934] 1962), who suggests that the self-concept develops out of social interaction and that the individual assumes the viewpoint (reflected appraisal) of the "other" and "generalized other" of the society of which he or she is a member. Expanding on these earlier formulations, Sullivan (as cited by Kuhn 1972) describes a specific "significant other" later defined by Denzin (1970) as a person "whose evaluations of his behavior and attitudes the individual holds in high esteem." These evaluations and/or reflected appraisals from both the "generalized other" (the community) and a specific significant other can be either positive or negative and thus may influence the individual's self-concept accordingly.

For the past 25 years, investigators have examined various factors in the sphere of the significant other's influence. Among these studies is the work of Haller and Woelfel (1972), who concentrated on developing an instrument that would identify significant others and measure their influence, simultaneously examining the influence of the significant other on the educational and occupational aspirations of high school students. These researchers conclude that their findings support earlier formulations by Mead and Sullivan that stressed the role of the expectation of other persons in determining the goal orientations of the individual, and that "significant other" is a precise and flexible concept currently available "for use in assessing interpersonal influence on orientation variables" (p. 591).

The significant other as a factor in the lives of black people has received attention in both theoretical formulations and empirical research. In suggesting reasons for his finding that black people, despite minority racial status, manage to achieve stability and social status, Billingsley (1968) includes reference to the influence of significant others—not only from the individual's family but from all segments of the wider community, the latter of whom function primarily as social supports. Whereas Billingsley's sample for the most part concentrated on blacks from established achieving families, Manns (1974) examined the autobiographies of blacks from low socioeconomic background and found that parents, other relatives, and nonrelatives were identified as significant others and that they influenced individuals in several ways. Other empirical research includes the work of Shade (1978), who examined the significant other influence of "disadvantaged Afro-American freshmen" and found that although both family and nonfamily members were identified, nonfamily significant others were more prevalent. There were questions, nevertheless, that persisted about the influence of the significant other. Accordingly, this chapter will share selected findings from an intensive study that focused on two areas: identification of the type of significant other, and delineation of the manner of the influence of the significant other.

The study participants included 20 black adult respondents, purposively selected according to the following criteria: education, minimum master's degree in social work; socioeconomic status of the family of origin, as determined by a modified version of the Hollingshead-Redlich SES scale; age between 40 and 65; and sex. The influence of the significant other was examined in terms of the respondent's educational and occupational achievement in order to anchor the influence to an observable event. In addition, because the perceived responses of others are more important than their actual responses (Quarantelli and Cooper 1966, 1972), the perception of the influenced individual was a perspective selected for identifying the significant other.

Number of Significant Others

The respondents identified a large number of significant others—212, approximately 10 per respondent. A persistent pattern in the data suggests that there is an association between respondent's societal status, as determined by race and socioeconomic background, and the number of significant others. In a larger comparative study that examined race and socioeconomic status as variables, it was found that there was a tendency for blacks to have more significant others than whites, and also for lower-class individuals to have more than did middle-class persons (Table 11.1). In addition, the low variability of the black middle class indicated group stability that supports the notion that minority racial status accounts for the difference between blacks and whites (Table 11.1). Finally, an accumulative effect was observed among black lower-class subjects, who, confronted with both minority racial status and low socioeconomic status, tended to have more significant others than did black middle-class subjects (Table 11.1).

The observed pattern implies that groups that are viewed as low status (blacks and the lower class) by the larger society tend to have more significant others than do higher-status groups (whites and the middle class). In order for low-status groups to achieve, they may require more specific significant others than high-status groups.

Black people, as a minority group, experience negative appraisals from the overall society (the "generalized other"). When individuals experience negative appraisals from the "generalized other," the specific significant other may take on special meaning. It is suggested that a sizable number of specific significant others compensate, in part, for the negative aspects of the minority experience. However, in order to achieve, lower-class blacks may require even more significant others than middle-class blacks, because they are confronted with negative life experiences from both minority racial status and low socioeconomic status.

TABLE 11.1 Frequency, Mean, and Standard Deviation of the Number of Significant Others by the Race and Socioeconomic Status of the Respondents ($N = 20$ black, 20 white)

Respondent Groups				
Race	SES	f	M	S.D.
White	middle	84	8.4	5.31
White	lower	93	9.3	6.37
Black	middle	98	9.8	3.32
Black	lower	114	11.4	6.43

Type of Significant Other and Mode of Influence

An initial grouping of the type of significant other as caretaker or parent, relative and nonrelative, was followed up with a more precise specification of both the relative and the nonrelative.

As a result of an analysis of the manner in which almost 400 significant others wielded influence, eight modes of influence categories were established: modeling, validation of self, emotional support, achievement socialization, learning elicitation, providing, disconfirmation of self, and negative modeling.

The pattern in which individual significant others used these modes varied. A specific significant other, for instance, may have influenced through validation or through validation and modeling—in other words, through two or more modes.

Caretaking Significant Other

Of 212 significant others identified by the black respondents, 15% were caretakers or parents. This proportion must be considered within the context of the parent pool, generally limited to two parents per individual. Actually, parent significant others were prominent among the respondents, especially those in the middle class. A total of 80% of middle-class respondents designated both parents as significant others, as opposed to only 50% reported by lower-class respondents.

The majority of the parents influenced respondents through the mode of achievement socialization (Table 11.2), in which the significant other incul-

TABLE 11.2 Percentage Distributions of Types of Significant Others of Black Respondents by Mode of Influence (N = 20)

Mode of Influence	Type of Significant Other %		
	Parent	Relative	Nonrelative
Modeling	39	52	35
Validation of self	6	13	33
Emotional support	23	17	12
Achievement socialization	71	22	13
Providing	39	17	21
Learning elicitation	6	15	18
Disconfirmation of self	0	7	15
Negative modeling	3	2	7
N	31	46	135

cates the achievement orientation in the individual, either by establishing an achievement atmosphere or by mandating achievement. The former was described by a middle-class male whose parents were both college graduates: "It was just something I grew up with. There was always the idea that I was to go to college and achieve something. I cannot break it down further. It was just a way of life."

In contrast, a mandate to achieve is a clear and explicit requirement. Directives of this nature sometimes were attributed to the family reputation. A middle-class mother told her son that "you have come from a family who has achieved . . . and you will be expected to achieve also." Another rationale was attributed to racism in society and can be seen through the statement of a female respondent who was an only child in a middle-class home. The mother had 3 years of college but added to the family income by taking in sewing. She "always said that 'as a black person, you really have to go to college and get an education in order to get a job.' I grew up with the idea." Although mandates to achieve appeared in both classes, the middle-class parents were more likely to establish an achievement atmosphere, whereas the lower-class parents were inclined to mandate achievement.

Historically, both middle-class and lower-class black parents have extolled achievement as the means of combating the negative aspects of minority status. The class difference found in the achievement socialization mode, however, is probably a function of the difference between the inter-personal environments. Middle-class parents are able to establish achieve-ment atmospheres (even casual ones) because of inherent support from their interpersonal environment: Parents and other significant persons are more likely to be educated than are significant persons in the interpersonal world of the lower class. Therefore, lower-class parents, who may be achievement oriented but are usually uneducated and lack support from the interpersonal environment, rely to a greater extent on mandating achievement. Irrespective of this class distinction, the parental emphasis on achievement was persistent and relenting.

Almost 40% of the parents influenced respondents through the mode of modeling (Table 11.2), in which the significant other projects a quality and/or performs in a manner that inspires the individual to emulate and/or to adopt the said quality and/or performance. A middle-class female described the exemplary life of her father, a physician:

> My father was extremely committed to anything he did; to his family, to the community, and to the institution that he served for many, many years. There was always the expectation that you would go to school, that you would develop a skill and thus prepare to be of service to others.

Accordingly, she selected social work as her life's work.

Parents exercised influence through other modes to a lesser extent (Table 11.2). Through emotional support, significant others sustained, supported, and/or nurtured. Interestingly, the parent significant others were described as sustaining and supportive, but they were not described as nurturing—a usual caretaking or parental function. Because the sample consisted of achievers only, it is assumed that a foundation of self had been established in early life and thus it is probable that nurturing on the part of the parents was either "lost in the unconscious" of the respondents or taken for granted and consequently not designated as significant. The fact, however, that parents were not described as nurturing merits further study.

Through providing, the significant other gives or makes available to the individual a concrete time, a service, and/or an opportunity. Of those using this mode of influence, lower-class parents were more prevalent than middle-class parents. A lower-class male offered a clue to the reason for this class difference. He described his father as a significant other because he "worked hard in a dirty job at the steel mill, but he always stuck with us and provided food, clothing, and a roof over our heads. He wanted me not to give up or quit." Lower-class respondents credited their parents for giving them things that the middle-class parents undoubtedly also provided their offspring. It is surmised that in the middle-class these items—basic to life—were taken for granted and hence were not designated as significant.

Learning elicitation involves a couple of subcategories, one of which is teaching—the significant other facilitates the acquisition of specific knowledge and skills. Very few of the parents influenced through teaching, although this finding is not supported by Jones (1981), who, in a study on a current group of low-income black mothers, identified a "range of teaching styles as characterizing [their] interaction with their children."

None of the respondents described his or her parents as influencing through disconfirmation of self, a mode in which the significant other manifests disapproval and/or rejection of the individual. More than likely, already confronted with minority racial status, blacks who also experience disconfirmation by a parent find the dual stress an intolerable trauma and tend to disappear from the achievement structure. Other findings indicate that this notion may be especially applicable to the black lower class, whose members face both minority and low socioeconomic status.

Almost all of the parents exerted influence during the respondents' early childhood and adolescent years, but a majority continued to have influence during a large part of the respondents' adult lives. (In fact, in the larger study it was found that black parents were more likely than white parents to exert influence during the respondents' adult years of 18 to 40, at a significant level.) In this group of achievers, black parents remained an important factor in their offspring's transitions to adulthood and during many of the years that followed.

Relative Significant Other

A total of 21% of the significant others named were relatives of the respondents other than their parents. As with the percentage of parents designated significant others, this finding must be considered along with the recognition that there is a limit to the number of relatives one can have. Other findings, nonetheless, clarify the extent of relative involvement. A total of 80% of the respondents mentioned at least one relative as a significant other.

From another perspective, some of the respondents (30%) who did not mention specific significant others referred to a number of their relatives as a group influence. Thus, although the majority of the respondents mentioned at least one relative significant other, only a few mentioned a number of them.

The array of relative significant other types that were found is extensive: aunt/uncle, sibling, grandparent, spouse, cousin, great-relative, and even in-law. The sibling, aunt/uncle, and grandparent were more likely to be named as significant others than were the latter four types. Thus, although most relatives had the potential for being significant others, those who were close in blood relationship were more likely to be viewed as significant others.

The majority of the relative significant others exerted influence by serving as models (Table 11.2). There were various aspects to the manner of the modeling, but whether the influence was through a projected quality or performance on the part of the significant other, almost all incidents of modeling (irrespective of the type of the significant other) reflected one major theme: the effort, planning, personal quality, and/or lifestyle that culminated in achievement (as measured by education and occupation). This tendency can be observed in the following description of an older brother:

> He was a kind of great guy; I really admired his ability to lead. When I was 11, I became a tenderfoot because he was the scout master. He managed to pass the civil service exam in 1939 and get a job in the postal service. He could have been a doctor, but it was during the Depression. Still, he did manage 2 years of junior college. Quite a feat for a poor black then.

There were a few instances of what might be called structural kinds of modeling, such as pairing. This occurred when cousins of the same age paired up and formulated mutual achievement goals and/or agreed to follow family expectations, as with two cousins who "went off to college together." The family "expected it because she was my pair." Pairing is characterized by friendly competition, reciprocal modeling, and a prolonged relationship. Also observed was a pairing that was not mutual (one-sided pairing); in fact, the significant other was unaware of its existence. Such cousins were not intimately close, and usually the significant other cousin "came from the side of the family that was better off financially." These respondents were often from the lower class and used the opportunity to observe that "it was possible within the family" to achieve and were inspired "to keep up."

The family ghost model was another instance of special modeling. These were family members who had achieved—sometimes a first for the family, or even the race. They related peripherally, if at all, to the respondents. Their deeds were known through family lore passed around to extended family members and down to succeeding generations. "Aunt _____ was important in my life. She always worked into every conversation that Poppa (her father and my grandfather) had gone to _____ College; had not graduated but had just 'gone.' But his children were all so proud." Hearing the story "reinforced my desire to get an education." No one had ever clarified how long "Poppa" had attended the college; it didn't matter—it was enough that he had "gone."

Although relatives influenced the respondents primarily through modeling, to some extent they also demonstrated other modes of influence (Table 11.2).

A wise and persistent grandmother exerted influence through validation of self as she set forth her expectations.

> My grandmother . . . conveyed to me that she had high expectations, and she saw me fulfilling aspirations for the family that other members of the family, like my father, had not been able to achieve. She talked to me about the importance of an education, the importance of staying in school. I was devoted to her.

And through this respondent's efforts, family "dreams deferred" were finally realized. This illustration calls attention also to the "grandparent factor" in black life (Manns 1977), which has been sensitively depicted in autobiographies (for example, Waters [1951] 1978; Angelou 1969) and fiction (for example, Walker 1970).

Older siblings sometimes influenced younger brothers and sisters through emotional support; some often really parented. A middle-class male whose father was dead and whose mother took a second teaching job in the evening spoke of his brother:

> My oldest brother was wonderful, just the end of the world for me; he was responsible for getting my sister and me our evening meal. At dinner, and after dinner while doing the dishes, he had a game of whistling. He would whistle songs and my sister and I had to guess the name. He read everything and retained everything; but in those hours together, we read everything, too. I still love to read and cannot go into a store without buying a book.

How nourishing this must have been during this man's crucial growth and development years. And what a beautiful way in which to learn to appreciate a basic achievement tool—the book. The older sibling has been more critical to black family life than has been recognized in either research or literature; this area merits study.

The majority of the relative significant others influenced the respondents when they were between the ages of 6 and 17. Some, however, continued their influence during the youth and adult years that followed, although at a decreasing rate. Nevertheless, 22% of the relatives influenced respondents when they (the respondents) were in their 40s.

Occasionally, a "great significant other factor" manifested itself. These were relatives who were described in superlatives, served as models in several ways (in contrast to the usual one-dimensional modeling of most significant others), and profoundly influenced the lives of the respondents. Thus the relative significant other, through modeling, represented sources of inspiration for other family members in their quest for achievement.

The black family, for some time, has been described as a vital force in its members' overall efforts to survive and cope, as well as in their efforts toward achievement (Billingsley 1968; Hill 1971). Recent studies, whether reporting on the middle-class family (McAdoo 1977) or perhaps less solvent families (Martin and Martin 1978), have delineated the support provided by the black family's kinship network.

The findings in this study generally support the notion of a black family support system, but they further clarify specific dynamics of the system. Relative significant others who influenced the achievement of the respondents were not as prevalent as the large, extensive kinship network that has been described as supporting overall survival and coping efforts. (However, in comparison with whites' significant others, the black relative significant other was more prevalent, at a significant level.) In addition, it was found that although almost all relative types were identified as being significant others, those closest in blood relationship were more likely to be so designated; and that although relative significant others influenced the respondents through a variety of modes, they tended to influence through modeling.

Nonrelative Significant Other

More than half (64%) of the significant others were nonrelatives, suggesting that, in addition to parents and other relatives, nonrelatives are greatly involved in the achievement of black family members. Furthermore, these nonrelatives were found in almost every segment of the respondents' lives.

The largest group of nonrelatives were education significant others (47%), of which the majority were teachers and professors, from grade school through graduate school. Other institutional personnel responsible for different aspects of the educational experience (counselors, administrators, and others) were also described, thus the source of the education significant other extended beyond that of the teacher-learner configuration.

Work significant others included administrators, supervisors, and work colleagues from the respondents' jobs. The appearance of this type of significant other (18%) focuses attention on the role of the work environment in the significant other's influence on the individual. It also indicates that this influence occurs during the adult years—a part of the life cycle frequently overlooked in discussions of significant others—and has implications for adult development theory that is emerging.

Mental health significant others included a playground instructor and a Boy Scout leader. Characterized as professionals and other helpers who relate to individuals around life coping efforts, these significant others were not prevalent (2%) among the respondents.

The religion significant others (8%) were ministers for the most part, but included persons outside church leadership, such as a minister's wife. Half of the respondents also mentioned that black ministers, as a group, influenced their achievement.

Thus 75% of the nonrelative significant others were from education, work, mental health, and religious settings—which underscores the importance of the structured institutional environment in the socialization process. Outside the family, such institutional arrangements reflect most of the areas of living. In addition, and particularly germane to black life, is the fact that many of these institutions are white dominated. Thus their potential as a source of significant others is a critical issue.

Close nonkin significant others (11%) included peers, family friends, and sweethearts who shared relationships qualitatively near to the intimacy usually ascribed to caretakers and close relatives. The majority were family friends and were found primarily in the middle class.

Three other types of significant others were categorized: neighborhood (4%), community (4%), and world-at-large (6%) significant others. Although only representing 14% of all nonrelatives, these types are noteworthy because, along with the significant others from institutional settings, their presence speaks to the extensiveness of the sources of possible significant others. The neighborhood and one of the subtypes of the world-at-large (the chance encounter) were found only in the lower class, indicating that lower-class respondents "required" significant others from a broader base than did middle-class respondents.

Unlike the parent and the relative, the nonrelative significant other did not tend to exert influence primarily through one mode (Table 11.2). Nonetheless, more than one-third influenced through modeling and/or validation (Table 11.2). Pairing and one-sided pairing, special kinds of modeling described earlier as being characteristic of some cousins, also appeared with a nonrelative—the peer. Pioneering was another instance of modeling in which the significant other penetrated educational and occupational areas previously closed to blacks and "showed that it could be done." After overcoming many obstacles, a lower-class male entered college but worried about job possibilities. One day he heard a black male social worker address a public forum. "He became a role model for job possibilities and opportunities open to blacks. So I switched to social work." A necessary condition for pioneering is a situation in which the significant other—a member of one's own group—can be observed achieving.

The cultural or lofty hero was another instance of modeling; in this group were persons of renown—gracious Marian Anderson of the concert stage and Joe Louis, beloved by his people for both his skill and his integrity. The element of pioneering was present also, because the lofty hero was often one of the first blacks to achieve distinction in his or her field and thus opened up new possibilities for other blacks.

There were several nuances within the validation of self mode of influence. The most frequently observed was that of positive defining, in which the significant other articulated a direct positive definition of the respondent. A teacher told a respondent's mother that " 'she was very bright and that she should attend college'; it reaffirmed that I was somebody." Along class lines an interesting difference was noted in the manifestations of positive defining. In the middle class there was a tendency for the positive definition, although appreciated, to serve as reinforcement of information already known to the respondent. In the lower class the significant other, in contrast, often offered information that was either unknown and/or not quite believed by the respondent. In the following instance, the respondent's father was dead and the mother, burdened with a large family, worked long, hard hours as a farm laborer. An interested high school teacher "raked me over for considering giving up a scholarship to college. It finally got through to me that I was getting information about myself, and it made me feel important. Maybe, I was worth something."

Another nuance of validation was heritage-reminding, in which the significant other advised the respondent of his or her racial background. One respondent recalled the first time a teacher who happened to be black "taught us black history. It inspired all of us. We really got a sense of what it was like really being black." Although heritage-reminding appeared infrequently as a nuance of validation of self, it was observed as an aspect of other modes. For example, modeling significant others, in demonstrating achievement, sometimes projected a sense of pride in black roots and the need to appreciate them.

More than a third of the nonrelative significant others influenced through validation of self, indicating that the nonrelative (Table 11.2) was important in meeting a human need—the need for positive appraisals (Rogers, cited in Maddi 1972).

As noted above, parent significant others exerted influence through the achievement socialization mode, either by *establishing* an achievement atmosphere or by *mandating* achievement. In contrast, the nonrelative influenced through achievement socialization by *stipulating* educational and occupational goals. Such incidents occurred primarily in the lower class, which indicates that these respondents may have required information on the options available to them from others outside their families.

Nonrelatives also influenced through one of the subcategories of learning elicitation: teaching. A respondent recalled her first boss, who "taught me administrative skills and how to handle budgets, committees, and boards." In addition to knowledge and skills, teaching sometimes emphasized the rudiments of everyday living. For example, a significant other may articulate thoughts on living in the form of a proverb, such as the one provided by a librarian who employed a respondent when she was a teenager, after school: " 'If anything is worth doing, it is worth doing well.' It helped me to incorporate a certain thoroughness in my work." The black elderly have been found to use a similar teaching tool the "maxim" in interactions with younger family members (Martin and Martin 1978).

Most of the family friend (close nonkin) significant others performed supplemental parenting roles—nurturing—through the mode of emotional support. A middle-class female, though loved by her two busy and task-oriented parents, remembered a close family friend who was uneducated but who saw me as a child always. She was one of those very good people who always give tender, loving care. She had the capacity to give and the capacity to love. She nurtured me; my mother did not. She gave me something to fall back on; somebody who was always there.

However, the respondent also described her mother as important in her life and a significant other, but for mandating achievement. This combined input of parent and nonrelative significant others illustrates a kind of partnership in parenting that may characterize some black families.

Numerous nonrelatives, persons outside the family system, influenced the respondents' achievement. Thus these findings support earlier references to the influence of the nonrelative significant other in the achievement of various groups of black individuals (Billingsley 1968; Manns 1974; Shade 1978). However, the findings additionally indicate that the nonrelative significant other was proportionally more prevalent than the relative and parent, combined, irrespective of class; that although nonrelative significant others came from almost all life areas, they were most likely to be from the structured institutional environment, especially education and to some extent the work arena; and that although they concentrated in influencing through modeling and validation of self, they were more inclined than the parent and the relative to exert influence in all of the various modes described above. We can conclude that the nonrelative significant other was an important and necessary presence in the achievement of the respondents.

A profile of the nonrelative significant other was developed. For the most part, the nonrelative significant other tended to be like the respondent on ascribed characteristics, race, and sex. Although nonrelative significant others were of both races—black and white—they tended to be black. As relative and parent significant others were also black, the majority of all significant others who influenced the achievement of the respondents were black. For influence on achievement, members of these black families were dependent primarily, but not exclusively, on their own race.

On achieved characteristics, nonrelative significant others were at higher educational, income, and community levels than were the respondents. In a sense, this finding supports an accepted definition of a significant other as someone the individual holds in esteem. Yet it also raises a question: To what extent are potential significant others who influence achievement available to members of the black lower socioeconomic class, who are often surrounded by people of the *same* or *lower* educational, income, and community levels? This question is particularly relevant considering the growing attention being directed toward the locked-in plight of a special group of the black lower class, the *underclass* (Glasgow 1980; Wilson 1978).

Nonrelative significant others were older in age than the respondents. Although nonrelative significant others appeared throughout a large part of the respondents' life cycle, they concentrated during the respondents' childhood, adolescence, and young adulthood, which underscores the importance of the black adult in black life.

This concentration on the influence of significant others is not intended to negate the role of black individuals' inner resources, or self-directiveness, which are also a factor in achievement. Rather, this discussion has focused on examining the influence of the many persons who contribute to that achievement and thereby participate in the socialization process of black families.

References

Angelou, M. 1969. *I Know Why the Caged Bird Sings*. New York: Random House.

Billingsley, A. 1968. *Black Families in White America*. Englewood Cliffs, NJ: Prentice Hall.

Cooley, C. H. [1902] 1964. *Human Nature and the Social Order.* New York: Schocken.

Denzin, N. K. 1970. *The Research Act*. Chicago: AVC.

Glasgow, D. G. 1980. *The Black Underclass*. San Francisco: Jossey-Bass.

Haller, A. O. and J. Woelfel. 1972. "Significant Others and Their Expectations, Concepts and Instruments to Measure Interpersonal Influence on Status Aspirations." *Rural Sociology* 35(December):591-621.

Hill, R. B. 1971. *The Strengths of Black Families*. New York: Emerson-Hall.

Jones, R. L. 1981. "The Effects of Person-Environment Fit, Locus of Control and the Mother's Perception of the Teaching Behaviors of the Significant Other on the Teaching Behaviors of Low Income Black Mothers." Ph.D. dissertation, Case Western University.

Kuhn, M. H. 1972. "Major Trends in Symbolic Interaction Theory in the Past Twenty-Five Years." In *Symbolic Interaction: A Reader in Social Psychology,* edited by J. Manis and B. N. Meltzer. Boston: Allyn & Bacon.

Maddi, S. R. 1972. *Personality Theories: A Comparative Analysis*. Homewood, IL: Dorsey.

Manns, W. 1974. "Significant Others in Black Autobiographies: An Exploration." Unpublished manuscript.

———. 1977. "Significant Others in Black Autobiographies." Paper presented at conference on Black Families: A Source of National Strength, sponsored by National Urban League's Project Thrive, Chicago, November.

Martin, E. P. and J. M. Martin. 1978. *The Black Extended Family*. Chicago: University of Chicago Press.

McAdoo, H. P. 1977. *The Impact of Extended Family Variables Upon the Upward Mobility of Black Families*. Final report to Department of Health, Education and Welfare. Washington, DC: Office of Child Development.

Mead, G. H. [1934] 1962. *Mind, Self and Society,* vol. 1 (C. W. Morris, ed.). Chicago: University of Chicago Press.

Quarantelli, E. L. and J. Cooper. 1966. "Self-Conceptions and Others: A Further Test of Meadian Hypotheses." *Sociological Quarterly* 7(Summer).

———. 1972. "Self-Conceptions and Others: A Further Test of Meadian Hypotheses." In *Symbolic Interaction: A Reader in Social Psychology,* edited by J. G. Manis and B. N. Meltzer. Boston: Allyn & Bacon.

Shade, O. 1978. "Significant Other Influences on the Educational and Occupational Goals of Disadvantaged Afro-American College Freshmen." *Dissertation Abstracts International* 38:7200-A.

Walker, A. 1970. *The Third Life of Grange Copeland.* New York: Harcourt Brace Jovanovich.

Waters, E. [1951] 1978. *His Eye Is on the Sparrow: An Autobiography.* Westport, CT: Greenwood.

Wilson, W. J. (1978). *The Declining Significance of Race: Blacks and Changing American Institutions.* Chicago: University of Chicago Press.

Out There Stranded?

Black Families in White Communities

BEVERLY DANIEL TATUM

According to a 20-year-old Black woman raised in a White suburb:

> [My parents] never presented an option for me as a Black female teenager. Say, "If you're going to a White school, well that's okay, but here are other Black outlets for you." So they never did anything. They just complained about it and saw how unhappy I was and how "White" I was, but they never did anything about it. . . . I'm really kind of resentful. . . . In retrospect, I think I could be dealing with a lot of different social situations with White people better if I knew I had a Black network to fall back upon. But when you don't have any kind of support group, you're kind of, like, out there stranded.

Out there stranded? Is that the essence of the experience of living in a White community for Black families and their children? Often such communities allow Black residents access to well-funded school systems, desirable housing, and economic opportunities, yet at what psychic cost?

214

Because of persistent residential segregation in the United States, these families represent less than 10% of the Black population (Landry 1987). Barely visible in the communities in which they live, ironically these families are also barely visible in the social science literature on Black families. Although there has been research on Black children in predominantly White school settings (St. John 1981; Slaughter and Johnson 1988; Miller 1989; Zweigenhaft and Domhoff 1991), typically these children are attending school outside their home communities. In addition, clinicians have contributed case examples to the literature on Black families in White suburban communities (Coner-Edwards and Spurlock 1988; Boyd-Franklin 1989; Hopson and Hopson 1990), as have contemporary essayists and journalists (Early 1993; Cose 1993; Hayes 1994). Only a few social scientists (Banks 1984, 1989; Tatum 1992a, 1993a, 1993b) have investigated the experiences of the small but growing population of Black children and their families who reside in predominantly White communities.

Their experiences are of interest because they are on the leading edge of housing desegregation and because the children of these typically middle- to upper-income families have unprecedented access to educational and economic resources that might prepare them for leadership positions in U.S. society. This leadership potential is an important resource for the development of African Americans as a group, if it is used for the benefit of Black communities. Yet if young men and women have been isolated from other Black people because of their living situation, will they feel connected in any significant way to the issues facing the larger Black community? If they are "out there stranded," how will their social and emotional growth be affected?

Brookins (1988) raises a similar question in discussing the marginalization of talented Black children attending an elite, predominantly White private school:

> If these Black students represent an important segment of the potential leadership of the Black community, how can they assume effective leadership roles if their experience in an important socializing setting during a critical developmental period accrues marginal status to them? (p. 17)

How much more salient is this question for children who spend most if not all their time (outside the family) in settings where they are racially isolated?

Assimilation Blues:
Parental Perspectives on Sources of Stress

Black parents who choose to live in White suburban communities are usually drawn there for educational or economic reasons (Tatum 1992b). Despite the material advantages such opportunities may represent, these parents often are quite ambivalent about their choice and its social implications for their children. Because many of these parents were reared in segregated or racially diverse communities, they usually do not have first-hand experience with growing up in a predominantly White community. Socializing children to live in this unfamiliar context represents a new challenge.

In my own phenomenological study of 10 two-parent, upwardly mobile, middle-class Black families living in a predominantly White community in California identified as "Sun Beach," most of the parents readily acknowledged that their town was a beautiful, quiet, and relatively safe place to rear children. Yet, with a Black population of less than 2%, it lacked the cohesiveness and relatedness of the Black communities in which they had grown up. Several of the 20 parents interviewed had very warm memories of the closeness of family and friends in their childhood, and they perceived this change as a real loss. One mother discussed it at length:

> I lived in a segregated community and then I came here. . . . In the community where I grew up, everybody was a part of my family. . . . Every female in that neighborhood was like my mother. . . . All the kids in the neighborhood belonged to everybody, so it was like you had this huge gigantic extended family and there was nowhere you could go where someone didn't know you and did not know who you belonged to, and did not know whether you were out of place, and nobody had any qualms about saying, "You know you're not supposed to be doing that," and no child would have even thought about saying, "Well, hey, you're not my mother, you can't tell me what to do," because they had every right to tell you what to do. . . .
>
> I guess part of the problem is the geographic structure. New people coming here don't even realize that there are Black people here because we're so spread out, they're all over the city. There is no Black community, there is no one area where there's more Black people than others . . . so you miss the advantages of the extended family. It's not there, so the kids will grow up today thinking, "Well, hey, where do you get off telling me what to do? You're not my mother." . . . I mean it could be your best friend's child . . . and when you go up and tell your friend she'll say, "Well, that's none of your business." Because

after all, that's not your child. And so the continuity is lost that you get when you live in a Black community. (quoted in Tatum 1992b, p. 66)

The absence of a strong community support network was exacerbated for some families in Sun Beach by the fact that they were geographically distant from their extended families. With the exception of one mother, all the parents in the sample were employed outside the home, some in more than one job. With so much energy expended in the maintenance of family income, there is little left for child rearing and household maintenance. Although this situation is common among Black middle-class families (McAdoo 1978; Boyd-Franklin 1989), it may be experienced more intensely among isolated Black families because they often do not have easy access to extended family support systems. Particularly for extremely busy parents, the lack of family assistance, especially in the area of child care, is a source of stress.

In addition, some parents were concerned about the effect of "hidden racism" on their families. Unlike the overt racism of segregation that they had learned to recognize in their own childhood, they found the racism in this community was more likely to be covert and therefore more difficult to confront. They frequently felt the pressures of tokenism (Kanter 1977) at their places of employment. Describing his situation, one man said:

Just being Black makes it hard, because people look at you like you're not as good as they are, like you're a second class citizen. . . . You got to always look over your shoulder like somebody's always watching you. At my job, I'm the only Black in my department and it seems like they're always watching me, the pressure's always on to perform. You feel like if you miss a day, you might not have a job. So there's that constant awareness on my part, they can snatch what little you have. . . . that's a constant fear, you know, especially when you've got a family to support. (quoted in Tatum 1992b, p. 99)

Again, these pressures are not unique to Black families in the suburbs (Davis and Watson 1982; Boyd-Franklin 1989; Edwards and Polite 1992; Cose 1993), but they may be intensified by their isolation.

Of even more concern to the parents in the sample, however, were the effects of racism on their children, particularly as the children experienced it in the schools. These parents observed little or no accurate representation of the historical contributions of Blacks in the school curriculum, and they noticed a tendency of teachers to neglect the individual needs of Black children in the classroom (that is, not calling on them in class). The majority

of the parents interviewed volunteered anecdotes about race-related incidents at school. Many were dismayed at the apparent belief held by some
school personnel that racial name-calling and other race-related hostility
cannot be prevented and therefore must simply be endured. The stress of
having to confront the problem was often compounded by anger at the
school's unsatisfactory response (Tatum 1992b).

Although the quality of the public schools is often one of the assumed
benefits of living in a White suburb, ironically, 4 of the 10 families interviewed in Sun Beach were sufficiently disillusioned by the racism in the
schools to place their children in private schools. Similar problems can and
do occur in those settings (Slaughter and Johnson 1988), but the parents who
chose this option felt they had more power to influence the school environment because the private schools seemed more responsive to their input. For
these parents, the increased feeling of control, combined with the belief that
the quality of education was higher in the private schools than in the public
schools, justified the financial burden of tuition payments.

And what about the child's life outside school? Many Black parents living
in White communities express concern about the nature of their children's
social relationships (Tatum 1992b; Early 1993; Boyd-Franklin 1989). Will
they have Black friends? Who will they date? Will they understand what it
means to be Black in a racist society? Will they get enough of what they need
in their social environment to have a positive sense of Black identity? What
should the nature of that identity be? Because the social context for their
children is so different from what the parents' was, the parents feel anxious
about rearing children in these uncharted waters.

In a collection of essays about race, identity, and the ambivalence of
assimilation, Loury (1993) describes the anxiety he felt after an afternoon
walk with his 3-year-old son, during which they observed a group of White
men playing ice hockey on a local pond:

> I sensed that we were interlopers, that if we had come with sticks and skates
> we would not necessarily have been welcome. But this may be wrong. . . . I do
> know that my son very much enjoyed watching the game, and I thought to
> myself at the time that he would, someday too soon, come asking for a pair of
> skates. I found myself consciously dreading that day. . . .
> My aversion to the idea of my son's involvement in that Sunday afternoon
> ritual we witnessed was rooted in my own sense of identity, as a Black American
> man who grew up when and where I did, who has had the experiences I have
> had. Because I would not have felt comfortable there, I began to think that he
> should not want to be a part of that scene either. I was inclined to impose upon

my son, in the name of preserving his authentic blackness, a limitation of his pursuits deriving from my life, but not really relevant to his. (pp. 10-11)

This father concludes that the fact that his children are part of an affluent White community means "it is inevitable that their racial sensibilities will be quite different" from his own, and this inevitability is not something to be feared.

Yet other parents do fear the possible consequences for a child who does not understand the continuing significance of race in this society. One of the fathers interviewed in Sun Beach commented:

> It becomes really damaging, if you somehow have a kid who fails to understand the reality of living in this kind of community. You can play with these kids, and you can be friends in school, and everybody will be happy and get along fine. But when you start talking about taking this girl out to some ice cream stand or basketball game, then you have the parental prejudices and racism come forward . . . that will create an unfortunate kind of situation, particularly if the kid's not prepared for that sort of racism. . . . We try to let them know that there is very definitely a great deal of racism here, that you've got to be prepared for it. You can't be overwhelmed when you see it. But that is something I am very much concerned about. (quoted in Tatum 1992b, p. 81)

The stress of trying to find the right balance between protecting children from the pain of racism and inoculating them against what will probably be unavoidable encounters is part of daily living for these families.

Although most, if not all, Black parents struggle with these issues (Peters 1988), Black families in a racially similar environment may have the additional support of the community as a buffer between the child and the negative messages of the dominant society (Barnes 1972; Jackson, McCullough, and Gurin 1988). Without such a buffer, families must find their own means for addressing their children's racial socialization. The socialization strategies observed among the Sun Beach families will be discussed later in this chapter.

Parental Sources of Support

Given these sources of stress, where do Black parents find support for themselves and, ultimately, for their children? Black churches have been and continue to be a traditional source (Taylor and Chatters 1991). Almost all the

Sun Beach parents interviewed had been part of a Black religious community in their childhood. They freely acknowledged the social as well as spiritual support they had received in this context, but only 4 of the 10 families had maintained religious involvement as part of their family life. For those 4 families, the church was still an important resource.

Those who no longer had ties to a church community attributed this to changes in lifestyle and general disinterest. Although it represents another loss in cultural continuity for their children, this finding is consistent with those reported by McAdoo (1979) and Jackson (1982). McAdoo (1979) found that only half her middle-class sample said religion was important to them, a significant decline from the previous generation. Jackson (1982) suggests there is a developmental cycle of family participation in churches, with the lowest participation occurring between the ages of 17 and 40. Given that the median ages of the men and women in my sample were 38 and 34, respectively, it remains to be seen whether patterns of church attendance will change as these families age (Tatum 1992b).

Close friendships are another potential source of support. It already has been pointed out that the Sun Beach families do not experience the neighborhood cohesiveness they knew in their communities of origin, but 14 of the 20 adults interviewed (70%) maintained close relationships with friends in Sun Beach that they considered to be "like family" (90% had such relationships in other locations). Most, but not all, of these relationships had been formed with other Black people, typically individuals who befriended them, or whom they befriended, shortly after they arrived in Sun Beach. Such fictive kin relationships have been discussed by others as an important aspect of Black family support networks (Nobles et al. 1976; Aoyagi 1978; Malson 1982).

Particularly in socially alienating situations, such friendships are very important. A strong peer support group can reduce the effects of tokenism. In fact, if there is enough support outside the situation, the challenge of being a token actually can be a positive one. To go where few have gone before and succeed can be a source of pride. If there is a place to unwind, where one can revert back from symbol of one's racial group to individual, then a potentially stressful situation can become an opportunity for positive growth (Kanter 1977). The greater likelihood that another Black person will share one's frame of reference and will understand what it is like to be the only Black person on the job, or in the neighborhood, probably fosters the high percentage of close intraracial, rather than interracial, friendships.

These friendship networks are important not only to adults but also to children, who find support among these caring adults and, if the adults have children, an expanded friendship network. It is a valuable object lesson for a child to observe the close "family" relationships that can develop between friends. It is perhaps axiomatic that isolated adults often have isolated children. It is certainly the case that among the 15 Sun Beach children interviewed, only 8 understood what I meant when I asked if they had any "play" relatives. Like all the adults, these 8 children understood right away and described relationships with "play" aunts or sisters or cousins. The other children were completely baffled by the phrase. When the term was explained, they all indicated that they did not have any relationships like that. In almost all cases, their parents indicated that they did not have any fictive kin relationships in Sun Beach, so it is not surprising that the children did not. Unlike their parents, however, the children do not share the idea that such relationships, commonly found in Black communities, are possible and desirable. To the extent that fictive kin ties can be considered an adaptive response to stressful circumstances for Black individuals and families, this apparently untransmitted concept represents another cultural loss for these particular children (Tatum 1992b).

Although fictive kin relationships clearly are important for those who have them, all the Sun Beach families relied primarily on the household unit as the primary source of support and rejuvenation in the face of daily stress. Most nonwork time was spent at home. Several parents described their families as being very close and inclined to keep to themselves, or, as one woman said, "We don't really bother people" (quoted in Tatum 1992b, p. 118). Consistent with McAdoo's (1982) findings, most of the families indicated that the nuclear family is the preferred source of support in times of crisis, followed by extended family members.

This heavy reliance on intimates for support is not surprising when it is understood that most of these families view their frame of reference as different from that of their White neighbors (Tatum 1992b). Families often respond to environmental uncertainty and unshared community frameworks by withdrawing into themselves and tightening their boundaries (Reiss and Oliveri 1983). How do these tight family boundaries expand or contract to allow for the development of children's relationships?

Race-Conscious Socialization as a Coping Strategy

The variation in socialization strategies among parents is most evident in their attitudes concerning their children's friendships. As discussed previously, Blacks who make the choice to live in predominantly White neigh-borhoods often worry about the social implications for their children. As Spencer, Swanson, and Cunningham (1991) point out, "Traditionally, the cultural experience of minorities in the United States requires they become not only marginal persons but also bicultural ones capable of demonstrating competence both in the larger society and within their own ethnic commu-nity" (p. 368). The emphasis that Black parents in White communities place on their children's school performance is intended to ensure that their children will be capable of demonstrating their competence in the larger society. But how is competence within their own ethnic community—that is, an appropriate sense of "Blackness"—ensured?

Concern about this issue leads some parents to create Black peer groups for their children (Spurlock and Booth 1988; Boyd-Franklin 1989; Randolph 1992). Among the 10 pairs of parents in the Sun Beach study, 8 said it was important that their children have Black friends, but only 4 had actually taken steps to encourage that outcome. Because the local Black population is so small, no peer group occurs naturally at school or in the neighborhood. If a Black peer group is going to exist, it must be created; parents must actively seek out other Black families with children in the surrounding areas, join organizations with Black membership (such as churches or social clubs), and, when possible, use extended family networks (such as sending children to visit relatives in Black communities). Characterized as "race-conscious," these parents were explicit about their intention to reinforce their children's sense of Black identity even in the midst of a White community. One race-conscious father said:

> Sure my kids have a Black peer group, because we make it a point, we have to import them in, or export them out. . . . I believe my children can have just as much as anybody else, but they also have to have reality in their life. They're going to face enough reality just by going to school with these people, but then there's also reality when they're going to have to be able to communicate to their own people and be with their own people. . . . Well, I know their best friends are Black, and we're going to keep it that way. And I was just for-tunate to be able to give them what they've had. . . . But what I'm saying is that still doesn't have us running away from the truth. (quoted in Tatum 1992b, pp. 79-80)

Those parents who said it was important for their children to have Black friends but had not actively worked to make such friendships possible often assumed that the situation could not be altered or would change naturally as their children got older. They adopted what Spencer (1985) calls a race-neutral approach, making no special efforts to influence their children's friendship patterns.

The responses of both the race-conscious and the race-neutral parents can be contrasted with the response of one parent who believes a Black peer group is not important for his children. He explained: "Their contacts are basically non-Black. I think it's more important that they have a socio-economic group than a racial peer group" (quoted in Tatum 1992b, p. 119). This perspective initially was classified as class consciousness, which minimizes the significance of race, but a subsequent investigation of family socialization frameworks suggests that some parents may be both race- and class-conscious, and those who de-emphasize racial group membership might be more accurately described as race-avoidant.

The finding that parents vary in their degree of race-conscious socialization is supported by the clinical observations of Boyd-Franklin (1989). She also describes parents who engage in proactive efforts to create social networks for their children, as well as parents who "have adopted a 'color blind' attitude in which they deny the impact of racial differences. Unfortunately, it is often their children who bear the brunt of the cultural isolation" (p. 217).

The issue that obviously emerges from this categorization of parental socialization responses is what difference it makes to the children. How are their experiences affected by their parents' approaches? Boyd-Franklin suggests that the children of the "color blind," or what I am now calling race-avoidant parents, are most negatively affected by the isolation. Certainly, without the active intervention of their parents, they are less likely to have Black friends. But if they have White friends, does this really matter?

A Black professor, struggling with guilt over his residential choice, suggested to his daughter that she should have more Black friends (Early 1993, p. xxiii). She replied: "Why do I have to have black friends? Just because I'm black?" He acknowledged to himself that he was more uncomfortable about her friendship pattern than she was. He then told her that when older she "could pay a price" for having a White social life. "Well, Daddy," she responded, "as you always like to say, nothing is free."

And what is the cost? Ultimately, this is a question only the children can answer. From their point of view, what do they need not only to survive but also to thrive in the situation in which they find themselves? What do they need to feel competent in both the larger society and within their own ethnic community?

The Children Speak

In the Sun Beach study, 15 children were interviewed about their perceptions of family life, school, and social relationships. They ranged in age from 6 to 14 and gave very brief responses to these questions. In general, they expressed enthusiasm for their community. The response of this 11-year-old girl was typical: "I love it [here]. What I like most about [Sun Beach] is that all my friends are here, and I just like it. It's real fun and stuff" (quoted in Tatum 1992b, p. 86). Unlike their parents, the children have had limited experience in any other community. More than half were born in Sun Beach, and the rest were just entering school or younger when they moved there. Perhaps more important, most had not yet entered adolescence, an important developmental transition and the period when issues of social isolation seem to become most salient for Black youth in White communities. "At this point, social barriers often become more evident and a child who may have felt 'accepted' at a younger age may now feel left out" (Boyd-Franklin 1989, p. 216). It seems the children in the Sun Beach study were not yet ready to address their parents' concerns.

In his research on Black youth in White communities, Banks (1984, 1989) concludes that the majority of children surveyed felt comfortable in their neighborhoods and at school and had positive attitudes toward their racial group. It should be noted, however, that adolescents had significantly more negative attitudes toward both their White neighborhoods and other Blacks than did younger children. One possible explanation is that, as Boyd-Franklin (1989) suggests, adolescents become more socially isolated in their communities and consequently like them less. They also may begin to internalize the negative messages about African Americans they receive from their White communities. And they may begin to encounter hostility from other Black youth, who accuse them of being "too White," which may result in a negative attitude toward other Blacks. The age range in Banks's sample population was 8 to 18, but the mean age was 12.8. As Spencer et al. (1991) and Parham (1989) point out, the process of ethnic/racial identity development is lifelong, but it unfolds in a critical way during adolescence. As in my earlier study (Tatum 1992b), the usefulness of Banks's findings may be limited by the age of the sample.

Beyond Childhood:
Coming of Age in White Communities

In an effort to answer some of the questions raised about the effects of parental socialization and community context, I conducted in-depth interviews with Black college students who had been reared in predominantly White communities (Tatum 1993a, 1993b). The students were recruited, by letter and through a "snowballing" method of personal referrals, from two elite, private coeducational colleges in New England. A total of 23 students volunteered to participate in in-depth individual interviews (approximately 2 hours long) about their family lives, school and peer relationships in their communities of origin, current level of racial awareness, and adjustment to their predominantly White college environment. All of those who volunteered were interviewed, but 6 of the 23 were children of interracial marriages, had been adopted by White families, or were recent immigrants to the United States. Clearly, the experiences of these young people are important to consider, but this discussion is limited to the remaining 17 subjects, all of whom had two Black parents and grew up in the care of at least one of them while residing in the United States.

The participants (5 men and 12 women) ranged in age from 18 to 22, with a median age of 20. The median annual family income was $60,000. All had lived in predominantly White communities and/or attended predominantly White schools since their elementary years. Probably primarily owing to the recruiting patterns of the colleges, all but two were from the East Coast, ranging as far south as Washington, D.C., and as far north as Massachusetts. The remaining two participants were from the Midwest.

The taped interviews were transcribed and analyzed thematically, with particular attention to details regarding parents' attitudes toward racial socialization (degree of race consciousness), school experiences, and changing self-perceptions regarding racial identity. Gender differences in the nature of their social experiences were also investigated. Although each person's story, told in response to very open-ended interview questions, is unique, clear patterns emerged.

Despite the fact that 11 of the 17 reported racist interactions, usually name-calling, during their elementary school years, most still remembered their childhood as relatively free of conflict. In two communities, however, where racial tensions were high because of White resistance to school desegregation, children were exposed to more negative incidents, sometimes initiated by adults. As one young man described life in his small New York suburb: "It felt normal. . . . I never knew anything different. I wasn't race-conscious until, say, sixth, seventh, eighth grade." Like this young man, most mentioned a change in their perceptions and experiences as they entered junior high or high school. Typically, this change meant entering a larger school that drew a more diverse student population from beyond the boundaries of their own neighborhoods.

In this context, 13 of the 17 respondents described feeling a sense of alienation from other Black teenagers. Of these 13, 9 experienced rejection from other Blacks because they were "too White" and criticism from Blacks for the way they talked, dressed, or achieved in school (Tatum 1993a). For example, one young woman from a predominantly White neighborhood in Baltimore said of her experiences in high school:

> That's when I got hit with racism again. But not from Whites but from Blacks. Oh you sound White, you think you're White, that sort of thing. . . . So ninth grade was sort of traumatic. . . . [The other Black women there] were not into me for the longest time. My first year there was hell.

This young woman responded by trying to "become Black," listening to rap music, even though she did not like it, so she would fit in.

Other respondents reacted by avoiding other Black students. Of the 13 who said they felt some alienation from other Blacks, 4 talked about it in terms of perceived differences in values and expectations for achievement. As a 21-year-old man from a Midwestern suburb explained:

> [School's] a very integrated environment, but in terms of those who you'd characterize as successful, [they] are overwhelmingly White. And since I wanted to be successful, I tended to hang out with people who, you know, I thought had similar interests. And so for the most part, my friends, um, were predominantly White all the way through [high] school.

Relying on a circle of White friends did not adequately resolve the problem of social interaction in high school, however, as 13 of the 17 respondents also described discomfort among their White peers because they were Black (Tatum 1993a). When asked what it was like to have mostly White friends in high school, the young man just quoted said: "It was always uncomfortable. . . . I tried to de-emphasize the fact that I was Black," a strategy of racelessness that Fordham (1988) finds common among academically successful Black adolescents (Tatum 1992a).

Another participant, a 20-year-old woman from the Philadelphia area, described some of her anger at White friends who implied that she was not like other Blacks, an exception to a stereotypical rule, or that she would not have to worry about getting into college because of affirmative action programs, not acknowledging her academic efforts (Tatum 1993b). In other cases, the source of discomfort was less easily located in particular statements or actions but resulted from a general feeling of not being understood by White friends, who did not know what it was like to be the only Black student in the class.

As indicated earlier, Black parents in White communities are often concerned about what their children's dating experiences will be like. Of the 12 young women interviewed, 5 (42%) dated little, if at all, in high school. For some of those interviewed, it was a very frustrating experience. One young woman described herself as "pursuing White guys all throughout high school" without success. As she said, "That prom thing was out of the question." Other nondaters seemed prepared to wait. Said one young woman: "I guess from my father's lectures, just study, study, study, and think about that later. And that's really what I did."

Although it was the perception of the young women that young Black men were more likely to date than they were, two of the five young men interviewed (40%) also had little dating experience in high school. One of these young men did at least attend his prom, along with his brother and their White dates. The number of male interviewees is too small to allow any definitive statements, but it seems that the young men who dated did so more frequently than the girls who dated. All of those who dated, men and women, had some experience with interracial dating. In general, both males and females who were involved in sports had more active social lives because they were invited to teammates' parties and other related social events. To the extent that boys are more likely to be involved in school athletics, it may be easier for them to find a social niche than it is for girls.

Of the 17 respondents, 10 came from families that could be characterized as race-conscious. That is, the families engaged in many or all of the following behaviors, as described by the children: expressed pro-Black attitudes, encouraged children to learn about African American history, maintained Black friendship networks, initiated conversations about race-related topics with their children, and urged their children to attend historically Black colleges.

Another 6 of the 17 were from families that I characterize as race-neutral. These families may share some of the same pro-Black attitudes as race-conscious families, but they do not operationalize them in the same way. Their approach is more passive. For example, one young woman said:

> I really can't remember her ever saying racial issues in particular, but I think that she just instilled in me certain values about myself that surpassed any barrier. . . . I think that's the way she chose to deal with it, letting me come to certain realizations rather than her saying, "Expect this."

Only one of the respondents came from a family that might be characterized as race-avoidant. She is quoted at the beginning of this chapter as feeling stranded in a school where she did not feel accepted, yet her family seemed actively to discourage her interaction with other Blacks. When she expressed interest in a more racially mixed high school, and subsequently a historically Black college, her parents convinced her that she would not fit in either place. Now as a college student at a prestigious White university, she still struggles with feelings of social rejection.

> My self-esteem has gone down the toilet since I've been here. . . . Being made to feel that you're never quite pretty enough, never quite smart enough, or even if you're all of these things, just being made to feel that you're different, something's not quite right. Obviously I know there's nothing wrong with me, but it's constant reinforcement of something's not quite right.

Based on their experiences in junior and senior high school, most of the respondents viewed the racial makeup of the colleges they considered as an important criterion for selection. Only 6 of the 17 participants seriously considered attending historically Black colleges. Of the remaining 11, 9 said they did not consider historically Black colleges for what I have called identity-related reasons. They were not sure that they would be able to fit in socially, afraid that once again they might be labeled "too White" (Tatum 1993a). As one young woman from a Maryland suburb explained, "I knew initially I didn't want to go to a Black college because I thought I would get the same shit I had gotten in high school." A male student from New York was also apprehensive about attending a historically Black college:

> It was exciting and frightening at the same time, of going to a school and sitting in a classroom, full of intelligent Black men and women, and entering in intelligent debates and academic talks, socializing and all that stuff, with other Black people. At the same time, because I hadn't done it before, I wasn't sure . . . how I was going to fit in. . . . This was the easier thing to do.

Of the 6 who initially considered attending historically Black colleges, 5 were from race-conscious families.

Of those interviewed, the young woman from the race-avoidant family seemed to be the most demoralized by her experience, and she still seemed to be seeking external validation from Whites in ways that the other students interviewed were not. In fact, she was the only interviewee who explicitly indicated a preference for a White marriage partner (9 indicated no preference, and 7 indicated a preference for a Black partner). It is interesting to note that 5 of the 7 who indicated a Black preference were from race-conscious families.

Perhaps particularly telling are the responses the young people gave to two questions: "What preparation, if any, do you think you received in your family for dealing with racial issues?" and "What, if anything, would you have wanted your parents to do differently?" Six respondents said they wished their parents had given more help or preparation. For example, in discussing her adjustment to college, one young woman said:

> Everything that I've gone through this year she knows about, and now I can talk about it with her and everything, but I just wish that she had spoken to me earlier about it. Like for instance, studying the Civil War in high school, I wish she had said, "Oh, did you learn anything interesting about Blacks in the Civil War?" And I didn't know Blacks were in the Civil War. You know, for her to say, "Look at this book. Bring this up to your teacher." I wish I would have had that knowledge to kind of dispute a lot of what I was taught in high school.

Of those who wished for more preparation from their parents, only one was from a race-conscious family. Of the 8 who felt quite satisfied with their family's preparation, 5 were from race-conscious families (3 of the 17 were unsure).

Despite the challenges that living and going to school in predominantly White environments presented to these Black students, 9 of the 17 said they would choose similar communities in which to rear their own children. The remaining 8 indicated they wanted to live in communities more racially mixed than the ones in which they grew up. Of the 9 who would choose suburban communities, 6 were from race-conscious families. This may suggest that their proactive families provided enough support to prevent their feeling "out there stranded" and that they foresee being able to do the same for their own children.

Discussion and Implications for Future Research

The design of this study and the small sample size necessitate caution in interpreting the findings. Similar questions need to be asked on a larger scale. Nevertheless, it seems that some tentative inferences can be made. The widespread descriptions of social difficulties with both Black and White peers suggest that these experiences have more to do with the community context than with family socialization patterns. Yet those young people who eventually were able to make positive connections with other Black peers experienced a sense of relief. To the extent that family socialization patterns encourage such connections, the young person benefits.

The facts that the children of race-conscious families were more willing to consider historically Black colleges and were more likely to express preferences for Black marriage partners suggest that they may feel more competent with their own ethnic group than do some of their peers. If this is the case, their families may have been able to accomplish the dual socialization goals identified by Spencer (1985), even in the context of a White community. Although race-neutral families also may be able to achieve these goals, it seems that in the face of the racial hostility found in some suburban communities, the more passive race-neutral stance may be an insufficient buffer. Bowman and Howard (1985) suggest that children of race-conscious families are more resilient in the face of racism and other stressors. Their finding seems consistent with the trends identified here.

More research needs to be done on the relationships among family socialization practices, community context, and the social and emotional adjustment of Black youth. There is still much to learn about Black families' experiences and coping strategies in the context of predominantly White communities. It is telling that none of the young people I interviewed complained that their parents talked too much about their heritage or provided them with too many social opportunities to connect with other Black children. In the absence of more information, it seems that families willing to be vocal in their affirmation of their children's cultural heritage may be able to reap the benefits of the opportunities that drew them to the suburbs without leaving their children stranded in the process.

References

Aoyagi, K. 1978. "Kinship and Friendship in Black Los Angeles: A Study of Migrants From Texas." Pp. 271-353 in *The Extended Family in Black Societies,* edited by D. B. Shimkin, E. M. Shimkin, and D. A. Frate. Chicago: Aldine.

Banks, J. A. 1984. "Black Youths in Predominantly White Suburbs: An Exploratory Study of Their Attitudes and Self-Concepts." *Journal of Negro Education* 53(1):3-17.

———. 1989. "Black Youth in Predominantly White Suburbs." Pp. 65-77 in *Black Adolescents,* edited by R. L. Jones. Berkeley, CA: Cobb & Henry.

Barnes, E. J. 1972. "The Black Community as the Source of Positive Self-Concept for Black Children: A Theoretical Perspective." In *Black Psychology,* edited by R. L. Jones. New York: Harper & Row.

Bowman, P. and C. Howard. 1985. "Race-Related Socialization, Motivation, and Academic Achievement: A Study of Black Youths in Three-Generation Families." *Journal of the American Academy of Child Psychiatry* 24(March):134-41.

Boyd-Franklin, N. 1989. *Black Families in Therapy: A Multisystems Approach.* New York: Guilford.

Brookins, G. K. 1988. "Making the Honor Roll: A Black Parent's Perspective on Private Education." Pp. 12-20 in *Visible Now: Blacks in Private Schools,* edited by D. T. Slaughter and D. J. Johnson. Westport, CT: Greenwood.

Coner-Edwards, A. F. and J. Spurlock. 1988. *Black Families in Crisis: The Middle Class.* New York: Brunner/Mazel.

Cose, E. 1993. *The Rage of a Privileged Class.* New York: HarperCollins.

Davis, G. and G. Watson. 1982. *Black Life in Corporate America: Swimming in the Mainstream.* Garden City, NY: Anchor.

Early, G. 1993. *Lure and Loathing: Essays on Race, Identity, and the Ambivalence of Assimilation.* New York: Penguin.

Edwards, A. and C. K. Polite. 1992. *Children of the Dream: The Psychology of Black Success.* Garden City, NY: Doubleday.

Fordham, S. 1988. "Racelessness as a Factor in Black Students' School Success: Pragmatic Strategy or Pyrrhic Victory?" *Harvard Educational Review* 58(1):54-84.

Gibbs, J. T. 1989. "Black American Adolescents." Pp. 179-223 in *Children of Color,* edited by J. T. Gibbs and L. Huang. San Francisco: Jossey-Bass.

Hayes, D. W. 1994. "Integration and the African American Family." *Black Issues in Higher Education* 10(23):34-35.

Hopson, D. and D. Hopson. 1990. *Different and Wonderful: Raising Black Children in a Race Conscious Society.* Englewood Cliffs, NJ: Prentice Hall.

Jackson, F. M. 1982. "Black Families, Children and Their Churches." Pp. F1-14 in *Studies on Black Children and Their Families*. Proceedings of the 6th Annual Conference of the National Council of Black Studies, March, edited by G. McWorter. Urbana: University of Illinois, Afro-American Studies and Research Program.

Jackson, J. S., W. R. McCullough, and G. Gurin. 1988. "Family, Socialization Environment, and Identity Development in Black Americans." Pp. 242-56 in *Black Families,* 2nd ed., edited by H. P. McAdoo. Newbury Park, CA: Sage.

Kanter, R. M. 1977. *Men and Women of the Corporation.* New York: Basic Books.

Landry, B. 1987. *The New Black Middle Class.* Berkeley: University of California Press.

Loury, G. C. 1993. "Free at Last? A Personal Perspective on Race and Identity in America." Pp. 1-12 in *Lure and Loathing: Essays on Race, Identity, and the Ambivalence of Assimilation,* edited by G. Early. New York: Penguin.

Malson, M. 1982. "The Social-Support Systems of Black Families." *Marriage and Family Review* 5(Winter):37-57.

McAdoo, H. P. 1978. "Factors Related to Stability in Upwardly Mobile Black Families." *Journal of Marriage and the Family* 40(4):761-76.

———. 1979. "Black Kinship." *Psychology Today,* May, pp. 69-70, 79, 110.

———. 1982. "Stress-Absorbing Systems in Black Families." *Family Relations* 31(October): 479-88.

Miller, R. L. 1989. "Desegregation Experiences of Minority Students: Adolescent Coping Strategies in Five Connecticut High Schools." *Journal of Adolescent Research* 4(April):173-89.

Nobles, W. W., et al. 1976. *A Formulative and Empirical Study of Black Families.* DHEW Publication OCD-90-C-255. Washington, DC: Government Printing Office.

Parham, T. A. 1989. "Cycles of Psychological Nigrescence." *Counseling Psychologist* 17(2):187-226.

Peters, M. F. 1988. "Parenting in Black Families With Young Children: A Historical Perspective." Pp. 228-41 in *Black Families,* 2nd ed., edited by H. P. McAdoo. Newbury Park, CA: Sage.

Randolph, L. B. 1992. "Browning the Suburbs." *Ebony,* January, pp. 36-42.

Reiss, D. and M. Oliveri. 1983. "Family Stress as Community Frame." *Marriage and Family Review* 6(Spring):61-83.

St. John, N. H. 1981. "The Effects of School Desegregation on Children: A New Look at the Research Evidence." Pp. 84-103 in *Race and Schooling in the City,* edited by A. Yarmolinsky, L. Liebman, and C. S. Schelling. Cambridge, MA: Harvard University Press.

Slaughter, D. T. and D. J. Johnson, eds. 1988. *Visible Now: Blacks in Private Schools.* Westport, CT: Greenwood.

Spencer, M. B. 1985. "Cultural Cognition and Social Cognition as Identity Correlates of Black Children's Personal-Social Development." Pp. 215-30 in *Beginnings: The Social and Affective Development of Black Children,* edited by M. B. Spencer, G. K. Brookins, and W. R. Allen. Hillsdale, NJ: Lawrence Erlbaum.

Spencer, M. B., D. P. Swanson, and M. Cunningham. 1991. "Ethnicity, Ethnic Identity, and Competence Formation: Adolescent Transition and Cultural Transformation." *Journal of Negro Education* 60(3):366-87.

Spurlock, J. and M. B. Booth. 1988. "Stresses in Parenting." Pp. 79-89 in *Black Families in Crisis: The Middle Class,* edited by A. F. Coner-Edwards and J. Spurlock. New York: Brunner/Mazel.

Tatum, B. D. 1992a. "African-American Identity, Achievement Motivation, and Missing History." *Social Education* 56(6):331-34.

———. 1992b. *Assimilation Blues.* Northampton, MA: Hazel-Maxwell.

————. 1993a. "Black Youth in White Communities." *Focus: Notes from the Society for the Psychological Study of Ethnic Minority Issues* 7(2):15-16.

————. 1993b. "Racial Identity and Relational Theory: The Case of Black Women in White Communities." Work in Progress No. 62, Stone Center Working Paper Series, Wellesley, MA.

————. Forthcoming a. "Growing Up Black in a White Community: Racial Identity Development of Black Middle-Class Adolescents." In *Adolescents, Schooling, and Social Policy,* edited by F. Miller. Albany: State University of New York Press.

————. Forthcoming b. "In Search of Connection: Young Black Women in White Communities." In *The Psychology of African American Women,* edited by A. Brown-Collins. New York: Guilford.

Taylor, R. J. and L. M. Chatters. 1991. "Religious Life." In *Life in Black America,* edited by J. S. Jackson. Newbury Park, CA: Sage.

Zweigenhaft, R. L. and G. W. Domhoff. 1991. *Blacks in the White Establishment? A Study of Race and Class in America.* New Haven, CT: Yale University Press.

African American Education

A Cultural-Ecological Perspective

JOHN U. OGBU

This chapter attempts to explain why Black children do less well in school than other children. I also discuss here the effects of perceptions and academic efforts on Black upward mobility, in particular, how school performance is related to Black perceptions of social, occupational, and educational opportunity structure. The first section outlines the problem and some of its current explanations, the second examines the structural context of the problem, and the third describes the cultural-ecological framework and the mechanisms of maintaining the disproportionately high rate of school failure. In the concluding section I consider some of the policy implications of the cultural-ecological perspective.

The Problem and Some Current Explanations

One baffling education problem in the United States is the persistence of low academic performance among Black Americans and members of other castelike minority groups, such as Chicanos, Native Americans, Native

234

Hawaiians, and Puerto Ricans. These groups not only do less well in school than White Americans but also do less well than other minorities, including Asian Americans. It is true that children from poor families of all groups do less well in school than children from affluent families; it is also true that a disproportionate number of Black children come from poor families. Nevertheless, differences between Blacks and Whites in academic achievement remain when children from similar socioeconomic backgrounds are compared (Jensen 1969, pp. 81-82; Baughman 1971, pp. 5-8; Jencks 1972, p. 154; Mayeske, Okada, Cohen, Beaton, and Wisler 1973; CEMREL 1978; Haskins 1980).

Since the 1960s, special efforts have been initiated to help "disadvantaged" Black and other children improve their school performance. There have been some positive results, but no significant change has taken place in the relative academic position of Black children, especially those from the inner city (CEMREL 1978; Ogbu 1978). The failure lies, in part, in the theories undergirding these efforts. In the 1960s, social scientists assumed that school performance depends on three factors: home environment, school environment, and genetic endowment (Bloom, Davis, and Hess 1965; Coleman 1966; Jensen 1969; Guthrie, Kleindorfer, Levin, and Stout 1971). It thus followed that Blacks were relatively unsuccessful in school because their home or school environment or their genetic endowment was less conducive to academic success. Social scientists continue to argue about the relative weight of each of these factors in influencing school performance. Policy makers generally have been more sympathetic to theories emphasizing the deficiencies of the home or school and consequently have based their programs for change on such theories.

In more recent years, a cultural difference or cultural discontinuity perspective has emerged to explain the disproportionately high rate of school failure among Blacks and other castelike minorities. This perspective argues that Blacks have their own culture and child-rearing practices through which distinctively Black instrumental competencies are inculcated, and schools do not recognize and use these competencies in the teaching, learning, and testing processes (Wright 1970; Gibson 1976; Boykin 1980).

Elsewhere, I have analyzed the strengths and weaknesses of these explanations (Ogbu 1978, 1980a, 1981a), and here I will briefly summarize the points most relevant to the present chapter. First, these explanations are not based on adequate comparative data. Using data from one type of minority group, castelike minorities, they fail to explain why other types of minorities with similar features of poverty and cultural differences succeed in the same schools. Second, although proponents of these views want to assist Black children in improving their school performance in order to obtain good jobs eventually, they usually do not consider how job discrimination against Black parents may affect their children's education. For example, how do Black perceptions of job discrimination influence their perceptions of and responses to schooling? On the whole, current explanations generally neglect the reciprocal influence of employment opportunities and schooling. Third, some of the explanations erroneously assume that the educational and economic problems of Black Americans are the same as those of lower-class Whites. This is a false assumption, because Blacks occupy a castelike position in a racial stratification system. Other weaknesses of these explanations will become apparent when we consider the structural position of Black Americans as the context for understanding their lag in school performance. Traditional education research has considered neither the collective historical experience of Blacks nor the structural barriers of the wider society.

I use the term *castelike minorities* here for two reasons. First, it contrasts this type of minorities with immigrant minorities in terms of both structural and school experiences in an effort to explain why some minorities do well in school and others do not. Second, I use the term in reference to some minority groups that are not racially different from the dominant group and yet are doing poorly in school. Chicanos, for instance, cannot as a group be racially defined as different from Whites; many call themselves White and are officially defined as White or Caucasian. In my analysis of structural barriers and school experiences, however, they qualify as a castelike minority group.

Racial Stratification as a
Structural Context for School Failure

Social scientists concerned with the problem of lower levels of school performance among Blacks have long recognized "race" as a variable, but not "racial stratification." If they consider American society stratified at all, their preferred model is class stratification (Coleman 1966; Jensen 1969; Jencks 1972; Mosteller and Moynihan 1972; Ogbu 1977, 1981b). There are ample data on parental education, occupation, and income showing that a disproportionate number of Black children come from "lower-class" backgrounds, and from this it is argued that school performance among Blacks is class related. But this class model is only one of several that can be constructed for American society, and it is probably not the one that most accurately reflects the position of Blacks, who are a racial caste. I am using the concepts of "caste" and "castelike" advisedly, as a methodological tool to emphasize the structural legacy of Black subordination, not in the classical Hindu sense. One question, then, is how the stratification of racial castes differs from class stratification.

Class Versus Racial Caste Stratification

In general, stratification of racial castes differs from class stratification with regard to closure, affiliation, status summation, social mobility, and cognitive orientation.

Closure and Affiliation

Class stratification is based on economic relations, an acquired characteristic, whereas racial stratification is based on "status honor," regarded as an inborn quality (Berreman 1977). Social classes are more or less permanent entities but have no clear boundaries; nor is their membership necessarily permanent, because people are continually moving in and out of them. Furthermore, children of interclass marriages can affiliate with the class of either parent. Racial castes, in contrast, are permanently and hierarchically organized into more or less endogamous groups, clearly bounded, publicly recognized, and named. Interracial/caste marriage is often prohibited, but where it is allowed there is usually a formal or informal rule as to with which parent's group the children must affiliate (Berreman 1967, pp. 279-80). For example, before their emancipation in 1871, the Japanese Buraku outcastes were legally forbidden to intermarry with the dominant Ippan group (Mitchell 1967); in South Africa, intermarriage between Blacks and Whites is legally forbidden (van den Berghe 1967); and in the United States, it was not until 1967 that the Supreme Court "finally declared unconstitutional those statutes (in 16 states at that time) prohibiting interracial marriage" (Higginbotham 1978, p. 41; see also Franklin 1971). In the United States the rule of affiliation has always been that any children of known Black-White mating must affiliate with the Black. In very rare cases, some "Blacks" covertly become "Whites" through the painful and noninstitutionalized process of "passing" (Warner, Havighurst, and Loeb 1941; Burma 1946; Eckard 1946).

Status Summation

In a class stratification, such as exists among American Whites, occupational and other status positions are based on training (for example, on formal education) and ability. This is much less true for racial minorities because of the job ceiling and other barriers. The job ceiling results from the highly consistent pressures and obstacles that selectively assign minorities (and women) to jobs at the low level of status, power, dignity, and income, while allowing White males to compete more easily and freely for the more desirable jobs above that ceiling on the basis of individual training and ability. The job ceiling and other barriers have been the object of racial minorities' struggle for equal social, economic, and political opportunities (Drake and Cayton 1970; Newman, Amidei, Carter, Kruvant, and Russell 1978; Ogbu 1978).

Social Mobility

Vertical social mobility is built into class stratification, and the means of achieving it are usually prescribed. Mobility from one racial stratum to the next is proscribed.

Cognitive Orientation

Class and racial castes differ in cognitive orientation (Berreman 1977). For instance, Blacks and other castelike minorities do not accept their low social, political, and occupational status as legitimate outcomes of their individual failures and misfortunes, whereas lower-class Whites often do (Sennett and Cobb 1972). Blacks see racial barriers in employment and education as the primary causes of their low social status and poverty. Most Black Americans, regardless of their class position, blame "the system" rather than themselves for their failure to get ahead as individuals and as a group, an orientation that underlies their collective struggle for equal employment and educational opportunity.

In contrast, there is neither a conscious feeling among White Americans of any given class "that they belong together in a corporate unity" nor a feeling that their common interests are different from those of other social classes (Myrdal 1944). Not even lower-class Whites share a collective perception of their social and economic difficulties as stemming from "the system." What distinguishes Black Americans and similar minorities from lower-class Whites is not that their objective material conditions are different, but that the way in which the minorities perceive and interpret their conditions is different.

Blacks, of course, are internally stratified by social class, as are Whites, but the respective classes differ in both development and attributes. They are unequal in development because historically Blacks have had less access to the numbers and types of jobs and training that facilitate class differentiation and mobility. Black social classes are also qualitatively different because the historical circumstances that created them and the structural forces that sustain them are different from those that created and sustain White social classes. For example, the narrow base of Black class differentiation began during enslavement rather than, as among Whites, with differences in education, ability, and family background.

During enslavement most Blacks had no access to schooling and were relegated to slave status, regardless of their individual abilities; among the few free Blacks, most were confined to menial jobs and social position through legal and extralegal mechanisms. After enslavement, racial barriers in employment—the job ceiling—continued to limit class differentiation and mobility. These collective experiences resulted in a shared perception of the lack of equal opportunity for Blacks of any social class; that is, Blacks came to believe that it is much more difficult for any Black than for any White to achieve economic and social self-betterment in the mainstream economy through free competition based on training and ability. Another reason for the qualitative difference is the forced ghettoization of Blacks. Until recent decades, Whites created and maintained clearly defined residential boundaries to which they restricted the Black population. Many relatively well-to-do Blacks who preferred to live elsewhere were forced to share the ghetto with poorer Blacks. This involuntary segregation further reinforced a shared sense of oppression.

In summary, the economic and education problems of Black Americans do not result merely from lower-class status. Instead, they are consequences of the double stratification of class and racial caste. As a result, lower-class Blacks share certain attributes common to all lower-class people everywhere, but they also have distinctive attributes because they belong to a subordinate racial caste. The effect of this double stratification is apparent in the Black status mobility system, described in a subsequent section.

Castelike Minorities Versus Other Minorities

Some minorities do relatively well in school, and it is important to distinguish them from those who do not. Generally, Blacks fit into the category of castelike minorities (Ogbu 1978), and one characteristic of groups in this category is a greater lag in school performance. Castelike minorities are distinguished from other minorities by four factors:

1. Castelike minorities have usually been incorporated into "their country" involuntarily and permanently. Blacks are a classic example, having been brought to America as slaves. As a result, they occupy a more or less permanent place in society from which they can escape only through "passing" or emigration, options that are not always available.
2. Membership in a castelike minority is acquired permanently at birth.
3. Castelike minorities have limited access to the social goods of society by virtue of their group membership rather than because they lack training and ability. More specifically, they face a job ceiling.
4. Having been incorporated into society involuntarily and then relegated to menial status, castelike minorities tend to perceive their economic and social problems in terms of collective institutional discrimination, which they view as more than temporary.

These structural features distinguish Blacks from Whites, poor Blacks from lower-class Whites, and Blacks from such immigrant minorities as Chinese or Japanese Americans, who came to the United States more or less voluntarily seeking social and economic betterment. The occupational and educational implications of the structural position of Blacks are expressed through their unique status mobility system.

Status Mobility and School Performance

A status mobility system is a way of getting ahead in a society or social group. Members of a society or group usually share a theory or assumptions about how the system works and how one gets ahead, however "making it" is defined (LeVine 1967). The theory or folk assumptions generally cover the range of available status positions (for example, types of jobs open to members), rules for eligibility to compete for the available positions, and how to qualify for successful competition. A status mobility system works insofar as the actual experiences of a large proportion of the population confirm the folk beliefs about it. And how the system works influences the values and practices of parents and others entrusted with the upbringing of children as well as how children themselves strive to be as they get older. People's theory about how their status mobility system works is the cognitive basis of their behaviors with regard to child rearing and schooling as well as strategies for subsistence and self-advancement (Ogbu 1980a, 1980b).

In a relatively open class system, such as exists among White Americans, differences in the status mobility systems of the different classes are minor. For stratified racial castes, however, such as Blacks and Whites, the system of each stratum is unique in many respects. For example, the status mobility system of the subordinate racial caste is distinctive in two ways that have important implications for schooling. First, the system offers access to fewer social goods, such as high-paying jobs, and, second, it embodies two sets of behavioral rules for achievement: one imposed by the dominant group and the other evolved within the subordinate population. In the United States, Whites "impose" education credentials on Blacks; as a consequence, Blacks have developed a number of alternative or "survival" strategies, including collective struggle, clientship, and hustling. Black Americans employ these two sets of rules differentially according to their circumstances.

Castelike minority schooling reflects these two features. On the one hand, the dominant group's perceptions of how minorities get ahead or should get ahead influence how it defines and provides for the minorities' educational needs; on the other hand, how the minorities perceive their opportunity structure and the role of schooling within it influences their response to schooling. For castelike minorities, schooling generally functions to prepare children to participate as adults in the minority's rather than the dominant group's status mobility system. From this point of departure, I would suggest that a clue to the differences in the education and school performance of Whites and Blacks lies in the nature of their status mobility systems. Specifically, that of caste-bound Blacks traditionally offers fewer jobs requiring upper-level schooling or credentials, embodies two sets of behavioral rules for achievement, and makes both Whites and Blacks behave in a manner that promotes Black school failure. Perceptions by dominant Whites of how Blacks should get ahead lead them to provide Blacks with inferior education.

For Blacks, their own perceptions of the limited opportunities to get ahead in the conventional economy and their perceptions of inferior education generate attitudes and behaviors that often are not conducive to school success.

Among the Black responses to the job ceiling and to inferior education discussed below are disillusionment and lack of perseverance because of low payoffs from education. Other responses are alternative or survival strategies that may require skills and attitudes incongruent with those required for classroom learning as well as hostility and lack of trust toward the public school. Let us briefly examine in more detail how White and Black responses cause the disproportionately high school failure among Blacks.

Inferior Education

Many public and private schools now profess to offer Blacks the same quality education provided Whites and have even established special pro-grams to enable Black children to "succeed" like Whites. These, however, are recent developments and should not mask the fact that before the 1960s there was no explicit or implicit goal to educate Blacks and Whites equally for adult occupational and social positions. Also, although it is true that education for lower-class Whites has always been inferior to that for middle-class Whites (Warner, Havighurst, and Loeb 1944; Hollingshead 1949; Sexton 1961), it is equally true that at every class level Blacks have been provided even more inferior education. For example, as late as 1972 the money spent by the school district of Washington, D.C., for each child decreased as the proportion of Black children in a given school increased (Hughes and Hughes 1973), a situation also documented for Chicago and other cities (Sexton 1968, p. 228).

In general, prior to emancipation Blacks were systematically excluded by law from formal education and thereafter were given inferior education in segregated schools. Segregation was legal nationwide, although it lasted longest in the South (Bond 1966, pp. 374-84; Bullock 1970; Weinberg 1977). In the separate schools, the inferiority of Black education was maintained through inadequate funding, facilities, and staffing; a shorter school year; and curricula that emphasized manual rather than academic training (Bond 1966, pp. 97-99; 1969, pp. 132, 235-65; Collins and Noblitt 1978). Blacks who attended integrated schools received inferior education through more subtle mechanisms: negative teacher attitudes and low expectations

(Knowles and Prewitt 1969; U.S. Senate 1972; Hobbs 1975), biased testing and classification (Mercer 1973; Children's Defense Fund 1974, pp. 101-14; Illinois Advisory Commission on Civil Rights 1974), tracking or ability grouping (Findley 1973; Ogbu 1974a, p. 169), and biased textbooks and inferior curricula (U.S. Senate 1972). They also generally received academic and career guidance that reinforced their preparation for inferior positions in adult life (Ogbu 1974a, p. 193; 1974b, p. 120), and extracurricular activities were race-typed. These subtle devices were also present in segregated schools.

Today, both gross and subtle mechanisms such as these still exist in many schools, as evidenced by many lawsuits for school integration and by protests against testing, tracking, and related matters in many cities (U.S. Commission on Civil Rights 1977). One subtle mechanism receiving increasing attention is the disproportionate labeling of Black children as having "learning handicaps" and channeling of these children into special education that prepares them for inferior occupations. In a court case brought by Blacks against the San Francisco school district in 1979, for instance, evidence was presented showing that Black children constituted only 31% of the school enrollment in the 1976–1977 school year, but 53.8% of all children in the educable mentally retarded classes. In the same year, in the 20 California school districts that enrolled 80% of all Black children in the state, Blacks constituted 27.5% of all students but 62% of the educable mentally retarded population. The judge in the case ruled against the school district, noting that the disproportionate placements could not have occurred by chance (*Larry P. v. Riles* 1979). The figures for San Francisco are similar to those for other large U.S. cities, including Chicago and New York.

Some evidence suggests that in many instances Blacks are provided inferior education deliberately. We find in the South purposive misappropriation of Black school funds for White schools, legislation to legalize such misappropriation, and employment of teachers for Black schools who are less qualified, at less pay, and with disproportionate workloads (Bond 1966; Bullock 1970).

Even northern philanthropists who helped make public school education more available to Blacks and Whites in the South endorsed explicit policies to give Whites superior academic education for superior jobs and other adult positions and to give Blacks "industrial" or manual education. They did, however, make some provision for a few Blacks to receive academic training to serve the Black community as preachers, teachers, doctors, and lawyers

(Harlan 1968, pp. 76-80; Bullock 1970, pp. 93-98). Interestingly enough, when industrial education became an asset to acquiring well-paying jobs and attracted state and federal financial support, Black participation was curtailed. Myrdal (1944, p. 877) explains this policy reversal by saying that southern Whites believed that Blacks should receive an industrial education so long as it did not mean preparing them to compete more effectively with Whites for skilled and economically rewarding jobs (see also Frazier [1949] 1957, p. 439; Bond 1966, p. 404).

In the North the policy of differential and inferior education has been more covert and, partly because records are not kept by race, less adequately documented, but it has existed as deliberate policy in many instances. Evidence presented in various desegregation court cases has shown the prevalence of inferior education for Blacks in the North (Sexton 1967, 1968; U.S. Commission on Civil Rights 1977). And many Blacks educated in the North who have discussed their experiences with me have recounted how they and other Blacks were channeled into "dead-end courses" in segregated and integrated schools.

The possibility of Blacks' receiving inferior education has also been reinforced by many school personnel who share the general folk assumptions of Whites that Blacks are less "intelligent" and therefore not capable of mastering the education required for more desirable jobs and social positions (Johnson 1930, p. 224; Conant 1961). These folk beliefs, which predate the invention of modern psychometric measures of "intelligence" (Bullock 1970, p. 68), have had considerable influence on the type of curriculum school personnel consider appropriate for Black children and on perceptions of how Black children should be treated. Another factor contributing to inferior education is well-meaning school personnel, who, aware of the limited chances for Black school leavers, have tended to channel Black pupils into educational programs that prepare them mainly for traditional "Negro jobs."

Black Responses

It would seem from their long history of collective struggle for equal education that Blacks view it as a means to improve their social and economic status, but their expectations have not been met, partly because their education has not been designed to do this. It appears that Blacks have responded to both inferior education and the job ceiling in ways that actually promote school failure and prepare them for marginal economic participation. These responses are considered next.

Disillusionment and Lack of Effort

Disillusionment is one response of Blacks to the job ceiling that has had adverse effects on academic behavior. Blacks do not believe that the United States is a land of equal opportunity: They often point out that racial discrimination has historically prevented them from obtaining desirable jobs, good wages, and promotions commensurate with their education and ability; discrimination has also prevented them from owning houses and living in better neighborhoods.

One result of this disillusionment is lack of perseverance in academic pursuits: "What's the use of trying?" From my own observations of Black children in the classrooms and wider community of Stockton, California, I have concluded that they do not take their schoolwork seriously even though they acknowledge that hard work is necessary for doing well in school. Furthermore, interviews with parents suggest that they may be teaching their children ambivalent attitudes. On the one hand, parents espouse the need to work hard in school and obtain more education than they did. On the other hand, the same parents teach their children verbally and through their own life experiences about unemployment, underemployment, and other discrimination, as well as through gossip about similar experiences among relatives, neighbors, and friends. In other words, through what they see at home and in the community, children learn that even if they succeed in school they may not make it as adults in the wider society. Eventually, Black children become disillusioned and "give up," blaming "the system" for their school failure, just as their parents blame "the system" for their own failures.

In the face of the historical barriers that have restricted educational payoffs, Blacks have not remained passive but have responded actively and creatively. The important consideration is whether the responses facilitate or hinder the successful pursuit of formal education. My observations indicate that some reactions are not congruent with the maximization of school efforts. It is my thesis that as structural barriers are removed and Blacks experience and perceive their elimination, they will respond with perceptions and behaviors that facilitate a greater degree of school success.

Survival Strategies

Another response to the job ceiling that has adverse effects on Black school performance is what Blacks call "survival strategies." These fall into two categories, one type directed toward increasing conventional economic and social resources of the Black community and obtaining conventional jobs and other social rewards. Strategies in this category include collective struggle or civil rights activities (Scott 1976; Newman et al. 1978) and clientship, or "uncle tomming" (Myrdal 1944; Dollard 1957; Farmer 1968; Powdermaker [1939] 1968; Ogbu 1981b). The other category is directed toward exploiting nonconventional economic and social resources, or "the street economy," and includes hustling and related means (Heard 1968; Milner 1970; Wolfe 1970; Bullock 1970; Foster 1974).

Within the Black community success in obtaining conventional jobs and other social resources often requires collective struggle (at least to make them available) and/or clientship, in addition to educational credentials. There also are alternative ways to make a living and achieve status without school credentials and conventional jobs. People who succeed in either the conventional economy or the street economy are "legitimately successful" in the eyes of the community, are admired, and influence the ways others, including children, try to make it. I suggest that some survival strategies may require knowledge, attitudes, and skills not wholly compatible with those required in White middle-class classrooms. I also suggest that children probably begin to learn survival strategies in the preschool years as part of their normal "enculturation." As a result, they may begin school with a potential disposition for academic and behavioral difficulties, but whether and to what extent these occur depends on their encounters with school personnel and other children.

Conflict and Distrust

A third response of Black people is hostility and distrust toward the public schools, feelings that have grown out of a long history of unpleasant experiences with the schools and White society in general. Blacks have learned to perceive their frequent exclusion from and discriminatory treatment by the schools as designed to prevent them from qualifying for the more desirable jobs open to Whites. Consequently, a significant thrust of Black collective struggle for more than a century has been to force Whites to provide Blacks with equal education.

Even in schools that are predominantly Black and with which one might expect Blacks to identify, their cooperation often has been undermined by society's perception of such schools as inferior to White schools. The feeling that the public schools cannot be trusted to educate Black children because of their gross and subtle mechanisms of discrimination frequently results in conflict with the schools, which often resort to various forms of control, paternalism, and contestation in response. The schools' responses, too, divert their efforts from educating Black children. Under these circumstances, which can be documented in many American cities, I would suggest that a relationship riddled with conflict and suspicion makes it difficult for Blacks to accept and internalize the schools' goals, standards, and teaching and learning approaches, and this situation contributes to the poor school performance of Black children.

Policy Implications

There seem to be three steps prerequisite to the elimination of the lag in Black school performance in the United States. The first is to recognize that stratification of racial castes exists in this society. The second is to view the disproportionately high rate of school failure as a kind of collective adaptation to the job ceiling and other features of the Black status mobility system. This adaptation was engendered and has been maintained by policies and actions of Whites and their institutions; it also has been sustained by Blacks' responses to their situation. The third step is to recognize that real change depends on opening up decent jobs and other opportunities to Black youths and adults, not on patching "deficiencies." The solution requires both short- and long-range policies. In the short term, remedies may include some current programs to assist the present generation of children who are experiencing difficulties in school. In the long term, the goal must be to develop policies and programs to ensure that future generations of Black children will not experience a disproportionately high rate of school failure, and this includes elimination of the job ceiling and the ultimate destruction of the caste system.

References

Baughman, E. 1971. *Black Americans*. New York: Academic Press.

Berreman, G. D. 1967. "Caste in Cross-Cultural Perspective: Organizational Components." In *Japan's Invisible Race: Caste in Culture and Personality,* edited by G. DeVos and H. Wagatsuma. Berkeley: University of California Press.

———. 1977. "Social Inequality: A Cross-Cultural Paradigm." Unpublished manuscript, University of California, Berkeley, Department of Anthropology.

Bloom, B. S., A. Davis, and R. D. Hess, eds. 1965. *Compensatory Education for Cultural Deprivation*. New York: Holt, Rinehart & Winston.

Bond, H. M. 1966. *The Education of the Negro in the American Social Order.* New York: Octagon.

———. 1969. *Negro Education in Alabama*. New York: Atheneum.

Boykin, A. W. 1980. "Reading Achievement and the Social Cultural Frame of Reference of Afro-American Children." Paper presented at the NIE Roundtable Discussion on Issues in Urban Reading, Washington, DC.

Bullock, H. E. 1970. *A History of Negro Education in the South: From 1619 to the Present*. New York: Praeger.

Burma, J. H. 1946. "The Measurement of Negro Passing." *American Journal of Sociology* 52:18-22.

CEMREL, Inc. 1978. *Minority Education 1960–78: Grounds, Gains, and Gaps,* vol. 1. Chicago: Author.

Children's Defense Fund. 1974. *Children Out of School in America*. Washington, DC: Washington Research Project.

Coleman, J. S. 1966. *Equality of Educational Opportunity*. Washington, DC: Government Printing Office.

Collins, T. W. and G. W. Noblitt. 1978. *Stratification and Resegregation: The Case of Crossover High School, Memphis, Tennessee*. Final Report, NIE Contract Grant 400-76-009. Washington, DC: National Institute of Education.

Conant, J. B. 1961. *Slums and Suburbs*. New York: McGraw-Hill.

Dollard, J. 1957. *Caste and Class in a Southern Town*. Garden City, NY: Doubleday.

Drake, S. C. and H. Cayton. 1970. *Black Metropolis: A Study of Negro Life in a Northern City,* vols. 1-2. New York: Harcourt Brace Jovanovich.

Eckard, E. W. 1946. "How Many Negroes Pass?" *American Journal of Sociology* 52:498-500.

Farmer, J. 1968. "Stereotypes of the Negro and Their Relationships to His Self-Image." In *Urban Schooling,* edited by H. C. Rudman and R. L. Featherstone. New York: Harcourt Brace Jovanovich.

Findley, W. G. 1973. "How Ability Grouping Fails." *Inequality in Education* 14:38-40.

Foster, H. L. 1974. *Ribbin', Jivin', and Playin' the Dozens: The Unrecognized Dilemma of Inner-City Schools*. Cambridge, MA: Ballinger.

Franklin, J. H. 1971. *The Free Negro in North Carolina, 1790–1860*. New York: W. W. Norton.

Frazier, E. F. [1949] 1957. *Negro Youth at the Crossways: Their Personality Development in the Middle States*. Washington, DC: American Council on Education.

Gibson, M. A. 1976. "Approaches to Multicultural Education in the United States." *Anthropology and Education Quarterly* 7:7-18.

Guthrie, J. W., G. B. Kleindorfer, H. M. Levin, and R. T. Stout. 1971. *Schools and Inequality*. Cambridge: MIT Press.

Harlan, L. R. 1968. *Separate and Unequal*. New York: Atheneum.

Haskins, R. 1980. "Race, Family Income and School Achievement." Unpublished manuscript.

Heard, N. C. 1968. *Howard Street*. New York: Dial.

Higginbotham, A. L. 1978. *In the Matter of Color: Race and the American Legal Process: The Colonial Period*. New York: Oxford University Press.

Hobbs, N. 1975. *The Future of Children*. San Francisco: Jossey-Bass.

Hollingshead, A. 1949. *Elmstown's Youth*. New York: John Wiley.

Hughes, J. F. and A. O. Hughes. 1973. *Equal Education: A New National Strategy*. Bloomington: Indiana University Press.

Illinois Advisory Commission on Civil Rights. 1974. *Bilingual/Bicultural Education: A Privilege or a Right?* Washington, DC: Government Printing Office.

Jencks, C. 1972. *Inequality*. New York: Basic Books.

Jensen, A. R. 1969. "How Much Can We Boost IQ and Scholastic Achievement?" *Harvard Educational Review* 39:1-123.

Johnson, C. S. 1930. *The Negro American Civilization*. New York: Holt.

Knowles, L. L. and D. Prewitt, eds. 1969. *Institutional Racism in America*. Englewood Cliffs, NJ: Prentice Hall.

Larry P. v. Riles. 1979. U.S. District Court for Northern California.

LeVine, R. A. 1967. *Dreams and Deeds*. Chicago: University of Chicago Press.

Mayeske, G. W., T. Okada, A. E. Cohen, A. E. Beaton, and C. E. Wisler. 1973. *A Study of the Achievement of Our Nation's Students*. Washington, DC: Government Printing Office.

Mercer, J. R. 1973. *Labeling the Mentally Retarded*. Berkeley: University of California Press.

Milner, C. A. 1970. "Black Pimps and Their Prostitutes." Ph.D. dissertation, University of California, Berkeley, Department of Anthropology.

Mitchell, R. H. 1967. *The Korean Minority in Japan*. Berkeley: University of California Press.

Mosteller, F. and D. P. Moynihan, eds. 1972. *On Equality of Educational Opportunity*. New York: Random House.

Myrdal, G., with R. Sterner and A. Rose. 1944. *An American Dilemma: The Negro Problem and Modern Democracy*. New York: Harper & Row.

Newman, D. K., B. K. Amidei, D. D. Carter, W. J. Kruvant, and J. S. Russell. 1978. *Protest, Politics and Prosperity: Black Americans and White Institutions, 1940–1975*. New York: Pantheon.

Ogbu, J. U. 1974a. "Learning in Burgherside." In *Anthropologists in the City,* edited by G. M. Foster and R. V. Kemper. Boston: Little, Brown.

———. 1974b. *The Next Generation*. New York: Academic Press.

———. 1977. "Racial Stratification and Education: The Case of Stockton, California." *IRCD Bulletin* 12(3):1-26.

———. 1978. *Minority Education and Caste*. New York: Academic Press.

———. 1980a. "Equalization of Educational Opportunity and Racial/Ethnic Inequality: A Cross-Cultural Perspective." In *Comparative Education,* edited by P. Altbach, R. Arnove, and G. Kelley. New York: Macmillan.

———. 1980b. "Societal Forces as a Context of Ghetto Children's School Failure." In *The Language of Children Reared in Poverty,* edited by L. Feagans and D. Darran. New York: Academic Press.

———. 1981a. "Minority Schooling and Transition to Labor Force." Paper presented at the seminar Youth Education and Employment: Policy Issues for the 1980s, Madison, WI.

———. 1981b. "Schooling in the Ghetto: A Cultural-Ecological Perspective on Community and Home Influences." Paper presented at the NIE Conference on Follow Through, Philadelphia.

Powdermaker, H. [1939] 1968. *After Freedom: The Portrait of a Negro Community in the Deep South*. New York: Atheneum.

Scott, J. W. 1976. *The Black Revolts*. Cambridge, MA: Schenkman.

Sennett, R. and J. Cobb. 1972. *The Hidden Injuries of Class*. New York: Random House.

Sexton, P. C. 1961. *Education and Income*. New York: Viking.

———. 1967. *Racial Isolation in the Public Schools: A Report*, vol. 1. Washington, DC: Government Printing Office.

———. 1968. "Schools: Broken Ladder to Success." In *Negroes and Jobs*, edited by L. A. Ferman. Ann Arbor: University of Michigan Press.

U.S. Commission on Civil Rights. 1977. *The Unfinished Business*. Washington, DC: Government Printing Office.

U.S. Senate, Select Committee on Education. 1972. *Report: Toward Equal Educational Opportunity*. Washington, DC: Government Printing Office.

van den Berghe, P. L. 1967. *Race and Racism: A Comparative Perspective*. New York: John Wiley.

Warner, W. L., R. J. Havighurst, and M. B. Loeb. 1941. *Color and Human Nature: Negro Personality Development in a Northern City*. Washington, DC: American Council on Education.

———. 1944. *Who Shall Be Educated? The Challenge of Equal Opportunity*. New York: Harper.

Weinberg, M. 1977. *A Chance to Learn: A History of Race and Education in the United States*. New York: Cambridge University Press.

Wolfe, T. 1970. *Radical Chic & Mau-Mauing the Flak Catchers*. New York: Strauss & Giroux.

Wright, N., ed. 1970. *What Black Educators Are Saying*. New York: Hawthorn.

Family, Socialization Environment, and Identity Development in Black Americans

JAMES S. JACKSON
WAYNE R. McCULLOUGH
GERALD GURIN

Family and environmental influences have been largely ignored in previous empirical work on personal and group identity development in blacks. The major research on group identification and self- and group attitudes is reviewed in the current chapter. We stress here the important role of the family and the socialization environment and discuss the possible nature of

AUTHORS' NOTE: We wish particularly to acknowledge Phillip Bowman, Clifford Broman, Ronald Brown, Patricia Gurin, Shirley Hatchett, Harold Neighbors, and M. Belinda Tucker, collaborators on our previous and ongoing research. They helped us to formulate our ideas on group identity and consciousness, and made major contributions to other substantial and theoretical areas as well. We appreciate the research support of the Ford and Rockefeller Foundations, Carnegie Corporation, National Institute of Mental Health, and National Institute on Aging. This chapter was revised while the first author was a Ford Foundation Senior Postdoctoral Fellow at Groupe D'Etudes et de Recherches Sur La Science, Ecole Des Hautes Etudes en Sciences Sociales, Paris, France.

their effects on the development of group identification in black Americans. We offer some explanations for the lack of an observed relationship between group and personal identity among blacks, and suggest that a negative or neutral relationship between black group identification and traditional measures of self-esteem may be the result of the pivotal role of the family in inculcating a strong and positive sense of black identity. Family socialization themes that emphasize the importance of racial group history and togetherness are antithetical to Western-oriented conceptualizations and measures of self-esteem. Analyses of data from the National Survey of Black Americans reveal that personal identity is weakly related to racial group identity and not related to group consciousness. We discuss below some possible reasons a strong sense of black group identity is not strongly related to measures of self that stress individual striving and a sense of personal achievement.

Over the past 40 years, much of the social and psychological literature on black Americans has addressed, directly or indirectly, issues of group identification and consciousness. This interest in group identity derives largely from the minority status of blacks in U.S. society. In any group experiencing discrimination, a central issue becomes how individual members relate to the group, to its history of discrimination, and, in the case of black Americans, to the current active collective struggle to overcome a racist system. Furthermore, how black Americans deal with their minority status has been viewed as a critical determinant of their general psychic health and functioning. Writers have differed on whether they have focused on the pathological consequences of discrimination or the strengths of coping in the face of it, but all have agreed on the central significance of this psychological relationship to the group, the individual's group identity.

Despite the universal unquestioned assumption of a link between group identity and psychological health, it is surprising that the actual documentation of this relationship is ambiguous, overly simplistic, and ill defined (Cross 1985). Reviews have noted that there is no consistent empirical support for the assumption that there is a simple positive relationship between group and personal identity (Cross 1985; Spencer 1985). Most studies in this area have had serious conceptual and measurement limitations (Banks 1976; Semaj 1985). There has also been conceptual confusion in the definition of personal and group identity and consciousness, as well as inadequate formulation of the conceptual links between the two sets of concepts (Harrison 1985). Measurement problems have followed largely, although not entirely, from these conceptual confusions.

As a result of the empirical findings and the conceptual and measurement limitations of earlier literature, much of the current work (see McAdoo 1985 for an exception) in this area has focused on the conceptual independence of self- and group identity, rather than on the relationship between the two concepts (Cross 1985; Harrison 1985; Peters 1985; Rosenberg 1985; Semaj 1985). This emphasis on the conceptual independence of the two concepts is consistent with the position that we presented in first edition of *Black Families*.

In this chapter we attempt to clarify the distinction between personal and group identity, and discuss some of the conceptual and measurement issues that remain unresolved. Also, although the literature continues to be sparse, we present some speculations on the role of the family and other socialization influences in the development of personal and group identity.

Group and Personal Identity

Black Family and Black Identity

Within our conceptualization, the rudiments of the self are conceived as emerging initially in infancy and early childhood. This evolving self is influenced primarily, but not exclusively, by the socialization practices of the family and insulated local community (Alejandro-Wright 1985; Peters 1985; Semaj 1985; Spencer 1985; Young 1970). Similarly, social group identity is conceived to be developed through a person's perceptions, filtered by the family and other primary groups, of the relationships and cleavages that exist in the larger society between and among various social, economic, and political groups (Tajfel 1982; Turner 1982). Both personal and group identity are viewed as essentially cognitive phenomena—one as the self-placement of the individual in relationship to the primary group and local community (Who am I?), and the other as the recognition by the individual of the societal placement of the group(s) to which he or she belongs within the stratification system that characterizes a particular society (Who are we? Who are they?). Related to these essential cognitive processes are the affective loadings that become attached to the person's individuality and to his or her group belongingness.

There is little systematic evidence regarding the buffering and insulating functions and the identity-nurturing roles served by the black family in fostering functional group or personal identity (Lipscomb 1975; Taylor 1976). Similarly, the coping strategies and situational adaptations derived from this identity and fostered in the familial context have only recently begun to receive theoretical and empirical attention (Bowman and Howard 1985; McCullough 1982; Peters 1985; Spencer 1985).

The minority family is the important agent of socialization, for it is within the family context that the individual first becomes aware of and begins to grapple with the significance of racism and discrimination (Alejandro-Wright 1985; Washington 1976). The intrafamilial socialization of group and personal identity has considerable bearing upon personal functioning in a society that cultivates negative conceptions of minority group members through direct interaction, the media, and institutional barriers (Allen and Hatchett 1986). An important social structural factor that we discuss in this chapter is racial homogeneity or heterogeneity of the socialization environment. How do such environments differentially affect the development and compartmentalization of group and personal identity? Our focus is not only on the degree of racial homogeneity of the socialization environment, but also on the timing of socialization and the elements of group and personal identity that are transmitted across generations.

Group and Personal Identity

The literature on black identification and personal functioning can be divided into two distinct periods demarcated by the civil rights movement of the 1960s. The studies antedating the civil rights movement focused almost exclusively on the supposedly negative effects of black identification. Identifying as black was seen as a "problem," because it meant identifying with an oppressed group and internalizing the negative group image from the dominant white society. Two types of studies predominated in this period: those based on intensive clinical material (Kardiner and Ovesey 1951) and empirical studies with young children, mostly around their choices of and reactions to black and white dolls. These latter studies were particularly influential in promoting the view that black identity implied self-hatred. Following the early work of Clark and Clark (1947), a number of these studies showed that, given one choice, a majority of black children tended to choose a white rather than a black doll and saw the white doll as "nice" and the black doll as "bad" (Goodman 1952; Landreth and Johnson 1953; Radke and Trager 1950; Stevenson and Steward 1958; Moreland 1962).

These choices were viewed as reflecting rejection of the group and self-hatred.

A critical characterization of these doll studies should be noted: They did not measure group identification and self-feeling as *separate* sets of variables. Rather, the choice of the white doll was seen as both group rejection and self-rejection. The relationship between group rejection and self-rejection was an unquestioned assumption, rather than a hypothesis to be tested empirically. This assumption was not peculiar to views of the psychic consequences of black identification; it was applied to the supposed internalization of negative group images held by the majority of individuals belonging to any minority group that was discriminated against. Many of the writers on black identification and self-rejection referred to Lewin's (1948) classic statement about Jewish identification; rejection of one's Jewishness was seen as automatically implying "self-hatred."

Literature on black identification published during the period after the civil rights movement differs from the earlier writings in two major ways. First, although some writers still stress negative black identity (e.g., Gitter, Mastophy, and Satow 1972), the majority of studies have focused on the positive psychic effects of black identification. This emphasis predominates in the speculative writings on the psychological impact of the movement as well as in the empirical research (Barnes 1972; Cross 1985; Hall, Cross, and Freedle 1972; Hraba and Grant 1970; McAdoo 1985; Spencer 1985; Thomas 1971; Ward and Braun 1972; Wyne, White, and Coop 1974). Although obviously different in tone, this literature nonetheless shares important conceptual similarities with the work conducted prior to the civil rights movement. Akin to the studies that tied negative group identity to self-rejection and other negative psychological consequences, much of the newer theorizing and empirical studies have tied positive identity to high self-esteem and other positive psychological consequences. Both perspectives assume, however, a simple, direct relationship between group identification and psychological outcomes.

Recently, some writers, in a further departure from pre-civil rights movement thinking, have directly attacked the assumption of any simple relationship between personal and group identity (Cross 1985; McAdoo 1985). For example, both Barnes (1972) and Peters (1985) indicate that earlier work projecting negative identity and negative self-image as almost automatic consequences of a powerless minority status neglects the role of family and community in mitigating the effects of the wider society on the developing child. The assumption that discrimination is internalized as self-hatred (rather than as hatred of the oppressing group, for example) represents the majority group's perspective (and wish). Zavalloni (1973) suggests that the relationship between a particular group identification and self-attitude cannot be automatically assumed, as any given group identification is only one aspect of a person's social identity.

McAdoo (1985) has also made this point, noting that very few studies have actually measured racial identification and self-feelings separately. When measured separately, the two have not consistently been related to each other. Whereas some empirical studies suggest that there is a positive relationship between black identification and positive self-concepts (Mobley 1973; Ward and Braun 1972), other empirical studies have found no such consistent relationship (McAdoo 1970, 1985; Sacks 1973). This lack of support in the empirical findings has been noted in several reviews of this issue (e.g., Cross 1979, 1985; Porter and Washington 1979).[1]

These inconsistencies in the empirical findings are reflected in some results from a national study of 2,107 black adults (Jackson, Tucker, and Bowman 1982; Jackson and Hatchett 1986) that investigated the relationships among self- and group identity and group consciousness. Self-identity was conceptualized and measured as self-esteem and personal efficacy. Group identity was conceptualized and measured as feelings of closeness to the ideas and feelings of a variety of black groups (Broman, Neighbors, and Jackson 1986). Group consciousness was assessed as the willingness to take action on behalf of the group (Gurin, Miller, and Gurin 1980; McCullough 1982; Pitts 1974).

As expected, both self-esteem and feelings of personal efficacy were positively related ($r = .26$). Group identity and group consciousness showed a moderate positive relationship ($r = 16$). Self-esteem and personal efficacy, however, were found to be differentially related to group identity and group consciousness. Self-esteem was moderately related to group identity ($r = .14$) and weakly related to group consciousness ($r = .05$). Personal efficacy was not related at all to either group identity or group consciousness. The pattern of results was not affected by any background or socioeconomic status factors. These findings suggest that certain aspects of self may be tied to feelings held toward the group; specifically, affective feelings about the self (self-esteem) are related to affective feelings about the group (group identity). This is consistent with some previous literature (Cross 1985). Group consciousness, on the other hand, is apparently not strongly related to feelings of self-esteem or self-worth. Feelings of personal efficacy, the belief that one has personal control over one's life, have absolutely no relationship to either group identity or group consciousness. This is in spite of the fact that self-esteem and personal efficacy are related to each other in an expected, positive manner. In short, the relationship between orientation toward the self and orientation toward the group depends on the particular self and group attitudes being measured.

These analyses highlight a major limitation in existing conceptualizations of group identification and consciousness: the simplistic "either/or" perspective, a person identifies or does not identify, feels pride in or rejects the group. This has been true in the writings on group identification and consciousness generally, not just in the literature specific to blacks. With few exceptions (e.g., Zavalloni 1971, 1973), the empirical literature has not dealt with the fact that feelings toward the group are usually a complicated mixture of positive and negative, and the process of identification usually involves identifying with some aspects of the group and attempting to disassociate oneself from others (McAdoo 1985). This is particularly true for minority group members, who, no matter the degree of their positive identification, have to confront psychologically the negative images of their group found in the majority culture (Tajfel 1982; Turner 1982).

In summary, the relationship between group orientation and self-orientation has been viewed as self-evident. It has seemed an obvious assumption, not requiring testing, that disassociating oneself from one's blackness implies some rejection of the self, that feeling pride about black people implies feeling pride in the self, that blaming blacks for their life conditions implies inappropriate blaming of the self. The literature has taken for granted a high degree of permeability between the boundaries of the group and the boundaries of the self, so that the view of the group automatically fuses with the view of the self. But, as we have already indicated, empirical evidence to support this seemingly self-evident assumption is lacking (Cross 1985; McAdoo 1985). Cross (1985), in a review of this literature, is particularly eloquent on this issue: "An entire people have been burdened with images of their children's self-hatred even though no empirical link between racial preference behavior and direct measures of low self-esteem has been demonstrated" (p. 165). The review by Porter and Washington (1979) also emphasizes this discrepancy.

Why has consistent empirical support not been found for assumptions that to so many have seemed self-evident and obvious? As we have indicated, the major problem is a conceptual one. The thinking in this area has been overly simplistic.[2] A more complex view is needed of the nature of an individual's relationship to the group, and of processes, such as the family and other major socialization influences, that make this relationship to the group relevant to an individual's self-concepts and personal functioning. In the following pages, we turn to a discussion of some of these possible family and socialization processes.

The Family and Socialization Environment and Functional Separation of Self From Group Membership

The compartmentalization of group and personal identity is viewed as psychically functional (Cross 1985; Turner 1982), permitting the individual to adapt to the variety of environmental situations he or she confronts. Simmons (1978) describes the possible psychological separation of self from minority group status:

> It is very possible that an individual may rate the black race less good in general than whites without feeling that he, himself, is less deserving as a total human being. While other minority members may be seen as deserving of societal prejudice, one may view oneself as an exception. . . . at some fantasy level, a person might prefer to be white or lighter skinned without feeling dissatisfied with himself as a total human being. Such fantasies may assume less significance than the fact that he is well-regarded by parents, teachers, and peers (most of whom are also black), or that he is skilled at highly valued activities. (p. 55)

Simmons's statement suggests several things. First, there is a distinction between personal identity and esteem and group identity that has important implications for psychological functioning. Second, the individual can actually identify with the out-group while still maintaining highly valued self-worth. And third, self-worth (personal identity) evolves out of the interaction with the primary group, family, peers, and teachers. If these conditions are likely, as much of the evidence leads us to believe, how is it possible that the compartmentalized identities develop and foster such development?

The suggestion that the socialization environment may have a bearing upon the development of identity has some empirical grounding. The optimal environments that foster independent identity development are suggested by the findings of several studies (Bowman and Howard 1985; McAdoo 1985;

McCullough 1982; Porter and Washington 1979; Wellman 1970). Hare (1977), in delineating general self-esteem from area-specific self-esteem (school, peer, and home), analyzed data collected from fifth-grade black and white students for the effects of socioeconomic status, race, and sex. He found that home and peer self-esteem were not significantly different by racial group; however, school self-esteem was significantly higher among whites. These findings indicate that the typical racially homogeneous settings (home and peer group) have nurturing effects upon self-esteem development. For blacks, only home area-specific esteem accounted for a significant amount of variance in general self-esteem. These data suggest both differences in racial groups and the influence of the socialization environment in the development of group and personal identity.

Family and Socialization Environment

As intimated earlier, self-esteem and other aspects of personal functioning are developed mainly in the context of an individual's immediate personal relationships, particularly those involved in early socialization in the family, but also peer relationships and those in the immediate community (Young 1970). For most blacks in our society this has meant an all-black setting for these formative personal relationships. Self-evaluations develop almost totally with other blacks as the comparative reference group. In contrast, group identification and consciousness develop out of the relationships of blacks to a broader set of influences and referents, specifically blacks' relationships and experiences in white-dominated environments. These differences in influences and reference points lead to different and possibly unrelated consequences in self- and group orientations. Porter and Washington (1979) point out that this may explain the suggestive findings in the literature antedating the civil rights movement that middle-class blacks were higher in personal self-esteem (for which they were comparing themselves predominantly with blacks as a group) but lower in racial esteem (for which they were using the majority world as their comparative referent). Cross (1985) also draws upon this difference to explain the findings that the civil rights movement seems to have wrought a great increase in black identification and consciousness but no apparent change in the personal self-esteem of black Americans.

The evidence previously cited suggests that the racial composition and degree and quality of intergroup contacts may affect the positiveness of personal identity development and its compartmentalization from group identity. If we presume that personal identity development (Who am I?) temporally precedes the internalization of group identity, the family serves at least two important functions in this early development. First, there is the development of self-worth and the personal frame of reference for achievement and other behaviors in this society. Second, the insulating function of the family serves to lessen the negative and often deleterious consequences of minority group status—for both personal and group membership.

It has been suggested that the racially homogeneous home environment may also serve an insulating or buffering role with regard to personal identity development (Hare 1977; Lipscomb 1975; McAdoo 1985; Peters 1985; Porter and Washington 1979; Simmons 1978). Self-worth and self-conceptions are formed under the auspices of the family/primary group. In the homogeneous racial environment there are fewer occasions than in the heterogeneous environment for negative messages regarding group membership to impinge directly upon personal identity development. Thus the homogeneous environment can help to foster a high degree of individual compartmentalization. Once the development of self is established, integrating conceptions of one's relationship to the group and understanding the group's status in society can be achieved through exposure to images such as art, stories, history, and culture.

Introduction to more racially heterogeneous environments (e.g., school, camp) consequently leads to a reduction of the buffering or insulating role played by the family. The family's filtering of input from the larger society is reduced as a broader range of experiences is encountered. As the minority individual gains more intergroup experience, however, the family has an increasing interpretive function. This translation role is critical for maintaining the integrity of the already developed early personal identity as well as the evolving conception of group identity (Bowman and Howard 1985; Peters 1985).

In comparison to the homogeneous environment, the racially heterogeneous environment may serve to hasten the development of the individual's group identity (McCullough 1982; McCullough, Gurin, and Jackson 1981; Porter and Washington 1979; Simmons 1978; Tajfel 1982). The categorical treatment that minority individuals receive (as distinct from interpersonal treatment based upon individual traits or characteristics) helps to place them within the bounds of the minority group and to discern their group's status with regard to the dominant group (Who are we? Who are they?). Other intragroup and intergroup comparisons help to define further the boundaries, commonalities, and other discrepancies between groups. It should also be pointed out that in a nonhostile, nonsegregated, and nondiscriminatory intergroup environment, the development of even a meager sense of belonging to a minority group would undoubtedly be difficult to foster.

We have mentioned little to this point relative to the role that family ideology about the society serves in identity development. We believe that it is through the enactment of parental ideologies that the external world is buffered and filtered through to the developing individual (Lipscomb 1975; Peters 1985). It is not very likely that black persons socialized to a strong sense of compartmentalized personal identity and a thorough understanding of their minority group status, in addition to the historical cultural underpinnings of their group, will hate themselves because they are black. For example, Bowman and Howard (1985), in an analysis of the Three-Generation Family Study data (Jackson and Hatchett 1986), found positive effects on personal efficacy and academic achievement in black youth who reported receiving strong black socialization messages. The possibility also exists that significant influences outside the family (e.g., peer group) affect the relative valences of personal and group identities (Hare 1977). This is most plausible in those circumstances in which parental ideologies are neither communicated nor grounded in the socialization that transpires.

It is also conceivable that minority group members, regardless of the racial homogeneity or heterogeneity of the environment, evolve with an incorporation of group and personal identities that are undifferentiated. Individuals reared in family and environmental settings devoid of an emphasis on separateness may develop an orientation in which their fate is inextricably linked to that of the group. The individual internalizes all images, characteristics, and treatments of the group as statements of his or her individual nature. This fatalism entails a total dependence upon the group for "individual definition." The lack of differentiating socialization by the primary group in the racially homogeneous setting or the unbuffered press (categorical treatment and characterizations) by the dominant majority may accentuate this effect.

It is possible that the strong inculcation of black pride and a sense of common fate with other blacks may negate any possible relationships between group identification and consciousness with frequently used measures of self-esteem. Some work suggests that negative relationships are most often demonstrated when group identity is related to highly individualistic, achievement-oriented, and Western value-dominated measures of self-esteem (Adams 1978; Gordon 1976; Nobles 1973; Taylor and Walsh 1979). Rasheed (1981) found in a study of black third graders that the highly positively identified youngsters demonstrated negative levels of self-esteem, and that the most negative relationships existed in those youngsters socialized in the highest black-consciousness home situations. This relationship was also found following experimental manipulations designed to increase group identification. If socialization attempts of parents to inculcate a strong sense of black group identity and consciousness are successful, then either negative or null relationships may be found with traditional measures of self-esteem, particularly those that are the most individually achievement oriented.

Conclusions

In this chapter we have reviewed some of the basic literature regarding the meaning, definition, and complexity of group and personal identity. In so doing, we have directed our attention to the observed relationships between group identification and personal functioning, most often operationalized as self-identity or self-esteem. We have noted some of the problems in the relationships between these concepts, most notably conceptual and methodological difficulties, and the failure of researchers to consider other major factors that may have important roles in the development of both personal and group identity in blacks. We have suggested that the family and community racial environment may be two important structural factors that mediate the link between self- and racial/social group conceptions. We have briefly reviewed the role of the racial environment in buffering, insulating, or confronting group membership and have noted the functions of the family as a filtering and supportive agent.

Finally, we have briefly discussed a possible reason current conceptualizations and measures of group and personal identity might consistently demonstrate a negative relationship with one another. Though speculative, some literature supports the view that parental inculcation of black pride and strongly held group images of survival might be antithetical to Western-dominated conceptions and measures of self-esteem that are commonly used in empirical studies. Under these circumstances, blacks who hold the strongest group identification might be less likely to endorse self-esteem items that stress highly individually oriented conceptions of self.

In conclusion, we believe that more empirical research is needed on those conditions that affect both group and individual orientations, and that make the group a salient element in the formation of personal identity. Special emphasis should be placed on the study of family relationships and socialization patterns, because, as we have suggested, the black family is the purveyor of both group and personal identity. Because of the simplistic nature of conceptualization in this area, there is a need for more refined and specified theory, rather than the testing of existing notions. Despite more than 40 years of studies and speculation on the relationship between black personal and social group identity, the complexities are only beginning to be recognized and conceptualized.

Notes

1. In addition to these two theoretical reformulations, some researchers have also raised methodological questions about the earlier work on negative black identity and self-concept. In a review of the studies on preference behavior in blacks, Banks (1976) points out that most of the studies indicate that preferences do not depart from change; he also questions whether they have demonstrated self-rejection and indicates that researchers need to appreciate the complexity of the issues. In a similar vein, Brand, Ruiz, and Padilla (1974), in an extensive review of studies of ethnic identification and preference, point up the questionable state of our knowledge in this area. They note that results vary according to method and nine other situational, contextual, and individual variables.

2. An engagement of personal values may also provide some explanation of this simplistic view. Cross (1979) makes an interesting comment on how difficult it is to challenge the assumption that there is a direct relationship between group identity and psychological functioning. After noting that we have not been able to demonstrate empirically any direct relationship between reference group orientation (RGO) and personal identity (PI), Cross notes, "During several recent lectures, this observer has found it difficult to even present the idea that RGO and PI may not be related, so emotional was the response of students and faculty in the audience" (p. 30).

References

Adams, B. A. 1978. "Inferiorization and Self-Esteem." *Social Psychology* 41:47-53.

Alejandro-Wright, M. 1985. "The Child's Conception of Racial Classification: A Social-Cognitive Developmental Model." In *Beginnings: The Social and Affective Development of*

Black Children, edited by M. B. Spencer, G. K. Brookins, and W. R. Allen. Hillsdale, NJ: Lawrence Erlbaum.

Allen, R. L. and S. J. Hatchett. 1986. "The Media and Social Reality Effects: Self and System Orientations of Blacks." *Communication Research* 13:97-123.

Banks, W. C. 1976. "White Preference in Blacks: A Paradigm in Search of a Phenomenon." *Psychological Bulletin* 83:1170-86.

Barnes, E. J. 1972. "The Black Community as the Source of Positive Self-Concept for Black Children: A Theoretical Perspective." In *Black Psychology,* edited by R. L. Jones. New York: Harper & Row.

Bowman, P. J. and C. Howard. 1985. "Race-Related Socialization, Motivation, and Academic Achievement: A Study of Black Youths in Three-Generation Families." *Journal of the American Academy of Child Psychiatry* 24:134-41.

Brand, E. S., R. A. Ruiz, and A. M. Padilla. 1974. "Ethnic Identification and Preference: A Review." *Psychological Review* 81:860-90.

Broman, C. L., H. W. Neighbors, and J. S. Jackson. 1986. "Racial Group-Identification Among Black Adults." Unpublished manuscript, University of Michigan, Ann Arbor, Institute for Social Research.

Clark, K. B. and M. P. Clark. 1947. "Racial Identification and Preference in Negro Children." In *Readings in Social Psychology,* edited by T. M. Newcomb and E. L. Hartley. New York: Holt, Rinehart & Winston.

Clark, M. L. 1985. "Racial Stereotypes and Self-Esteem in Black Americans." Unpublished manuscript, Wake Forest University, Department of Psychology, Winston-Salem, NC.

Cross, W. E. 1979. "Black Families and Black Identity Development: Rediscovering the Distinctions Between Self-Esteem and Reference Group Orientations." Paper presented at the International Seminar on the Child and the Family, Gustavus Adolphus College, St. Peter, MN, August.

———. 1985. "Black Identity: Rediscovering the Distinction Between Personal Identity and Reference Group Orientation." In *Beginnings: The Social and Affective Development of Black Children,* edited by M. B. Spencer, G. K. Brookins, and W. R. Allen. Hillsdale, NJ: Lawrence Erlbaum.

Gitter, A. G., D. J. Mastophy, and Y. Satow. 1972. "The Effect of Skin Color and Physiognomy on Racial Misidentification." *Journal of Social Psychology* 88:139-43.

Goodman, M. E. 1952. *Race Awareness in Young Children.* Reading, MA: Addison-Wesley.

Gordon, V. V. 1976. "Methodologies of Black Self-Concept Research: A Critique." *Journal of Afro-American Issues* 4:73-81.

Gurin, P., A. H. Miller, and G. Gurin. 1980. "Stratum Identification and Consciousness." *Social Psychology Quarterly* 43:30-47.

Hall, W. S., W. E. Cross, and R. Freedle. 1972. "Stages in the Development of Black Awareness: An Exploratory Investigation." In *Black Psychology,* edited by R. L. Jones. New York: Harper & Row.

Hare, B. R. 1977. "Racial and Socioeconomic Variations in Preadolescent Area-Specific and General Self-Esteem." *International Journal of Intercultural Relations* 1:1-59.

Harrison, A. O. 1985. "The Black Family's Socializing Environment: Self-Esteem and Ethnic Attitude Among Black Children." In *Black Children,* edited by H. P. McAdoo and J. L. McAdoo. Beverly Hills, CA: Sage.

Hraba, J. and G. Grant. 1970. "Black Is Beautiful: A Reexamination of Racial Preference and Identification." *Journal of Personality and Social Psychology* 16:398-402.

Jackson, J. S. and S. J. Hatchett. 1986. "Intergenerational Research: Methodological Considerations." In *Intergenerational Relations,* edited by N. Datan, A. L. Greene, and H. W. Reese. Hillsdale, NJ: Lawrence Erlbaum.

Jackson, J. S., M. B. Tucker, and P. J. Bowman. 1982. "Conceptual and Methodological Problems in Survey Research on Black Americans." In *Methodological Problems in Minority Research,* edited by W. Liu. Chicago: Pacific/Asian American Mental Health Center.

Kardiner, A. and L. Ovesey. 1951. *The Mark of Oppression.* Cleveland: World.

Landreth, C. and B. C. Johnson. 1953. "Young Children's Responses to a Picture and Inset Test Designed to Reveal Reactions to Persons of Different Skin Color." *Child Development* 24:63-79.

Lewin, K. 1948. *Resolving Social Conflict.* New York: Harper & Row.

Lipscomb, L. 1975. "Socialization Factors in the Development of Black Children's Racial Self-Esteem." Paper presented at the annual meeting of the American Sociological Association.

McAdoo, H. P. 1970. "Racial Attitudes and Self-Concepts of Black Preschool Children." Ph.D. dissertation, University of Michigan, Ann Arbor (University Microfilms No. 71-4677).

————. 1985. "Racial Attitude and Self-Concept of Young Black Children Over Time." In *Black Children,* edited by H. P. McAdoo and J. L. McAdoo. Beverly Hills, CA: Sage.

McCullough, W. R. 1982. "The Development of Group Identification in Black Americans." Ph.D. dissertation, University of Michigan, Ann Arbor.

McCullough, W. R., G. Gurin, and J. S. Jackson. 1981. "Racial Identity and Consciousness: The Socialization of Ingroup and Outgroup Orientations." Paper presented at the annual meeting of the American Psychological Association, Los Angeles (ERIC Document Reproduction Service No. ED 212687).

Mobley, B. 1973. "Self Concept and Conceptualization of Ethnic Identity: The Black Experience." Ph.D. dissertation, Purdue University.

Moreland, J. K. 1962. "Racial Acceptance and Preference of Nursery School Children in a Southern City." *Merrill Palmer Quarterly* 8:271-80.

Nobles, W. W. 1973. "Psychological Research and the Black Self-Concept: A Critical Review." *Journal of Social Issues* 29:11-31.

Peters, M. F. 1985. "Racial Socialization of Young Black Children." In *Black Children,* edited by H. P. McAdoo and J. L. McAdoo. Beverly Hills, CA: Sage.

Pitts, J. P. 1974. "The Study of Race Consciousness: Comments on New Directions." *American Journal of Sociology* 80:665-87.

Porter, J. R. and R. E. Washington. 1979. "Black Identity and Self-Esteem: A Review of Studies of Black Self-Concept." *Annual Review of Sociology* 5:53-74.

Radke, M. J. and H. G. Trager. 1950. "Children's Perceptions of the Social Roles of Negroes and Whites." *Journal of Psychology* 29:3-33.

Rasheed, S. 1981. "The Development of Ethnic Identity and Self-Esteem in Bilalian (Black) Children." Ph.D. dissertation, University of Michigan, Ann Arbor.

Rosenberg, M. 1985. "Summary." In *Beginnings: The Social and Affective Development of Black Children,* edited by M. B. Spencer, G. K. Brookins, and W. R. Allen. Hillsdale, NJ: Lawrence Erlbaum.

Sacks, S. 1973. "Self-Identity and Academic Achievement of Black Adolescent Males: A Study of Racial Identification, Locus of Control, Self-Attitudes, and Academic Performance." Ph.D. dissertation, Columbia University.

Semaj, L. T. 1985. "Afrikanity, Cognition and Extended Self-Identity." In *Beginnings: The Social and Affective Development of Black Children,* edited by M. B. Spencer, G. K. Brookins, and W. R. Allen. Hillsdale, NJ: Lawrence Erlbaum.

Simmons, R. B. 1978. "Blacks and High Self-Esteem." *Social Psychology* 41:54-57.

Spencer, M. B. 1985. "Cultural Cognition and Social Cognition as Identity Correlates of Black Children's Personal-Social Development." In *Beginnings: The Social and Affective Develop-*

ment of Black Children, edited by M. B. Spencer, G. K. Brookins, and W. R. Allen. Hillsdale, NJ: Lawrence Erlbaum.

Stevenson, H. W. and E. C. Steward. 1958. "A Developmental Study of Race Awareness in Young Children." *Child Development* 29:399-410.

Tajfel, H., ed. 1982. *Social Identity and Intergroup Relations.* Cambridge: Cambridge University Press.

Taylor, M. C. and E. J. Walsh. 1979. "Explanations of Black Self-Esteem: Some Empirical Tests." *Social Psychology Quarterly* 42:253-61.

Taylor, R. L. 1976. "Black Youth and Psychosocial Development: A Conceptual Framework." *Journal of Black Studies* 6:35-72.

Thomas, C. 1971. *Boys No More: A Black Psychologist's View of Community.* Beverly Hills, CA: Glencoe.

Turner, J. C. 1982. "Towards a Cognitive Redefinition of the Social Group." In *Social Identity and Intergroup Relations,* edited by H. Tajfel. Cambridge: Cambridge University Press.

Ward, S. and J. Braun. 1972. "Self-Esteem and Racial Preference." *American Journal of Orthopsychiatry* 42:644-47.

Washington, V. 1976. "Learning Racial Identity." In *Demythologizing the Inner-City Child,* edited by R. C. Granger and J. C. Young. Silver Springs, MD: National Association for the Education of Young Children.

Wellman, B. 1970. "Social Identities in Black and White." *Sociological Inquiry* 41:57-66.

Wyne, M. D., K. P. White, and R. H. Coop. 1974. *The Black Self.* Englewood Cliffs, NJ: Prentice Hall.

Young, V. H. 1970. "Family and Childhood in a Southern Negro Community." *American Anthropologist* 72:269-88.

Zavalloni, M. 1971. "Cognitive Processes and Social Identity Through Focused Introspection." *European Journal of Social Psychology* 1:235-60.

———. 1973. "Social Identity: Perspectives and Prospects." *Social Science Information* 12: 65-91.

Gender Relations Within
African American Communities

This section provides an overview of the roles and attitudes that Black males and females hold toward one another, an issue that has attracted much attention within the community. An overview of marital relations is followed by a discussion of male-female relations; Black women's values regarding marriage are then examined, and the final chapter discusses Black women's attitudes toward childbearing.

In the first chapter, Robert Staples gives an overview of race and marital status and their effects on Black families. He provides a historical basis for the present relationship between Black males and females and explains some of the unique patterns that are sometimes found. The egalitarian relationship between Black men and women, the role overload of women, and the greater independence of women within the family stem from historical and financial reasons and may have implications for marriage relations. Regardless of these pressures, African Americans are heavily committed to marriage, with postponement occurring in younger age groups that is consistent with trends in other populations. Staples explains the increasing level of Black single-hood as well as the structural restraints on marriage faced at the lower- and middle-income levels. The complexity of relations in the pair-bonding process is noted by Staples and detailed by Heiss and Harrison in their chapters in this section.

In Chapter 16, Audrey Chapman explores relationships between male and female African Americans, an area of growing concern both inside and outside marriage. She shows how stereotypes have played havoc, how the pressures build, as both males and females seek to survive economically in a society that is growing toward more high technology. She points to the need for African Americans to maintain positive relations between the sexes. Chapman sees as key elements in this effort both the choices made by and the joint responsibility of both women and men.

Jerold Heiss presents in Chapter 17 a clear articulation of the different points of view that have been presented in the literature about the association of family values and race or SES. He uses a national probability sample to test Ladner's hypothesis that Black women reject society's expectations and create alternative family forms that result in different values. He tackles the difficult task of looking at family and marriage values from several perspectives: Is race associated with values? If race does matter, then what is the effect of differential SES? Which is greater? And if one controls for all other variables, is race still important? Heiss begins with the premise that SES, not race or culture, is the key variable, and he reports that racial differences are minor, indicating a divergence (as projected by Glick in Chapter 7) of values and structure. Instrumental concerns are more salient for Black women in terms of marriage partners, and SES has less influence on Blacks than on whites. Heiss finds no race differences in attitudes toward divorce and an increase in the acceptance by Blacks of out-of-wedlock parentage.

In Chapter 18, Algea Othella Harrison points to the importance of parental role expectations, how they have changed, and how they affect the procreational attitudes of Black adults. Although she has found little in the literature about the male role in parenting and in procreation planning, she reviews many studies about women. She notes that Black families have been found to provide modeling that leads children toward androgynous roles. The importance of the active maternal role, as noted also by Staples, and the centrality of children in the woman's life often lead to subsequent prioritization of the mother role over the wife role. Harrison also concludes that the decline in fertility levels and the increase in the use of effective birth control, along with the delay in parenting of younger career-oriented women, will have an influence on pair-bonding among Blacks and on their attitudes toward procreation in the future.

An Overview of Race and Marital Status

ROBERT STAPLES

Relationships between Black men and women have had a peculiar evolution. Unlike the white family, which was a patriarchy sustained by the economic dependence of the female, the Black dyad has been characterized by more egalitarian roles and economic parity in North America. The system of slavery did not permit the Black male to assume the superordinate role in the family constellation, as the female was not economically dependent on him. Hence, relationships between the sexes were ordered along socio-psychological factors rather than economic compulsion to marry and remain married. This fact, in part, explains the unique trajectory of Black male-female relationships.

In the postslavery era, the economic parity of Black men and women continued. Due to the meager wages of most Black males, women were forced to enter the labor market and contribute to the maintenance of their households. Such a strong economic role in the family had certain consequences for the marital relationship. The stability of the white, patriarchal family was based on the economic dependence of the female spouse, forcing her into the prescribed role of a passive, subordinate female. Because Black

269

females were more economically independent, many developed attitudes of freedom and equality unknown to most women in the nineteenth century. Although this trait may be currently perceived as a healthy predecessor to the modern women's liberation movement, it produced tensions in Black marriages that were less prevalent in white marriages. The independent woman, in the past and the present, is more likely to be party to a dissolved marriage than is her more reliant and passive counterpart.

Economic factors, however, provide only the foundation for dyadic conflict, which is subject to the interplay of other psychosocial forces. Another cause of Black male-female conflict consists of the often ignored consequences of the dual role Black women play in the family: worker and mother. The heavy concentration of Black women in domestic service often meant that they held the unenviable position of caring for two households: their own and those of their employers. It has seldom been questioned that the negative effects of doing double duty in two households could create competition between obligations to the two households and could tear at the fabric of the Black woman's marital relationship. Certainly, it could lead to role overload that might compound the difficulties of prosaic marital interaction. It might be noted that this same role overload continues to be extant, albeit in a slightly different form. Many Black women remain burdened by the multiple roles they must play—worker, mother, and wife. Surely this partly explains the resultant tension and high rate of marital dissolution among many Black couples.

Despite the problematic aspects of marriage, Blacks continued to marry in record numbers. When one looks at the marital status of Black women over the age of 65, only 3.5% had never married, in comparison to 6.5% of white women.[1] However, the younger group of Blacks appear to have abandoned marriage as a viable institution. At least, the figures that show only a minority of them married and living with a spouse indicate that to be the case. Upon closer inspection, it seems that the desire to marry and remain married has not diminished—only the conditions for doing so have altered.

One can best understand the high rate of singlehood among Blacks by examining the phenomenon along class and gender lines. The basic causes are structural constraints and ideological preferences. Among lower-income Blacks, the structural constraints consist of the unavailability and undesirability of Black males in the eligible pool of potential mates. Due to the operational effects of institutional racism, large numbers of Black males are incarcerated, unemployed, or narcotized, or have fallen prey to early death.

There may actually be an excess of 3 million Black women without the opportunity to find available or desirable mates. As a result, many Black women have children out of wedlock and raise them with the assistance of extended family members and their children's biological father.

Similar structural constraints are operative among the Black middle class. Assuming a desire for homogeneity in mate selection, it is not possible for every Black female college graduate to find a mate among her peers. In 1975, there were 68,000 more Black female college graduates than Black male college graduates. Overall, the ratio of single college-educated Black women to similar men is 2 to 1. In certain categories the ratio is as low as 38 women to every male. This gap, although currently wide, will continue to widen, as there are 150,000 more Black women than Black men currently enrolled in college. A very different demographic picture exists among whites, where there are a million more white male college graduates than white female college graduates. The origins of this difference can be attributed to the historical practice of Black families' sending their daughters to college because their sons had a wider variety of occupations open to them. The daughters either went to college and became schoolteachers or went into domestic service, an occupation fraught with risks for young Black women in the postbellum South.

However, it is among this middle-class group that ideological preference—that is, the desire not to marry—is more prevalent. Because the women in this group earn 90% of a similar male's income, they do not need to marry for economic support. It is more often the satisfaction of psychological needs that is the dominant reason for entering into marriage. Yet the satisfaction of psychological needs is not the forte of American males. Moreover, the greater a woman's educational level and income, the less desirable she is to many Black males. Whereas a male's success adds to his desirability as a mate, it detracts from a woman's. Hence the women in this group are less likely to marry; if they do marry, they are less likely to remain married. This is a classical case of success in the labor market and failure in the marriage arena.

Relationships between Black men and women are probably more complex than can be spelled out in this brief overview. Certainly the dominant factors are contained in the interplay of institutional racism with individual traits. The problems of conflict between Black males and females are ultimately a function of political and economic forces beyond their control. Even within the context of economic and racial oppression, many Black men and women share happy moments with each other. For many, their relationships last a lifetime. There are also those for whom the tension of living in a racist society filters into their most intimate relationships. Relationships between the sexes are, at best, fragile in a society undergoing such rapid social change as is occurring in the United States. Rapid social change, no matter in what direction, can cause dislocation in individuals and institutions. The dyadic relationships of Blacks, the group in America most vulnerable to economic and political change, are most sensitive to those changes.

Note

1. All figures are from Staples (1981).

Reference

Staples, R. E. 1981. *The World of Black Singles.* Westport, CT: Greenwood.

The Black Search for Love and Devotion

Facing the Future Against All Odds

AUDREY B. CHAPMAN

With all the recent media attention given to the plight of the Black family, it would be hard to ignore the fact that great problems still exist between Black men and women. It is a mistake to view these problems in a vacuum, however. Any objective observer can see that family relations have changed throughout U.S. society as a whole, not just among Blacks. Yet it is probably true that economic and social conditions compound the problems in the Black community more so than in the White community. A thorough discussion of the future of the Black family calls for an honest examination of the chasm between Black men and women. Powerful controlling myths surround the relationship, and those myths still influence the thinking and behavior of many Black individuals. It is baffling to contemplate that some of the myths that took hold during slavery still cripple us today.

In her edited volume *The Black Woman,* Rodgers-Rose (1980) indicates how devastating the stereotypes of the shiftless male and the hostile woman have been to Blacks, who internalize these feelings and bring them into their relationships. Many women say that Black men cannot be counted on because they have met a few who neglect the needs of their women and children. Another persistent damaging myth is that of the controlling Black woman, who is supposed to be "super-strong," self-reliant, totally independent and aggressive, and hostile to Black men.

These stereotypes are two examples of myths from the past that continue to plague relationships today. Ideas like these have been perpetuated by society, and Black males and females collude in them, consciously and subconsciously. Thus they continue to struggle with one another rather than unite against the external forces that keep them in turmoil. Some Blacks remain focused solely on racism rather than devoting their energies to controlling their lives. Although no one would deny the role of racism in the problems confronting the Black community, it is a powerless position to concentrate on our victimization instead of a search for love and commitment.

Since the 1960s, Blacks have experienced numerous external negative pressures at a time when many expected to be doing better. The social changes that occur in the larger society filter into the Black community and affect it as well. The sexual revolution, a climbing divorce rate, and a return to conservatism and subtle racism have brought new challenges for Black families. Although many have surmounted these pressures, others still languish in the hopelessness of the situation. Obviously, these factors greatly affect relationships. As Black Americans, we witness the fallout every day.

Black men complain that Black women always want control, like the character Sapphire who dominated Kingfish in *Amos 'n' Andy*. In the literature of the 1990s, Black women complain about the failures of Black men. In the best-seller *Waiting to Exhale*, Terry McMillan (1992) explores the lives of a group of Black women who seem to be in a desperate search for love but more often feel emotionally abused or used. The struggles described by McMillan often affect the way men and women romantically connect and ultimately bring on the male bashing that we hear so often from women who are angry at their men. Some women have chosen to go on without male partners. Black women often feel they bear both the burden and the responsibility for how their partners feel about being committed and loving with them. Black men often feel they are blamed for all the problems that exist in their relationships.

Perhaps the best way to explore where Black male-female relationships stand is to examine the current condition of the Black family in America. The family is changing, and the balance in relationships is in flux. Households headed by females increased from 28% to 41% between 1970 and 1982, partially as a result of the rising divorce rate and partly due to the growing number of unwed mothers. In 1992, 52% of Black households were headed by a single female. In 1982, 49% of Black children lived with one parent, and 8% lived with neither parent. William Julius Wilson of the University of Chicago has predicted that by the end of the century, 70% of Black men will be unemployed.

The *New York Times* reported in 1982 that the divorce rate had doubled for Black women since 1970, rising to 257 divorces for every 1,000 marriages, a 104% increase. For Black males, there were 151 divorces to every 1,000 marriages, up from 62 in 1972. The difference between the genders comes from the fact that divorced Black men remarry sooner and at higher rates than do divorced Black women, and remarriages are counted as marriages in the census statistics.

The divorce rate accounts for the second-largest category of singles in this country. The first is people who have never married, and marriage is being postponed for longer periods today than in the past. The economy tells only part of the story. The birth control pill gave all women the ability to determine pregnancy, and the sexual revolution in the 1970s relaxed social attitudes about having children outside marriage. In every economic group, Black women are from two to six times more likely to have children before marriage than are White women. According to the U.S. Census Bureau, in 1992 32% of the White females in this country were unwed mothers, compared with 66% of Black females. The decision to be a single mother has a bearing on the trend toward resisting marriage altogether among Black women (and some men). According to Gilligan and Brown (1992), in 1990, 20% of Black women were married, compared with 40% of White women. In what looks like a "marriage shift," U.S. Census officials report that less than 75% of Black females are likely to marry, compared with 90% of White females.

Part of this imbalance is due to the excess of women in the Black population, which is estimated at 1 million, but another factor is the criteria middle-class Black women use in selecting a mate. Many Black men are considered "unacceptable" unless they are good looking, have college degrees, are professionals, earn at least $90,000 annually, own BMWs or Jaguars, and have other such resources. The many men who fall into the "undesirable" category are confronted with too many women to date.

To cite these facts is not an attempt to "blame the victim" for all the problems in the Black community, but we must begin to face some painful realities if we are going to find and make lasting relationships. In the economic arena, although some Blacks have made great strides, many have not gained access to the economic equality they need in order to take care of their families. The past decade has not been kind to African Americans, especially couples trying to make it. For example, in 1991 Black males earned on average $12,962 annually, compared with $21,395 for White males. Black women earned the lowest income, $8,816, compared with $10,721 for White women (U.S. Bureau of the Census, 1992). How can a man feel competent or capable of taking care of responsibilities when he is underemployed or unemployed? This dynamic sets up competition and disloyalty between the sexes, creating polarities that cause a sense of mistrust and disappointment. These economic facts are interesting because one of the greatest sources of conflict between Black men and women is the myth that the women are doing so much better economically. In reality, neither gender group is faring very well in this society.

Another relevant statistic is that a disproportionate number of male African Americans are either in prison or dead. Although Blacks represent only 12% of the U.S. population, Black men accounted for 44% of the inmates in state prisons and local jails in 1991. This social dynamic, along with the rise in open homosexuality, leaves many Black women facing life alone.

In the 1970s it was called the "male shortage"; in the 1990s, we refer to "love phobia." Whatever term is used, today as a century ago, there is still fear of commitment, lack of trust, and emotional game playing. Those who do marry face tensions because of competing career and gender roles, balance-of-power issues, remarriage, and problems with stepchildren. These couples must identify ways to find time and energy for healthy loving.

A recent *Newsweek* article (August 30, 1993) notes that the sexual revolution in the 1970s was the second shift that changed Black families. The first was that Black women delayed marriage or denied its benefits because they were uncertain there would be men to marry, but they continued to have children. Many are making the conscious choice to educate themselves, get jobs, buy homes, and have children before they are beyond their childbearing years. Although family life is very much connected to African culture and is highly valued within the Black community, many men and women are finding it difficult to make relationships work.

The Situation Today

In recent years, Blacks have assumed a "yo-yo" or approach-avoidance mentality regarding relationships. More single men and women are interacting briefly and often in a solely physical way. If married, some focus less on intimacy and more on superficialities.

In *Future Shock* (1970), Alvin Toffler attempted to prepare Americans for the "SuperIndustrial Revolution," suggesting that this phase would place more emphasis on "freedom" than on commitment. Whereas previous generations stayed in marriages because of societal expectations, Americans today espouse the new attitude of "doing your own thing."

The rift between Black males and females begins early in their social development. The same internal and external forces of family and society that encourage young Black females toward scholastic achievement discourage young Black males from this same goal. Instead, society pressures Black males to prove their manhood through excelling in sports, music, and hustling. Therefore, some young men learn dysfunctional patterns early in life as a way to gain status in a hostile system. Among Black male adolescents, there are high rates of homicide, suicide, incarceration, and substance abuse.

Between 1976 and 1981, the number of Black women with doctoral degrees rose 29%, and the number with first professional degrees increased 71%. The number of Black men with doctoral degrees decreased 10%, and the number with first professional degrees dropped 12%. In 1991, 11.97% of Black females earned a bachelor's degree, compared with 11.88% of Black males. An estimated 40% of the Black male population is functionally illiterate. One depressing consequence of these circumstances is that a large number of Black women are unable to find suitable Black mates and thus focus more on their education and the acquisition of material goods. At the same time, Black men seem confused about how to provide what the "new Black woman" wants. Black men in the professions are not plentiful, and others risk rejection because they do not meet certain standards. Many respond to the new Black woman with a distant approach and mixed feelings about relating to her. Some men who are "acceptable" seem not to be interested in bonding, and others fear approaching women, yet they also fear going through life alone.

Although women feel less powerful in unhealthy relationships, they often stay in them because the opportunity to find another man is not great. Furthermore, because many Black women feel responsible for the outcomes of their relationships, they persevere in unsatisfying situations just to keep peace, only to discover that this behavior creates other dynamics, such as pain and confusion. The reaction on the women's part may be rivalry, jealousy, and competition, resulting in hostility toward men. Many experts believe that the desire of women for more rights and freedom has caused many men to feel so intimidated that they have withdrawn any open demonstration of intimate feelings. Whatever the reasons, many Black men and women feel great emotional divisions and distance, and too many are still struggling to gain control, get attention, and have quality time and loving experiences.

Many Black men and women have a "throwaway" style of relating in brief emotional ties. One reason may be the women's movement, which seems to have created feelings of autonomy and less need for permanent commitments. Sexual liaisons have become "in" and intimacy "out." One consequence has been a sense of unfulfillment caused by lack of emotional connections. Even Black women who have not been active in the women's movement have adopted some aspects of this new lifestyle, and many experts believe that the demographic imbalance between the sexes aggravates the problem.

Although there is general concern about the apparent chasm between men and women and the resulting ill effects on the family, many individuals have been slow to acknowledge the powerful social changes that have occurred in the past decade. The resulting confusion among and violence against Black individuals and within families has resulted in what Americans are witnessing today. Many Black men and women struggle without really understanding the underlying reasons for the new tensions between them, and this lack of understanding makes change or improvement very difficult.

Mansharing Revisited

In the research for my book *Mansharing: Dilemma or Choice?* (Chapman 1986), 2,000 women throughout the nation were interviewed on why mate selection is difficult. More than 75% (1,580) reported fewer problems meeting men than in identifying someone who would fulfill many of their needs. Most of the women indicated that "it's not who he is, but what the possibilities are for him to gain access to power." Because of unequal economic factors, many Black men are not likely to fit that category.

As noted earlier, aside from their economic unsuitability, Black men are in short supply due to high rates of mortality, incarceration in prison or mental hospitals, and drug addiction, as well as military service (overseas) and homosexuality (recently more visible in the Black community). All these factors reduce the eligible pool, which means that there are more women who desire partners at an age when fewer exist.

The imbalance promotes an interesting social structure sometimes referred to as mansharing. This occurs when two or more women share one man. They may be married or single, aware or unaware of this status. In 1982, a workshop on the topic was offered for women in Washington, D.C., and 120 attended the first session, either to learn what it was about or because they had chosen to share men. The women ranged in age from 35 to 45 and were divorced or widowed. They were in search of companionship, not marriage. They tended to view mansharing as a dilemma and were in conflict and depressed about their lack of exclusive relationships. One interesting reaction was that some women stated their opposition to sharing but gave information that they had shared many times.

Harriette McAdoo (1983) studied single mothers in Washington, D.C., to determine how they felt about sharing men. Her research shows that although these women reported having difficulty with sharing, there were discrepancies between what they said and their behavior. Although only a small proportion reported agreeing to sharing arrangements, almost four times that number had participated nonetheless.

In *Too Many Women* (1983), Secord reports that whenever there is an excess of females in society, marriage and monogamy are devalued. In 1986 a sexual survey conducted by *New Woman* magazine revealed that 65% of the men and 34% of the women surveyed admitted being unfaithful to a spouse or lover. Given the ratio of Black men to women, it seems that many women unknowingly share partners. Robert Staples, in *The World of Black Singles* (1981), notes that because of the surplus of Black women, it is a "buyer's market" in the marital arena for Black men.

Another factor is that Blacks as well as Whites confront the issue of changing gender roles with much anxiety. Christopher Lasch suggests in *The*

Culture of Narcissism (1979) that Americans have taken flight from "feelings" and have entered an era of sexual warfare. It seems that relationships involve more sexual freedom but fewer emotional returns. Americans are living for the moment.

The Struggle to Bond

The attitude that everything that happens between a man and woman is okay, and that "everything" includes anything, has become a tempting illusion for many, resulting in an escalating tension between men and women. Much of this tension stems from the collapse of "chivalry ethics." Lasch (1979) describes the outcome when men and women pursue sex for itself: "The efficient contraceptive, legalized abortion, and a realistic and healthy acceptance of the body have weakened the links that once tied sex to love, marriage and procreation. Men and women now pursue sexual pleasure as an end in itself, unmediated even by the conventional trappings of romance."

So both sexes, in order to survive in an era of detached unions, must work hard to manipulate their emotions to protect themselves against pain and rejection. That is why relationships appear so unstable that they cannot accommodate mutual demands or expectations—not to mention commitment and monogamy. Both sexes invest in playing it safe and in behavior that will control the other person so that they are less vulnerable.

In my counseling practice, Black men and women reveal that they feel lonely, sad, and scared about the lack of stable relationships with members of the opposite sex. This awareness usually occurs after they have spent many years on the unfulfilling social circuit. When they begin to realize that developing loving bonds need not be so frightening, they can learn that positive relationships are at the root of strong families for Black people. Some Black couples have managed to avoid the trends of the 1970s and 1980s. A closer investigation of how they are faring is essential to developing a model for those still seeking a new way to interact emotionally with the opposite sex.

Making Love and Devotion Happen

Many people struggle with the question of how to maintain "good" relationships. Love is a natural and basic need; every living being desires it.

Some believe that friendship supersedes sexual union, social commitments, and short-term affairs. Once men and women discover the importance of spiritual bonding, they experience what love and friendship really are. Some are aware that what was abandoned in the 1970s needs to be rediscovered for survival in today's world. Many realize that a good friendship forms the basis of a strong, durable relationship.

Many couples take their relationships so seriously that they structure time for communication, relaxation, and spiritual union. They relate as friends long after the glow is gone, and they work very hard on fairness within the union. For example, I know of one couple whose high-powered jobs involved extensive travel; they decided to hold weekly family meetings just to keep communications open and conflict at a minimum in their household.

For married couples in the past, friendship was the basis of their commitment to each other. They learned how to understand each other's needs, likes, and dislikes. They learned the process of give-and-take and the ability to be less selfish. There was an acceptance of the total person that allowed patience and endurance during trying times. Black men and women need to relearn some of the "old ways."

Many single women form support groups to unite around common concerns or needs. This allows them to share and not compete with other women over personal relationships. It allows them to know they are not alone in their experiences. Black men have formed several groups around the country to address the need for support of single heads of household. Concerned Black Men and Adopt a Family are just two examples. Civic organizations, sororities, singles' associations, and church groups also provide ways for individuals to meet and develop friendships. Friendships provide important support networks when families are far away. Cross-sex friendships are another way of extending oneself, but they can be difficult to formulate, mainly because few role models for doing so exist. Many patterns of cross-sex friendship once existed. For example, if a man was working away from his family, in another town, a male friend of his might oversee the man's household's needs while he was away, interacting as a friend with the man's wife and children. Examples of this type occur in the Black community today, but the community needs to be much more accepting of them.

Another trend in relationships today for some Blacks is crossing the color line. As of the 1984 U.S. Census, in the total population of 46 million White males, 64,000 were married to Black women. Among the nation's 3.5 million Black couples, 100,000 Black men were married to White women. In a study by Robert Staples (1981), 85% of Black men reported having had at least one interracial experience. In informal interviews conducted with 350 Black single women, 205 stated that they had dated White males, and the others believed they would at some point. When asked why, they all said they wanted more economic options and a chance to identify partners with whom they believed there would be fewer hassles than with Black men.

Information on the educational status of Black Americans in the 1985 College Board Report indicates that most interracial couples are White males paired with Black females. It is argued that as more Black women obtain higher education and move further up in status, they may move away from Black men. Thus loss of the traditional Black family unit is a real issue for the future, and the educational and psychological status of Black men has serious implications for the survival of Black family life. If Black males continue to be an endangered species through social oppression and Black females continue to succeed, there is potential for the gulf to widen between the sexes. This may mean more power struggles for future generations, but it also may promote more creative ways to relate, such as older women seeking younger men at greater rates, communal households of women and children (divorced and unwed) joining together for support, and the selection of mates from the cross-cultural pool. More fear provoking, however, is the possibility that the Black population may end up with single, unwed women (adolescent or adult) as the only ones producing families, while those in the middle class postpone marriage due to careers or the search for "Mr. or Ms. Right."

Blacks need to recognize that they still have choices. We need to challenge the awful myth that Black men and women cannot get along. The statistics do not have to be strong indicators of the future unless we allow them to be. Blacks must strive toward empowerment, making decisions based upon what is real in America rather than on what they would like to experience or on false expectations. Material gain alone will not erase the problems. The middle class must reach back and invite those less fortunate to come along.

Blacks must become more comfortable with the fact that total dependence upon the system that oppresses the race will never set Blacks free. Blacks must also realize that they will survive more effectively if they support one another. They must applaud those who are making professional strides, because eventually they may have the clout to make the difference for the race as a whole. By their gains, everyone gains.

Black men and women must realize their joint responsibility for today's tensions in relationships and strive to join together to create more balanced and loving connections. Values and ethics have been challenged in the past few years. Sexual health problems and lack of closeness and intimacy may cause many to consider a return to the old-fashioned style of relating. Even though these ways were not perfect, they did create relationships of substance. If Blacks want successful relationships, they must be willing to take some risks. This may mean that, even if the male shortage continues, people will recommit themselves to mutually monogamous relationships. Conceptualizing love as based on equality and a more balanced way of sharing power will support more devotion and create realistic love bonds.

Love is the pulse of spirituality and bonding. No race of people has ever succeeded without it. Blacks have always gotten through difficult times with a strong sense of brotherhood and sisterhood. Once Blacks accept total responsibility together, Black women can be relieved of bearing the social burdens alone and Black men can stop feeling undervalued and threatened. With this in mind, Black men and women must reexamine their own values and needs. Put simply, they must decide to structure their personal lives in more respectful and loving ways for the future of the race. The next generation's very existence depends upon it.

References

Chapman, A. B. 1986. *Mansharing: Dilemma or Choice?* New York: William Morrow.

Gilligan, C. and L. Brown. 1992. *Meeting at the Crossroads.* Cambridge, MA: Harvard University Press.

Lasch, C. 1979. *The Culture of Narcissism.* New York: Warner Communications.

McAdoo, H. 1983. *Extended Family Support of Single Black Mothers.* DHSS Research Report No. NIMH 5701, MH32159. Washington, DC: Government Printing Office.

McMillan, T. 1992. *Waiting to Exhale.* New York: Viking.

Rodgers-Rose, L. F., ed. 1980. *The Black Woman.* Beverly Hills, CA: Sage.

Secord, P. 1983. *Too Many Women.* Beverly Hills, CA: Sage.

Staples, R. E. 1981. *The World of Black Singles.* Westport, CT: Greenwood.

Toffler, A. 1970. *Future Shock.* New York: Random House.

U.S. Bureau of the Census. 1992. *Marriage and Household Statistics.* Washington, DC: Government Printing Office.

Values Regarding Marriage and the Family From a Woman's Perspective

JEROLD HEISS

After a number of years of sociological investigation, it is now clear that the distributions of several family variables differ for Blacks and Whites. Black families, for example, tend to be somewhat larger, are more likely to be headed by a female, and are more likely to be extended in form (Angel and Tienda 1982; Beck and Beck 1989; Heiss 1975; Hofferth 1984; Tienda and Angel 1982). The reasons for these racial variations remain unclear, however. Some authors argue that there are important differences in family values, and they see the differences in family behavior as a reflection of these psychological differences. Others contend that Blacks and Whites have the same values and that variation by race occurs because their situations differ in ways that produce differential access to the resources required to live by those values.[1]

Ladner (1972) expresses the "attitude difference" view when she says that many of the girls in her study of the lower class "reject larger societal expectations of them and realistically adapt to as well as create their own alternatives and norms" (p. 247). Peters and de Ford (1978) express a similar sentiment when they list three family values to which they say Black families subscribe, "unlike most families in the dominant culture" (p. 193) (see also Schoen and Kluegel 1988). And, of course, the value difference view is held by many who place the sources of the contemporary Black family in Africa and/or slavery (see, for example, Nobles 1978; Herskovits 1941).

Scanzoni (1971), by denying attitudinal differences, states part of the "situational" view when he argues that "the dominant family form through-out western society at the level of values . . . is what the majority of adults (black and white) prefer" (p. 3). Along the same lines, Hannerz (1969) suggests, in speaking of lower-class Blacks, that "there is an idealization of the mainstream model of marriage. People get married and hope to make a go of it largely along its lines" (p. 71). Similarly, "no ghetto-specific model for a male-female union has anything close to the normative validity which the mainstream model enjoys in the ghetto as well as outside it" (p. 102).

According to these authors, the differences in family form emerge from situational differences. Hannerz (1969) contends, for example, that conflict and disruption arise in lower-class Black families because "the rights and duties prescribed in the mainstream model are applied to the situation so that facts of limited access to resources are transformed into ambiguities and deviations in the definition of the conjugal relationship. . . . In such cases the influence of the mainstream model prevents a stable settlement on the basis of ghetto-specific macro-structural conditions" (p. 89) (see also Hofferth 1984; Liebow 1967; Rainwater 1970; Staples 1978, 1985).

Cutting across the lines drawn by the two positions just described is a difference of opinion that relates to the contribution of socioeconomic status (SES) to the differences between the races. Some of those who posit the existence of attitudinal differences see them as a function of the differential distribution of SES. In their view this is the major factor affecting these attitudes, whereas others suggest that the racial differences would remain even if the races were the same in SES. They argue that the experiences that cause the supposed attitudinal differences are associated with racial status at all SES levels, though perhaps to different degrees.

Similarly, those who focus on situational factors may claim that the situations of Blacks tend to differ from those of Whites regardless of social class, or they may posit that racial differences reflect social status differences between the races (see Billingsley 1968; Cherlin 1981; Frazier 1939; Jackson 1973; Udry 1966).

My goal in this chapter is to examine these matters by considering data drawn from a national sample of women. It will not be possible to settle the issue completely, but we can test the "attitude difference" theory by directly comparing the attitudes of women of the two races. Furthermore, when differences are found, we can estimate the degree to which they are a function of SES by comparing the attitudes of the racial groups with SES held constant.[2]

In addition, I attempt to push the matter somewhat further by examining the independent effects of race, SES, and other variables upon the variation in attitudes.[3] By comparing the magnitude of these various effects, we can determine the relative significance of the racial effect. In sum, and more specifically, the research to be reported here is intended to provide answers to six questions:

1. Do Black and White women differ in their attitudes regarding family-related issues?
2. Are any differences the result of differences in SES between the races?
3. Are the SES or racial effects greater?
4. If the racial groups showed the same distribution on SES and other variables (age, religion, current marital status, number of children, and work status), would they differ in their responses?
5. If any racial differences remain after the effects of other independent variables are ruled out, are they larger or smaller than any SES differences that remain when the other independent variables are controlled?
6. After race and SES have explained as much of the variance in responses as they can, how much more of the variation is explained by the other variables?

Answers to these questions will allow us to estimate the independent effects of racial status and will provide us with standards by which to judge the relative significance of these effects. The data will also permit us to determine the relationship between SES and the dependent variables for each race separately. This will allow us to discover if the patterning of responses is the same in the two races—that is, if variables that affect attitudes in one race have similar effects in the other. If this is the case, it would suggest that if the races become more similar in social status, they would probably become more similar in family attitudes. Also, because surveys conducted in 1974 and 1979 asked some of the same questions, it will be possible to determine whether the attitudes of the races are converging or diverging.

Hypotheses

The basic hypothesis is that the attitude differences between the races are of minor significance. It is expected that they will be rather small in absolute size, that they will be no larger than those associated with SES and the other demographic variables, and that they are at least partially a function of the differential distribution of SES and the other variables to be considered. It is my belief that the family values held by an individual are a result of his or her particular socialization experiences, and that the relevant experiences are not strongly affected by race and the other demographic variables used in this study.

This view rejects the "Africanist" and "slavery" positions. Certainly, African ancestry and the experience of slavery represent two major differences between Blacks and Whites. I believe, however, that these differences have relatively little direct effect on the family attitudes that are taught contemporary Blacks. Furthermore, consistent with research (Gutman 1976), it is my assumption that if there is any remaining effect of slavery, it does not push in the direction of a markedly distinctive set of family values.

This is not to deny that there are relevant differences in the recent histories of Blacks and Whites. Racial status is a significant element in the lives of people in U.S. society, and it is quite probable that race has an effect on the family attitudes people encounter and on the choices they make among the attitudes presented to them. At the same time, however, I would note that both races are constantly exposed to the general American culture, and this would serve to reduce the differences between them.

It also seems likely that some of the differences in the experiences of Blacks and Whites are as much a function of differences in SES and other demographic variables as they are of racial status per se. Thus one would expect that the differences between the races would be reduced when SES and the other demographic variables are controlled. Given this, and the known relevance of some of the other variables (for example, age and marital status), one would expect that the independent effect of racial status is very small and no greater than the independent effects of the other factors.

A further assumption is that SES is related to family attitudes in a similar manner in both races. This hypothesis rests on the supposition that the situations of Blacks and Whites are sufficiently alike to ensure that the implications of possessing particular traits are the same in both races, even if the magnitude of the effect is not the same in all cases. For example, regardless of race, people who are well educated are likely to have important socialization experiences that differ from those of people who are less well educated. The former, for example, are more likely to be economically secure. Such differences may very well be reflected in similar intraracial SES effects.

Finally, I expect to find that the races came closer together on family attitudes between the two surveys. This prediction is based on the assumption that societal events brought many additional Blacks into the mainstream of American life. This would have the effects of further reducing the influence of the relevant parts of Black culture, increasing Blacks' exposure to the secondary agencies of socialization, and reducing the differences between their life experiences and those of typical Whites. All of these would lead to a convergence in attitudes over time.

Methods

The data to be examined here were obtained from surveys of national samples conducted in 1974 and 1979 under the sponsorship of Virginia Slims cigarettes. A multistage, stratified, probability design was used to choose sampling units to the level of blocks, and beyond this level there was a combination of random and quota methods. (The quotas were for sex, age level, and employment status.) The subjects of this study are the 2,566 White women and the 318 Black women of the 1974 survey and the 2,607 White women and 296 Black women questioned in 1979.

The SES scale is a factor-analytic score using respondent's education, family income, and a complex occupational prestige code. This code uses the respondent's occupation if she was unmarried and employed, the husband's occupation for married women not in the labor force, and a composite of the husband's and the respondent's occupation for married women who held outside employment. The factor analysis and scoring were done separately for the 1974 and 1979 samples so that changes in the distribution of socioeconomic characteristics in the society would not produce a higher set of scores for the 1979 respondents.

Results

The first set of questions bears on motivations for marrying. Respondents were given a list of 10 possible reasons and asked to choose the 2 or 3 they considered the most important. The responses were analyzed by means of factor analysis, and a clear expressive-instrumental factor emerged. Those who scored high on this factor tended to choose items that related to responsibilities, income, and quality of life. High scorers were less likely than other respondents to choose reasons related to being in love, liking and wanting to be with a particular person, having children, and so forth.

The respondents were also asked to rate 13 marital outcomes in terms of their importance "for a good marriage," and their responses provide us with an index of their motivations for marriage.[4] When these responses were analyzed, two useful factors were found: an expressive factor, reflected in items that had to do with sexual relationships and the survival of love, and a companionship factor, indexed by items dealing with understanding the spouse's life, sharing the humorous side of things, and the sharing of feelings. The analysis that follows uses these factors plus two items that did not weight heavily on either factor: the necessity of financial security and children for a good marriage.

My goal in this section is to test the general validity of Ladner's (1972) conclusion that the motivations that led the lower-class Black women in her sample to marry differ from those of Whites. Ladner states that the former enter marriage after "a more realistic cold assessment of the chances of its succeeding. . . . Love, emotional security, etc. are actually 'luxury' reasons for getting married. Thus, Black females . . . are using more sophisticated and rational reasons for entering the marriage contract" (p. 247).

The data bearing on this issue are presented in Table 17.1. Because they are complex and presented in a somewhat unusual format, I will provide a detailed reading of the data bearing on the first dependent variable to ensure that the reader can follow the argument in later sections of this chapter, where cursory references are made to the tables. Section I of the table presents Pearson correlations among race, SES, and the dependent variables. The

TABLE 17.1 Analysis of Responses to Questions Bearing on Marital Motivations and Goals

			Motives and Goals		
Statistic: Variable; Constants	(A) Instrumental[a]	(B) Expressive[a]	(C) Companionship[a]	(D) Financial Security[b]	(E) Having a Child[b]
I. Correlation: race	.18	-.01	-.10	.12	.02
SES	-.13	-.01	.06	-.13	-.16
II. Beta: race; SES constant	.16	-.01	-.09	.10	-.02
SES; race constant	-.09	-.02	.04	-.11	-.16
III. Final beta: race	.15	-.03	-.11	-.10	.00
SES	-.07	-.03	.04	-.10	-.13
IV. R: race + SES	.20	.02	.11	.17	.16
R added by 5 other variables	.04	.09	.04	.01	.12
V. b: SES; no variables constant					
Black	-.10	-.03	-.04	.01	-.09
White	-.09	-.01	.04	-.07	-.10
VI. b: SES; 5 variables constant					
Black	-.04	-.06	-.06	.05	-.06
White	-.06	-.02	.04	-.06	-.08
VII. Trend, 1974–1979[c]					
Black	-.14	-.11	-.11	+1.8%	-6.9%
White	-.03	-.06	-.08	+8.3%	-5.2%

a. For numerical scores a positive sign indicates that Blacks or higher-status persons tended to get the higher scores.
b. For nonnumerical variables a positive sign means that Black or higher-status respondents were more likely to say the goal was important.
c. A positive sign means that people in the 1979 study had higher scores or a greater likelihood of saying the goal was important.

figures in column A show that race and SES are both weakly related to the number of instrumental reasons for marriage chosen by the respondent. Blacks are more likely than Whites to choose such reasons ($r = .18$), and the higher the SES, the smaller the number of instrumental reasons chosen ($r = -.13$).

The numbers in Section II are the standardized regression coefficients (betas) for race and the dependent variable controlling for SES, and for SES and the dependent variable controlling on race. In column A we see that when SES is controlled, the association of race and instrumental score is about the same as it was when SES was not held constant, and the relationship for SES is reduced slightly when race is controlled (compare Sections I and II). This means that race and SES are weakly related to the score independent of each other, and that a small part of the association between SES and instrumentality that was seen in Section I was owing to racial differences among the SES groups.

The figures in Section III are the betas for race and SES when they and age, religion, marital status, number of children, and employment status are all in the equation. For instrumental score these betas are approximately equal to the SES and race betas without the other variables held constant. This means that the "other" variables do not explain the effects of SES and race on the dependent variable.

The first row of Section IV presents the multiple correlation of race and SES with the dependent variable. In the case of instrumental score, the multiple correlation is quite small. When taken together, race and SES explain only a small amount of the variation in instrumental scores.[5] The second row of Section IV shows how much the other five variables add to the multiple correlation if they are put into the equation after race and SES have been entered. In this case, the addition of the other variables does not raise the multiple R very much. The other variables do not increase our ability to explain variations in instrumental score. In summary, none of the variables is strongly related to variations in response to the measure of instrumental motivations, but race has a somewhat stronger effect than SES, and the other five variables do not increase the correlation by any significant amount.

Sections V and VI present unstandardized regression coefficients (bs) for SES for each race separately, with and without the other variables held constant. These figures tell us how SES affects the dependent variables in each race, another way of judging the extent to which the races are similar or different. The data in column A suggest that for instrumental scores the patterning by SES is similar in the two races. The coefficients for SES and instrumental score are in the same direction for Whites and Blacks, and they are about the same in magnitude. Controlling the other variables reduces both coefficients, but the reduction is slightly greater for Blacks. The general conclusion is that there are similar differences between SES groups in both races, that the differences are small, and that they are partially a result of the associations among SES, age, and so forth.

The trends from 1974 to 1979 are presented in Section VII. As is indicated by the negative signs, both races had lower instrumental scores in 1979 than they had in 1974. It is important to note, however, that the change is somewhat greater for Blacks. As the Blacks had higher scores than the Whites in the 1974 study, this means there was a small convergence of the races between 1974 and 1979.

The items bearing on the criteria for a good marriage show a variety of patterns. Section I indicates that neither SES nor race is related to choosing expressive criteria (column B). In fact, none of the independent variables shows a substantial association with this dependent variable. Compared with Whites, however, Blacks do show a tendency to give less importance to companionship (column C), and they emphasize financial security more than do Whites (column D), even when other variables are held constant. The racial effect on the rating of companionship is stronger than the SES effect; for financial security it is the same strength. And the ratings on the importance of children for a good marriage (column E) are related to SES but not to race.

This diversity makes it difficult to present a general conclusion, but it does seem that there are small racial differences on some marital goals and motivations. Just as Ladner (1972) has suggested, Blacks tend to be more instrumental. The differences are small, to be sure, and they are not found on all variables, but they do seem to exist, and it is important that none of them is a reflection of racial differences in SES or the other variables being considered here.

In general, the social status patterns are about the same in the two races. For two of the variables, the signs of the *b*s are different, which implies that in one race high-SES people tend to have higher scores and in the other race lower-status people have the higher scores. But for both variables the effects are small.

The time trends are all in the same direction for the two races and generally do not differ much in magnitude. This suggests that there is neither convergence nor divergence. The financial security item is an exception, however. Both races rated this higher in 1979 than in 1974, but the increase was greater for Whites. This caused the races to converge on this matter, given that in 1974 the Blacks were more likely to respond that financial security was important.

Turning now to other matters, we note that many authors have reported that the structural patterns prescribed by the mainstream model of the family are followed less often by Blacks than by Whites.[6] For example, married Black women whose husbands are present are somewhat more likely to be employed outside the home than is the case for similar White women (Blau and Ferber 1986), the Black rate for nonmarital parenthood is higher (Ahlburg and De Vita 1992; Farley and Allen 1987; Jaynes and Williams 1989), Black families are more likely to be headed by females (Ahlburg and De Vita 1992; Rodgers-Rose 1980), and there is a greater likelihood that the Black household will contain people who are not members of the nuclear family (Angel and Tienda 1982; Beck and Beck 1989; Farley and Allen 1987; Hill and Shackleford 1978).

The data in Table 17.2 relate to whether there are attitudinal differences behind the structural differences in families. Column A analyzes the responses to an item that asked about preferences in family form. For our purposes the item was dichotomized into "mainstream" and "nonmainstream" categories. The first comprises those who chose the option of a nuclear family with a "traditional" division of labor, and the second comprises primarily people who preferred a nuclear family with an equal sharing of responsibilities for housework, children, and "breadwinning."[7] The item considered in column B asked the respondents whether they would respect more, less, or about the same a man who stayed home and did the housework while his wife worked, compared with a man who was a wage earner. The remaining two variables also deal with variant family forms: cohabitation without marriage (as an option for one's child) and parenthood without marriage.[8]

Despite the behavioral differences that exist, the races show very little attitude difference for these items. None of the racial correlations is above .10, which indicates that Blacks are not substantially more accepting of these "nonmainstream" family forms.[9] It is also clear that this failure to find racial differences is not due to a lack of patterned variation. The SES differences are all .10 or above, even when other variables are held constant. In addition, the demographic factors, particularly age, add a reasonable amount to the multiple Rs for three of the variables.

TABLE 17.2 Analysis of Responses to Questions Bearing on Acceptance of "Nonmainstream" Family Forms

	Family Forms Accepted			
Statistic: Variable; Constants	(A) Accepts Nontraditional Forms[a]	(B) Respects Househusband[a]	(C) Kids Without Marriage[b]	(D) Accepts Child Who Cohabits[a]
I. Correlation: race	.04	-.10	.07	-.04
SES	.15	.23	.11	-.14
II. Beta: race; SES constant	.08	-.05	.11	-.08
SES; race constant	.17	.22	.14	-.16
III. Final beta: race	.06	-.05	.08	-.05
SES	.10	.21	.10	-.10
IV. R: race + SES	.17	.24	.15	.16
R added by 5 other variables	.20	.02	.14	.16
IV. b: SES; no variables constant				
Black	.12	.16	.13	-.06
White	.09	.12	.08	-.16
VI. b: SES; 5 variables constant				
Black	.11	.18	.08	-.01
White	.05	.12	.06	-.11
VII. Trend, 1974–1979[c]				
Black	+3.0%	—[d]	.16	+13.7%
White	+7.6%	—[d]	.04	+12.2%

a. For nonnumerical variables a positive sign means that Blacks or higher-status respondents were more likely to say the form was acceptable.
b. For numerical scores a positive sign indicates that Blacks or higher-status persons tended to get the higher scores.
c. A positive sign means that people in the 1979 study had higher scores or a greater likelihood of saying the form was acceptable.
d. The question was not asked in 1974.

The patterns of response are generally the same for both races (Sections V and VI). The only notable difference is that SES has less of an independent effect on attitudes toward cohabitation for Blacks than for Whites. This notwithstanding, these data give further evidence of the similarity of the races.

The data for trends over time show that for two of the three items for which there are data, the movement is in the same direction at about the same speed. Blacks, however, increased their acceptance of parenthood without marriage to a greater degree than did Whites. Because Blacks were originally more accepting, this produces a small widening of the gap between the races.

With the exceptions noted, it may be concluded that the hypotheses of this study are generally supported by the data on acceptance of "nonmainstream" family forms.

Finally, we turn to the subject of divorce, a matter about which there has been considerable controversy. That Blacks have higher divorce rates than Whites is beyond dispute by now (see Ahlburg and De Vita 1992; Heiss 1975; Norton and Miller 1990, 1992; Ross and Sawhill 1975), but we still do not know for certain if this is due to a greater acceptance of divorce by Blacks or to situational factors that make it more difficult for Blacks to achieve stable marriages (Cherlin 1981; Hannerz 1969; Heiss 1975; Liebow 1967; Ross and Sawhill 1975).

We will first consider responses to a general item that asked respondents whether they favored or opposed divorce as a solution to a marriage that was "not working out." The second variable is the number of reasons the respondent accepted as valid for divorce. (The list referred to such reasons as the loss of love, different ideas about how children should be reared, and a severe drinking problem.) Thus we can determine whether the races differ in their general willingness to resort to divorce if a marriage is defined as bad, and we can also determine their reactions to particular kinds of problems. The final two variables are factor-analytic scores that group the reasons into an expressive group, which included items such as the feeling that the romance is gone from the marriage, and a conflict group, which contained items dealing with such matters as conflict over how money should be spent.

My discussion of Table 17.3, which contains the relevant data, is brief, for the races show no differences on any of the items. Thus several of the other questions lose their relevance. I note simply that SES differences are also quite trivial, although they are generally larger than the race differences; that the races are quite similar in their patterning of responses; and that from 1974

TABLE 17.3 Analysis of Responses to Questions Bearing on Attitudes Toward Divorce

	Divorce Attitudes			
Statistic: Variable; Constants	(A) Accepts Divorce[a]	(B) Number of Reasons Accepted[b]	(C) Expressive Reasons[b]	(D) Conflict Reasons[b]
I. Correlation: race	-.02	.01	.06	.01
SES	-.05	.09	.01	.13
II. Beta: race; SES constant	-.03	.03	.06	.05
SES; race constant	-.06	.10	.02	.14
III. Final beta: race	-.01	.01	.05	.03
SES	-.05	.09	-.01	.14
IV. R: race + SES	.06	.10	.06	.14
R added by 5 other variables	.10	.09	.10	.06
V. b: SES; no variables constant				
Black	-.02	.29	.01	.14
White	-.03	.29	.03	.13
VI. b: SES; 5 variables constant				
Black	.01	.39	.03	.14
White	-.03	.25	-.01	.13
VII. Trend, 1974–1979[c]				
Black	+3.0%	—[d]	—[d]	—[d]
White	-0.1%	—[d]	—[d]	—[d]

a. For nonnumerical variables a positive sign means that Blacks or higher-status respondents were more likely to say the reason was acceptable.
b. For numerical scores a positive sign indicates that Blacks or higher-status persons tended to get the higher scores.
c. A positive sign means that people in the 1979 study had higher scores or a greater likelihood of saying the reason was acceptable.
d. The question was not asked in 1979.

296

to 1979 there was essentially no change in acceptance of divorce for Whites or Blacks.

Summary and Conclusion

The data suggest the following answers to the questions posed earlier.[10]

First, although there are differences between the family attitudes of Black and White women, the evidence of this study suggests that their size is trivial more often than not. The prime exception to this generalization seems to be that Black women are more instrumental in their motivations for marriage and in their marital goals. Even here, however, the racial correlations are not large.

Second, the differences found do not seem to reflect SES differences. The control for SES does not typically reduce the race-attitude correlations, even though race and SES are correlated.[11]

Third, there is not much difference in the magnitude of the race and SES differences; race is certainly not more important than SES. In fact, in most cases the SES betas are somewhat larger.

Fourth, as noted before, the racial differences are quite small, but in almost no case are they made significantly smaller by controlling for the other variables considered in this study. The racial differences are not due to differences in these social characteristics.

Fifth, when the other variables are controlled, SES still seems to have a somewhat greater independent effect than race.

Sixth, in general, the other variables do not add much to the multiple correlations obtained by using only SES and race. Variations in the dependent variables are not strongly related to any of the independent variables for which there is information in these surveys.

In addition, it should be noted that SES tends to show similar relations to the dependent variables in both races, and that between 1974 and 1979 the races did not change their relative positions very much. There is, however, more evidence for convergence than for divergence.

The major general conclusion to be drawn from the study presented above is that the differences in the history and present experiences of Blacks and Whites have not produced major differences in their attitudes toward the family matters considered here. Despite their different situations, there is a common core of experience, and that core seems to include exposure to the "mainstream model." It is clear that racial status does not hold the key to family attitudes. In some cases, for example, the SES differences within each race are considerably larger than the difference between the races. Undoubtedly, racial differences in family attitudes are neither as large nor as important as some have claimed.

Finally, it does not seem likely that attitudinal differences of the size shown here could account for the differences in family behavior that have been reported in other studies. It seems extremely likely that much of the racial variance in family behavior is a function of situational and resource differences rather than attitude differences.

Notes

1. A more accurate term would perhaps be the "stereotypical model," for less than 15 percent of contemporary American homes are of this type.

2. There is, of course, a basic problem involved in the attempt to control for SES when racial comparisons are being made, for people of different races who are equal on objective indicators of SES do not necessarily occupy comparable positions in the status hierarchy (see Dodson, this volume; Heiss, 1975; Jackson, 1973). There does not seem to be an adequate operational solution to this problem, though the use of a composite indicator such as is used here does reduce its magnitude. The reader should keep in mind that when we speak of comparisons with SES controlled, we are not in fact dealing with groups that are equal in social status, broadly conceived.

3. The "other" variables are age, religion, current marital status, number of children, and work status.

4. For these questions, the subjects were asked to rate the importance of each item. They were not asked to choose the few they considered most important, as in the previous set.

5. To make the figures in the table more comparable, R rather than R^2 is presented. The increase in variance explained is, of course, indicated by R^2.

6. No value judgment is implied by this statement. We do not believe that it is necessarily desirable for a group to live by the mainstream model (see Heiss, 1975).

7. This category also includes those who choose other forms such as the communal family. However, over 90 percent of the subjects chose one of the responses that involved a nuclear family unit.

8. The latter variable was a factor-analytic scale. Some of the items which loaded heavily on this factor referred to single people having children, and others asked about them raising children. A question that asked if a couple should marry for the sake of the child if the woman was pregnant did not load heavily on this factor.

9. The strongest correlation is found for the item that asks about respect for a man who keeps house. It is negative, which means that blacks are a little less favorable to this variant form.

10. It should be emphasized that these conclusions should not be generalized to aspects of family life not covered here. Even within the areas we have considered we have found that the findings are not totally consistent.

11. The reductions do not occur because in most cases when there is a correlation between race and attitude, the correlation of SES and the attitude is quite small.

References

Ahlburg, D. A. and C. J. De Vita. 1992. "New Realities of the American Family." *Population Bulletin* 47(2)A.

Angel, R. and M. Tienda. 1982. "Determinants of Extended Household Structure: Cultural Pattern or Economic Need?" *American Journal of Sociology* 87:1360-83.

Beck, R. W. and S. H. Beck. 1989. "The Incidence of Extended Households Among Middle-Aged Black and White Women: Estimates From a 5-Year Family Study." *Journal of Family Issues* 10:147-68.

Billingsley, A. 1968. *Black Families in White America.* Englewood Cliffs, NJ: Prentice Hall.

Blau, F. D. and M. A. Ferber. 1986. *The Economics of Women, Men, and Work.* Englewood Cliffs, NJ: Prentice Hall.

Cherlin, A. 1981. *Marriage, Divorce, and Remarriage.* Cambridge, MA: Harvard University Press.

Farley, R. and W. R. Allen. 1987. *The Color Line and the Quality of Life in America.* New York: Russell Sage Foundation.

Frazier, E. F. 1939. *The Negro Family in the United States.* Chicago: University of Chicago Press.

Gutman, H. G. 1976. *The Black Family in Slavery and Freedom, 1750–1925.* New York: Pantheon.

Hannerz, U. 1969. *Soulside.* New York: Columbia University Press.

Heiss, J. 1975. *The Case of the Black Family.* New York: Columbia University Press.

Herskovits, M. J. 1941. *The Myth of the Negro Past.* New York: Harper & Row.

Hill, R. B. and L. Shackleford. 1978. "The Black Extended Family Revisited." Pp. 201-6 in *The Black Family: Essays and Studies,* edited by R. E. Staples. Belmont, CA: Wadsworth.

Hofferth, S. L. 1984. "Kin Networks, Race, and Family Structure." *Journal of Marriage and the Family* 46(4):791-806.

Jackson, J. J. 1973. "Family Organization and Ideology." Pp. 405-45 in *Comparative Studies of Blacks and Whites in the United States,* edited by K. S. Miller and R. M. Dreger. New York: Seminar.

Jaynes, G. D. and R. M. Williams, eds. 1989. *A Common Destiny: Blacks and American Society.* Washington, DC: National Academy Press.

Ladner, J. A. 1972. *Tomorrow's Tomorrow: The Black Woman.* Garden City, NY: Anchor.

Liebow, E. 1967. *Tally's Corner: A Study of Negro Street Corner Men.* Boston: Little, Brown.

Nobles, W. 1978. "Africanity: Its Role in Black Families." Pp. 19-26 in *The Black Family: Essays and Studies,* edited by R. E. Staples. Belmont, CA: Wadsworth.

Norton, A. J. and L. F. Miller. 1990. "The Family Life Cycle: 1985." In *Work and Family Patterns of American Women. Current Population Reports,* Special Studies Series P-23, No. 165. Washington, DC: Government Printing Office.

———. 1992. "Marriage, Divorce, and Remarriage in the 1990's." *Current Population Reports,* Special Studies Series P-23, No. 180. Washington, DC: Government Printing Office.

Peters, M. and C. de Ford. 1978. "The Solo Mother." Pp. 192-200 in *The Black Family: Essays and Studies,* edited by R. E. Staples. Belmont, CA: Wadsworth.

Rainwater, L. 1970. *Behind Ghetto Walls: Black Families in a Ghetto Slum.* Chicago: Aldine.

Rodgers-Rose, L. F. 1980. "Some Demographic Characteristics of the Black Woman: 1940 to 1975." Pp. 29-41 in *The Black Woman,* edited by L. F. Rodgers-Rose. Beverly Hills, CA: Sage.

Ross, H. L. and V. Sawhill. 1975. *Time of Transition.* Washington, DC: Urban Institute.

Scanzoni, J. H. 1971. *The Black Family in Modern Society.* Boston: Allyn & Bacon.

Schoen, R. and J. R. Kluegel. 1988. "The Widening Gap in Black and White Marriage Rates: The Impact of Population Composition and Differential Marriage Propensities." *American Sociological Review* 53:895-907.

Staples, R. E. 1978. "The Black Family Revisited." Pp. 13-18 in *The Black Family: Essays and Studies,* edited by R. E. Staples. Belmont, CA: Wadsworth.

———. 1985. "Changes in Black Family Structure: The Conflict Between Family Ideology and Structural Conditions." *Journal of Marriage and the Family* 47(4):1005-13.

Tienda, M. and R. Angel. 1982. "Headship and Household Composition Among Blacks, Hispanics, and Other Whites." *Social Forces* 61:508-31.

Udry, J. R. 1966. "Marital Stability by Race, Sex, Education and Occupation Using 1960 Census Data." *American Journal of Sociology* 72:203-9.

Contraception

Practices and Attitudes in the Black Community

ALGEA OTHELLA HARRISON

Two important components of the fertility rate in the black community are childlessness among married couples and births among never-married adolescents. These two groups will be the focus of this discussion, after an examination of practices and attitudes toward contraception in the black community. The latest data from the National Center for Health Statistics will be used in the section on birth control. There are concerns among professionals and others about the lack of birth control among adolescents and the social problems this creates. Also, the discussion of these issues is pertinent because improvements in scientific technology and health care delivery systems make it possible for blacks to choose childlessness and other ways to limit their number of offspring.

Birth Control Practices Among Blacks

A Historical Overview

The studies of birth control use among blacks in the latter part of the nineteenth century are controversial (McFalls and Masnick 1981). Many demographers attribute the sharp decline in black fertility rates from 1880 to 1940 to health factors, particularly venereal disease, rather than family planning by black women. The willingness of social scientists to accept this explanation long prevented more thorough examination of the issue. Recent studies, however, suggest that blacks used birth control during that period at a much higher rate than previously believed. Furthermore, because contraception and induced abortion were practiced in Africa and among slaves, black women had some knowledge of techniques to control fertility (Ross 1992). According to Ross (1992), "The midwifery culture among African American slaves maintained centuries old African folk knowledge about contraceptives (pregnancy preventers) and abortifacients (pregnancy terminators)" (p. 275). Slave journals and narratives and the limited amount of scholarly research available on slave life note trends in births and ascribe some types of abortion and birth control techniques to the slave community. Folk methods practiced among blacks at the end of the nineteenth century included alum water douches, poultices of petroleum jelly mixed with quinine, douches made from boiling rusty nails, quinine tablets, or turpentine (orally or as a douche), and plant compounds such as pennyroyal and papaya seeds.

After World War II, increased health and medical services, urbanization, and improved general living conditions affected birth control among blacks (Farley 1970). There were, however, demographic differences, with more favorable attitudes reported by urban compared with rural females and more positive orientations the higher the educational level (Furstenberg, Gordis, and Markowitz 1969; Ladner 1972; Valien and Fitzgerald 1949). Urban black middle-class females preferred smaller families, used the most effective available birth control method (pills and the IUD), and had lower fertility rates. In contrast, poor urban and rural females also preferred smaller families but used less effective methods (preparations available at drug stores and condoms) and had higher fertility rates than they desired (Furstenberg et al. 1969; Linn, Carmichael, Klitenick, and Webb 1978; Westoff 1970). Moreover, there is evidence that both partners wanted to use some type of contraceptive and felt the decision should not be the sole responsibility of one partner (Johnson and Staples 1979; Vadies and Hale 1977).

More recent studies indicate that some black women are poorly informed about the human reproductive system and birth control. In an assessment of family planning among low-income, undereducated black clientele at a prenatal clinic, Johnson and Snow (1982) found that the majority of the women had at least one unwanted pregnancy due to their lack of knowledge. Furthermore, there were gender differences in motives to act to control family size.

Data from the 1970s indicate that feelings of powerlessness, attitudes about the value of children, and fear of racial genocide were important variables in explaining and predicting birth control use among black males (Bauman and Udry 1972; Treadwell 1972; Tobin, Clifford, Mustian, and Davis 1975). In contrast, surveys of poor black females in 17 cities failed to support the idea that high feelings of powerlessness lead to the selection of poor or no contraceptive methods (Morris and Sison 1974). The reasons for wanting to limit family size cited most frequently by black females were economics and desire to control their lives (Cochrane, Haney, and Michielutte 1973; Gustavos and Mammen 1973; Treadwell 1972).

Historically, black women have tried to control fertility (Ross 1992) through the use of abortion and birth control. The best predictors of birth control use among black females have been information about contraceptives, past experiences of failure with birth control methods, and intention to act (Haney, Michielutte, Vincent, and Cochrane 1974; Kothandapani 1971; Linn et al. 1978). Hence, despite gender differences among blacks in terms of motivations to practice birth control, the desire to limit family size with the use of effective methods has been the prevailing attitude.

A Current Overview

The most recent estimates of contraceptive use in the United States are from data collected in 1988 (National Center for Health Statistics 1990; Mosher and Pratt 1990). A report by Mosher and Pratt (1990) in which they compare data collected in 1973, 1982, and 1988 reveals that black women were more likely than white women to use the two most effective female methods, sterilization and the pill. In 1983, among female contraceptors, 38% of blacks in comparison to 26% of whites used female sterilization; for the pill, the respective figures were 38% and 30%. Between 1982 and 1988, among black contraceptors, the use of female sterilization increased from 30% to 38%; among white contraceptors the increase was from 22% to 26%. Nonetheless, the data indicate that black women were less likely to use contraception than were white women (52% in comparison to 57% in 1982; 57% and 62%, respectively, in 1988). The gap has remained approximately the same during the past decade. Similarly, black women (10%) were more likely than white women (6%) to have had intercourse in the past 3 months before the interview without using any birth control method.

Overall, the proportion of married couples using sterilization (male and female) as a method of contraception rose between 1973 (15%) and 1982 (30%) and continued to rise until 1988 (38%). Between 1982 and 1988, for both racial groups the largest increase in use of female sterilization occurred among formerly married contraceptors, rising from 39% to 51%. For currently married contraceptors, the increase was from 27% to 31%. Black contraceptors, in comparison with white contraceptors, were less likely to use male sterilization (1% and 14%, respectively), the diaphragm (2% and 6%, respectively), and the condom (10% and 15%, respectively). Overall, the total number of current condom users increased from 4.1 million in 1982 to about 5.8 million in 1988, or from about 7% of all women aged 15-44 in 1982 to 10% in 1988.

For this same age group and period, there was an increase in the number of contraceptors among black women (Mosher 1990), rising from 6.985 million in 1982 to 7.679 million in 1988. In the latter year 57% of all black women were contraceptors; 38.1% used female sterilization, 38% the pill, 3.1% the IUD, 1.9% the diaphragm, 10.3% condoms, 0.9% male sterilization, and 7.8% other methods. A close examination reveals an increase in the proportion of black women classified as sterile, from 23.7% in 1982 to 29.6% in 1988. Mosher (1990) classified a married woman as sterile if she reported that it was impossible for her to have a baby or for her husband to father a child, for any reason, including a sterilization operation or other causes. An unmarried woman was classified as sterile if she reported that it was impossible for her to have a baby or if her current method of contraception was male sterilization. Of those so classified in 1988, 27.8% were surgically sterile (completely sterile due to an operation) compared with 22.2% in 1982. Of the surgically sterile in 1988, 22.1% were contraceptively sterile and 5.7% were noncontraceptively sterile. A woman was classified as nonsurgically sterile if she reported that it was impossible for her to have a baby, or for her husband to father a child, for any reason other than surgical sterilization.

Nonsurgical reasons included menopause and sterility from accident, illness, congenital causes, or unexplained inability to conceive. In 1982, 1.5% of black women between the ages of 15 and 44 reported being nonsurgically sterile, compared with 1.8% in 1988.

In 1982 the proportion of nonusers of contraceptives was 29.6%, which decreased to 26.9% in 1988. These were women who reported not using contraceptives because they were sterile, pregnant or postpartum, seeking pregnancy, or had had intercourse only once. In 1982, 36% of black women used nonsurgical contraceptives, compared with 35% in 1988. These differences may be explained by the increase in those years of women who were surgically sterile. Among those who used nonsurgical techniques, there was a change in contraceptives of choice between 1982 and 1988. Use of the IUD declined (from 4.7% to 1.7%), as did use of the diaphragm (from 1.8% to 1.1%), foam (from 1.4% to 0.6%), periodic abstinence (from 1.6% to 1.2%), douche (from 0.7% to 0.2%), and other methods (from 1.7% to 1.6%). Increases occurred in the use of condoms (from 3.2% to 5.8%) and the pill (from 19.8% to 21.6%).

Thus the major change in birth control practices over approximately the past two decades among black women aged 15-44 has been the greater use of surgical sterilization, pills, and condoms. Condom usage grew from 6% to 10% among male and female black contraceptors. Regardless of race, the proportion of condom users among never-married contraceptors rose from 12% in 1982 to 20% in 1988 and from 2% to 6% among formerly married contraceptors. Among black contraceptors the female was the gender of choice for sterilization; only 1% reported reliance on male sterilization. For all races, there was an increase between 1982 and 1988 in the proportion of women never or formerly married who were classified as sterilized. For the never married, the figures were 3.7% in 1982 and 6.4% in 1988; for the formerly married, 39.2% in 1982 and 50.7% in 1988. Among the currently married for both races, the figures were 26.9% in 1982 and 31.4% in 1988.

Summary

Black women brought contraceptive techniques from Africa, and they have continued to practice birth control. Between Reconstruction and World War II, fertility rates declined in the black community, and the explanations given by social scientists and government officials were controversial. After World War II, due to increased health and medical services, urbanization, and improved general living conditions, the usage of contraceptives grew. There were demographic differences between poor urban and rural women and middle-class urban women, who preferred to limit family size and used the most effective available contraceptives to accomplish that goal. Attitudinal and motivational factors also contributed to variations in birth control usage. According to the most recent national survey, there has been an increase over the past two decades in the number of women who can be classified as contraceptors. Female sterilization and the pill are the most frequently cited birth control techniques among black women ages 15-44. There also has been an increase in the use of condoms.

Attitudes Toward Contraception

Social scientists have become more interested in the attitudes of blacks toward contraception due to the increase in teenage pregnancies, female heads of households, and the incidence of AIDS in the black community. Both professionals and laypersons have written extensively about these issues and have offered empirical findings and suggestions for addressing the perceived social problems with intervention and prevention programs. In addition, with the growth in education and economic opportunities for blacks, there has been a parallel increase in voluntary childlessness and voluntary female sterilization among black married couples. The following literature review is limited to and organized around studies of two black groups, adolescents and married couples, and their attitudes and behaviors related to contraception.

Adolescents

Black persons aged 10-19 years constitute 16% of the youth population in the United States and 17.6% of the African American population. This group is sexually active. In 1988 black women between the ages of 15 and 19 had the highest rate of sexual activity (61%) compared with their Hispanic (49%) and white (52%) counterparts (Forrest and Singh 1990). Moreover, 58% of these young black women reported having had two or more sex partners, and nearly 25% reported having had four or more partners. Teenage black males reported younger ages at first intercourse than did their Hispanic or white counterparts (Sonnenstein, Pleck, and Ku 1991): 20% had intercourse before age 13, and 35% before age 14. In the sexually active 18 to 19 age group, 50% reported multiple partners within a year (Forrest and Singh 1990). The result has been an equally high incidence of pregnancy and childbearing among these young persons, which is an indirect indicator of the lack of contraceptive usage. In 1988, 58.4% of births to teens younger than 15 years were to blacks (National Center for Health Statistics 1990), and 92% of black teen mothers were not married at the time of delivery (National Center for Health Statistics 1990); 30% of the births were not the first for that mother.

In a study of contraceptive-related behavior, St. Louis et al. (1991) report on national research into HIV infection among adolescents in the Job Corps, a federal training program for disadvantaged youth. The authors found that the infection rate was 3.2 per 1,000 among poor applicants between ages 17 and 19, a possible indicator of failure to use barrier-type contraception. The Centers for Disease Control (1992) reports higher rates of AIDS for blacks and Hispanics than for whites. Blacks represent 12% of the U.S. population yet account for 29% of the AIDS cases reported for adults/adolescents, 37% of the cases reported for adolescents aged 13-19, and 53% of the reported pediatric (younger than 13 years) cases. The latency period of 10-15 years for AIDS has to be considered when looking at the statistics on incidence among the age group 20-29 years (Hein 1989). In a 1992 report, the Centers for Disease Control noted that one-fifth of persons in this age groups had AIDS and speculated that they were infected during adolescence.

These figures suggest that contraceptives are not used consistently by sexually active black adolescents. Social scientists have postulated that early first intercourse, substance abuse, risk-taking behaviors, and poor environmental conditions are contributing factors. When intercourse is initiated at an early age, contraceptive use is less likely (Brooks-Gunn and Furstenberg 1989; Forest and Singh 1990). In a study of inner-city black males in a large eastern city conducted by Jemmott and Jemmott (1990), the majority (78%) of the subjects stated they had not used contraceptives during their first intercourse, and 54% reported not using any during their most recent intercourse. Adolescent females have less knowledge about contraception and reproduction and therefore are more likely to become pregnant during initial intercourse. Handler (1990) examined factors associated with nonvirginity among a sample of 13-year-old black females in an urban neighborhood. Relevant variables were being the daughter of a teenage mother, educational level of the adolescent's mother, and climate of the school the subject attended. A school in which the peer norm was a more liberal attitude toward premarital sex and a stated young age at which it was desirable to have a baby was associated with subjects who were nonvirgins.

A relationship also has been found between problem behaviors and failure to use contraception. Several studies have documented the connection between substance abuse and sexual activity (Irwin 1993). For example, crack cocaine use affects the sexual behaviors of black adolescents. Fullilove et al. (1993) investigated crack cocaine use and sexual risk behaviors among black youth in an urban area and found a significant difference between users and nonusers. Compared with male nonusers, adolescent males who used crack had sex at an earlier age, had a higher number of sexual partners per year, were more likely to engage in sex under the influence of drugs or alcohol, exchanged sexual favors, had used no condom during the most recent sexual episode, and had a history of pregnancy. Adolescents in this study lived in environments where risk-taking behaviors were common. The greater the prevalence of risk behaviors in an individual's immediate environment, the greater the likelihood he or she will engage in one of these behaviors (Newcomb and Maddham 1986).

Risk-taking behaviors have been defined as volitional actions for which the consequences remain uncertain but that may result in identifiable negative health outcomes (Irwin 1993). Social scientists consider risk taking to be a component of normal adolescent development. Major changes occur in all the domains of development during adolescence (cognitive, emotional, social, and physical), and experimentation and exploration increase among all socioeconomic and racial/ethnic groups at that time. According to Irwin (1993), the timing of biological maturation, cognitive scope, self-perceptions, perceptions of the social environment, and personal values affect adolescent risk taking. The social environment in which a large percentage of black youth live increases the likelihood that they will engage in sexual activity, a risk-taking behavior for adolescents. In 1989, 44% of all black children under the age of 18 lived in poverty, and 50% (compared with 17.5% of whites) lived in mother-headed households (U.S. Bureau of the Census 1993). It is generally known that violence is greatest in large U.S. cities in which the majority of residents are poor and belong to ethnic populations.

The prevalence of high-risk behaviors in poor neighborhoods and the effects of these behaviors on young persons have been illustrated in a survey by Vanderschmidt, Lang, Knight-Williams, and Vanderschmidt (1993). Boston University's Youth at Risk program is designed to reduce these behaviors among a sample of students from grades 6 to 8 in four inner-city public schools; the students are from predominantly minority, low-income families. The subjects completed a questionnaire that included items about violence (physical fights, carrying knives and guns), sexual activity, alcohol consumption, illicit drug use (marijuana, cocaine, and crack), and cigarette smoking. For each of the five risks, the pattern of response was analyzed to identify no risk (never) and current or past risk (ever). If there was no response or an inconsistent pattern, the risk was undefined (can't tell). Analysis revealed high prevalence (ever) for all the risk behaviors: violence, 53.5%; sexual activity, 46.2%; drinking, 40.4%; illicit drug use, 22.5%; and smoking, 29.4%. Females were consistently less likely than males to engage in violence, sexual activity, drinking, and the use of illicit drugs, with risk differences that varied from 36% to 2%. The largest increase in sexual activity occurred between the seventh and eighth grades, which supports the view that problem behaviors facilitate the early initiation of sexual activity.

Schubiner, Scott, and Tzelepis (1993) examined the effects of frequent exposure to violence on the quality of life among a predominantly black inner-city sample, ages 14-23, in a large midwestern city. The subjects were surveyed regarding their exposure to and participation in acts of violence: 44% reported they could obtain a gun within one day, 42% had seen someone shot or knifed, and 22% had seen someone killed. In the preceding 3 months, 18% had carried a gun and 32% had been in a physical fight. A total of 34 of these subjects were rated by the psychologists as at high risk for involvement in violent acts in the future. That group also was rated as at high risk for sexually transmitted disease and pregnancy in comparison with members of a low-risk group. These findings are similar to results from surveys in other large U.S. cities. For young blacks living in these environments, decisions regarding sexual activity and contraception have a high probability of negative outcomes—sexually transmitted diseases, pregnancy, childbearing, dropping out of school, limited mate availability, and so forth (Dryfoos 1990).

Yet living in a community with high clusters of risk-taking behaviors is not always an indicator that an individual will engage in self-damaging behavior. There is ongoing research on the risk and protective factors that guide the behaviors of young persons in highly stressed environments, such as the work of Rutter (1979, 1987). Social scientists have initiated studies to identify adaptive or protective factors that may compensate for the risk elements prevalent in the lives and environments of young persons in troubled neighborhoods (Garmezy 1993). Among the terms used to catego- rize these young persons are *resilient* and *stress resistant*. Empirical findings suggest that resilient youngsters may overcome their high-risk environments owing to (a) dispositional attributes of the individual, such as activity level and sociability; (b) affectional ties within the family that provide emotional support in times of stress; and (c) external support systems at school, work, or church that reward the individual's competencies and determination and provide a belief system by which to live (Garmezy 1985; Werner 1989). In other words, cultural values and beliefs as well as individual inclinations affect sexual attitudes and behaviors for some adolescents.

Generally, the black community is accepting of sexual activity as a natural expression of self and as a source of pleasure. Historically, the black com- munity has not stigmatized children born out of wedlock, so there is consid- erable tolerance of nonmarital childbearing (Moore, Simms, and Betsey 1987). Thus the fear of community rejection if one becomes pregnant or impregnates someone is not great, and teen pregnancy is viewed as a normative event (McGowan and Kohn 1990). Many blacks believe that birth control is dangerous and may negatively affect one's sexuality (Horn 1983), that condoms spoil the pleasure of sex, and that being daring and aggressive in sexual encounters is an expression of one's masculinity (Dalton 1989) or femininity. These beliefs filter down to adolescents. Zabin, Stark, and Emerson (1991) examined reasons for the delay in using the contraceptive services of a health clinic by two samples of black junior and senior high school students. The members of one group were interviewed before being enrolled in an education intervention program, and their answers were compared with those given by members of a second group that had been exposed to an organized prevention program for 2 years. Both groups cited as reasons for delay the fear that contraception was dangerous, the fear of parental discov- ery, and waiting for a closer relationship with someone.

These findings suggest that attitudes toward contraception prevalent in the community sometimes persist even after educational intervention. Interest- ingly, Jemmott and Jemmott (1991) found that personal knowledge some- times overrules community norms. In their study of unwed black female college students, the subjects' own attitudes and above-average AIDS knowl- edge influenced their determination to use condoms in the next 3 months. Nevertheless, these subjects had been told by their sexual partners and their mothers that condom use would have a negative effect on their sexual enjoyment.

There are also attitudes in the black community that discourage sexuality. In one study, Hendrick and Fullilove (1983) found that the members of a control group of black adolescent males who had never been fathers were more likely to go to church and to practice birth control than were members of the comparison group of fathers. Religiosity has been found to be a significant intervening variable in the less permissive sexual attitudes found among blacks in comparison to whites and Hispanics (Langer, Zimmerman, and McNeal 1992). Similarly, in a study of high school students in a large southern city, Langer et al. (1992) found that sexual intercourse was less likely among black subjects with a higher level of religiosity, females with high educational aspirations, and persons with greater perception of their interpersonal skills. Subjects who were not living with both parents were more likely to have had intercourse. The researchers suggest that intervention programs may need to focus less on knowledge and attitudes and more on the social environment.

Yet results from a 3-year study of a school-based clinic involving 17,000 students in grades 7 through 12 indicate that girls involved in the program were more likely to postpone first intercourse, to seek birth control before first sexual intercourse, and to attend birth control clinics than were girls who were nonparticipants (Zabin 1986). In other studies, it has been found that a number of young mothers began to have sexual relations willingly because of emotional involvement, curiosity, or simply because they did not see any reason for waiting (Harrison 1990).

Jemmott and Jemmott (1990) examined attitudes toward contraception and related behaviors among a sample of black male junior and senior high school students in the inner city. Only 2% reported not having intercourse. Subjects with higher levels of sexual knowledge and positive attitudes toward contraception were more likely to report having used contraceptives during intercourse. Nathanson and Becker (1986), in a study of 2,884 black adolescent females between the ages of 11 and 19, found that their subjects reported using alternative support strategies in seeking contraceptive information. If a young woman's parents were involved in forming her attitudes and behaviors toward sexual activity, they were more likely to accompany the adolescent to a family planning clinic. If the parents were not involved, the teenager was more likely to involve peers in the trip to the clinic for contraceptive information.

Although condom use has increased, there are gender differences in attitudes regarding the practice. Johnson et al. (1992), for instance, discovered that black males are more likely to react with anger during negotiations about condom use than are females. In their sample, which consisted of black college students in the southeastern United States, males expressed more intense anger than females regarding the perception that their partners might not reach orgasm if a condom is used, that condoms will interrupt foreplay, and that condoms interfere with sexual pleasure. Males also felt more strongly about a partner's refusal of sex unless a condom is used and partner rejection if questions are asked about previous sexual contacts. Men who had multiple sex partners and who engaged in more than one risk behavior were less likely to want to use condoms. Thus knowledge about and attitudes toward contraception continue to play an important role in the lives of black adolescents.

Married Couples

Marriage rates for all races and ethnic groups in the United States have undergone change in recent decades. Among blacks, 13.8% of women between the ages of 20 and 23 were married in the mid-1980s, compared with 51% in this group in 1940 (Mare and Winship 1991). Indeed, currently only 50% are expected to marry by age 28 (Lichter, McLaughlin, Kephart, and Landry 1992). The major determinants of this change have been the focus of considerable debate. Suggested causes are a limited supply of economically attractive and available men (Wilson 1987), public assistance as a disruptive factor (Lichter LeClere, and McLaughlin 1991), the effect of growing up in female-headed households (Avery, Goldscheider, and Speare 1992), and the increasing educational status and economic independence of women (Mare 1991).

Lichter et al. (1992) examined these explanations with data from a representative sample of the noninstitutionalized U.S. population of young women ages 18 to 28, the National Longitudinal Survey of Youth (NLSY). Data were selected from a pool of female blacks and whites who were not Latina and were age 18 or older in the 1979 through 1986 waves of the NLSY files. Analysis provided no support for the explanation that decline in marriage rates is related to the increasing economic independence of women or to public assistance. The results were consistent with the view that economic independence either makes women more attractive marital partners or provides them with the financial resources necessary for marriage and childbearing. In the 1980s, black women with the most economic resources were the most likely to marry. Mate availability in local marriage markets is a significant factor contributing to delayed marriage or nonmarriage among black women.

Among blacks who do marry, there has been an increase in the use of contraception. The methods of choice increasingly are surgical sterilization, pills, and condoms, the most effective techniques. The data suggest a serious commitment on the part of wives to controlling fertility, given that surgical sterilization is performed on the female 99% of the time. One determinant of this choice may be the division of household responsibilities. Wilson, Tolson, and Kiernan (1990) examined household maintenance, child-care duties, and parental punishment behavior in a sample of 64 black families in an East Coast region. They found that mothers were designated as responsible for more than 60% of the child-care and household tasks, and fathers generally elected not to use corporal punishment with children. Thus mothers have more to gain in quality of life by preventing pregnancy.

Also, the timing of first childbirth is a factor in the stability of black marriage, as Wineberg (1988) found in analyzing data from the 1985 Survey of Population. Wineberg notes that there was a similarly high risk of marital dissolution among black women who conceived premaritally and gave birth postmaritally and those who had their first child during the second year of marriage. Conversely, black couples whose first childbirth occurred 8-12 or 25-41 months after marrying had a low probability of marital dissolution. Thus the desire to stabilize a marriage is a strong motivator for becoming a contraceptor. Another is the desire to remain childless.

Childlessness in the black community has been a controversial subject. In the white community it has been viewed as voluntary, whereas in the black community it has been considered as involuntary and caused by poor health, poverty, and sexually transmitted diseases (Farley 1970). Other factors posited by analysts include growing education and economic opportunities, urbanization, and the availability of birth control. Nevertheless, historians and demographers have attributed the increase in childlessness rates in the black community to external factors rather than to the deliberate agency of black women (Ross 1992). Yet a proportion of black women have chosen childlessness as a strategy for upgrading their status in the education and economic markets. When this decision is mutual to both marriage partners, a closer examination becomes pertinent for understanding the attitudes of blacks toward birth control.

Boyd (1989) has examined the issue of minority status and childlessness in the black community from the theoretical framework of Goldscheider and Uhlenberg. These theorists hypothesize that black and white differences in childlessness can be explained by the effects of blacks' minority status in the United States. The environmental conditions that promote childlessness among a minority group are established when the group achieves or desires acculturation, when minority-majority socioeconomic characteristics converge along with minority ambitions for social mobility, and when the minority group has no pronatalist ideology and no norm proscribing contraception. To test these ideas, Boyd used 1970 census data published in 1973 by the U.S. Bureau of the Census. The birth cohort was 1926–1935, a group of black Americans who had been exposed to the Great Depression, World War II, and new opportunities in the postwar economy, yet who married before the civil rights movement of the 1960s.

Boyd selected a sample using the following criteria: (a) once-married wives (age 35-44), with spouse present and employed in an urban occupation; (b) wives in the labor force who married at age 22 or older; (c) husbands and wives who had at least a high school diploma and husbands with white-collar jobs; and (d) family income in the three highest categories. The sampling restrictions eliminated racial differences in childlessness, which was 15.6% for blacks and 15.2% for whites, in contrast to 11.4% for blacks and 7.5% for whites in the full census sample. A comparison of college-educated black and white couples was used to evaluate the theory of Goldscheider and Uhlenberg. In all three income categories, black couples with one or more years of college were more likely to be childless than were comparable white couples. Thus, according to Boyd (1989), the data supported the theorists.

Boyd also examined data for 1975 and 1985 and found a decrease in childlessness for blacks and an increase for whites. Boyd attributed the trend for blacks to improvements in the health and socioeconomic status of disadvantaged blacks, which reduced childlessness due to involuntary causes, and to antidiscrimination programs that promoted assimilation and advancement, which led to a decline in voluntary childlessness. These trends are not new, as one can see if one examines fertility rates in the black community historically. At the end of the nineteenth century, approximately 50 years after emancipation, half of all married educated black women had no children, and one-fourth of all black women, the majority of them rural and uneducated, had no children (Giddings 1984). Historically, black women have had a unique voice in family planning and in civil rights activities regarding reproductive rights. They have combined support for birth control and abortion with an opposition to forced sterilization and coercive efforts of social and government agencies (Ross 1992).

Summary

Approximately 18% of the black population may be categorized as adolescent, and a high rate of sexual activity has been documented among members of this group. The failure of many to practice effective birth control can be inferred from the high incidence of teenage pregnancy and HIV/AIDS infection. Of black teens who gave birth in 1988, 92% were not married at the time of delivery. Social scientists speculate that early onset of first intercourse, substance abuse, risk-taking behaviors, and poor environmental conditions contribute to the failure to be a contraceptor. Cultural values and beliefs as well as individual disposition affect sexual attitudes and behaviors among adolescents. In the black community, sexual activity has been viewed as natural and desirable, and children born out of wedlock have not been stigmatized. The beliefs that birth control is dangerous and spoils the pleasure of sex and that masculinity and femininity are related to unsafe sex circulate in the black community. These mores have discouraged contraceptive usage, yet there are also community values that discourage sexual activity. High religiosity and educational aspirations have been found to dampen sexual activity and to increase the likelihood of birth control. Interpersonal skills and knowledge of health and birth control are personal attributes that also contribute to the use of contraceptives.

In the 1980s, black women with the most economic resources were the most likely to marry. Continuing a historical trend, these women were the most likely to practice birth control to limit the size of their families or to be childless by choice. The division of household and child-care responsibilities in black couples has contributed to women's being contraceptors, because their quality of life is most directly affected by family size. Currently, the contraceptors of choice for black married couples are female sterilization, the pill, and condoms.

Conclusion

Since arriving in America from Africa, black women have practiced birth control. The techniques have varied depending upon the economic and technological resources available. As family planning has become more effective and legal, blacks have sought access to the safest and best techniques. Thus it has never been a question of whether but of how blacks practice contraception. Demographic data indicate that educated, married couples historically have been the most consistent contraceptors. Currently, the most widely used methods are female sterilization, the pill, and condoms. Environmental conditions and external as well as internal determinants contribute to the failure of sexually active adolescents to practice birth control. Involvement in religious activities, educational aspirations, and sex education help to increase birth control among never-married adolescents.

References

Avery, R., F. Goldscheider, and A. Speare, Jr. 1992. "Feathered Nest/Gilded Cage: Parental Income and Leaving Home in the Transition to Adulthood." *Demography* 29:375-88.

Bauman, K. E. and J. R. Udry. 1972. "Powerlessness and Regularity of Contraception in an Urban Negro Male Sample: A Research Note." *Journal of Marriage and the Family* 34(1):112-14.

Boyd, R. L. 1989. "Minority Status and Childlessness." *Social Inquiry* 59(2):331-42.

Brooks-Gunn, J. and F. F. Furstenberg. 1989. "Adolescent Sexual Behavior." *American Psychologist* 44:249-57.

Centers for Disease Control. 1992. *HIV/AIDS Surveillance: U.S. AIDS Cases Reported Through March 1992.* April. Atlanta, GA: Author.

Cochrane, C. C., V. C. Haney, and R. Michielutte. 1973. "Motivational Determinants of Family Planning Clinic Attendance." *Journal of Psychology* 84(May):33-43.

Dalton, H. 1989. "AIDS in Blackface." *Daedalus* (Summer):205-28.

Dryfoos, J. 1990. *Adolescents at Risk: Prevalence and Prevention.* New York: Oxford University Press.

Farley, R. 1970. *Growth of the Black Population.* Chicago: Markham.

Forrest, J. and S. Singh. 1990. "The Sexual and Reproductive Behavior of American Women, 1982–1988." *Family Planning Perspectives* 22(September/October):206-14.

Fullilove, M., M. Thompson, E. Golden, R. E. Fullilove III, R. Lennon, D. Porterfield, S. Schwartz, and G. Bolan. 1993. "Crack Cocaine Use and High-Risk Behaviors Among Sexually Active Black Adolescents." *Journal of Adolescent Health* 14:295-300.

Furstenberg, F., L. Gordis, and M. Markowitz. 1969. "Birth Control Knowledge and Attitude Among Unmarried Pregnant Adolescents." *Journal of Marriage and the Family* 31(1):34-42.

Garmezy, N. 1985. "Stress-Resistant Children: The Search for Protective Factors." Pp. 213-33 in *Recent Research in Developmental Psychopathology* (*Journal of Child Psychology and Psychiatry* Book Supplement 4), edited by J. E. Stevenson.

————. 1993. "Children in Poverty: Resilience Despite Risk." *Psychiatry* 56(February):127-36.

Giddings, P. 1984. *When and Where I Enter: The Impact of Black Women on Race and Sex in America.* New York: William Morrow.

Gustavos, S. and K. Mammen. 1973. "Black-White Differentials in the Family Size Preferences Among Youth." *Pacific Sociological Review* 16:107-19.

Handler, A. 1990. "The Correlates of the Initiation of Sexual Intercourse Among Young Urban Black Females." *Journal of Youth and Adolescence* 19:159-70.

Haney, C., R. Michielutte, C. Vincent, and C. Cochrane. 1974. "Factors Associated With the Poverty of Black Women." *Sociology and Social Research* 59(1):40-49.

Harrison, A. 1990. "High Risk Sexual Behavior Among Black Adolescents." Pp. 175-88 in *Ethnic Issues in Adolescent Mental Health,* edited by A. R. Stiffman and L. E. Davis. Newbury Park, CA: Sage.

Hein, K. 1989. "Commentary on Adolescent Acquired Immunodeficiency Syndrome: The Next Wave of the Human Immunodeficiency Virus Epidemic?" *Journal of Pediatrics* 114:144-49.

Hendrick, L. E. and R. E. Fullilove. 1983. "Locus of Control and the Use of Contraception Among Unmarried Black Adolescent Fathers and Their Controls: A Preliminary Report." *Journal of Youth and Adolescence* 12(3):225-33.

Horn, B. 1983. "Cultural Beliefs and Teenage Pregnancy." *Nurse Practitioner* 3(9):35-39.

Irwin, C. E., Jr. 1993. "Adolescence and Risk Taking: How Are They Related?" Pp. 7-28 in *Adolescent Risk Taking,* edited by N. J. Bell and R. W. Bell. Newbury Park, CA: Sage.

Jemmott, L. S. and J. B. Jemmott. 1990. "Sexual Knowledge, Attitudes, and Risky Sexual Behavior Among Inner-City Black Male Adolescents." *Journal of Adolescent Research* 5(3):346-69.

————. 1991. "Applying the Theory of Reasoned Action to AIDS Risk Behavior: Condom Use Among Black Women." *Nursing Research* 40(4):228-34.

Johnson, E. H., L. Gant, Y. A. Hinkle, D. Gilbert, B. A. Willis, and T. Hoopwood. 1992. "Do African-American Men and Women Differ in Their Knowledge About AIDS, Attitudes About Condoms, and Sexual Behaviors?" *Journal of the National Medical Association* 84(1):49-64.

Johnson, L. and R. E. Staples. 1979. "Family Planning and the Young Minority Male: A Pilot Project." *Family Coordinator* 28(October):535-43.

Johnson, S. M. and L. F. Snow. 1982. "Assessment of Reproductive Knowledge in an Inner-City Clinic." *Social Science Medicine* 16(19):1657-62.

Kothandapani, V. 1971. "Validation of Feeling, Belief, and Intention to Act as Three Components of Attitude and Their Contributions to Prediction of Contraceptive Behavior." *Journal of Personality and Social Psychology* 19(September):321-33.

Ladner, J. A. 1972. *Tomorrow's Tomorrow: The Black Woman.* Garden City, NY: Anchor.

Langer, L. M., R. S. Zimmerman, and R. McNeal. 1992. "Explaining the Association of Race and Ethnicity With the HIV/AIDS-Related Attitudes, Behaviors and Skills of High School Students." *Population Research and Policy Review* 11:233-47.

Lichter, D. T., F. B. LeClere, and D. K. McLaughlin. 1991. "Local Marriage Markets and the Marital Behavior of Black and White Women." *American Journal of Sociology* 96:843-67.

Lichter, D. T., D. K. McLaughlin, G. Kephart, and D. J. Landry. 1992. "Race and the Retreat From Marriage: A Shortage of Marriageable Men?" *American Sociological Review* 57: 781-99.

Linn, M., J. Carmichael, P. Klitenick, and N. Webb. 1978. "Fertility Related Attitude of Minority Mothers With Large and Small Families." *Journal of Applied Social Psychology* 8(January/March):1-14.

Mare, R. D. 1991. "Five Decades of Educational Assortative Mating." *American Sociological Review* 56:15-32.

Mare, R. D. and C. Winship. 1991. "Socioeconomic Change and the Decline of Marriage for Blacks and Whites." Pp. 175-202 in *The Urban Underclass,* edited by C. Jencks and P. E. Peterson. Washington, DC: Urban Institute.

McFalls, J. F. and G. S. Masnick. 1981. "Birth Control and the Fertility of the U.S. Black Population, 1880 to 1980." *Journal of Family History* 89(Spring):89-105.

McGowan, B. G. and A. Kohn. 1990. "Social Support and Teen Pregnancy in the Inner City." Pp. 189-207 in *Ethnic Issues in Adolescent Mental Health,* edited by A. R. Stiffman and L. E. Davis. Newbury Park, CA: Sage.

Moore, K. A., M. C. Simms, and C. L. Betsey. 1987. *Choice and Circumstance.* New Brunswick, NJ: Transaction.

Morris, N. and B. Sison. 1974. "Correlates of Female Powerlessness: Parity, Methods of Birth Control, Pregnancy." *Journal of Marriage and the Family* 36(4):708-13.

Mosher, W. D. 1990. *Use of Family Planning Services in the United States: 1982 and 1988.* Document HE 20.6209/3:184, Vital and Health Statistics of the National Center for Health Statistics. Hyattsville, MD: U.S. Department of Health and Human Services.

Mosher, W. D. and W. F. Pratt. 1990. *Contraceptive Use in the United States, 1973-88.* Document HE 20.6209/3:182, Vital and Health Statistics of the National Center for Health Statistics. Hyattsville, MD: U.S. Department of Health and Human Services.

Nathanson, C. A. and M. H. Becker. 1986. "Family and Peer Influence on Obtaining a Method of Contraception." *Journal of Marriage and the Family* 48(3):513-25.

National Center for Health Statistics. 1990. *Advance Report of Final Natality Statistics, 1988.* Monthly Vital Statistics Report (August Supplement). Washington, DC: U.S. Department of Health and Human Services.

Newcomb, M. and E. Maddham. 1986. "Risk Factors for Drug Use Among Adolescents: Concurrent and Longitudinal Analyses." *American Journal of Public Health* 76:525-31.

Ross, L. J. 1992. "African-American Women and Abortion: A Neglected History." *Journal of Health Care for the Poor and Underserved* 3(2):274-84.

Rutter, M. 1979. "Protective Factors in Children's Responses to Stress and Disadvantage." Pp. 49-74 in *Primary Prevention of Psychopathology,* vol. 3, *Social Competence in Children,* edited by M. W. Kent and J. E. Rolf. Hanover, NH: University Press of New England.

———. 1987. "Psychological Resilience and Protective Mechanisms." *American Journal of Orthopsychiatry* 57:316-13.

St. Louis, M. E., et al. 1991. "Human Immunodeficiency Virus Infection in Disadvantaged Adolescents: Findings From the U.S. Job Corps." *Journal of the American Medical Association* 266(November):2387-91.

Schubiner, H., R. Scott, and A. Tzelepis. 1993. "Exposure to Violence Among Inner-City Youth." *Journal of Adolescent Health* 14:214-19.

Sonnenstein, F., J. Pleck, and L. Ku. 1991. "Levels of Sexual Activity Among Adolescent Males in the United States." *Family Planning Perspectives* 23(April):162-67.

Tobin, P. W., W. Clifford, R. Mustian, and A. Davis. 1975. "Value of Children and Fertility Behavior in a Tri-racial, Rural County." *Journal of Comparative Family Studies* 6(Spring): 46-55.

Treadwell, J. 1972. "Is Abortion Black Genocide?" *Family Planning Perspectives* 4(1):4-5.

U.S. Bureau of the Census. 1993. *Statistical Abstracts of the United States: 1993.* Washington, DC: Government Printing Office.

Vadies, E. and D. Hale. 1977. "Attitudes of Adolescent Males Towards Abortion, Contraception, and Sexuality." *Social Work in Health Care* 3(Winter):169-74.

Valien, P. and A. Fitzgerald. 1949. "Attitudes of the Negro Mother Toward Birth Control." *American Journal of Sociology* 55(3):279-83.

Vanderschmidt, H. F., J. M. Lang, V. Knight-Williams, and G. F. Vanderschmidt. 1993. "Risks Among Inner-City Young Teens: The Prevalence of Sexual Activity, Violence, Drugs, and Smoking." *Journal of Adolescent Health* 14:282-88.

Werner, E. E. 1989. "High Risk Children in Young Adulthood: A Longitudinal Study From Birth to 32 Years." *American Journal of Orthopsychiatry* 59:72-81.

Westoff, C. 1970. "Contraceptive Practice Among Urban Blacks in the United States, 1965." *Milbank Memorial Fund Quarterly* 48(2):215-33.

Wilson, M. N., T. F. Tolson, and M. Kiernan. 1990. "Flexibility and Sharing of Childcare Duties in Black Families." *Sex Roles* 22(7-8):409-25.

Wilson, W. J. 1987. *The Truly Disadvantaged: The Inner City, the Underclass, and Public Policy.* Chicago: University of Chicago Press.

Wineberg, H. 1988. "Duration Between Marriage and First Birth and Marital Instability." *Social Biology* 35(1-2):91-102.

Zabin, L. S. 1986. [Article]. *Children and Teens Today* (Newsletter of the Alan Guttmacher Institute) 6(12):2-4.

Zabin, M., H. A. Stark, and M. R. Emerson. 1991. "Reasons for Delay in Contraceptive Clinic Utilization: Adolescent Clinic and Nonclinic Populations Compared." *Journal of Adolescent Health* 12(3):225-32.

PART V

Advocacy and Family Policies for African American Families

Marian Wright Edelman of the Children's Defense Fund begins this section with a chapter that lists some positive steps that can and should be taken to improve the current state of Black families. Whenever one makes lists of all that ails Black families, the tendency is to become depressed and to feel powerless. Instead, Edelman provides positive, manageable, and definitive actions that are within the ability of all families. She presents her premises for effective advocacy in a form that can be disseminated to local parent and community groups. Her major premise is that nothing will be done for Black families except what they do for themselves. Edelman outlines the ground rules of each institution that must be mastered and then used to advantage, with an effective focus of energy. Family members should not expect rapid change; they must be prepared to fight a long battle for what they want. Edelman emphasizes the need for unity and for focus on real enemies.

In Chapter 20, Rose Merry Rivers and John Scanzoni describe the roles of fictive and blood kin in providing support for the basic needs of Black families. The goal of promoting family protection is a major policy thrust. These authors give an example of one family's attempt to obtain intensive support and outline the social policy of expanding family support beyond the extended family through bonding with the wider community.

The effects of welfare policies on African American families are highlighted in an excellent chapter by Robert Hill. He describes many federal programs and provides pertinent statistics covering public assistance, social insurance, foster care, and child support programs. Despite much political debate regarding policy changes, many programs have continued much as they have in the past because of increasing costs and alterations of the political agenda. The fact that most programs target individuals and not families leads to further crises for families. As Rivers and Scanzoni point out in their chapter, there is a strong need to extend support beyond the family into government programs that address the issues faced by families.

An Advocacy Agenda for Black Families and Children

MARIAN WRIGHT EDELMAN

A Portrait of Inequality

A Black child still lacks a fair chance to live, learn, thrive, and contribute in America. A Black baby is three times as likely as a White baby to have a mother who dies in childbirth and to be born to a mother who has had no prenatal care at all. A Black infant is nearly two and a half times as likely as a White infant to be born at a low birth weight and twice as likely to die during the first year of life. The Black infant mortality rate in 1991 was about the same as the White infant mortality rate 20 years earlier.

Black teenagers and young adults die from HIV infection at nearly five times the rate of their White counterparts, and Black preschoolers die from HIV infection at seven times the rate of White preschoolers. As of June 1993, there were three and a half times as many cumulatively reported AIDS cases among Black as among White preschoolers.

Black children are more likely to be sick because they are more likely to be poor. Black school-age children are at least one and a half times as likely as White school-age children to have fair or poor health, two and a half times as likely to have no regular source of health care, and likely to be more seriously ill when they finally do see a doctor.

AUTHOR'S NOTE: Sections of this chapter are reprinted from *Portrait of Inequality: Black and White Children in America,* by permission of the Children's Defense Fund, 122 C. Street, N.W., Washington, DC 20036.

Every year more Black babies face a losing struggle to escape poverty throughout childhood. A Black baby has nearly one chance in two of being born into poverty and is four times as likely as a White child to live below half of the poverty level. A Black child in a mother-headed family has one chance in five of living doubled up with other families. More than one in six Black households live in dilapidated homes, and one in five Black families lives in public housing.

A Black child's mother is more likely to go out to work sooner, to work longer hours, and to make less money than a White child's mother. As a result, young Black children are far more dependent on full-time day-care arrangements than are White children.

A Black man over age 24 is twice as likely as a White male to be unemployed, and when Black men find work, they bring home $168 a week less than White men. In fact, a Black preschool child is twice as likely as a White preschooler to live below the poverty level if he or she depends solely on the father's income.

A Black child is four and a half times as likely as a White child to live with neither parent, two times as likely to be born to a teenage mother, two and a half times as likely to have parents who separate, and three times as likely to live in group quarters.

A Black child is three times as likely as a White child to live in a single-parent home. A Black preschool child is five times as likely to depend solely on a mother's earnings. Because the Black woman still faces discrimination as an African American and as a woman, she is the lowest paid among workers, and the family she heads alone is the poorest in the nation.

A Black child is one and a half times as likely as a White child to grow up in a family whose head did not finish high school and is two and a half times less likely to grow up in a family whose head graduated from college.

In school, a Black child faces nearly one chance in three of being in a racially isolated school and is nearly three times as likely as a White child to be suspended or given corporal punishment, two times as likely to be labeled educable mentally retarded, but only half as likely to be labeled gifted.

The longer a Black child is in school, the farther behind he or she falls. A Black teenager between age 18 and 19 is two and a half times as likely as a White counterpart to be behind grade level and one and a half times as likely to have dropped out of school. A Black teenager is two times as likely as a White youth to be unemployed. A Black high school graduate is nearly one and a half times more likely to be unemployed than is a White high school dropout, and a Black student who graduates from college is nearly twice as likely to be unemployed than a White high school graduate with no college.

One out of every four juvenile arrests is of a Black child. Black children are five times as likely to be arrested for violent crimes as are White children and are twice as likely to be arrested for property crimes. A Black male teenager and young adult is nine times as likely as a White male teenager to be a victim of homicide—the conclusion of a winding, uphill struggle to beat the odds against success.

Eleven Premises for Effective Advocacy

Become an active and effective advocate for Black and poor children. We all must take a stronger, more systematic, and more programmatic interest in alleviating the problems that affect Black children. No one has a greater stake than we do in whether our children read, write, think, survive, and grow up healthy. If the widespread nutrition, health, child-care, education, and employment needs described are to be met, Black parents and leaders must constantly raise them in public, organize to challenge them, and vote for leaders who will do something about them.

Become well-informed about the needs of Black children and families in your area and nationally. We will not help Black children if we are uninformed. We must argue with facts as well as with emotion. We must teach as well as preach. Homework is a key to effective change. We must take the time to define specifically the problems facing children in our communities. We must then analyze and seek a range of appropriate remedies within our own families and institutions and through appropriate policy changes in other institutions. Those who care about Black children and families should hold study groups in churches and in women's, civic, and social clubs; invite speakers knowledgeable about and active on behalf of children; and find out how to achieve specific positive policies for children.

Don't give or accept excuses for doing nothing. Too many of us hide behind excuses:

"Whatever I do won't make a difference anyway."
"I've already done my bit or paid my dues. Now I'm going to get mine."
"It'll just get me and my child into trouble."

These and other do-nothing excuses are an abnegation of personal responsibility for one another and for our children. We are not out of the woods because some of us have two cars, a big mortgage, and several charge accounts. Any Black person who thinks this way is courting danger and jeopardizing our children's future.

The Black community today stands poised between progress and regression. We should heed Frederick Douglass's (1972) warning about how fragile change is:

> I know that from the acorn evolves the oak, but I know also that the commonest accident may destroy its potential character and defeat its natural destiny. One wave brings its treasure from the briny deep, but another sweeps it back to its primal depths. The saying that revolutions never go back must be taken with limitations. (p. 284)

The hard-earned progress of the 1950s and 1960s is not a keepsake that can be taken for granted. Indeed, it is threatened daily. There is a growing resistance to affirmative action, programs targeted for the poor, increased government spending, and strong federal regulations. There is a defense budget that is regarded by many as a trade-off for children's futures. And there is a national impatience that resents the fact that the effects of centuries of segregation and discrimination did not disappear quietly and cheaply in a decade or two. The revival of Ku Klux Klan activity, increasing clashes between the police and Black communities, and threatened retrenchment of Black political power through restrictive judicial interpretation of the Voting Rights Act of 1965 are all causes for concern.

The Black community must be constantly vigilant lest our rights and our children's futures are undermined by subtle and not-so-subtle means. Today's atmosphere, against the end of the Reconstruction era and the backsliding on equal opportunity during several presidential administrations, should be adequate warning.

Understand clearly that nobody is going to give us or our children anything. Frederick Douglass (1972) put it bluntly: "Men may not get all they pay for in this world, but they must certainly pay for all they get" (p. 200). Whatever we achieve for Black children and families will depend more on what we do with our votes and political power than on what those in power do on their own. We must vote strategically and intelligently and, through our example and leadership, encourage Black youths to participate in the political process.

Even as we seek additional resources and laws, we must constantly monitor the enforcement of laws already on the books, help weed out those that do not work, and see how existing money can be used better to reach the children intended to be served. For example, only one-sixth of the children eligible for Medicaid get the Early and Periodic Screening, Diagnosis and Treatment (EPSDT) services to which they are entitled (U.S. Department of Health, Education and Welfare, 1979). These children are disproportionately Black. Tens of thousands more children could receive needed health services now if their families knew of the program's availability and if Black organizations demanded better enforcement of that law by states and the federal government.

Recognize that the ground rules for achieving change are different now from what they were 5 or 10 years ago. The resource pie is contracting. The burden of proof and the level of competence required of groups seeking social change have increased. We cannot represent the interests of children and families effectively simply by asserting that what we want is morally right. We cannot look at children's or poor people's or civil rights programs and simply ask for more money.

We must gain greater technical proficiency in how bureaucracies work, how programs are administered, how services are delivered, and how budget decisions are made at the federal, state, and local levels. We must be aware of and learn to influence the complicated trade-offs that are made by those in power. "Whoever controls the budget controls policy and will have a critical impact on jobs and services for Black families in the decade to come" (Children's Defense Fund, 1980).

Focus attention and energies. We should always maintain our vision and work toward longer-range goals for Black children and the Black community. But we must break down our big goals into manageable, practical pieces for action. Too much of our current effort is diluted by our failure to set priorities and stick with them until they are accomplished. Too many possible, incremental gains are overlooked while we focus on long-term agendas we cannot accomplish in the foreseeable future. We must act now to deal with our children's immediate needs for adequate nutrition, education, child care, health care, and family stability. They only grow up once. Another generation should not be sacrificed while we work toward ideal solutions. A child health bill that we can help pass now, for instance, is worth a lot more than a national health insurance program that may or may not pass in the next 5 years or at all. We must set specific immediate, intermediate, and long-range goals and go systematically, step by step, until we achieve them.

Expend energy on real issues, not symbolic ones. We must not be bought off by appeals to vanity or status. We must avoid a treadmill of endless consultations and meetings that result in little or no action. Consultations, conferences, and commissions are not substitutes for programs and money. We must set substantive goals, think about how to achieve them, and choose the means that get us there.

There is another, more important dimension to this substance versus symbolism issue for the Black community. Nannie Burroughs (1972), a leading Black churchwoman, spoke of the need for Black people to organize "inside" and to teach our children "the internals and eternals rather than the externals. Be more concerned with putting in than getting on. We have been too bothered about the externals—clothes or money. What we need are mental and spiritual giants who are aflame with a purpose." In the 1990s, we must focus more on what is in our children's heads and hearts and less on what is on their backs and feet. Black people have always brought a special dimension to our nation because of our struggle for freedom and equality. We must not squander it by buying into the materialistic values of the culture and abandoning the commitment to serve others that our past has dictated. We have not come so far to seize so little.

Persist and dig in for a long fight. Recognize that a major agenda for Black children and families is possible and essential, but it will not be achieved overnight. There are no miracles on the horizon to make the dream of equal opportunity a reality for Black children. There are no Moseses or Kings in the wings to lead us to light. We must each take the responsibility for lifting ourselves and bringing along others. Everything we have earned as a people— even that which is our own by right—has come out of long struggle. The latest civil rights movement did not start in the 1950s. It started in the 1930s with a small band of brave parents and lawyers plotting to challenge legal segregation. As in past decades, nothing is more likely to bring about change now for our children than determination and persistence.

Use what you have to do what you must. Don't hide behind lack of education or wealth as a reason for inactivity or despair. To do so is to betray a central quality of our history and key to our futures. Our attitude must be like that of the father on a plantation in Issaquena County, Mississippi, who said, when his child's Head Start center did not appear to have any chance of being re-funded, "If there is no way, we'll find a way anyway" (Greenberg 1969, p. 1). And they did.

Sojourner Truth, a woman who could neither read nor write, pointed the way for us. She never gave up talking or fighting against slavery and the mistreatment of women, not even against odds far worse than those we and our children face today. Once a heckler told Sojourner that he cared no more for her talk "than for a fleabite." "Maybe not," was her answer, "but the Lord willing, I'll keep you scratching" (Lerner 1972, p. 524). Her retort should be ours today and tomorrow to a nation that keeps turning its back on our children. Although many politicians, voters, schoolteachers, corporations, and unions do not really want to hear or act on the problems of our families and children, Black parents and leaders have got to "make them scratch" all over the nation. Every single person can be a flea and can bite. However poor, however unlearned, everybody can stand up for a child who is mis-treated. Enough fleas for children can make even the biggest dogs mighty uncomfortable. If they flick some of us off and others of us keep coming back, we will begin to get our children's needs heard and attended to.

Attack the right enemy. Stand united. We remain our own worst enemies. Some Black people spend more time fighting with and picking at each other than confronting the real opponents of Black children and families. Too many of us are forever looking over our shoulders to see who else is doing some-thing. People who always look over their shoulders are not looking ahead. The facts make plain that there is plenty for all of us to do without stepping on each other's toes. Let us pull together. It is Black children who lose from our ego-tripping and fragmentation. How can we expect other people to place our children's needs higher than their own interests if we ourselves do not? And how can we ask others to invest more time, energy, and service than we do? Our ideas will not work unless we do.

Teach our children our history so that they can gain confidence, self-reliance, and courage. I recall hearing Mary McLeod Bethune, who founded Bethune-Cookman College, talking about the need to arm ourselves with the facts of our past so that we and our children could face the future with clear eyes and sure vision. Yet there are some Black youngsters in our urban schools who have never heard of Martin Luther King, Jr. There are talented Black students in Ivy League universities who complain about how tough it is to get an education. There are Black youths who know neither who Benjamin Mays is nor what he went through to get from the town of Ninety Six, South Carolina, to Bates College, to become the president of Morehouse College (see Mays 1971). Too many Black students in Black colleges today do not know the debt they owe John Lewis or that Andrew Young earned his way to fame by way of the jailhouse and the billy club. They have not basked in the eloquence of Frederick Douglass, Countee Cullen, or James Weldon Johnson, or escaped slavery and death with Harriet Tubman. They do not know the "Negro national anthem," "Lift Ev'ry Voice and Sing," which many Black adults learned before "The Star Spangled Banner." They have not flared up indignantly against discrimination with Sojourner Truth or laughed with Langston Hughes's "Simple" or raged with Claude McKay (see, for example, Hughes 1965). They are unaware of the contributions Charles Drew and Ralph Bunche made to world health and peace. Too many of our children are not anchored in the faith of a Bethune, who could envision and start a college on a dump heap and promised down payment of five dollars that she did not have. They do not sense or share deeply enough the sorrowful despair channeled into song and sermon that allowed our grandparents, fathers, and mothers to keep going when times were so tough. They are missing the pride, confidence, and purpose of a Nannie Burroughs, who boasted about specializing "in the wholly impossible" (Lerner 1972, p. 132).

More critically, too many of our middle-class children do not know the dangers of taking anything for granted in America or what remains to be done to achieve justice, because we adults are not sufficiently teaching them and leading the way. That is the task before us now if the portrait of inequality drawn here is to develop into a portrait of hope.

The 1990s may look complex and bleak, but they cannot be as complex and bleak as what the Tubmans, Truths, Douglasses, Bethunes, Du Boises, Everses, Parkses, and Kings faced when they began to stand up for our children and for the justice to which the Black community is entitled. That is what each of us must do now: Find the ways to help those of our Black—and White and Brown and Red—children still left behind and to guide the nation away from the moral shame, the ongoing toll of dependency, lost talent, forgone productivity, and unrealized promise that ignoring our children brings.

An Action Agenda for Black Children and Families

This agenda is by no means all-inclusive. It focuses on specific goals to help Black children that are critically important and that can be accomplished immediately or in the near future. It calls not only for new legislation and more resources, but also for better enforcement of laws and more efficient administration of programs already on the books. It calls for improving some programs, like the EPSDT program, that are not working well. It calls for expanding others, like Head Start, that are successful. It also calls for the enforcement of new laws—such as the Adoption Assistance and Child Welfare Act of 1980, which holds promise for getting Black and other children out of costly, long-term, and discontinuous foster and institutional care. In sum, we must analyze what we have, eliminate practices and programs that do not work, build on those that do, and improve or redirect those that could be made to work better.

In looking at specific problems of and programs for children, we do not ignore the overarching importance of adequate jobs and income to Black family stability and to Black children's well-being. We will continue to lend our support to civil rights, labor, and other proponents addressing these important issues. But jobs and income alone are not enough to meet children's needs. We must, in addition, find specific remedies to alleviate the education, health, child welfare, child-care, and housing problems daily facing millions of Black children and families. Equally important, we must change the negative attitudes and expectations that so many who teach and come into contact with Black children hold and transmit to them.

No one institution—the family, Black churches, corporations, the government—has all of the power and responsibility to meet all the needs of Black children and families. To blame or place responsibility on government or business alone would be as much a mistake as blaming parents or communities for all the problems their children face in schools, health clinics, and a range of other institutions over which they can exercise little or no control (see, for example, Keniston and Carnegie Council on Children 1977; National Academy of Sciences 1976; U.S. Department of Health and Human Services 1985). Rather, we call for the primacy of Black parents in making decisions affecting their children. They can and must exercise responsibility for their children. But public and private officials and institutions must be more sensitive to Black children and families. They must ensure that their policies and practices are fairly administered and implemented and help rather than hurt, strengthen rather than undercut, parental roles and children's well-being.

Included in this agenda are two kinds of activities: those that can be undertaken by local organizations (often using existing resources) and those that require changing the policies and practices of other institutions. Both are critically important. Do not be overwhelmed by all that needs to be done. Take one issue or set of problems that is most pressing in your community or that most concerns your church or organization. Make a plan and begin to learn who can help you. Reach out to friends, neighbors, and local groups for support. Call the Children's Defense Fund for assistance.

References

Burroughs, N. H. 1972. "Unload Your Uncle Toms." Pp. 522-53 in *Black Women in White America: A Documentary History,* edited by G. Lerner. New York: Vintage.

Children's Defense Fund. 1979. *It's Time to Stand Up for Your Children: A Parent's Guide to Child Advocacy.* Washington, DC: Author.

———. 1980. *Where Do You Look? Whom Do You Ask? How Do You Know? Information Resources for Child Advocates.* Washington, DC: Author.

———. 1985. *Black and White Children in America: Key Facts.* Washington, DC: Author.

———. 1987. *A Children's Defense Budget: An Analysis of the President's FY 1988 Budget and Children.* Washington, DC: Author.

Douglass, F. 1972. "The Mission of War" and "If There Is No Struggle, There Is No Progress." In *The Voice of Black America,* edited by P. Foner. New York: Simon & Schuster.

Greenberg, P. 1969. *The Devil Has Slippery Shoes.* Toronto: Macmillan.

Hughes, L. 1965. *Simple's Uncle Sam.* New York: Hill & Wang.

Joint Center for Political Studies. 1980. *The National Black Agenda for the 80's: Richmond Conference Recommendations.* Washington, DC: Author.

Keniston, K. and Carnegie Council on Children. 1977. *All Our Children: The American Family Under Pressure.* New York: Harcourt Brace Jovanovich.

Lerner, G., ed. 1972. *Black Women in White America: A Documentary History.* New York: Vintage.

Mays, B. E. 1971. *Born to Rebel: An Autobiography.* New York: Scribner's.

National Academy of Sciences. 1976. *Toward a National Policy for Children and Families.* Washington, DC: Author.

U.S. Bureau of the Census. 1979. "Voting and Registration in the Election of November 1978." *Current Population Reports,* Series P-20, No. 344. Washington, DC: Government Printing Office.

U.S. Department of Health and Human Services. 1985. *Report of the Secretary's Task Force on Black and Minority Health.* Washington, DC: Government Printing Office.

U.S. Department of Health, Education and Welfare. 1979. *Data on the Medicaid Program: Eligibility/Services/Expenditures.* Washington, DC: Government Printing Office.

Social Families Among African Americans

Policy Implications for Children

ROSE MERRY RIVERS
JOHN SCANZONI

Background

The Helping Tradition

A number of scholars (African American and European American) from a variety of disciplines (history, anthropology, sociology, and psychology) have argued that a "helping tradition" exists among Blacks (for example, Martin and Martin 1985; Jewell 1988; Cheatham and Stewart 1990; Billingsley 1968; Stack 1974). They claim that this tradition existed among tribes from which Africans were stolen into North American slavery, persisted during slavery as a means of survival, and after emancipation continued for another century—at least through the 1960s.

This tradition consisted of cultural values and norms prescribing that persons should "help out" others in their community, not merely in their own households, particularly with "bottom-line" material needs (McAdoo 1981, 1988). Helping out consisted of providing services (including shared shelter), goods, and money as well as meeting intangible needs, such as emotional support for adults in coping with a harsh and oppressive environment and participation in the socialization of children.

It is important to note that helping out was not restricted to blood kin. It meant concern also for other persons, whom some scholars have labeled "fictive kin." These "social families" and "social parents" contributed significantly to both the material and emotional well-being of many disadvantaged Blacks (adults and children) for a century following emancipation. Furthermore, analysts assert that Black churches were very often the "structural locus" for social families (Caldwell, Greene, and Billingsley 1992; Martin and Martin 1985), the place where persons needing family met other persons needing family. Out of that mutual need, those persons began to forge the bonds of family.

At the same time, scholars concur that the structural forces of industrialization and the anonymity of urbanization, to which Blacks were increasingly exposed throughout the late nineteenth and early twentieth centuries, had a negative effect on the formation and maintenance of social families. Furthermore, certain federal programs of the 1930s and 1960s were additional structural factors that tended to reduce the perceived need for, and thus significance of, social families. Ironically, the "Reagan revolution" of the 1980s brought the elimination of and/or sharp reductions in the kinds of federal programs that had weakened the need for social families. These were the very programs upon which less advantaged urban Blacks had come to depend for survival and well-being (Jewell 1988).

Household Composition

Although social families often contributed toward the maintenance of husband-wife households within the Black community, scholars concur that this was not their overriding rationale. Help was extended to households (such as those headed by females) located within the scope of the social family, regardless of their composition. During the 1960s, Moynihan (1965) and other White social scientists focused on census data showing that a much larger proportion of Black than White female-headed households existed in urban areas. Policy makers began to adopt the view that solving what Moynihan called the "tangle of pathology" within the urban Black community (divorce, illegitimacy, poverty, dropping out of school, unemployment, and so on) required the promotion of stable husband-wife marriages. For example, the success of federal income maintenance programs in the early 1970s was to be measured by the degree to which they reduced the incidence of divorce. The programs were soon abandoned, however, one reason being the finding that receiving material aid actually increased the likelihood of divorce (Hannan, Tuma, and Groenveld 1977).

Since that time, the number of urban Blacks born into and living within husband-wife households has continued to decline sharply. Moreover, drug abuse, AIDS, youth unemployment, and violent crime have made living conditions in urban Black communities extremely tenuous (Wilson 1987). The 1992 Los Angeles riots are said to have been symptomatic of the frustration caused by such conditions. At the same time, politicians and policy makers have reiterated the earlier theme that promoting husband-wife households might solve a variety of problems within the Black community, including adolescent childbearing and welfare dependency (Christensen 1990).

Broad Demographic Trends

The theme of family, as laudable as it is, must be placed in the broader context of what is occurring within the White community (Bumpass 1990), which now is experiencing the same kinds of demographic trends once largely restricted to Blacks (Peters and McAdoo 1983). Among others, these include an increase in the number of children born to never-married women, a decrease in first marriage and remarriage rates, an increase in cohabitation, an increase in separation and divorce, an increase in the likelihood of women's employment, an increase in solo parenting by women, and an increase in the number of children growing up in other than two-parent households. Furthermore, these trends are by no means restricted to North America and are occurring throughout virtually all Western societies (Espenshade 1985). Scandinavian societies, for example, have long been viewed as being in the vanguard of a wide range of changes among Western families (Glendon 1989). Evidence for these changes is also emerging from former Eastern European societies (Mozny and Rabusic 1992).

Public Policies

No one debates the assertion that the overriding goal of public policy should be the material and emotional well-being of children and adults, but the divergent programs put forth by numerous advocates to address that goal are the subject of passionate and acrimonious conflict (Bauer 1986). Some Black analysts contend that the historical experience of African Americans suggests that the notion of social families may be a feasible means of contributing to that goal, for any number of reasons. Promoting social families is a workable way not only to assist adults and children but also to "empower" them. Hence analysts assert that we ought to consider, first, whether social families make sense for both Black and White citizens for the 1990s and the decades ahead. Second, if they do make sense, then we ought to promote them as a major social policy goal.

The last thing that has any attractiveness within the volatile social and political climate of the mid-1990s is yet another federal program requiring infusions of tax dollars and/or professional service personnel. Scholars report that prior to the 1930s and 1960s, Blacks themselves made social families work for them in their own communities quite apart from any government assistance whatsoever. The current political appeal of programs that do not require extensive government intervention and are driven primarily by what groups do for themselves should be obvious indeed.

Nevertheless, let there be no misunderstanding: The policy goal of rejuvenating and promoting social families can in no way be construed as diverting attention away from the need for quality education, good jobs, adequate medical care, and affordable housing for all citizens. Rather than being viewed as a proxy for any of those structural matters, social families themselves should be seen as an additional structural issue. We view social families as operating in precisely the same ways they have historically: They provide a structural means for helping both adults and children cope with and perhaps even manage the often capricious circumstances of their everyday existence. Social families enable adults and children to take advantage of whatever level of social opportunity is available to them, whether those opportunities are declining or expanding.

Networks and Families

Cochran, Larner, Riley, Gunnarsson, and Henderson (1990) conducted an extensive multiyear investigation of what they call "social networks," which are similar to what others (such as Stack 1974) have termed fictive kin or social families. These networks were groups of parents (some solo, others dual) who exchanged varying levels of tangible (goods, services, money) and/or intangible resources (companionship, emotional support, advice, and so on) with other parents in the group. The researchers identified a continuum of networks: primary, functional, and peripheral. A *primary* network included persons identified by the parent as "especially important" to him or her:

> [They] were not always kinfolk, but the feature they had in common was high perceived value to the parent. [They] were likely to be tied to the parent with multiple strands—to serve a variety of functions. They were also apt to be available with emotional support, if needed. . . . This portion of the parent's network has impacts on the childrearing process, and must be articulated in any model of environmental factors affecting the parenting role. (p. 266)

A *functional* network consisted of parents with whom relatively few resources were exchanged intermittently. A *peripheral* network was a set of persons among whom exchange was possible but seldom occurred.

In short, available evidence suggests that support networks and social families are not necessarily the same thing. Very likely, however, they exist on a continuum, and over time the latter may develop out of the former. But in what ways are they distinct? If differences exist, are the distinctions conceptually significant? Are the differences important in terms of public policy and programs?

A Study of a Social Family

During spring 1993 one of the authors observed and conducted in-depth interviews with members of an African American social family located in a north-central Florida community with a population of fewer than 1,000. The conceptual scheme guiding the research is spelled out elsewhere in considerable detail (Scanzoni and Marsiglio 1993; Scanzoni 1995; Bernardes 1986; Gubrium and Holstein; Smith 1993; Wilson and Pahl 1988). The other author was exploring the general notion that "family" is a socially constructed reality as opposed to the more conventional notion that it is based on formal ties of blood and marriage.

The Family Members

The social family Rivers studied was made up of five women and one man, each residing separately from the others:

1. Ms. D is 30 years old, divorced, and resides with her two young sons. She recently graduated from nursing school and is awaiting state board results. Her 1992 gross income was $9,600.

2. Ms. C is 33 years old, has a high school diploma, is married but separated from her spouse, and resides with three children. She earns money as a foster parent, teacher's aide, and housecleaner. Her 1992 gross income was $20,000.

3. Ms. B is 41 years old, married, and lives with her spouse and a young son. She has completed the ninth grade, and she makes and sells crafts as well as sells Avon products. She and her husband produced a 1992 gross income of $25,000.

4. Ms. DP is 48 years old, divorced for many years, and lives alone. She works as a housecleaner and had a 1992 gross income of $5,000.

5. Ms. BH is 55 years old, has a high school diploma, is widowed, and lives alone. She has a small farm and runs a small thrift shop located in her residence. Her 1992 gross income was between $5,000 and $6,000. She is also Ms. D's biological mother.

6. Mr. A is 38 years old, has a GED, attended one year of college, and has a certificate in electrical wiring. Because his health is not good, he does occasional odd jobs and random electrical work. He resides with his wife and two teenage daughters. He and his wife had a combined 1992 gross income of $48,000.

Despite the fact that some of these are low-income households, none draws welfare. They all maintain their own homes and have created ways to survive in the face of scarce resources.

Rivers approached family members by first remarking that they seemed to have a unique and very positive set of group relationships. She observed to them that they have learned how to rely on one another for financial, physical, and emotional support. She indicated that she was studying "social families" and would very much like to ask them questions and learn more about their unique group. It is vital to note that the use of the construct "family" to characterize the group relationship created no dissonance for the respondents. They indicated that they themselves had for some time perceived of their group as "a family."

The Development of Family

Rivers verified existing literature arguing that the Black church has been the structural site for the formation and maintenance of social families (Billingsley 1968; Jewell 1988; Caldwell et al. 1992; Martin and Martin 1985). Each of these six persons belonged to the same church, where they had met and begun to forge the bonds of family. Weston (1991) argues that the phenomenon of "families we choose" (as opposed to "families we're born with") tends to emerge out of persons' perceiving one another as existing within shared disadvantageous social conditions. Although Weston studied the social families of urban gays and lesbians, she draws also from the literature describing social families among Blacks. She compares these (and other) settings and argues that persons who are disadvantaged vis-à-vis the larger society cling to one another in a manner that goes beyond support network and even beyond "mere" friendship. For example, studies have shown that persons in the traumatic later stages of HIV infection are sometimes ignored by their blood kin, especially if the persons who are ill are homosexual. The social families of which they are a part provide the emotional, physical, and material support they sorely need (Levine 1990; Lovejoy 1990). Giallombardo (1966) provides another example of clusters of disadvantaged persons constructing families, in this case women prisoners.

Friendship

Rivers found that the family members perceived themselves as existing in a shared situation of relative economic disadvantage. The four women who first became family described the sequential history of their relationship in a manner that verified Stack's (1974) earlier classic study of Black urban women. Over time, beginning in 1987, Ms. C, Ms. DP, Ms. BH, and Ms. D gradually became friends. (Recall that the two latter women also have a blood tie, although this tie seemed to have no significant bearing on the formation and later development of their broader social linkages.) Initially, the friendship consisted of companionship, but it was not long before these four women engaged in mutual self-disclosure, shared anxieties and hopes, and exchanged other forms of emotional support—a second and more profound dimension of friendship known as "shared emotional intimacy" (Allan 1989; Rubin 1985).

A Support Network

After a while, these four friends began to exchange services, along with tangible goods and monetary aid (this verifies Stack's account). In effect, they were developing into a "mutual support network." At this time Mr. A gradually became admitted into the network. He had been friends with each of the four women but previously had not participated in tangible exchanges with them. Along with friendship (exchanges of intangible gratifications), he gradually began to participate in the network's tangible exchanges. He suffered from very low self-esteem due to his poor health, which kept him from full-time employment, and had no male friendship networks; his spouse had a well-paying full-time job. The network of women became the chief place where Mr. A gained a sense of belonging and acceptance. He reported that a number of community members wondered how he could not be sexually involved with one or more of the women, and his spouse, who was not a member of the group, felt particularly threatened and jealous. He was able to assure her and others, however, that the group tolerated no sexual involvement among any of its members.

Soon after Mr. A joined, Ms. B became the sixth member of the support network. Like Mr. A, she resides with her spouse (who is not a group member) and is not employed full-time. She, too, first was friends with the other four women, followed by her gradual absorption into their complex set of tangible and service exchanges.

A Sense of Family

The intriguing question is how this support network eventually developed into something more. By what means did it gradually come to define itself (and be defined by outsiders) as family? Rubin (1985) argues that her research among middle-class Whites reveals a critical distinction between persons who are merely friends and those who are family. Many of Rubin's respondents said, "I'd go to my friends for anything, with any kind of problem" (p. 22). They and their friends self-disclosed deeply felt concerns, sorrows, joys, fears, aspirations, disappointments, and anxieties. In short, as friends they intertwined their innermost selves. They also shared good times together—they were companions. Despite such positive intimacy and sociability, Rubin reports that "there's a limit to what we expect from friends, a certain amount of care with which we . . . ask for their help." Although Rubin's respondents held profound friendships, "the family is the bottom line, the people you know you can always count on, no matter what" (p. 22).

The Bottom Line

Unlike Rubin, Lindsey (1981) sought to show how friends might construct families. She asserts that, alongside spouses, "we can choose all of our family" (p. 12). Ironically, like Rubin, Lindsey found that tangible (that is, extrinsic) exchanges are "the most important" or bottom-line criterion for distinguishing friends from family. The bottom line, for Lindsey, was the complex loop of extrinsic exchanges shared by her respondents across households—goods, services, and money. In Rubin's view, however, there is also a sub-bottom line, namely, a blood tie: People linked by blood will always help each other out, "no matter what."

Reality is not that comforting. AIDS victims are sometimes neglected by their blood kin. And the expression *granny dumping,* describing how, by one means or another, persons sometimes forsake their elderly blood relatives, has become part of everyday language. Offspring may neglect or physically abuse elderly parents (Steinmetz 1988). Moreover, parents all too often abuse and neglect their biological children. Adolescents sometimes sue to rid themselves of their biological parents. And kin sometimes may wish to help out but lack the resources to do so, which frequently has been the case in the Black community (Jewell 1988). Very often, economically disadvantaged Blacks simply do not have the particular kinds of extrinsic resources needed at particular times by their blood kin; consequently, people turn elsewhere for Rubin's bottom line—to be helped out and to help out.

The study that Rivers conducted illuminates this point. Even though the persons in her study lived near many of their blood kin, they considered their social family "closer-knit than blood relatives." When Rivers probed this statement, respondents told her that being blood relatives does not guarantee either personal closeness (intrinsic gratification) or help in time of need (extrinsic benefits).

Moral Obligation

An investigation of White working-class British blood families by Wilson and Pahl (1988) carries us a significant step further. These researchers explain why some persons may not wish either to be helped by or to help their blood kin, even when the kin have the material resources to assist them during times of need. Wilson and Pahl (and Finch 1989) say that the absolute bottom line underlying extrinsic exchanges within blood families is a moral obligation to give and to receive. Because family members are always giving and receiving, they are always paying off debts and collecting debts. If they keep on giving and receiving, they can never get out of the family loop, as

Rubin suggests. Wilson and Pahl report that certain family members sometimes feel coerced and hemmed in by these obligations, so they gradually cease to fulfill them. As a result, the family "expels" them, no longer defines them as being in the exchange loop. When certain members fail to maintain their moral obligations, other family members feel released from theirs as well.

Based on their research, Wilson and Pahl conclude that it is too simplistic to state that blood ties inevitably and always mark the boundaries of families. Rather, a family is "socially constructed," and it "grows and declines over time." People cannot choose their blood relatives, but they can and do choose how much they will participate with their blood kin. Family, in other words, is not necessarily blood kin and can be socially constructed; it is by no means biologically determined.

It follows that if blood families are socially constructed (or deconstructed) based on the manner in which members do or do not fulfill their moral obligations, then the same must hold for social families. Indeed, Rivers found this to be so. Family members not fulfilling their obligations to give and receive were placed on "condition red" status (feeding with a long-handled spoon); that is, they were placed on probation for 3 months and forfeited the right to participate in group decision making. After that period, the group decided whether the person should be restored to the family as sister or brother or be treated as "distant kin," who may expect only limited help from the family. To escape probation and/or distant kin status, a person must actively contribute to family needs. Rivers found that a distant kin who fails to participate fully in giving and receiving for an extended period is likely to be perceived as no longer belonging to the family and eventually will be "expelled," as Wilson and Pahl (1988) found to be the case in their study of blood families.

In effect, Rivers verifies Finch (1989), who argues that when a member of the family (social or blood) announces to the others, "I need," the others feel compelled to respond in appropriate fashion. For some, the legitimate response is "I cannot," meaning, "I genuinely don't have the resources." Any member who does have the needed resources (such as time, goods, energy, money) is expected by all the others to respond in a positive fashion. In Rivers's study, for example, Ms. D devised a way to reward her sons monetarily for good school grades. Ms. C lacked the resources to reward her son in similar fashion, but she desperately wished she could do so. Hence Ms. D provided the financial resources Ms. C needed to reward her son for his grades. In turn, Ms. C is now further obligated—not specifically to Ms. D, but to the entire family. At the same time, the entire family is also indebted to Ms. D for helping out as she did.

Ekeh (1974), drawing from Lévi-Strauss (1957), labels such complex webs of obligations "general exchange." This usually involves three or more persons (but not always, for example, a parent and a child) and is sharply different from restricted exchange between merely two persons, such as a couple in a committed sexual relationship (Scanzoni and Marsiglio 1993). Rivers's findings verify the proposition that within a general exchange setting, if any member with adequate resources fails to help out, two things occur. First, his or her right to receive help in the future from any of the other group members becomes relatively limited. Second, those other members are likely to feel less bonded with her or him. Their feelings of we-ness become somewhat eroded.

We-Ness:
The Essence of a Primary Group

Families—whether blood or social—are primary groups. As pioneer sociologist Cooley (1909) puts it, a primary group "is a 'we'; it involves the sort of . . . mutual identification for which 'we' is the natural expression" (p. 23). Faris ([1937] 1957) agrees that the essence of a primary group is that it generates a powerful sense of *we,* or *we-ness.* That sense of bonding supplies the group's members with identity, meaning, security, and belonging. Scheff and Retzinger (1991) believe that "everyone requires a minimal sense of belonging, a web of secure bonds" (p. 14). Rosenberg and McCollough (1981) add that when a person feels that he or she matters to another person or persons, that feeling contributes greatly to his or her mental health.

Figure 20.1 shows that friendship networks, support networks, and families (social or blood) are located on a continuum of we-ness, or sense of bonding. Friendship and support networks are primary groups but are not families. Over time, the group that Rivers studied eventually became family owing to the powerful feelings of we-ness the members slowly developed among themselves. They came to share a common identity and the feelings of unity usually reserved for blood families. Why did their bonding gradually become so intense? Rivers attributes their sense of family both to their intrinsic attachments and to the ways in which they fulfilled their "bottom-

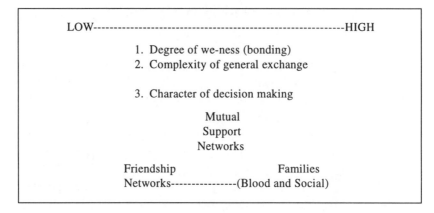

Figure 20.1. A Continuum of Primary Groups Based on the Strength of a Perceived Sense of We-Ness, on the Complexity of General Exchange, and on the Character of Decision-Making Patterns and Processes

NOTE: Networks and families consist usually, but not always, of three or more persons. These kinds of primary groups are sharply distinctive vis-à-vis ongoing primary relationships based on restricted (e.g., sexual) exchange (see Scanzoni and Marsiglio 1993). Families may sometimes consist of merely two persons, such as a parent and a child. For further elaboration of this figure, see Scanzoni (1995).

line" extrinsic obligations. They viewed their general obligations to one another as moral and thus fulfilled them accordingly (Ellis 1971).

Rivers also found that assessing whether members were fulfilling their obligations appropriately involves a certain degree of significant and serious group decision making (sometimes involving conflict and negotiation), as described above in connection with "condition red." The emergence of significant decision making is part of the set of complex reasons families are distinctive vis-à-vis friendship and support networks (Scanzoni 1995). A great deal is at stake in families. Members have a lot invested in their families and expect an appropriate return, at least from the other adults in their families. Failure to reciprocate appropriately is a catalyst that gives rise to some sort of group decision making, and the way in which that decision making takes place (whether implicitly or through explicit problem solving and/or negotiation) is a major influence affecting a person's sense of we-ness (Scanzoni 1995). Because a perception that the other group members are being fair enhances the person's sense that "they care about me," then that person's feelings of bonding with the group are strengthened. Conversely, a perception that others are not "playing fair with me" or are "limiting me" (as in Wilson and Pahl's study, cited above) tends to erode the person's feelings of we-ness with that group.

Implications for Children's Well-Being

"A World Without Fathers: The Struggle to Save the Black Family," declares the *Newsweek* cover (August 30, 1993). Accompanying stories amass the numbers documenting, among other things, the long-term decline in Black husband-wife households. Two cacophonous themes dominate the stories. One is that Black children are suffering because of the absence of males in their lives; the other is that no one seems to believe anything will be done about it anytime soon. Yet little attention is paid to the added demographic realities cited earlier in this chapter: Trends once concentrated within the Black community are becoming increasingly pervasive through-out North American White society as well as the entire Western world. The picture is further complicated by the continuing spread of dual-earner as well as dual-career households. Even if two adults are present in the home, it is exceedingly difficult for them to pay adequate attention to their children, partners, and occupations all at the same time.

Rivers found that the children belonging to the social family she studied are well protected because all of the adults feel a sense of obligation to monitor and/or discipline one another's children as if they were their own. The male in the group has been instrumental in serving as a role model and counselor for the younger male children. The small children as well as the teenagers are comfortable discussing their concerns with Mr. A. Further, the family members have found a way to minimize the effects of broken family ties resulting from factors such as divorce, father absence, and a history of low self-esteem. These people have been able to move away from the overwhelming incentives to be dependent on others for their livelihood. They have developed interdependent relationships instead. They buy into both giving and receiving.

Wilson and Pahl (1988) observe that, throughout the twentieth century, researchers, policy makers, and most citizens have been preoccupied with what has come to be known as the "modern" family (Bell and Vogel 1960). Although many features contribute to its ambiance, one of the most salient is the equation of family with a single household. Prior to the past two centuries, clusters of households (including blood kin and sometimes social kin) were much more relevant to the common, everyday understanding of family (Mintz and Kellogg 1988). According to Cheal (1991) and others, the modern family experienced its own "Big Bang" during the 1960s and 1970s. As we move into the twenty-first century and the postmodern era, varieties of families and households are becoming part of the everyday experience of a growing number of ordinary citizens. Nevertheless, the modern family model (Hofferth, 1985, calls it the "benchmark"; Smith, 1993, labels it "SNAF—Standard North American Family") remains the chief cultural ideal.

Naisbitt (1984) argues that policy is a vision of the desirable—that is, a broad state of affairs and a framework of general goals that an organization or society wishes to achieve. One such goal is that every adult who begets and/or resides with a child should be economically autonomous (Scanzoni 1995). This simply means that the adult should be able at the very least to provide for the child's economic well-being. This long-term goal is inextricably tied to policies regarding gender and sexuality, as well as to education and employment policies. Currently, there is little hope that programs politically acceptable to both liberals and conservatives can be devised in the near term to address the range of emotionally charged policies involved. The reality is that a growing number of adults of all races will find themselves increasingly pressed to take care of the economic and emotional needs of their children.

And that returns us to the policy goal of expanding our image of family beyond individual households to clusters of households. That expanded vision requires the notion that family cannot be confined to a single household or to ties of blood and marriage. No one wishes to undermine these kinds of ties or to minimize their significance. Cochran et al. (1990, p. 256) remark that no one desires to "usurp" the family by advocating the importance of primary networks/families. Instead, they suggest that social families may be thought of as meso-level structures mediating between unpredictable macro forces and the needs of individual micro-level households. The overriding objective is to place ties of blood and marriage into a much broader (yet pragmatic) framework: What works for ordinary adults and children in their everyday lives? Historically, social families worked for certain African Americans. Today, there is evidence that social families may work for some Blacks, as well as for other citizens who experience social and cultural disadvantage (Weston 1991). The awesome challenge is to take an ancient value—the helping tradition—and translate it into structural patterns that make sense for the twenty-first century.

Currently, research is being planned that will address those complex issues. The initial basic segments of the project will build on existing work, such as Rivers's study reported here and the research of Cochran et al. (1990), and seek to replicate it throughout a major U.S. city. Building on that research, the demonstration segments will then consider the conditions under which social families might be constructed and investigate their presumed benefits for both children and adults.

References

Allan, G. 1989. *Friendship: Developing a Sociological Perspective.* Boulder, CO: Westview.

Bauer, G. L., ed. 1986. *The Family: Preserving America's Future.* Washington, DC: White House Working Group on the Family.

Bell, N. W. and E. F. Vogel, eds. 1960. *A Modern Introduction to the Family.* New York: Free Press.

Bernardes, J. 1986. "Multidimensional Development Pathways: A Proposal to Facilitate the Conceptualization of 'Family Diversity.' " *Sociological Review* 34:590-610.

Billingsley, A. 1968. *Black Families in White America.* Englewood Cliffs, NJ: Prentice Hall.

Bumpass, L. L. 1990. "What's Happening to the Family? Interactions Between Demographic and Institutional Change." *Demography* 27:438-98.

Caldwell, C. H., A. D. Greene, and A. Billingsley. 1992. "The Black Church as a Family Support System: Instrumental and Expressive Functions." *National Journal of Sociology* 6:21-40.

Cheal, D. 1991. *Family and the State of Theory.* Toronto: University of Toronto Press.

Cheatham, H. E. and J. B. Stewart. 1990. "Retrospective and Exegesis: Black Families Reconceptualized." Pp. 395-99 in *Black Families: Interdisciplinary Perspectives,* edited by H. E. Cheatham and J. B. Stewart. New Brunswick, NJ: Transaction.

Christensen, B. J. 1990. *The Retreat From Marriage: Causes and Consequences.* Lanham, MD: University Press of America.

Cochran, M., M. Larner, D. Riley, L. Gunnarsson, and C. Henderson, Jr. 1990. *Extending Families: The Social Networks of Parents and Children.* New York: Cambridge University Press.

Cooley, C. H. 1909. *Social Organization.* New York: Scribner's.

Ekeh, P. 1974. *Social Exchange Theory.* Cambridge, MA: Harvard University Press.

Ellis, D. P. 1971. "The Hobbesian Problem of Order: A Critical Appraisal of the Normative Solution." *American Sociological Review* 36:692-703.

Espenshade, T. J. 1985. "Marriage Trends in America: Estimates, Implications, and Underlying Causes." *Population and Development Review* 11:193-246.

Faris, E. [1937] 1957. "The Primary Group: Essence and Accident." In *Sociology Theory,* edited by L. A. Coser and B. Rosenberg. New York: Macmillan.

Finch, J. 1989. *Family Obligations and Social Change.* Oxford: Basil Blackwell.

Giallombardo, R. 1966. *Society of Women: A Study of a Women's Prison.* New York: John Wiley.

Glendon, M. A. 1989. *The Transformation of Family Law: State, Law and the Family in the United States and Western Europe.* Chicago: University of Chicago Press.

Gubrium, J. F. and J. A. Holstein. 1990. *What Is Family?* Mountain View, CA: Mayfield.

Hannan, M. T., N. B. Tuma, and L. P. Groenveld. 1977. *A Model of the Effect of Income-Maintenance on Rates of Marital Dissolution: Evidence From the Seattle and Denver Income-Maintenance Experiments.* Research Memorandum No. 44. Stanford, CA: Center for the Study of Welfare Policy.

Hofferth, S. 1985. "Updating Children's Life Course." *Journal of Marriage and the Family* 47:93-116.

Jewell, K. S. 1988. *Survival of the Black Family: The Institutional Impact of U.S. Social Policy.* New York: Praeger.

Levine, C. 1990. "AIDS and Changing Concepts of Family." *Milbank Quarterly* 68:33-58.

Lévi-Strauss, C. 1957. "The Principle of Reciprocity." Pp. 840-94 in *Sociology Theory,* edited by L. A. Coser and B. Rosenberg. New York: Macmillan.

Lindsey, K. 1981. *Friends as Family.* Boston: Beacon.

Lovejoy, N. C. 1990. "AIDS: Impact on the Gay Man's Homosexual and Heterosexual Families." *Marriage and Family Review* 14:285-316.

Martin, J. M. and E. P. Martin. 1985. *The Helping Tradition in the Black Family and Community.* Silver Springs, MD: National Association of Social Workers.

McAdoo, H. P. 1981. "Upward Mobility and Parenting in Middle-Income Black Families." *Journal of Black Psychology* 8:1-22.

———. 1988. "Transgenerational Patterns of Upward Mobility in African-American Families." Pp. 148-68 in *Black Families,* 2nd ed., edited by H. P. McAdoo. Newbury Park, CA: Sage.

Mintz, S. and S. Kellogg. 1988. *Domestic Revolutions: A Social History of American Family Life.* New York: Free Press.

Moynihan, D. P. 1965. "Employment, Income, and the Ordeal of the Negro Family." *Daedalus* 8:745-69.

Mozny, I. and L. Rabusic. 1992. "Unmarried Cohabitation in Czechoslovakia." *Czechoslovak Sociological Review* 28:107-17.

Naisbitt, J. 1984. *Megatrends.* New York: Warner.

Peters, M. F. and H. P. McAdoo. 1983. "The Present and Future of Alternative Lifestyles in Ethnic American Cultures." Pp. 288-307 in *Contemporary Families and Alternative Lifestyles,* edited by E. D. Macklin and R. H. Rubin. Beverly Hills, CA: Sage.

Rosenberg, M. and B. C. McCullough. 1981. "Mattering: Inferred Significance and Mental Health Among Adolescents." In *Research in Community and Mental Health,* vol. 2, edited by R. G. Simmons. Greenwich, CT: JAI.

Rubin, L. B. 1985. *Just Friends.* New York: Harper & Row.

Scanzoni, J. 1995. *Contemporary Families and Relationships: Reinventing Responsibility.* New York: McGraw-Hill.

Scanzoni, J. and W. Marsiglio. 1993. "New Action Theory and Contemporary Families." *Journal of Family Issues* 14:105-32.

Scheff, T. J. and S. M. Retzinger. 1991. *Emotions and Violence: Shame and Rage in Destructive Conflicts.* Lexington, MA: Lexington.

Smith, D. E. 1993. "SNAF as an Ideological Code." *Journal of Family Issues* 14:50-65.

Stack, C. B. 1974. *All Our Kin: Strategies for Survival in a Black Community.* New York: Harper & Row.

Steinmetz, S. K. 1988. *Duty Bound: Elder Abuse and Family Care.* Newbury Park, CA: Sage.

Weston, K. 1991. *Families We Choose: Lesbians, Gays, Kinship.* New York: Columbia University Press.

Wilson, P. and R. Pahl. 1988. "The Changing Sociological Construct of the Family." *Sociological Review* 36:233-72.

Wilson, W. J. 1987. *The Truly Disadvantaged: The Inner City, the Underclass, and Public Policy.* Chicago: University of Chicago Press.

Social Welfare Policies and African American Families

ROBERT B. HILL

For almost 60 years, the cornerstone of social welfare policies in the United States has been the Social Security Act. Signed into law on August 14, 1935, this broad-ranging legislation was enacted in response to the devastating effects of the Great Depression on the lives of millions of Americans. It was specifically designed to prevent or reduce economic hardships due to recession, unemployment, disability, and death. Two kinds of income maintenance programs were established by the act: social insurance and public assistance. Each of these types of income transfer programs may be subdivided into those that provide (a) direct cash assistance and (b) noncash or in-kind benefits.

Social insurance programs were intended to provide economic benefits to individuals who were at risk due to unemployment, old age, and disability. The benefits were to be based largely on their own financial contributions to the insurance systems, *not* on their economic need. The primary social insurance programs that provide cash assistance are Old Age and Survivors Insurance (OASI), Disability Insurance (DI), Unemployment Insurance (UI), Workers' Compensation, Veterans Disability Compensation, armed forces pensions, and civil service retirement pensions. The only social insurance programs that provide in-kind benefits are Medicare's Part A (Hospital Insurance, HI) and Part B (Supplementary Medical Insurance, SMI), which were enacted by Congress in 1965.

In contrast, public assistance (or "welfare") programs were specifically designed to provide benefits to individuals and families based mainly on economic need. The main public assistance (or "means-tested") programs providing cash aid to low-income families and individuals are basic Aid to Families with Dependent Children (AFDC), primarily for poor single mothers; AFDC-Unemployed Parent (AFDC-UP), for poor two-parent families; Supplemental Security Income (SSI), for poor aged, blind, and disabled individuals; child support; and foster care. The major income transfer programs that provide in-kind benefits to poor individuals and families are food stamps, Medicaid, school lunches at reduced price or free, public housing, subsidized rent, day care, and energy assistance (U.S. Social Security Administration, 1993).

Most Americans feel that the overwhelming majority of poor people do not experience severe economic hardship today because government income support programs for the poor reach most of those in need. Accordingly, they do not believe that there are hungry children and families in this country. In fact, because much of the public thinks there are too many "loafers" on welfare, especially among Black families, general sentiment is that the public assistance rolls need to be reduced markedly.

What is the economic status of African American families today? To what extent do they make use of government income maintenance programs? Based on national unemployment and poverty data, one has to conclude that large segments of the Black community have experienced acute economic distress during the early 1990s. Although the official jobless rate for all Blacks was 14.1% in 1992, the National Urban League's Hidden Unemployment Index reveals an unemployment rate of 24.9%. In other words, one in four Blacks was jobless in 1992, which is equal to the highest unemployment level reached during the depression of the 1930s. If that level among Whites was sufficient to be characterized as the "Great Depression," then African Americans clearly have been in a depression—not a recession—during most of the past two decades.

Moreover, while the proportion of Black families in poverty edged up from 29% to 30% between 1971 and 1991, the number of poor Black families soared from 1,484,000 to 2,343,000, the highest figure since the U.S. Census

Bureau began collecting these data by race in 1967. Although Black families (30%) are three times more likely to be poor than are White families (9%), the number of poor White families also rose sharply over the past two decades, from 3,751,000 to 5,022,000, the highest figure since 1964 (U.S Bureau of the Census 1992b). Clearly, contrary to popular belief, economic hardship is pervasive among Black—and White—families today.

I have three aims in this chapter: first, to describe the extent to which Black families participate in key income support programs; second, to assess the effects of these programs on African Americans; and third, to offer suggestions for enlightened social welfare policies that are likely to enhance the economic self-sufficiency of Black families. Before I begin the discussion of the degree of participation of African Americans in specific programs, however, it is important to provide some background on the role of institutional racism in supporting social welfare policies that exacerbate the economic disadvantage of Blacks.

Structural Discrimination

Racism has two components: attitudes and behavior. Whereas racist attitudes are referred to as prejudice, racist behavior is termed discrimination. Racism can occur at both individual and institutional levels. Although national opinion polls and surveys suggest that individual racism has declined, there is mounting evidence that institutional racism has increased. Moreover, as Carmichael and Hamilton (1967) note, institutional racism can be unintentional as well as intentional. Downs (1970) underscores the declining significance of intentions as the overriding criterion for determining racism:

> Racism can occur even if the people causing it have no intention of subordinating others because of color, or are totally unaware of doing so. Admittedly, this implication is sure to be extremely controversial. Most Americans believe racism is bad. But how can anyone be "guilty" of doing something bad when he does not realize he is doing it? Racism can be a matter of result rather than intention because many institutional structures in America that most whites do not recognize as subordinating others because of color, actually injure minority group members far more than deliberate racism. (p. 78)

Almost 50 years ago, Merton (1948) identified "unprejudiced discrimination" as a form of racism that had been neglected by social scientists. I contend that social forces or policies that have disproportionate adverse effects on minority groups are discriminatory by result, whether intended or not. In short, we are moving into an era of increasing discrimination by institutional or structural proxies. This chapter will demonstrate that many well-intentioned social welfare policies have negative effects on African Americans because of the role of structural discrimination, that is, the disparate adverse consequences of societal trends and policies that may not have been explicitly designed to have racially discriminatory effects (Hill et al. 1993).

Two examples are the disproportionate effects of "structural" and "cyclical" unemployment on Black workers and their families. Many analysts acknowledge that Blacks are affected disproportionately by structural unemployment as a result of industrial shifts from high-paying and unionized manufacturing jobs to low-paying and nonunionized service jobs. Furthermore, many of the industries with the sharpest declines in jobs have been those in which Blacks were overrepresented, such as the auto, steel, rubber, and apparel industries. Although such technological shifts were not designed to affect Black workers, they have had acute effects nevertheless.

Similarly, Blacks were affected disproportionately by "cyclical" unemployment during the 1970s and 1980s. In recent decades the United States has experienced five recessions (1970–1971, 1974–1975, 1980, 1981–1982, and 1990–1992). Because of the "last hired, first fired" syndrome, Blacks were more likely to lose their jobs than were Whites. Consequently, the jobless gap between the races has widened markedly over the past two decades. We shall now examine the role of structural discrimination in maintaining social welfare policies that have disparate adverse effects on African Americans.

Social Insurance

Social Security

Among all income transfer programs, social security reaches the largest number of Americans. Because Blacks are a much younger age group than Whites, smaller proportions of African Americans participate in this program for the elderly. Whites made up 88% of the 41.5 million social security recipients in 1992, and Blacks accounted for only 10% (U.S. Social Security Administration 1993).

In 1983, Congress raised the eligible retirement age for full social security benefits to ages 66 and 67, effective in 2000 and 2022, respectively. Given that the overriding purpose of this legislation was to increase the solvency of the trust fund for future retirees, it was racially neutral in intent. Nevertheless, this act will structurally discriminate against Blacks, especially males, because their life expectancy (64.8) is 8 years lower than that of White males (72.7). Thus this policy change will prevent most Black men from receiving full retirement benefits even at age 65. Moreover, given that the life expectancy for all Blacks declined from 69.7 to 69.4 years between 1984 and 1985—while the life expectancy for Whites continued to rise—this new law will have disparate adverse effects on Black workers and their families throughout the twenty-first century (Hill 1989).

Unemployment Insurance

Unemployment Insurance (or compensation) was established by Congress in 1935 as the primary income support for unemployed workers. About 97% of all workers today are in industries or companies that are covered by the regular UI program, but coverage and eligibility are not the same. An unemployed person can work in an industry covered by UI and still not be eligible to receive jobless benefits. Contrary to popular belief, the majority of unemployed workers in this nation are not eligible because they (a) are reentering the labor force to find work (such as housewives), (b) are seeking work for the first time (such as recent school graduates or dropouts), or (c) voluntarily left or quit their last jobs. In general, to qualify for UI benefits, a worker needs to have been laid off from his or her last job.

Yet being laid off does not automatically qualify workers for UI benefits if they (a) have not accumulated enough weeks or earnings to have a "sufficient" attachment to the workforce, (b) have been discharged for bad or otherwise poor work conduct, (c) are not "available" for work, (d) are not "actively" seeking work, (e) have refused "suitable" work without "good cause," or (e) have voluntarily left their jobs without "good cause." Because Blacks are more likely than Whites to be overrepresented in each of these disqualifying categories, such eligibility criteria structurally discriminate against Black workers and their families. Thus Blacks accounted for only 11% of the 6.5 million unemployed workers who received UI in 1991, although they constitute about 22% of all jobless workers in the nation.

According to the Black Pulse Survey conducted by the National Urban League, 7 out of 10 unemployed Black workers did not receive any UI in 1979. Only 11% of Blacks were receiving UI, whereas 18% had exhausted their benefits because of their long period of joblessness. Among unemployed Black workers who had been laid off, 56% did not receive any jobless benefits, 20% were receiving UI, and 24% had used up their benefits (Hill 1980). Because structurally discriminatory UI eligibility criteria screen out Black jobless workers, Blacks are more likely than Whites to rely on public assistance for economic support.

Public Assistance

Such programs as basic AFDC, AFDC-UP, and general public assistance (which is paid for completely by the states) are what most Americans think of as "welfare." Many observers contend that the "easy" availability of public assistance is the major reason for the sharp growth in female-headed Black families. Contrary to the conventional wisdom, however, the majority of people receiving public assistance today are White. Of the 4 million families receiving such aid in 1991, Blacks accounted for only one-third (35%) (U.S. Bureau of the Census, 1992a). This marks a sharp decline from 1978, when 40% of all families receiving public assistance were Black (Hill et al. 1993).

Furthermore, only a small minority of all Black families are on public assistance at any one time, about one in five (18%) in 1991. Once again, contrary to popular belief, this marks a sharp decline since 1971, when 25% of Black families were on public assistance. In short, whereas the proportion of single-parent Black households increased from 31% to 46% between 1971 and 1991, the proportion of Black families on welfare decreased from 25% to 18%. Obviously, welfare has not been a major contributor to the growth in female-headed Black families, given that the two trends have been going in opposite directions.

Ellwood (1988) conducted an in-depth test of the hypothesis that the level of welfare assistance is strongly related to the formation of female-headed families. He found a negative correlation: Whereas the purchasing power of welfare grants declined sharply during the 1970s and 1980s, the proportion of single-parent families rose steadily. Other researchers have also found little support for the popular view that welfare is a major causal factor in the growth of female-headed families.

AFDC

Aid to Families with Dependent Children is the major cash support program for economically disadvantaged families with children. A "dependent" child is under the age of 16; is deprived of parental support or care by reason of the death, incarceration, abandonment, or physical or mental incapacity of one parent; and is living with a father, mother, or other relative. Most (90%) AFDC families (that is, the basic program) are headed by single mothers.

AFDC is jointly funded by federal and state governments, with the latter paying, on average, about 46% of total program costs. This point is important in understanding the magnified effect of state budget reductions on low-income families. Each state dollar that is cut reduces the benefits provided to poor families by at least two dollars.

Because there is no federally prescribed minimum, states set their own AFDC benefit levels as well as eligibility requirements. In order to qualify for AFDC, a family's income must fall below a "needs standard"; this standard varies from state to state. Because federal law does not require states to pay families at the needs standard, however, payment standards usually are below states' own need standards. In the typical (median) state, the benefit in 1992 for a family of three with no other income was $372 a month, or 41% of the poverty line. Even when food stamps are included, the combined benefits in the median state equaled only 72% of the poverty threshold for families with no other income. Moreover, because states are not required to adjust their AFDC payment standards regularly, the real value of the grants has declined markedly over the past two decades (Center on Budget and Policy Priorities 1993).

Of the 3.8 million families that received AFDC in 1989, Blacks accounted for 40%. This was a decline from 45% in 1969 and 43% in 1979 (U.S. House of Representatives 1991). Furthermore, Black families are still reeling from the devastating "antipoor" AFDC policies instituted in the early 1980s. At the initiative of the Reagan administration, Congress enacted the Omnibus Budget Reconciliation Act of 1981 (OBRA), which significantly reduced the number of families on AFDC and cut the benefits to those who remained on the rolls. The working poor on AFDC (in which group Black families were overrepresented) were hit hardest by several policy changes: the imposition of a gross income limit of 150% of a state's needs standard for AFDC eligibility; a cap on the deduction for child-care costs at $160 monthly per child; a standard deduction of $75 a month for other work expenses; and, most important, an end to the work incentive disregard for working recipients after their first 4 months on a job.

An analysis by the U.S. Department of Health and Human Services of OBRA's effects revealed that 408,000 families were removed from the AFDC rolls, and 299,000 families lost benefits while remaining on the rolls. These changes saved federal and state governments about $1.1 billion in 1983, which implies an average loss in benefits per family of $1,555 per year. Moreover, an in-depth evaluation of OBRA conducted by the U.S. General Accounting Office found that the working recipients who were eliminated from the AFDC rolls were disproportionately Black and had a longer attachment to the workforce than those who remained on the rolls (U.S. House of Representatives 1991). Clearly, the OBRA policy changes structurally discriminated against working poor Black families.

AFDC-UP

A program usually omitted from most analyses of welfare is AFDC-Unemployed Parent. Although it has been in existence since 1961, most Americans are still unaware that there is a welfare program for poor two-parent families. When this program became permanent in 1967, unlike the mandatory basic AFDC program, Congress made AFDC-UP optional for all states. Thus, prior to 1988, only about half (26) of all states elected to have the program, and none of these states were in the South.

A major reason for omitting AFDC-UP from most analyses of welfare recipiency is its relatively small size. In nonrecessionary periods, AFDC-UP constitutes only about 5% of the total AFDC caseload in the nation. Yet the federal and state dollars paid to AFDC-UP families are far from insignificant. In fiscal year (FY) 1988, about $1.4 billion went to 210,000 AFDC-UP families, totaling almost 1 million recipients. These payments were equivalent to a monthly average of $560 per family.

The size of the AFDC-UP rolls is strongly correlated to the state of the economy. After the 1981–1982 recession, the number of AFDC-UP families fell from 285,000 to 210,000 between FY 1984 and FY 1988. Due to the

1990–1992 recession, the number of recipient families rose to about 317,000 (1.3 million persons) in FY 1992. But the main reason the program is small is that it has stringent eligibility requirements. To qualify, the principal wage earner in a poor two-parent family must have a stable work history, be eligible for UI benefits but have exhausted them before applying for UP, have no UI disqualifications, have been unemployed at least 30 days before receiving UP benefits, and not work more than 100 hours per month.

Such criteria disproportionately screen out unemployed Black fathers, because they are more likely than unemployed White fathers to have erratic work histories, to be ineligible for UI benefits, and to have UI disqualifications. Consequently, only 25% of poor two-parent Black families received AFDC-UP in 1984, compared with 40% of poor two-parent White families (Hill 1989).

Although the Family Support Act of 1988 made AFDC-UP mandatory for all states effective October 1, 1990, it gave the new UP states the option of placing a time limit (usually 6 months) on the benefit period. Furthermore, this new legislation maintained the restrictive eligibility requirements for AFDC-UP that will continue to contribute to the dissolution of a higher proportion of two-parent Black families than two-parent White families.

In-Kind Programs

To what degree are African Americans recipients of in-kind benefits for low-income families? The key programs examined here are Medicaid, food stamps, public housing, and school lunches at reduced price or free.

In general, the extent to which Black families participate in these noncash programs is strongly related to their representation among the poor (35%). According to 1985 U.S. Census Bureau data, Blacks accounted for 30% of the 8.2 million Medicaid recipients, 32% of the 6.8 million food stamp recipients, 34% of the 3.8 million recipients of public or subsidized housing, and 33% of the 5.7 million households with children receiving school lunches at reduced price or free.

Contrary to conventional wisdom, only a small fraction of Black families receive these in-kind benefits for low-income people. Only about one-fourth of all Black families received Medicaid (25%), food stamps (22%), or public or subsidized housing (24%) in 1985, although about half (49%) of the families with children received school lunches at reduced price or free.

More surprising is the fact that poor Black families do *not* receive these benefits. U.S. Census Bureau data for 1985 reveal that only 39% of Black families in this category received public or subsidized housing, and only three out of five received Medicaid (57%) or food stamps (57%). The school lunch program had the largest participation, with 80% of poor Black families being recipients.

Most Americans also believe that low-income families receive multiple benefits from the income support programs for the poor, but national studies do not support this. To test the thesis, the Black Pulse Survey conducted by the National Urban League developed the Index of Economic Benefits for the Poor by combining seven public assistance programs: welfare, SSI, Medicaid, public housing, rent subsidy, food stamps, and free school lunches. It was found that about half (45%) of all Black households received no benefits from any of these seven major programs, and 58% of those who were recipients participated in no more than two of the programs (Hill 1980). Subsequent analyses by the Census Bureau also found little support for widespread multiple participation by low-income families in programs for the poor. For example, half of all poor families do not receive any cash public assistance (U.S. Bureau of the Census 1992b).

What effects do policies related to these income support programs have on African Americans? Some of the major changes in both cash and noncash programs for the poor occurred at the height of the 1991–1992 recession, when declining revenues prompted 40 states to freeze or reduce AFDC benefits for FY 1992. In FY 1993, however, 44 states again froze or reduced AFDC grants, and 6 of these states cut basic benefits below the previous year's levels. Overall, reductions pushed several million AFDC families deeper into poverty (Center on Budget and Policy Priorities 1993).

Moreover, the SSI supplements for elderly persons living alone were frozen in 17 states in FY 1993, and the maximum was reduced in nine others, lowering the purchasing power of SSI supplements because they were not adjusted for inflation. Furthermore, because Medicaid recipiency is tied to AFDC eligibility, the Medicaid rolls experienced a sharp decline as a result of the stringent requirements for AFDC imposed in 1992 and 1993. Many states also sharply cut general assistance (for individuals and families who do not qualify for federal programs) in 1991 and 1992 by eliminating people from the rolls or by reducing specific benefits, especially health care coverage. All these actions disproportionately affected both working and non-working poor families, in both of which groups Blacks are overrepresented.

Child Support

Many child support policies structurally discriminate against Black mothers and fathers. The family court is the basic government entity for providing child support to single parents of whatever socioeconomic status. It establishes responsibility for payments, sets amounts, and attempts to enforce obligations. Yet the family court has a number of shortcomings that have disparate effects on Black and low-income families. First, family courts often fail to order any awards at all. Only three out of five mothers (58%) eligible for child support received awards in 1989 (U.S. Bureau of the Census 1991).

Second, the probability of obtaining child support varies with marital status. Although three out of four divorced mothers (77%) were granted awards in 1989, only half of separated mothers (48%) and one-fourth of those never married (24%), who are disproportionately Black, had awards.

Third, child support awards are relatively low and constitute only a small fraction of the custodial parent's income. In fact, the mean award of $2,995 in 1989 accounted for only one-fifth (19%) of the total mean income ($16,171) of the custodial parent.

Fourth, child support figures vary widely from state to state, and the amounts awarded are often inequitable and regressive. In Wisconsin, for example, noncustodial fathers with annual income less than $5,000 were ordered to pay child support amounting to 41% of their income, whereas noncustodial fathers earning $40,000 or more were ordered to make payments that were only 19% of their total income (Hill et al. 1993). As low-income fathers often pay a higher proportion of their income for child support than do fathers with income in the middle or high bracket, Black noncustodial fathers are more adversely affected than are White noncustodial fathers.

Fifth, low-income noncustodial fathers are more likely to be arrested for nonpayment than are their higher-income counterparts. Because Black fathers are more likely to have low income than are White fathers, they are disproportionately affected by structural discrimination.

Finally, new "deeming" regulations related to the counting of income for AFDC eligibility also may have disparate adverse effects on Black households with extended family members. Thus the income of *all* household members (including grandparents and nonrelatives), even those who are not legally responsible for providing support to children, will be counted in determining the amount of the AFDC grant. Moreover, for the first time, all support payments for children who are not part of the AFDC unit are to be included in determining the AFDC grant. Such insensitive policy changes may cause (a) extended family members who provide vital support services to move out of these households and (b) noncustodial fathers who faithfully pay child support to prevent their children from going on welfare to discontinue those payments (U.S. House of Representatives 1991).

Foster Care

Numerous policies in the areas of foster care and adoption structurally discriminate against African Americans. For example, many agencies have the following criteria for potential adoptive parents: husband and wife, middle-class, can afford agency fees, childless, and younger than 45 years. In contrast, many studies have revealed that Black families most interested in adopting are single, working-class, have children of their own, and are older than 45 (Hill 1977). Thus thousands of Black children languish in the limbo of foster care for many years because nontraditional families are screened out by structurally discriminatory practices.

Although Black children in foster care are less likely than White foster children to have physical disabilities, they are less likely than White children to be adopted. Thus sizable numbers of Black children, especially males, are likely to "age out" of foster care and "graduate" to welfare and correctional systems. In short, many well-intentioned foster care and adoption policies may be contributing unwittingly to tomorrow's "underclass" or long-term poor.

Policy Implications

Several strategies can lead to enlightened social welfare policies that could significantly enhance the social and economic functioning of African American families.

Remedying Disparate Effects

It should be clearly understood that many legal remedies are available to combat structural or unintentional discrimination. The basic legal precedent is the 1971 *Griggs v. Duke Power Co.* decree, in which the U.S. Supreme Court declared a company's employment tests unconstitutional and discriminatory because of their "disparate adverse impact" on the hiring of minority workers—even though such consequences were unintentional. Furthermore, in renewing the Voting Rights Act in 1982, Congress overwhelmingly passed the "effects" standard to ensure that consequences, not intent, would be the overriding criterion for determining the constitutionality of specific electoral processes. Important legal strides also have been made in combating housing policies with unintended adverse effects on racial minorities. Family and child welfare advocates should give serious consideration to using these legal precedents to fight structural discrimination in the social welfare field.

Family Impact Analyses

Unfortunately, most public policies are targeted at individuals, not families, and those that focus on families are usually fragmented and not coordinated with one another. There is a vital need for a comprehensive and coordinated approach to providing assistance to individuals within a family context.

Government agencies should conduct periodic analyses of the intended and unintended consequences of potential or actual policies and legislation on the structure and functioning of families from a variety of class, racial, and ethnic backgrounds. The Black Family Impact Analysis program of the Baltimore Urban League should be used as a model.

Social Security

To counteract the racial inequity of the Social Security Amendments enacted in 1983, the eligible age for full retirement benefits should be made commensurate with life expectancy. Thus Black men should be eligible at about age 60, 5 years earlier than their life expectancy of 64.8 years. Similarly, Black women and White men should be eligible at about age 67 and White women at about age 75. If and when the life expectancy gap narrows between the races, the respective ages for full retirement benefits should be raised accordingly.

AFDC-UP

Although the Family Support Act of 1988 mandated the AFDC-UP program for all 50 states, it permits newly participating states to place a 6-month limit on the time that unemployed fathers and their families can receive benefits. This restriction should be eliminated so that the UP program in the new localities would have the same open-ended time period as in the original 26 states. Although many studies reveal that AFDC-UP recipients tend to remain on the rolls for relatively short periods, most of these families need help for more than 6 months.

Furthermore, the regressive AFDC-UP eligibility criteria, including the infamous 100-hour rule, should be eliminated completely. The requirements for participation should be the same as for the basic AFDC program for single parents, namely, that they be poor and unemployed. Economic disadvantage and not prior work history or labor force attachment should be the overriding criterion. This change would have the very important effect of enhancing the bonds of poor fathers with their families. If this nation is serious about strengthening two-parent families, enlightened change in the AFDC-UP program would be an appropriate start.

Child Support

Most studies reveal that low-income fathers pay higher proportions of their income for child support than do fathers in middle and upper brackets. More states should consider applying the income-sharing concept to set child support obligations, because it is based on the noncustodial parent's ability to pay. Although noncustodial fathers, especially those who are young and jobless, should be encouraged to provide in-kind services for their children, under no circumstances should this aid be "cashed out" to reduce the welfare grant to those families. More federal and state funds should be targeted to enhance the employability of young noncustodial fathers, especially those who are high school dropouts and lack work experience.

Foster Care and Adoption

According to conventional wisdom, a major reason that Black children languish in foster care is the decline in extended families. Yet studies continue to reveal that the proportion of Black extended families has steadily increased. Between 1970 and 1990, the proportion of these households jumped from 23% to about 40% (Billingsley 1992).

Moreover, 800,000 of the 1 million Black children living without either parent today are informally adopted by relatives; the remaining 200,000 are in foster care (Hill et al. 1993). The government has difficulty finding placements for 20% of these children, but the Black extended family has successfully found homes for 80%. Government policy needs to allocate resources in a way that makes greater use of extended family networks in finding well-functioning foster care and adoptive homes for Black children.

References

Billingsley, A. 1992. *Climbing Jacob's Ladder.* New York: Simon & Schuster.

Carmichael, S. and C. Hamilton. 1967. *Black Power.* New York: Vintage.

Center on Budget and Policy Priorities. 1993. *The States and the Poor.* Washington, DC: Author.

Downs, A. 1970. "Racism in America and How to Combat It." In *Urban Problems and Prospects.* Chicago: Markham.

Ellwood, D. 1988. *Poor Support.* New York: Basic Books.

Griggs v. Duke Power. 401 U.S. 424 (1971).

Hill, R. B. 1977. *Informal Adoption Among Black Families.* Washington, DC: National Urban League, Research Department.

———. 1980. *The Myth of Income Cushions for Blacks.* Washington, DC: National Urban League, Research Department.

———. 1989. "Critical Issues for Black Families by the Year 2000." Pp. 41-61 in *The State of Black America, 1989,* edited by Janet Dewart. New York: National Urban League.

Hill, R. B. with A. Billingsley, E. Engram, M. R. Malson, R. H. Rubin, C. B. Stack, J. B. Stewart, and J. E. Teele. 1993. *Research on the African American Family: A Holistic Perspective.* Westport, CT: Auburn House.

Merton, R. 1948. "Discrimination and the American Creed." Pp. 99-126 in *Discrimination and the National Welfare,* edited by R. M. MacIver. New York: Harper.

U.S. Bureau of the Census. 1991. *Child Support and Alimony: 1989.* Washington, DC: Government Printing Office.

———. 1992a. *Money Income of Households, Families and Persons in the United States: 1991.* Washington, DC: Government Printing Office.

———. 1992b. *Poverty in the United States: 1991.* Washington, DC: Government Printing Office.

U.S. House of Representatives, Committee on Ways and Means. 1991. *Overview of Entitlement Programs: 1991 Green Book.* Washington, DC: Government Printing Office.

U.S. Social Security Administration. 1993. *Social Security Bulletin, Annual Statistical Supplement, 1993.* Washington, DC: Government Printing Office.

Index

364

About the Editor

Harriette Pipes McAdoo is Professor of Family and Child Ecology, Michigan State University. She formerly taught at Howard University in the School of Social Work, and was Visiting Lecturer at the Smith College School for Social Work, the University of Washington, and the University of Minnesota. She received the B.A. and M.A. from Michigan State University and the Ph.D. from the University of Michigan, and she has done postdoctoral study at Harvard University. She has served as Director of the Groves Conference on Marriage and the Family, as National Adviser to the White House Conference on Families, and as Director and President (in 1994) of the National Council on Family Relations (NCFR), and she has been a member of the Governing Council of the Society for Research in Child Development.

Dr. McAdoo was the first person honored by NCFR with the Marie Peters Award for Outstanding Scholarship, Leadership, and Service in the Area of Ethnic Minority Families. She is also a recipient of the Helms Award from Carolina University Teachers College, and is a Fellow of the Institute of Children, Youth and Families at MSU. She has published widely on racial attitudes and self-esteem in young children, Black mobility patterns, coping strategies of single mothers, and professional Kenyan women. She is coeditor of *Services to Young Families: Program Review and Policy Recommendations* and *Black Children: Social, Educational, and Parental Environments.* She is coauthor of *Women and Children, Alone and in Poverty.* She is the widow of John Lewis McAdoo, and has four children and three grandchildren.

About the Contributors

Audrey B. Chapman, an active family therapist in private practice and at the Howard University Counseling Center, Washington, D.C., has conducted training workshops on male-female relations and support groups. She received the B.A. from Goddard College and the M.A. from the University of Bridgeport, and is a candidate for a Ph.D. in clinical psychology. She has appeared on several national talk shows and has been widely quoted in major magazines and newspapers. She is the author of *Mansharing: Dilemma or Choice?* (1986) and *Getting Good Loving: How Black Men and Women Can Make Love Work* (1996). She is also host of a radio talk show, "All About Love."

Jualynne Elizabeth Dodson is Associate Professor of African American and Religious Studies in the Department of Ethnic Studies at the University of Colorado, Boulder. She has been Center Director of Research and Demonstration at the Atlanta University School of Social Work, Dean of Seminary Life at Union Theological Seminary in New York City, and principal investigator on several research projects concerning African American families and religious life. She collaborated in the production of *Developing Cultural Competence in the Prevention and Treatment of Child Abuse and Neglect,* a publication of the National Center for Child Abuse and Neglect. Her current research focuses on religious activities of communities of the African American diaspora. She is married and has two children.

Marian Wright Edelman, President and Founder of the Children's Defense Fund, received the B.A. from Spelman College and the LL.D. from Yale. She has directed the Harvard Center for Law and Education and the Legal

Defense and Education Fund of the NAACP. She is the author of *Portrait of Inequality: Black and White Children in America,* and most recently of *Families in Peril: An Agenda for Social Change.* She is Chair of the Spelman College Board and a MacArthur Foundation Prize Fellow. She is married and the mother of three sons.

John Hope Franklin holds the James B. Duke Chair Emeritus at Duke University. He graduated from Fisk University and received the M.A. and Ph.D. in history from Harvard University. Formerly John Matthews Manly Distinguished Service Professor and Chair of the Department of History at the University of Chicago, he has served on the faculties of Fisk, St. Augustine's, North Carolina at Durham, Howard University, and Brooklyn College. He has been Visiting Professor at Harvard, the University of Wisconsin, the University of California, and Cambridge University in England. He was a Fulbright Professor in Australia and has held both a Rosenwald Fellowship and a Guggenheim Fellowship. He is a former president of the American Historical Studies Association, the Southern Historical Association, the Organization of American Historians, and Phi Beta Kappa. He has just completed 52 years of teaching. Among his books are *From Slavery to Freedom: A History of Negro Americans* (6th edition, 1987), *The Free Negro in North Carolina; The Militant South, 1800–1860; Reconstruction After the Civil War: The Emancipation Proclamation; Southern Odyssey;* and *Racial Equality in America.* He is married and has one son.

Paul C. Glick was Adjunct Professor of Sociology until his recent retirement from Arizona State University, where he continues to work closely with graduate students. He served with the U.S. Census Bureau from 1939 to 1981 and was Senior Demographer for 10 years. He received the M.A. and Ph.D. in sociology from the University of Wisconsin at Madison and the B.A. from DePauw University. DePauw established an annual award in his name, and he presented the first award in 1988. A former president of the National Council of Family Relations and Population Association of America, he is coauthor of *Marriage and Divorce* and is renowned for his many publications on family demography. He was married for many happy years to Joy, who has passed, and is the father of two sons.

Gerald Gurin is a research scientist at the Institute for Social Research and Professor of Higher Education, University of Michigan. He received the

Ph.D. from the University of Michigan. He has worked and published extensively in the area of group identity and consciousness. He is married and has three children.

Algea Othella Harrison is Professor of Psychology at Oakland University in Rochester, Michigan, and currently is Visiting Professor at Free University of Amsterdam, the Netherlands. She received the B.S. degree from Bluefield State College in Bluefield, West Virginia, and the M.A. and Ph.D. from the University of Michigan. She has been a visiting professor and scholar at the Universities of Illinois, Nanjing, Zimbabwe, California at Los Angeles, and the Virgin Islands. Her scholarly activities in developmental psychology have focused on prosocial development among African American children and interrole conflicts among African American women. She has written several book chapters and has published articles in various professional journals, including *Child Development* and *Psychology of Women Quarterly*. She is well-known for her efforts as a member of various committees for the Society for Research in Child Development and as a member of the Planning Committee for the Empirical Conference on Black Psychology. Her recent research centers on cross-cultural investigations of adolescents' perceptions of their social networks and HIV prevention techniques with incarcerated female sex workers. She is the mother of two children.

Jerold Heiss is Professor of Sociology at the University of Connecticut. He received the Ph.D. from Indiana University. His books include *The Case of the Black Family: A Sociological Inquiry* and *The Social Psychology of Interaction*. He is the father of two daughters.

Robert B. Hill is Director of the Institute for Urban Research at Morgan State University in Baltimore, Maryland. Previously, he served as Research Director for the National Urban League. He received the B.A. from City College, City University of New York, and the Ph.D. from Columbia University. His publications include *The Strengths of Black Families* and *Informal Adoption Among Black Families*. He is the father of two children.

James S. Jackson is Professor of Psychology and Faculty Associate at the Institute for Social Research, University of Michigan. He also is director of a nationwide, three-generation study on Black families and is Associate Dean in the Rackham Graduate School at the University of Michigan. He received the Ph.D. in social psychology from Wayne State University and was a Ford Foundation Senior Postdoctoral Fellow at Groupes d'Etudes en Science Sociales in Paris. He is married and has two daughters.

Leanor Boulin Johnson is Associate Professor in the Department of Family Studies and Director of African-American and African Studies in the Department of Psychology at Arizona State University. She received the Ph.D. in sociology from Purdue University and has taught at Florida State and Howard Universities. Formerly a senior research associate at the Urban Institute in Washington, D.C., and Westat, Inc., in Maryland, she was a Senior Postdoctoral Ford Foundation Fellow. She has paarticipated in numerous national studies and served as principal investigator on a work-family stress study funded by the National Institute of Mental Health. Her publications focus on marriage and family and on human sexuality. She and Robert Staples coauthored the 1993 textbook *Black Families at the Crossroads: Challenges and Prospects.* She lives in Scottsdale, Arizona, with her husband, mother-in-law, and two sons.

Wilhelmina Manns, Professor in the School of Social Work at Howard University, has taught at Case Western Reserve and Cleveland State Universities. She has now retired from teaching. She received the B.A. from Ohio State University, the M.S.W. from Case Western Reserve University, and the Ph.D. from the University of Chicago in the Human Development Program. She maintains an active clinical social work practice and has participated in the development of national tests for accredited social workers. She has four grown children and four grandchildren.

John L. McAdoo, who died October 25, 1994, was Professor of Family and Child Ecology, Michigan State University. He also served on the faculty of the University of Maryland School of Social Work and Community Planning. He received the B.A. from Eastern Michigan University and the M.S.W. and Ph.D. from the University of Michigan. He did postdoctoral study at Harvard University, was a postdoctoral fellow in the Johns Hopkins University School of Public Health, and was a summer fellow at the Institute of Survey Research, University of Michigan. He published in the area of parent-child interactions, parenting by Black fathers, and fear of crime among the elderly. He and his wife, Harriette Pipes McAdoo, coedited *Black Children: Social, Educational, and Parental Environments.* An editor for and on the planning committee of the Empirical Conference of Black Psychology, which for 20 years has mentored young professionals, he received the Lifetime Achievement in Scholarship Award from the Association of Black Psychologists. He is survived by his wife, four children, and three grandchildren.

Wayne R. McCullough is currently manager of market research for IBM, where he has worked in personnel research, management development, and employee relations. He received the Ph.D. in social psychology from the University of Michigan. Formerly an adjunct faculty member at New York University, he is currently conducting research in group identity and consciousness and organizational commitment. He is married and has one child.

Wade W. Nobles received the Ph.D. from Stanford University. A former President of the Urban Institute for Human Services, he also was Director of the Black Family Research Project at Westside Community Mental Health Center. He has written widely on the Black family and African American continuities. He is married and the father of five children.

John U. Ogbu, a native of Nigeria, is Professor of Anthropology at the University of California, Berkeley, where he received the Ph.D. in anthropology. He was previously a Research Associate with the Carnegie Council on Children and Distinguished Visiting Professor at the University of Delaware. His major publications include *The Next Generation: An Ethnography of Education in an Urban Neighborhood* and *Minority Education and Caste: The American System in Cross-Cultural Perspective.* He has published widely on the cultural contexts of the educational achievement of African American children. He is married and has four children.

Marie Ferguson Peters, who died on January 8, 1984, was on the Faculty of Human Development and Family Relations at the University of Connecticut and principal investigator for Toddler and Infant Experiences Studies. She received the B.A. from Fisk University and the Ed.D. from Harvard University. She served as Secretary of the National Council on Family Relations (NCFR), as Director of the Groves Conference on Marriage and the Family, and as editor of the *Journal of Marriage and the Family* special issue on the Black family in 1978. She conducted research on socialization, stress, and development of children in Black families, and she has been memorialized by the NCFR with an award named in her honor. Posthumously, she was made a member of the Academy of the Groves Conference on Marriage and the Family. She had a strong influence on the socialization of Blacks and other ethnic minorities into professional organizations and existing networks of the family and child development fields. She was survived by her husband, James Peters, Ph.D., and three children and three grandchildren.

William Harrison Pipes, who died on August 10, 1981, was Professor Emeritus, American Thought and Language, Michigan State University, and the author of *Say Amen, Brother! Is God Dead?* and *Death of an Uncle Tom.* He received the B.A. from Tuskegee Institute, the M.A. from Atlanta University, and the Ph.D. from the University of Michigan, the first U.S. Black to obtain a degree in speech. He served as President of Alcorn State University and as Dean of Philander Smith College. He also spent time on the faculties of Southern University, Fort Valley State College, and Wayne State University. He was active in directing college theater productions and debate teams. His recordings of rural Georgia old-time Negro preachers, made during World War II, now archived at the University of California, Berkeley, are considered among the few existing remnants of this unique preaching style. He married Anna Howard Russell; was the father of Harriette Ann, Willetta Ada, and William Howard; and had six grandchildren, Michael, John, Julia, David, Kahmara, and Paul Russell.

Rose Merry Rivers is Director of Nursing for the Surgical Team, Shands Hospital, University of Florida, Gainesville, where she recently completed requirements for a Ph.D. in nursing science, with a major in adult health nursing and a minor in sociology. She received an associate degree in nursing from Central Florida Community College in Ocala and the B.S. in nursing, with high honors, from the University of Florida, Gainesville, where she also completed the M.S. in nursing. She is married and the mother of three children.

John Scanzoni is Professor and Chair, Department of Sociology, University of Florida, Gainesville. His current research interests center on "social families" in urban environments, and his most recent book is *Contemporary Families and Relationships: Reinventing Responsibility.* His previous publications include *The Black Family in Modern Society: Patterns of Stability and Security, Family Decision-Making: A Developmental Sex Role Model,* and *Sex Roles, Women's Work and Marital Conflict.* His articles have appeared in a variety of journals, including the *Journal of Marriage and the Family, American Sociological Review,* and *American Journal of Sociology.*

Robert Staples is Professor in the Department of Social and Behavioral Science at the University of California, San Francisco. He has previously served on the faculties of Howard University, Fisk University, California State University at Haywood, and Bethune-Cookman College. He received the Ph.D. from the University of Minnesota. He is the author of *Black Women in America, Introduction to Black Sociology, The Lower Income Negro Family in St. Paul,* and *The World of Black Singles,* and editor of *The Black Family: Essays and Studies* (3rd edition). A former Director of the National Council on Family Relations, he was the second recipient of its Marie Peters Award for Outstanding Scholarship, Leadership, and Service in the Area of Ethnic Minority Families.

Niara Sudarkasa (formerly Gloria A. Marshall) is President of Lincoln University in Pennsylvania. She was formerly Professor of Anthropology and Director for Afroamerican (which is the way they spelled it) and African Studies at the University of Michigan, where she also served as Associate Vice President for Academic Affairs. She received the B.S. from Fisk University and the Ph.D. from Columbia University. She has published widely on the migration of Africans around the world and on women, trade, and family organization among the Yoruba of Nigeria and other West African countries. She is married, the mother of one son, and has two grandchildren.

Beverly Daniel Tatum is Professor of Psychology and Education at Mount Holyoke College in South Hadley, Massachusetts. She received the B.A. from Wesleyan University and the M.A. and Ph.D. from the University of Michigan. The author of *Assimilation Blues: Black Families in a White Community,* she is currently involved in research on racial identity development among Black youth in predominantly white settings. She is married and the mother of two sons.